MAKING
WISE DECISIONS
IN A SMART WORLD

Responsible Leadership in an
Era of Artificial Intelligence

Student Edition

MAKING
WISE DECISIONS
IN A SMART WORLD

Responsible Leadership in an
Era of Artificial Intelligence

Student Edition

Peter Verhezen

University of Antwerp, Belgium

 **World Scientific**

NEW JERSEY · LONDON · SINGAPORE · BEIJING · SHANGHAI · HONG KONG · TAIPEI · CHENNAI · TOKYO

Published by

World Scientific Publishing Co. Pte. Ltd.

5 Toh Tuck Link, Singapore 596224

USA office: 27 Warren Street, Suite 401-402, Hackensack, NJ 07601

UK office: 57 Shelton Street, Covent Garden, London WC2H 9HE

Library of Congress Cataloging-in-Publication Data

Names: Verhezen, Peter, 1960–   author.

Title: Making wise decisions in a smart world : responsible leadership in an era of
    artificial intelligence / Peter Verhezen, University of Antwerp, Belgium.

Description: Hackensack, NJ : World Scientific, [2023] |
    Includes bibliographical references and index.

Identifiers: LCCN 2022056895 | ISBN 9789811268052 (hardcover) |
    ISBN 9789811269424 (paperback) | ISBN 9789811268069 (ebook) |
    ISBN 9789811268076 (ebook other)

Subjects: LCSH: Leadership. | Artificial intelligence. | Industrial management--
    Technological innovations. | Decision making. | Social responsibility of business.

Classification: LCC HD57.7 .V47 2023 | DDC 658.4/092--dc23/eng/20221128

LC record available at https://lccn.loc.gov/2022056895

British Library Cataloguing-in-Publication Data

A catalogue record for this book is available from the British Library.

For any available supplementary material, please visit
https://www.worldscientific.com/worldscibooks/10.1142/13437#t=suppl

Desk Editors: Poornima Harikrishnan/Jiang Yulin

Typeset by Diacritech Technologies Pvt. Ltd.
Chennai - 600106, India

Printed in Singapore

In memory of my parents and my sister
who compassionately guided and accompanied me on my earthly spiritual journey and possibly beyond.

This book is dedicated to a few women who made me smarter and probably a little wiser:

my mam Annie-Charlotte (†) and my sister Klara (†),
"istriku" Linda, "anak perempuan saya" Nadya,
"keponakan saya" Charlotte, Camille and Julie,

... and the numerous sensitive and sensible women whom I had the chance to meet and learn from ...

About the Author

D
r. Peter Verhezen is a Professor of strategy, sustainability and corporate governance at the University of Antwerp and the Antwerp Management School (Belgium), and he also leads a consultancy firm in Southeast Asia that specializes in *Coaching & Advising Corporations* and their *Boards on Risk Management and Corporate Governance.* He was a former award-winning Associate Professor for global corporate governance at the University of Melbourne and Adjunct Professor at Melbourne Business School (Australia), and a Research Fellow for Governance at the Ash Institute of the Harvard Kennedy School (USA).

Peter published in the field of ethical leadership, corruption and business in emerging markets, sustainability and corporate governance in academic journals, and wrote so far six books. He also trained and coached top executives and new incoming board members on *Governance & Ethics* in Singapore, Hong Kong and Shanghai on behalf of the Australian Institute of Company Directors. He has been a guest speaker or visiting professor at a number of institutes like Fudan University in Shanghai, Insead Singapore, Singapore Management University, Hong Kong University, IBS Moscow, Hanoi Banking Institute, the World Bank in Washington, Stockholm University, Budapest Corvinus University, Neoma Business School in France, and Institut Teknologi Bandung, IPMI, Universitas Indonesia, ECGL and UPH in Indonesia to name a few.

He started his advisory career at SWIFT on behalf of IBM consultancy in the early nineties. As a practitioner, Peter worked as senior consultant in the field of corporate governance for IFC–World Bank in Asia Pacific, and as a debt negotiator-advisor for IBRA–IMF during the (1998–2001) "Asian crisis". In 1993, he co-founded and ran an IBM spin-off software company, Cimad Pacific, for more than 15 years in Southeast Asia and Australia till it was acquired by another international consultancy.

Peter studied Economics & International Relations (ME), Management-Finance (MBA) and Philosophy (MA & PhD). He lives with his family part-time in Bali, Indonesia, and part-time in Antwerp, Belgium.

Wising Up Amidst a Turbulent Future

"The world we have made, as a result of the thinking we have done thus far, creates problems we cannot solve at the same level of thinking at which we created them".

Albert Einstein

"Great minds discuss ideas. Average minds discuss events. Small minds discuss people".

Eleanor Roosevelt

"The future cannot be predicted, but future can be invented".

Dennis Gabor, Nobel Prize-winning physicist

"It's not because things are difficult that we don't dare. It's because we don't dare, that things are difficult".

Seneca

How to achieve your edge in an increasingly digitized *Industry 4.0*? The Boston Consulting Group recently claimed at Davos 2022 that only 11 percent of companies found the value from artificial intelligence (AI) they were seeking, mainly because the remaining 89 percent underestimated the human factor or the learning agenda within the organization. BCG estimates that 10 percent of the value created by AI comes from the algorithm and 20 percent from the (digital data) tech side. *Focusing on the people side of change* is actually where about 70 percent of the value is found when implementing AI[1]. Artificial intelligence is indeed about efficiency and productivity, ideally helping to improve learning and collaboration in the organization – all vitally important to retain best talent and keep a competitive advantage. Smart organizations become *learning* organisms within a broader interpreted *ecosystem* that will be both *digital* and *physical* in which *creativity* and *resilience* will be key features of success. But will being smart and adaptable be enough *to get the job done* and help resolve our challenges today? Implementing AI will likely be hugely beneficial for organizations, but not without focusing on responsible leadership.

In November 2014, I was invited by an international executive search company, Amrop, for a kick-off meeting at IMD Business School in Lausanne. The objective was to explore whether a new kind of corporate leadership could be defined to address the growing entangled and sometimes wicked problems in our world: *"What kind of new (corporate) leadership is needed to prepare the future?"* The collaboration resulted in *a "wise decision-making" model.* In 2017, I subsequently got involved in a heated debate that erupted around the potential of automating executive search through the use of AI algorithms, resulting in an attempt to rethink our current leadership model, published in seven related "Amrop" papers on "Wise Leadership" that I co-authored. However, I felt compelled to go a step further and analyze the reasoning behind this wise decision-making model more in detail. As a corporate governance "expert" dealing with fiduciary duties and boardroom functioning, I was initially compelled to take a board's perspective to answer that question on the role of AI in our daily lives, but I broadened the target a little.

Indeed, we all could agree that there is a need for a corporate leadership that is more fit in our changing business world. Making smart decisions is necessary but likely not sufficient to address our current challenges.

1. From Smart to Wise Decision-Making

Wising up means literally, according to the Cambridge dictionary, "to (cause to) learn the right information", as in having "the ability to understand what happens and decide on the right action". In that sense, this book concerns how to apply the best use of "limited" and often biased and noisy information in making good decisions at boards and in organizations. Creating value also implies to infuse *meaning.* Organizations are more than just a *nexus of contracts*, they also function as a *nexus of relations.*

Good and smart decisions should be distinguished from wise decision-making – especially in the age of AI where algorithms are increasingly used to automate business processes or to augment the accuracy and speed of decisions. I will argue why *consciousness* and *enhanced conscience* are crucial to make wise decisions – with consciousness to be clearly distinguished from intelligence. Also, why AI is plausibly able to help us making smart(er) decisions but definitely unable to make us wise(r). In essence, optimizing a desired output will require a balanced approach with cognitive awareness and ethical reflection, with the use of intuition and algorithmic thinking, encompassing short-term profit and longer-term envisioning.

1.1. A Future That Is Digital and "Relational"

Questions of any kind, are not really about getting the right answer, but rather about solving problems, especially entangled problems under high uncertainty. Asking questions is about making choices. This book isn't different. Eventually, the "new" leadership we envisage may embrace AI that can augment our ability to make *better and smarter* decisions. But only *conscious* humans are able to intentionally make wise decisions. And to be wise is to see through, to self-regulate and to generate profound insights.

Some people are afraid of an uncertain future, while others sense opportunities. What drives someone to be scared of uncertainty and ambiguity, while someone else embraces it? How do entrepreneurs, executives and boards – who are expected to take informed decisions about risks – make "good" decisions that positively affect the future of an organization? These risk-takers at firms are not exactly casino-dwellers but careful decision-makers. They watch trends and take risky "strategic bets" that will likely determine our future.[2] *How does top leadership use its power in the organization they are steering, directing and managing in an accountable and responsible manner?* Or more succinctly formulated: How to *create value without doing harm?* The answer in a nutshell: it will require smart but, above all, wise leadership.

Without question, boards but also citizens and governments should become better stewards and custodians of our socio-economic ecosystem in which interdependent relations cannot be ignored. At the same time, the ongoing digital transformation will fundamentally affect our daily lives. Current digitization such as cloud technology, blockchain technology and AI could be the turbo put on technological innovation. Companies that cannot take full advantage of AI will be sidelined by those that can. Most contemporary unicorns are linked to AI and cloud network applications in one way or another.

Gouverner, c'est prévoir. This book is ultimately about *mindful leadership, power in organizations* and *governing organizations* under high uncertainty, aiming to "foresee" and experiment how to steer organizations to create value, and this is in era of hyped AI and heavy pressure to resolve some of *socio-ecological challenges.* It is an attempt to show the boundaries of old (management) practices while indicating some initial contours of new suggested recommendations for corporate leadership in a *future* that is expected to be both **digital and relational**.

1.2. Global Digitalization and Socio-Ecological Degradation: Back to Our Human Roots?

How to survive an immanent fierce battle for both the mind and the heart of fickle customers who want personalized products and services that are also socio-ecologically sustainable? How to prepare for a digital transformation with the promise of higher profitability? This strategic battle to conquer thorny and entangled problems such as *global digitalization* and *ecological degradation* can sometimes be quite existential. Think about it. Climate warming and ecological disasters, growing inequality and fear for losing one's job, all are pressing matters that directly concerns boards at organizations. How to address these risks and how to think them through in a more holistic and potentially "wiser" manner? These often wicked problems require not just technological, but socio-ethical, political and organizational innovations. *A purely scientific and technological solution may help but will not solve these thorny socio-ecological challenges.* That many AI experts may search for a technical and quantitative solution to the identification of biases, fairness challenges, or even looking for codified and measured "certainty" in AI ethics, is all understandable. The truth, however, is that many socio-ethical challenges are not reducible to quantitative metrics or KPIs.

How does organizations' leadership make *reasonable* and *responsible* decisions at a time when AI capabilities seem to be (over)promised. How do boards take decisions that create value for those who have *stock* and/or *stake* in the organization while at the same time advocate a human approach that recognizes the deep respect for a systemic interdependent ecosystem.

We do not shun heuristics as found in our grandmother's wisdom or centuries-old "craftsmanship" – in its "love for wisdom" or *philo-sophia*. Such wisdom has stood quite well the scrutiny of time and could be refined for contemporary contextual usage. Hence, why the notion of *"wise decision-making"* is reintroduced, not as platitude to cover anything and thus at the end nothing, but rather as an attempt for decision-makers to become more mindful and responsible for their investments and organizational activities. *Attempting to become a wiser decision-maker*, I must not confuse the world *as it is* with the world as we *may wish to be*. Call it "pragmatic realism"[3]. For leaders – and human beings in general – the reality is not constituted by *"facts"* or data only, but by *possibilities* or what business euphemistically calls "opportunities". Seeing or creating such a *potential* definitely requires smart(er) and wise(r) decision-making. This new-found mindfulness may function as guiding brushstrokes on the new canvas that may inspire boards and executive leadership to come up with some new perception and interpretation of a changing world in an era of transformative technological digital transition.

As our focus is organizational but also related to the individual ability to make "good" decisions, boards and their leadership need to reflect about what it really stands for, and take action accordingly. Likely, it means that the *fiduciary duties* of boards and management will need to be *reinterpreted* and *realigned* with the goal of more meaningful creation of (sharing) organizational value.

2. Reasonable and Responsible Decision-Making

Taking business risks is about taking informed decisions that bridge the gap between what is going on today and an aspiring (normative or prescriptive) future that leadership wants to materialize. Improving our grasp of current reality means that we are confronting the world's challenges every day and trying to learn from our mistakes, and fast if possible.

2.1. Boards "Seeing" and Creating a Sensible Future

This book is a reflection on *how mindful boards can have a positive impact on their business and society*. The question begs how management and boards can optimize the benefits of a potentially transformative *digitization* in their respective organizations while minimizing the *analog degrading* effects that organizations still impose on our ecological and socio-ethical environment. The use of AI could possibly result in more efficient and effective production processes with hopefully less negative impact on our society and environment.

Who should read this book? Anyone who is excited about the future opportunities of digital technology and AI in particular to help making companies more competitive, and able to produce products and services that are more personalized and "sustainable". How did I get involved in this debate?

Just after obtaining my MBA and my postgrad studies in economics and international relations, but before completing my postgrad studies in philosophy, I was expected, to immediately start my PhD program in the overlapping field of business/economics and ethics. After visiting Singapore–Indonesia for a short period of two years, I moved away from academia for almost two-and-a-half decades to pursue a career in business, before returning part time to academia in my late forties.

Despite a career path that has not been straightforward or linear in any way to say at least, my passionate commitment to align responsibility and accountability to take action in pursuing innovative solutions has been an inspiring beacon in my professional and personal activities – though I may not have always succeeded. Be it during a short stint as a young academic and as a young MBA director of a fast-growing business school in Jakarta in the late eighties, and shortly thereafter as an IBM consultant at SWIFT-banking in Brussels early in my career, or subsequently in the early nineties as an entrepreneur and co-founder of a software company in Singapore–Indonesia from which we operated with our clients throughout Southeast Asia and Australia for more than a decade and a half before the firm was merged into a bigger international strategic consultancy.

The principles of accountability and responsibility definitely guided me when I became a financial expert and debt negotiator for the International Monetary Fund (IMF) and the Bad Debt Bank (IBRA) reporting to the Minister of Finance in Indonesia during the Asian financial crisis in 1997–2001. They also came of help when I was learning to combine profit and societal goals at the International Finance Corporation (IFC World Bank group) in Asia Pacific just after the global financial crisis in 2012, where I joined the corporate governance team operating out of Hong Kong and Jakarta for a couple of years. That experience taught me a lot about stock-holding investors that create value for those who have a real stake in the company. Influenced by these experiences as a practitioner, very often in emerging markets where uncertainties and ambiguities became even more obvious, my desire to understand – the impact of – changing realities prevailed.

Indeed, after two-and-a-half decades in business, I drifted back (part time) to my first passion of integrating information, knowledge and experience into a more coherent intellectual framework. And yes, I was fortunate and lucky do this at a number of reputable academic institutes: first in Australia at the University of Melbourne and the Melbourne Business School (during a period of 14 years on a part-time basis), then in the USA during an exciting gig at the Harvard Kennedy School, and part time during weekend MBA courses at the University of Indonesia and at the business schools IPMI, SMB–ITB, UPH and ECGL in Jakarta. During these years, I was also invited as a guest professor at a number of schools in France, Sweden, Russia, Singapore, Hong Kong, China, Malaysia, Thailand and Vietnam, and finally back to my country of origin, Belgium, first at the Vlerick Business School and now at one of my Alma Maters, the University of Antwerp and the Antwerp Management School.

The daily experience to deal with risks and to grab great business opportunities, but also the deep almost innate desire to survive adversity and crises I experienced as an entrepreneur have deeply shaped my thinking. My professional duties as an advisor-consultant during the Asian monetary crisis at IBRA–IMF and during and after the global financial crisis at IFC Asia Pacific, triggered my interest and got me focused on the following recurring theme: *How to make wise(r) decisions in duress or amidst uncertainty and disruptive technology (as AI)*, and ultimately, *how to create (sustainable) value allowing organizations to thrive (without harming others)?* Today, I advise boards and top leadership in attempting to answer that question, and share some of those ideas with my MBA business and economics master students or when I train or advise executives. This book is an attempt to describe this process of **making wise(r) decisions**.

If businesses want to be part of the solution instead of being part of the problem, then the leaders' mindset needs to interpret the context more holistically and open-mindedly. If boards don't change track, governments and courts may do it for them. Organizations should retake the initiative to innovate in a sensible manner while creating value to risk-taking *shareholders* and to minimally satisfy engaged but also concerned *stakeholders*. It can be easily argued that executives, managers and business leaders and their organizations need to "**wise up**"; they need to embrace a future that will be *digital* and thus "*connected*", but equally deeply (analog) *relational*, acknowledging the interdependency of us all. A digital future here refers to the way AI and deep learning machines are profoundly affecting our daily lives. However, most humans only really thrive when the "relational" aspect – cementing the feeling of belonging and genuine respect – has become part of an organization's DNA.

2.2. Why Making Wise Decisions Is Crucial Today?

The *homo sapiens* – literally the *wise man* – embraces innovation but is not reduced to it. *Making Wise Decisions* implies a verb that refers to an activity after reflection. It never relies on a pre-determined codification of specific rules and regulations only, but it's rather principle- (or purpose-) driven action(s). The *homo sapiens* understands that the *homo faber* – the builder and the plumber – needs to build a material economic sound and efficient "system". However, thorny entangled problems cannot be resolved by mere mathematical calculations only, but require a visionary imagination and a strategic foresight.

Smart leaders do resolve concrete problems as **plumbers** do. But crucially, these leaders also inspire and wisely *give meaning* to a future in an almost **poetic** visionary narrative. To realize such a "poetic" possible reality, some form of wisdom may be needed to guide share- and stakeholders on that journey [...] to steer an organization on that path of fulfilling certain expected objectives and desired financial goals, but also aligned to "higher goals" with possible short-term trade-offs.

Making Wise Decisions involves qualitative assessments and (normative) judgements on what is important for us *hic et nunc*, and what kind of society we morally *imagine* to live in. It's about narrating a story of "potentiality" about how companies can make a real difference and have a genuine positive impact in an increasingly complex and interdependent world. Being *intelligent* won't be enough; being aware and highly *conscious* of intentional motivations, consequences of action, and values-laden vision, the power of giving meaning, all count. More than ever, it will require clear and wise choices.

The book encompasses five major themes around *wise decision-making in an era of AI amidst uncertain and often turbulent times*. These five themes contain 30 chapters, which can be independently read.

The first part, **The Future Is "Relational": Wise Decision-Making at Boards,** emphasizes why and how boards and executives should and can make reasonable and responsible decisions. The idea is that making reasonable decisions is necessary but not sufficient in the current business context. Boards and their business need to aim for a transition *from smart to wise decision-makings*. Why? Reasonableness still prevails in decision-making but need to be enhanced and possibly embedded in a more holistic framework in which responsibility starts to play a more important role.

The subsequent three parts focus on AI. The second part, **The Future Is Digital: Wise Decision in an Era of Artificial Intelligence,** focuses on the benefits of AI in business. But it also highlights the darker side of AI that should not be omitted in discussions at boards. The *good*, the *bad* and the *ugly* of AI will continue to emerge and to evolve.

In the third part – **A Neuroscientific Perspective on Learning In Vivo et In Silico** – we go through the crux of the matter and argue why humans are still superior in decision-making compared to machine learning. We decipher the major difference between machine learning and AI in comparison with human learning. Basically, we argue that human intelligence – embedded in human consciousness and conscience – transcends cognitive reasonableness, by expanding the model and incorporate a socio-moral pathway to understand and to make decisions about a future world.

In a subsequent fourth part **Artificial Intelligence as the New Oracle of Delphi in an Uncertain Future**, we advise boards to take advantage of the enormous capabilities of both AI and human creativity and intelligence to improve decision-making. In a connected networked and increasingly digital future, well-aligned AI–human collaboration will become crucial. Particular tasks will be replaced by AI, automating the processes and also augmenting the decision power of humans. The power of AI has also generated a fierce geopolitical battle for supremacy in this field, especially between the two superpowers, China and the USA.

The final fifth part is concerned with questioning how to make better decisions: **Making Wiser Decisions Through Paradoxal and Algotuitional Thinking**. It details some of the processes that business leaders and managers can apply to make wiser decisions, by combining the complementary forces of tacit and explicit knowledge, of intuitive and analytical logic and algorithms. I emphasize *the relational interdependencies in business and thus subsequently how to achieve wiser decisions amidst uncertain, turbulent and ambiguous times*.

The problem is usually not so much an excess of technology – such as AI-driven robots or other AI tools – as a lack of real wisdom in making "good", reasonable and responsible decisions. Boards and the organization's leadership have duties and obligations but also the power granted to make decisions, to change the course where necessary and appropriate. Now is the time to use that power wisely. Too much is at stake and leadership better gets it right, surviving the upcoming digital competition onslaught – led by AI algorithms *augmenting* the executives' abilities to predict and find previously unknown or unseen patterns, and smart robots who may initiate an *automation* process never seen in human history before. You add the degradation of its ecological environment and socio-ethical context, and boards are in for a hell of a time to steer organizations away from threatening obstacles towards more sensible business opportunities.

I like to thank the global executive search company, Amrop, who initiated the project to re-think (corporate) leadership and stimulated me in trying to formulate a framework to better determine the profile of "a new leader of the future". Also, a thank you to all my MBA and master students and executives with whom I could discuss the relevance of those notions during seminars and classes. It goes without saying that the completion of this book would have been impossible without the socialization of ideas I received from my professors in economics-business, international relations and philosophy, and without the mentoring of a few persons I was lucky to meet in places where I spent considerable time like Belgium, Indonesia, Singapore–Thailand–Hong Kong, USA and Australia. To all those wonderful people I was lucky to meet and learn from over the years in business and academia: Thank you.

This book is dedicated to the female side of my family who taught me to "see the bigger picture" beyond the mere rational approach (of profit maximization in organizations), to their subtle nudging to embrace a different way of thinking. Thank you so much; without you, I would not be here today – strongly believing in balancing and harmonizing efficiency with caring, who appreciates the dialectic process of analysis and synthesis, of spiritual sensitivity or intuitive feelings and an analytical ratio, two sides needed for any symbiotic harmonious organizational entity or community.

I am well aware of the limitations trying to reflect and attempt to write about or describe the thorny entangled and in-depth challenges that boards face in this context of disruptive digitization and the demand for more sustainability. Progress occurs through trial and error. This book is not different. Although I am standing on the shoulders of numerous intelligent and wise giants – both recent and contemporary as well as far back in human history – the errors should be attributed to me only. I humbly accept my own limitations and hopefully learn from them as well. That is what reasonable, mindful and responsible decision-making is meant to be. Hopefully, you the reader may feel inspired to participate in foreseeing and creating those future possibilities that may give us, intelligent and conscious human beings, more meaning and purpose.

Peter Verhezen
Herenthout – Antwerp (Belgium) and
Canggu – Bali (Indonesia)
9 August 2022

CONTENTS

Making Wise Decisions in a Smart World
Responsible Leadership in an Era of Artificial Intelligence

PART I:
The Future Is "Relational": Making Wise Decisions in the Boardroom

Today, the *Zeitgeist* is definitely changing. I am convinced that our present paradigm may need some reengineering or dramatic revamping, allowing us to take a different viewpoint, or enabling us to see things differently and more holistically. At the end of the day, this new *Zeitgeist* may push us to move into a new paradigmatic framework that focuses on more *connectivity* and *relationship interdependency*.

More concretely, over the past decade, the world has been challenged and transformed by three powerful forces: (1) *social tension* as result of rising *inequality* within developed and emerging countries[1] that could easily turn into economic nationalism, populism and anti-globalization, (2) a *technological revolution* among which internet of things, *connectivity* and *artificial intelligence* with its successful machine learning narrative that has resulted in a number of *beneficial applications* in our daily lives, but that also created the fear among many to *lose their jobs to "smart robots"* in the not-too-distant future, or to become dependent on less-than-ethical-techno-oligarchies that may satisfy less benign objectives, and (3) and possibly the most daunting challenge of *crossing our system-ecological planet boundaries* that may jeopardize our prosperity and well-being on the planet as we know it[2]. These challenges can rightfully be described as *global, technological* and *socio-ecological*. Our focus will be on the technological challenge though indirectly touching upon the global ecological boundaries and societal concerns: we will assess how boards and corporate leadership create value through technological and digital innovation (AI) that benefits stockholders. But we won't neglect those who have a stake in the organization and how they can play a contributing role. In a recent survey by PWC consultancy, it has become clear that *sustainability* and *digitization* are holding the key to long-term value creation, both in family businesses[3] as well as in multinationals. Having *advanced technology* (like AI) and *scaling* (getting fast to a high volume to benefit from learning to reduce costs) gives any organization an ace to outcompete any competitor. So it is obvious that AI and its digitization of data allow organizations that have implemented and clearly aligned AI with human fair objectives would enormously benefit society.

Today, our evolution is not focusing on a struggle of existence, but rather "a cooperative dance in which creativity and constant emergence of novelty are the driving forces"[4]. With the emergence of new socio-ecological demands and new exciting technology such as artificial intelligence, the emphasis is shifting to understanding networks, complexity and patterns of organizations within an eco-system. In other words, a more *systemic* interrelated and thus an integrative dialectical thinking may be advisable. We claim that evolution is forcing organizations to acknowledge the interdependencies within the eco-system. And shareholders' dependencies (despite sometimes opposing goals) or stakeholders' objectives that affect the organization. Consequently, we suggest a slightly different narrative in comparison with mainstream economics of profit maximizing, emphasizing other "invisible" factors such as purpose, relations and meaning in business.

The fetish of economic growth at any price spares politicians the need for contentious debates about morally controversial questions or longer term goals. People do not seem to agree on "what is important in life" as we disagree on the meaning of human flourishing, in politics[5], international relations[6] as well as in business[7]. Consequently, that makes it difficult to agree on some consensus on ecological health or other normative insights or valuations. Tensions and antagonisms in society will not disappear; they may even form the driving energy to strive for better [strategic] positioning ... Transforming these *antagonisms* – interpreting the other as an enemy to beat as in a zero-sum game – into more manageable *agonisms* – seeing the other as an adversary to compete with and potentially seek compromises as in a win-win over a longer period – will require some form of wise decision-making. We refer to the metaphor of Nietzsche's arrow which can only be shot through the use of the tension of the bow, where opposing forces allow action and creativity to unfold.

We face incredible daunting challenges amidst tense, turbulent and ambiguous times: a global pandemic undermining international business practices, climate change starting to affect businesses, new business opportunities rooted in the technological progress of smart computers, cloud technology and other innovation that also have aggravated the inequality between haves versus have-nots. It seems that we are bound to go through some fundamental transformation on all levels, likely profoundly affecting how businesses are governed and run. However, if business wants to be part of the solution instead of the problem, business and political leadership will need to adapt a new style of governing and managing organizations[8]. Business needs to revise its current paradigm to prepare for a profound transformation and regain trust from society, probably evolving into a new evolutionary-driven paradigm that focuses both on digital efficiency and interconnectivity in a virtual world, as well as the impact it may have on the relations in the analog world of organizations, creating value for its customers and other stakeholders.

This first part around the notion of **"wising up"** – making wise(r) decisions – addresses this potentially more holistic perspective of corporate and political leadership addressing some of those global challenges.

Chapter One

Why Governing Business "Relations" Is on the Board's Radar Today?

"It is time we begin to pay for nature and understand that its 'services' – clean air and water, the beauty and abundance of nature, the fertility of the soil – are just as much assets as the products we create from those assets. […] The need to appreciate the complexity and brilliance of the natural world could not be more important".

Cambridge Prof. Dasgupta from The Economics of Biodiversity of the Dasgupta Review, 2021

"Almost everything worthwhile carries with it some sort of risk, whether it's starting a new business, whether it's leaving home, whether it's getting married, or whether it's flying into space".

Chris Hadfield, former NASA astronaut

"It is not the strongest of species that survive, nor the most intelligent, but the one most responsive to change".

Charles Darwin

The world is changing fast, and the role of business is being redefined. Business cannot expect their past linear expectations and performances to persist continuously. Companies adapt to changed realities and innovate through creating value for their customers. We have found new ways of creating value. Having a clear purpose that answers the *why* is a clear starter[9]. In addition to the why, coherently communicating the *what* and the *how* is becoming a decisive factor of acceptance among customers, employees, suppliers and other engaged stakeholders. What I'm interested in is answering *How to successfully and responsibly embrace a new **digital** reality within our eco-physical **analog** interdependent world?*

1. Aligning Cognitive Learning with Socio-Moral Learning […]

We must develop a sense of socio-relational learning. *Wising up* is both a perspective and an activity that encompasses ecological, socio-ethical and governance criteria in their performance evaluation. The old "thick" notion[10] "*wisdom*" sits at the roots of this activity of *wising up*; it reflects the ability to consciously reflect upon and *learn* with the aim to resolve problems[11] – often based on experience and practice, rooted in our cognitive abilities but also embedded in a genuine ability of empathy[12] – that is likely a source of any relation and socio-moral thinking. Learning is about acquiring knowledge, but equally about deepening our comprehension of facts and values, and how they are interlinked. Learning organizations are led by boards that have *confident humility*[13] to continuously rethink their assumptions and beliefs. Boards that foster a climate of respect, trust and openness – without individuals fearing for reprisals in case of failure[14] – are factors that hugely contribute to sustainable economic performance.

1.1. Being Intelligent Is Making Reasonable Decisions

All firms aim for making intelligent and reasonable informed decisions that create and capture value. Today, smart computers typically try to copy smart decision-makers, which can be brought back to a logic of our cognitive abilities, translated and transformed in explicit knowledge that can be coded in binary numbers[15]. The interdisciplinary "cognitive revolution" treats intelligence as merely internal computations in our brain. But this cognitive approach also remains quite "mechanistic" and (pre)determined. This is an approach that remains based on a cognitive oversimplification attempting to reduce intelligence and consciousness to a pure biochemical brain-process – which Part III will attempt to deconstruct and falsify. Equating a smart computer with a conscious mind is pure science fiction[16]. And let us not forget either that the notions of "intelligence" and "consciousness" are not interchangeable as often is done. **Consciousness**[17] is here understood as our *personal experience of phenomena, akin to being aware*, whereas **intelligence** can be interpreted as *achieving particular objectives* and/or *resolving certain challenges*. The incessant interplay between intellect (or cognition) and feelings produces what we call *consciousness* – as in being aware of your beliefs, assumptions and thoughts. Such inference to equate consciousness with the functioning of our brain remains a philosophical normative (and speculative) argument, not an objective neutral[18] scientific description.

1.2. Being (Self-)Aware and Being Wise Equal Making Responsible Decisions

Corporate leadership and boards need to adapt to a new mindset[19] that goes beyond cognitive intelligence[20]. The current rather mechanistic models found their birth in the Enlightenment period that served us well to "take control" over our socio-economic environment over the past two hundred fifty years. However, this perspective may have become outdated and in need for an urgent update. We concur that technology is neutral, and the way humans apply it, however, can be either benevolent or malicious. It is the responsibility of humans in charge to guarantee that AI technology or any other form of innovative technology is used to create a better life without harming others. Having a better understanding[21] of AI also resulted in a more refined understanding of ourselves, including our relationships with each other in business.

Wise decision-making, therefore, brings an additional set of critical variables into the equation of decision-making. **Wising up** enables managers to be commercially savvy, to make *reasonable* smart decisions, but also to commit to *responsible* behavior that distinguishes smart from wise leadership. Wise decision-making broadens the cognitive perspective to a framework in which a new synthesis of digital transformation and sustainability get a place. Non-financial criteria need to become part of such a new mindset. Organizational performance is not reduced to mere measurable financial objectives, but also contains soft elements that constitute the glue for an effective framework that is agile and flexible, adopting to changing contexts. Making wise decisions definitely implies a *relational* factor that is often grounded in tacit knowledge[22] – a knowledge that can also be linked to an ethical and socio-ecological component. *Values* and *responsibilities* are part of the factors in this decision-making process. It counts not only in optimizing stockholders' value, but also in satisfying legitimate stakeholders' concerns.

2. Responsible Decisions Enhancing (Intertwined) Relationships

Our research about this "new" kind of leadership concludes that conscientious "intelligent executives" – we labelled it a new breed of wise leaders – and their organizations will (1) embrace and cultivate some form of (assumed harmonious) *disciplined collaboration*[23] between the different kinds of intelligence[24] – including artificial intelligence – that transforms operations, markets, industries and the workforce with these new skills. This new more conscious leadership also (2) envisions a more meaningful and thus *purposeful* future that shows stakeholders what the organization can look like and guide or enable the organization to pursue that goal by appropriately *evoking emotions* that make those stakeholders want to support this overall goal in a passionate manner, which can be channelled to enhance organizational and ultimately shareholder value, and finally (3) by upholding the genuine *fiduciary duties* as *custodians*[25] instil profitable progress whilst making the society a better place to live.

2.1. Conscious Leaders Evoke Responsible Decision-Making That Focuses on "Relations" of the Business

That executives and board members need to commit to wiser decisions developing relationships[26] with stakeholders that matter is not just a luxury anymore, but it has become a necessity. Remaining competitive today involves embracing ambiguities and not oversimplifying the complexity of running and governing a business. Such leadership remains sensitive to the different relevant opinions and genuine stakes as well as the different time perspectives to remain sustainable. Taking care of those stakeholders requires a clear idea of strategy and a well-intentioned collaboration with crucial partners. In other words, boards and their executives will incentivize to build not just networks but also deep-seated collaborative relationships with some crucial stakeholders such as suppliers, employees and customers.

Apart from deepening the existing relationships, a collaborative relationship-oriented framework can also open opportunities for potential new relationships. IKEA's competitive advantage, for instance, is based on its trusting long-term relationships with its suppliers and partners to closely collaborate and co-create joint innovative investments[27]. Also, like the Schindler Group, a German manufacturer of escalators, walkways and elevators, who also understood the value of creating long-term trusted relationships with important prominent (potentially loyal) customers. Productive conversations between Schindler and a prospective customer, a multinational construction, property and infrastructure company, led to cost-saving initiatives, improved product quality and increased safety levels. In two years, the infrastructure company saved more than USD 16 million, and as a result, not only was Schindler awarded a large portion of its business, but it was also granted full visibility into its customer's 10-year project pipeline allowing to pre-empt innovative adaptations in collaboration with its new important customer[28]. However, those synergies connotated with business relationships are potentially still quite instrumental, and in that sense merely cognitively interpreted. I guess that the "relations" I am referring to are more deeply embedded into the eco-system. Organisms and organizations are interrelated and dependent on each other in the value chain to thrive. Developing and enhancing those more "fundamental" *interdependent systemic relations* are profound and necessary to sustain and to survive.

2.2. The Fiduciary Duties Imply to Take Care of the Organization and Its "Relations"

Developing and enhancing relations with business partners requires a "broader" and more systemic perspective in creating value. Wise leaders care for their employees, customers, investors and communities. They focus on increasing the willingness to pay and the willingness to supply[29]. It requires a broad systemic view in which *relations*, *duties* and *obligations* play their respective role. And yes, holders of shares should be rewarded for taking significant financial risks in providing capital without any guarantee. However, the legal community has awarded ownership in return for taking such risks, with allegedly full legal voting and cash flow rights power in the company. A debatable decision, nonetheless, according to a number of (legal) scholars[30]. Today, the shareholders are perceived to be the legal and legitimate owner of a business entity. It has been different before, and it may be again …

A. Should Fiduciary Duties Result in Smart Decisions? Or Wise Decisions?

The major difference between smart and wise leaders lies in the fact that (1) ethical and ecological normative values – i.e. "space" broadening – are incorporated in the decision-making, and/or (2) a long-term perspective is explicitly added. These values often express *socio-ethical relations* about respect for engaged *people*, a *planet* in harmony, and economic *prosperity*. This also implies a sense of intergenerational justice. *Wising up* contains (1) the ability to simultaneously think in terms of short-term results and long-term vision – the "time"-factor perspective – and (2) to optimize the shareholders' value while extending the fairness principle to those who have a real stake in the organization such as employees, customers, suppliers and potentially the community in which it operates, all relevant and concerned stakeholders. Most likely, this capability to hold two time perspectives at the same "*time*" and keeping different and sometimes opposing goals of different "*stake*"-holders[31] in mind may be one of the more challenging paradoxes for any board member who is responsible to look after the annual performance of the organization while preparing for an economic but also eco-social sustainable future.

If the objective of business is linked to creating organizational value through providing customers with a great experience, service or product, then strategy could be considered the blueprint for organizing such creation of value within the organization, and metrics as the bricks and wood of the organization. However, an organization can easily lose sight of its strategy and focus singlehandedly on one or two preferred metrics like a return on equity for instance, instead of understanding what the metrics represent. There are many unfortunate cases – often the result of surrogating metrics for strategy and cutting corners to achieve those desired metric objectives or measurements: be it Wells Fargo, or Enron, or World.Com. And the list is long … Any company should guard against *surrogation* of strategy by financial short-term metrics[32]. The danger of investor surrogating a strategy with focusing on quarterly accounting results (i.e. net operating income) is real.

B. Just One Bad Apple or Systemic "Greed"?

Let's just reveal the more recent case of *Theranos*, a notorious corporate scandal played out in the media today. The demise of the medical device company Theranos can be seen as the antipode of what I would consider wise decision-making. Its unethical and illegal practices – from board members over executives down to managers – were revealed to the outside world by two young managers of conscience who really cared about scientific standards, patient safety and family values. Despite the enormous financial and career stakes involved and thus the incredible pressure, these two young managers (Tyler Schultz and Erika Cheung), who on paper were relatively powerless, were courageous enough to withstand the intimidation and took the wise decision to dispose the scam. In a nutshell, Elizabeth Holmes, a young brilliant Stanford undergraduate, got the bright idea of a new method for blood testing, envisioning a high-tech device that would take a single drop of blood from a finger prick and use it to run multiple tests. Elizabeth subsequently established Theranos with the aim to change the health industry. If the elegant idea would prove to function, it would allow her to dominate the multibillion-dollar blood-testing market. She was able to convince high-profile stakeholders to join her board, including the dean of Stanford School of Engineering, senior diplomat and statesman Henry Kissinger, senator Sam Nunn, statesman George Schultz and a number of other high-profile kingmakers. It gave her company credibility and access to capital and connections. At the end, her "blood-testing device" scam – thriving on the Silicon Valley dreams of high-tech and high financial stakes – had attracted enormous flows of capital and capitalization. But in June 2018, after finally being exposed, Elizabeth Holmes, the founder and CEO, and her accomplice, COO Balwani were indicted[33]. Theranos formally ceased operations a few months later. All the well-connected relations were nothing but hiding walls used to hide selfish and irresponsible behavior under the veil of high-tech Silicon Valley expectations and "magic", underpinned by Wall Street egocentric "greedy" behavior. It is not unfair to say that irresponsible and unethical behavior were Theranos' undoing …

Responsible leaders are committed to appropriate accountability and responsibility, to transparency and fairness, and to a more ecological and inclusive organization and surrounding. Such desired kind of leadership functions as (moral) integrators who create value over a longer period for both *share-* and *stake*holders.

Some thoughts to take away:

- This chapter explores the notion of responsible leadership and how it differs from reasonable decision-makers.

- It's crucial to re-interpret this idea of wise or responsible decision-making in a swiftly changing business context where sustainability advocates that businesses are connected and embedded in a more holistic eco-system. Naturally, business and their boards may like to re-address the old traditional goals and provide a more appealing narrative to the younger more conscious generation.

- The chapter delineates the boundaries of a framework we imply for making wiser or more responsible decisions in business. It explains why the *future will be more "relational"* in a hyperconnected and increasingly digital reality – in which connectivity and social media relations will play an increasingly determining role.

Chapter Two

From Smart to Wise Decision-Making

"We believe that we are at an inflection point in the history of business. It is high time to think broadly and creatively about how business can achieve its full potential and how we can avoid its historical weaknesses. […] By focusing on the most powerful word in our language, 'AND', we can take giant steps toward making the business world more responsible".

Ed Freeman, Kirsten Martin & Bidhan Parmar, 2020

"Everything has been said before, but since nobody listens, we have to keep going back and beginning all over again".

André Gide, French novelist

*S*mart or *reasonable* decision-making[1] is crucial and a pre-condition for *wise* decision-making. We empirically researched this in a global Amrop survey published anno 2017[2]. We hypothesized a model – as shown in Figure 1 – in which smartness is necessary, but not enough to gain track in a very competitive and increasingly susceptible business context in which customers and other stakeholders – such as suppliers, advertisers and influencers, for instance – want more than just "good products". Increasingly, these stakeholders also care for the environment and the communities in which firms are operational, and thus, the way decisions are (ethically) made. Employees want to be part of an organization that is embedded in a narrative with a clear purpose, allowing them to be proud of being part of such an organization.

Wise leaders go a step further than mere smart intelligent decision-making. They incorporate more *"relational"* factors and *broader (time)* perspective in their decision-making. Ignoring these relational and time factors often creates moral hazards. Externalizing pollution is a typical example of such a hazard, although proving that this "pollution" causally result in life-threatening or a degrading situation is not always (scientifically) easy. Let us not forget that corporate governance and its fiduciary duties have been installed to counter the potential misuse of power of those who have asymmetric information about the firm's activities and its ramifications – which they might use for their own short-term benefit and not in the interest of the organizational longer-term goals[3]. A shift

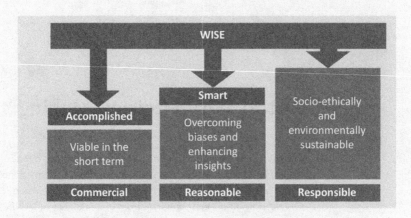

Figure 1: From smart to wise decision-making

Source: Verhezen, P. & S. Gande – Amrop (2018), *Wise Leadership and AI*

from smart to wise decision-makers will require a more holistic perspective that emphasizes the *interdependent relations* of our eco-system. Some refer to this more holistic view as "deep-time humility", or as a "transcendental legacy mindset" who thinks real long term, or even as "intergenerational justice" to indicate the moral hazards we create for those coming after us[4].

1. In Essence, What Is Business All About?

Our starting point is that any organization is and should be focused on creating value. But value *for whom* and *for what*? The traditional mainstream corporate governance view will tell you that it is the fiduciary duty to maximize profitability, mainly benefiting the shareholders and top leadership – who will receive bonuses and stock options for good performance – and in best case, governance experts will tell you that value creation is focused on the organization. Again, who represents the organization? It is here that the perspectives start to significantly differ. Do we take *an outside-in view* that emphasizes how much the value created by the organization benefits others like customers and communities[5]? Or do we focus on how management and leadership – and if you're generous, you include employees – have fulfilled their fiduciary duties for which they should be well remunerated, as in *an inside-out view*? Boards and their members should combine an outside view with an inside approach, not an *either or* approach that often interprets the world as a zero-sum game.

1.1. Value Creation Is the Aim of Any Business

Should we start with focusing on value first, and subsequently asking who will benefit from the various activities of the organization, really? Poor metrics – that measure achievement of goals but without creating real substantial value for customers and other relevant stakeholders – should be avoided. If you are a supplier and you aim to optimize that shipments reach the customer, then measuring whether the shipments left your warehouse according to the schedule (an inside-out view) may suit your objectives, but it hardly adds any value to the customer who is interested when it arrives in time at the customers' warehouse who urgently needs the equipment (an outside-in view)[6].

A. *Efficiency in Value Creation Is What Business Is All About …*

Value creation is more than maximizing output with minimum input – which is described as efficiency[7]. When creating value, we should aim to create an output that really benefits others – customers to start with – done in an efficient manner while simultaneously providing high quality. It gets even more complex when we add (moral) values to the value-creation equation, often ignored by the top leadership solely focused on optimizing profitability or shareholders' value. Such "moral values" are often intertwined in an organizational value creation that aims to "benefit the other". *Wise leaders* will be able to *create corporate shared value*[8] by emphasizing the interdependencies of a firm's objectives and the societal objectives, instead of the traditional focus on the tension between these objectives.

B. *… While Balancing an Inside-Out Perspective and Outside-In View*

What makes wise decision-making so distinctive from smart decisions? Wise corporate leaders obsessively focus on value creation. They will almost always integrate an *outside-in view* that emphasizes the importance of loyal customers, trustworthy suppliers and generous communities, with an *inside-out perspective* emphasizing the importance of engaged and productive employees, and obviously committed capital providers. You could even argue that those risk-taking founders of companies feel compelled to keep shareholders' primacy, merely because their inside view focuses on the specific circumstances that led them to invest money in an organization and the confidence that "one will make it". Any outside (presumably more objective) view could be seen as a distraction for those risk-takers. My own experience of having established a commercial for-profit organization confirms this psychological feeling of excitement and the need of feeling confident enough "to make it happen". Our subjective feeling to succeed in our venture is so strong that we would ignore any outside (likely more pessimistic) perspective. It seems that most of us almost psychologically deliberately omit the fact that potential "unknown unknowns" could and often occur in a longer-term projects[9].

As any entrepreneur knows, you need to be little obsessed with your own idea, and the possibility (not necessary the probability that usually is lower than expected) to have success. In other words, an outside view with higher validity is often ignored, especially if it looks incompatible with your personal (subjective) impressions of a case or venture: "In the competition with the inside view, the outside view doesn't stand a chance[10]". And yes, that preference for an inside view sometimes carries moral overtones, especially if that view – reward shareholders with a well-deserved return for the risks taken that no one else would take – has become mainstream among like-minded entrepreneurs and owners.

Again, my aim is not to provide a lengthy and detailed explanation on how to become smarter decision-makers – as in being less biased, more inventive and better informed. Most business schools and business management authors will tell you how to do this. For a better understanding in the details of smart decision-making, I would strongly recommend the incredible, insightful and substantiated work by the Nobel prize winner in Economics, Daniel Kahneman, especially his quite accessible and hugely eloquent *"Thinking, Fast and Slow"*. What a marvel that should be made mandatory for any business student[11]. Allow me to repeat: I am using the notion of smart decision-making as a condition or as a stepstone to move to a next state in which (philosophical or socio-ethical thinking or) wisdom gets on that stage – a crucial ingredient that is often lacking in business decisions. Let us return to the complexity of (smart) decision-making before we move to the core of my argument: making wise decisions.

1.2. Making Reasonable and Responsible Decisions

Smartness alone, then, is unlikely to equip leaders to address the complex business circumstances affecting society today. The global challenges we now face, beg for policy-makers and executives not just to be *smart* – as in allocating scarce resources in the most effective, efficient and innovative way – but also to act *wisely*. Call it a form of enlightened self-interest. In situation that may cause moral hazards or contribute to a more harmonious collaboration, responsible leaders can really make a difference. They are aware of the biases and errors that haunt presumed rational efficiency thinking. Making judgements in these cloudy and often fuzzy areas will require business executives to think as *reasonable* **and** *responsible* optimizers within "bounded rationality"[12].

Responsible leaders need to help their teams, managers, peers and board members to broaden their perspective, giving them the tools to become more mindful and the courage to address the difficult grey areas that require a *tough but fair* and thus *reasonable* **and** *responsible* decision. These leaders need to think as human socio-relational beings whose decisions may affect not only themselves, their organization and their subordinates but also the communities and possibly even humankind in general. Is this not the golden rule – sometimes also referred as *the rule of karma* – that we all (should) bear the consequences for our own actions? By extension, that applies to organizations as well.

In a nutshell, smart leaders turn into wise leaders when they can help themselves and others to holistically address and resolve the difficult socio-ethical dilemmas we all face in business. Over a longer period, the "return on responsible behavior" can be significant[13], because customer and other stakeholders would (start to) trust such an organization (again). However, I acknowledge that "doing good" – taking that broader view by combining an inside-out view with an outside-in view – is not necessarily or automatically resulting in higher profitability, both short and long term. Business is much more complex and difficult than adding or deducting some variables or notions into the economic equation or in the business model. Doing good can result in doing well – if the strategy is well thought through and executed – but there is no guarantee at all. Ignoring this truth often leads to "greenwashing", using sustainability as an advertising campaign to mislead ignorant or naïve investors and other stakeholders alike.

2. Smart Decision-Making Creating Value

Let's briefly decipher some of the variables that constitute smart decision-making. How to comprehend the subtle differences between smart and wise decision-making. The "metaphor" of smart decision-making is meant to initiate some ingredients that are necessary to optimize decisions that create value – and why that is distinguishable from wise decision-making in mainstream economics.

2.1. The Triangle of Smart Decision-Making

My starting assumption is that *smart decision-making*[14] combines three necessary features to perform well and achieve a certain level of commercial success:

1. the ability to *adapt to a changing context* because smart executives enable their teams to improve business results from investing in innovative product and services. These teams produce on average more insightful ideas that they translate in innovative products;
2. the propensity to sense, and to foresee, or *"predict" the future* as knowing how to make less errors, and reduce chaos and uncertainty – potentially with the use of smart computers or AI, allowing to become better predictors about the future and thus be able to react and/or respond in a speedier manner, while finally
3. having the *sensible grit or resilience* to withstand adversity or crises, an attitude without which it would be hard to withstand any form of negativity or hay wind. *Resilience* and *sensible grit*[15] reflect how leadership deals with adversity.

The recent Covid-19 pandemic and the subsequent global recession brought home not only the importance of resilience, grit[16] and agility in business, but also the ability to sense or even predict new business opportunities. Being self-confident allows us to have a balanced (self-)esteem and to feel a level of resilience that withstands pressure. Being resilient is an (psychological and philosophical) attitude that gets us through the chatter of negative gossip and noise around us. The Roman philosopher and statesman Seneca was convinced that "it is a rough road that leads to the heights of greatness". In a volatile, uncertain, complex and ambiguous world, resilience is a *sine qua non*, without which it is hard to survive.

In summary, these three features of *adaptability, predictability* and sensible grit or *resilience*[17], all characterize smart decision-making. All the three features

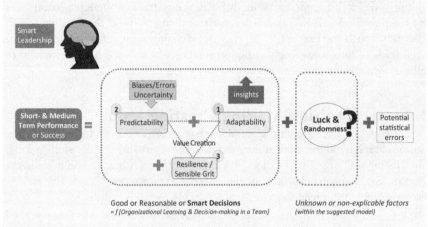

Figure 2: Smart decision-making that aims to optimize *stockholder* value

are interlinked and necessary to create organizational value, visualized hereunder (see Figure 2). Let me try to translate those variables of smart decision-making in terms of intelligence – that I will need to deconstruct the kind of intelligences encountered in AI algorithms.

2.2. IQ and RQ Constituting Smart Decision-Making

Indeed, I concur the argument that boards and teams making smart decisions require three fundamental features to be able to predict the future more accurately, to be flexible enough to adapt to changing contexts, and to be resilient in a smart way to withstand difficulties, ambiguities and even crises. Being smart can therefore be translated in the simplified sum of two crucial *cognitive abilities* or *different intelligences*. We distinguish a form of generic intelligence (**IQ** or intellectual quotient) – to make reasonable decisions – from the ability to assess risks (**RQ** or risk quotient) – or *making* "informed" *reasonable decisions* in uncertain situations.

A. Why T-Shaped Directors on Boards Are Desirable?

In her excellent book on governance, the economist and international board member Dr. Dambisa Moyo describes the need for "T-shaped directors"[18]. Basically, I reinterpret this T-shaped knowledge of generic intelligence on one hand and a specialized competency on the other hand, as leaders who have both a high level of IQ and RQ. This T-shaped board member has a broad enough knowledge and expertise to contribute to the bigger picture of (entangled) problems and challenges at the board, but this member has also a specific "deep" capability or competence in a particular area. That specific capability obviously varies from (explicit) knowledge such as AI development, reducing waste in operations or being specialized in option trading, if being at the board of a corporate investment bank, for instance.

Business schools prepare their participants to get a good grip on those different specialities, all needed to run a business efficiently and effectively. I group all these forms of (specialized) capabilities under the general flag of **IQ**. At the same time, these board members are expected to be able to foresee profitable possibilities as in knowing to take *informed* decisions about an uncertain future, which I have labelled as a high level of knowing to assess specific risk-oriented activities or **RQ**. This kind of intelligence simplifies and models a certain "measurable" probability and multiplies it with the possible impact that previously was considered "uncertain".

B. *Fundamental Uncertainty, Randomness and the (Un)Known (Un)Knowns*

Sometimes, the future remains fundamentally uncertain and random. Randomness contains an element of unpredictability. Fate, "fortune", randomness or luck is independent of the actions of the key actors in the organization. Further, the notion of luck or randomness may also have potentially significant consequences either on the upside (positive) or downside (negative).

However hard we put a probability "number" on a potential foreseen event – one we pinpoint down on a measurable event – it can obviously be digitized. Although we never can undo luck or randomness, we can use the notion of risk as in statistical and algorithmic thinking as a proxy for addressing these uncertain situations. This can also be considered when analyzing companies, those who were successful did not have more luck than anyone else, but they were better able to capitalize on the luck that they got, the luck that any company or person can expect over a long-time horizon.

From risk management literature and experience, we know that if we cannot *prevent* these potential negative events, we may need to *prepare* for those unlikely but impactful events to be reduced or mitigated. Or in case of positive potential events, you want to be prepared to *capture* them when "luck" actually pops up – an approach occasionally applied in financial or real option trading for instance[19]. Indeed, people or organizations who are successful recognize potential in fortuitous opportunities and capitalize on them[20]. In the case of a negative unfortunate downside, these organizations are better prepared to deal with such downturns. Smart executives are usually better prepared to embrace this "luck" or deal with their (un)fortune.

When a board does not know "*unknown knowns*" (i.e. we know we don't know) or "*unknown unknowns*" (i.e. we are not even aware that we don't know), they may consider scenario-building or war gaming for possibly catching certain risks or addressing the unknown knowns. All those activities fall under the notion of RQ. Some individuals are much better than others in foreseeing the future[21], which is a crucial ability to steer an organization.

We explicitly mention the often forgotten variable of **luck** or **randomness** in this "equation" because not everything today can be scientifically explained or clarified. This notion of luck is an important piece of non-explainable "truth" behind success and performance. Statistically, it is the non-explained part that evades the descriptive predication of scientific hypothesis-testing.

This notion of randomness[22] is to be distinguished from pure (statistic) inaccuracies or even plain errors. Randomness seems to escape the human desire to be fully controlled. Smart leaders acknowledge the role of randomness in business. However, most decision-makers are prone to biases, especially overconfidence and potential hubris, completely negating the impact of luck in our life. It is also true that optimistic and confident individuals play a disproportionate role in shaping our daily lives, be it inventors, entrepreneurs, politicians or military leaders. Sure, they are likely quite talented and skilful, but they also have been most likely luckier than the average[23]. One of the main benefits of an optimistic approach is that it encourages persistence in the face of obstacles, that can be transformed into resilience or grit. But despite the importance to be gritty, it should also be noted that persistence can be quite costly due to "persistent cognitive biases" or hubris in making decisions. Aren't we familiar with the fact that the outcome of a start-up depends as much on achievements of its competitors[24] and changes in the market as on its own efforts.

Smartness is necessary but not sufficient to sustain business success. Good decision-making will need some additional elements to allow business to prepare for the future and touch not just the minds of their stakeholders but also the hearts and the souls. Business cannot deny their embeddedness in such a broader *relational* eco-system. We attempt to characterize this systemic framework as a combination of capabilities that allow us to be logic-analytical and insightful while also being prescriptive[25] through ethical values. Prescribing a certain vision or future direction implicitly assumes a certain "model" or values[26] that underpin our mindset – the topic of Chapter 4. Before addressing this more in detail, let's pause for a few minutes and assess why the current prevailing financial economic model of maximizing shareholders' value is now widely and critically interpreted as part of the current problem, instead of a possible solution to the challenges we face today.

Some thoughts to take away:

- This chapter deciphers the transition from smart to wise decision-making. This generic framework of smart and wise decision-making is linked to the different forms of intelligence that are required to meet both stockholders' and stakeholders' expectations.

- *Smartness* is necessary, but *wising up* will make the difference of thriving, surviving or perishing over a longer period. Some elements of smart decision-making are assessed, and in addition, the crucial connecting and appealing narrative around a meaningful purpose is added to constitute the link with a more sustainable form of competitiveness of firms.

- We distinguish two constitutive forms of intelligence to make smart decisions: IQ (to run a business effectively and efficiently) and RQ (to make informed strategic decisions about an uncertain future). In addition, smart decision-makers acknowledge the importance of randomness or luck that indicates that portion that is not explained by a scientific "objective" statistical methodology, a part that seems to escape our "controlling" oriented business understanding.

Chapter Three

Why Shareholders' Primacy Is Under Scrutiny Today[1]?

"Not that everything that counts can be counted, and not everything that can be counted, counts".

Albert Einstein

"What shall it profit a man if he gains the world and loses himself".

Luke 9: 24–25

"Purpose creates a unifying vision for all of a company's stakeholders, including its employees, customers, partners and shareholders. [...] Climate risk is investment risk that has become something of a mantra at BlackRock, and our leaders are generating greater value – and reducing risk – for our clients as a result. [...] they are creating new funds to bring private capital into emerging markets to finance sustainable infrastructure. They are living our purpose".

Larry Fink, Co-founder and CEO of BlackRock, 2019

That the board as the custodians of the organization is expected to take smart decisions that financially benefit the organization goes without saying. It's the basis of our (liberal) market capitalist system. Indeed, commercially savvy and smart executives take pragmatic actions by minimizing errors and transcending biases while optimizing innovative insights that result in competitive strategies – strategies that exploit the current advantages and explore new innovative solutions that will generate future net cash flow.

The orthodoxy in decision theory has always claimed the scientific high ground, pointing to its assumed sophisticated mathematical underpinnings. These mathematical formulas have always been a rough and simplified representation of an economic phenomenon. Secondly, while making judgements, the decision-maker will be counted for its actions. Nowadays, a computer does not just perform some calculations. With artificial intelligence, organizations can tweak and refine the mathematical model it is using without taking full responsibility. Confronting uncertainty and ethical dilemmas, we should pace cautiously and tentatively.

Especially in settings where *data is scarce* and the *situation is volatile*, machine learning is not very helpful. Boards usually make decisions in a setting of pure (un)measurable uncertainty. A pure calculating approach based on probability information may not suffice. Instead, boards and their executives may resort to scenarios and story-telling with a clear vision and purpose, creating an appealing future that can be materialized – within the legal and socio-ecological boundaries that governments and regulators should impose on all business participants. Unfortunately, government often fail to do so.

Maynard Keynes claimed that economics is a science of thinking in terms of models joined to the art of choosing models that are relevant to the contemporary world. He was convinced that economics is essentially a moral science and not a natural science[2]. In other words, it employs introspection and judgement of value to understand economics and business. My assumptions here – following Keynes' belief – are that these ethical presumptions and value judgements are comprehensively embedded in economics, in many varied and often subtle ways.

Why do organizations exist? To create value and make money in the process is the often heard adage. If you follow the legal interpretation of the Delaware Corporate Law – under which 70 percent of all US-based companies are incorporated – then directors have the fiduciary duty of care, loyalty and good faith to both the corporation and its shareholders. This has led to the prevailing theory of shareholders' primacy today. Is this the end of the business story, making money in the most efficient manner under the rule of law, and that's it? Not quite.

1. Shareholders' Short-Term Value "Versus" Sustainable Value?

Yes, we observe that naturally humans are "groupish" as well as "selfish"[3]. But because of those natural instincts, we also have survived as groups. Probably, the unilateral legal interpretation of fiduciary and this feeling of "groupishness" has led to this economic paradigm of business as maximizing profitability for their shareholders. Today, that idea of profitability at all costs is not cutting it anymore. A board and their executives today are supposed to being able to be superb managers while also being visionary leaders. It's about being ruthlessly focused on profitability and efficiency and simultaneously being open to care for a sustainable world and its needs.

1.1. Creating, Capturing and Sharing of Value Results in Optimization of Profit

Entrepreneurs and business people know that without clients and talent, there is no sustainable business possible. Creating value encompasses (1) *customers* who are willing to pay a price for those products and services, (2) managerial and creative *talent* that is willing to supply knowledge and labor that drives innovation and (3) *producers* of services and material in the supply chain that are willing *to supply* as in manufacturing and shipping those intermediary products and material at a fair price. At the end of the process, after all contractual agreements are met, a net return on invested capital as a residue will go to the providers of capital, i.e. the owners and investors of the organization. Logically, focusing only on the capital providers may have seriously limited the enormous potential of business. But it also enabled to provide a strong sensible model to provide a (fair) return on invested capital at risk. Wising up broadens the perspective and is more inclusive without omitting the focus on generating cash flow and investment of scarce resources[4]. A short explanation of this underlying context of more inclusiveness in business is necessary for making reasonable inferences on the technology of artificial intelligence[5] that is part of this envisaged broader and more holistic context[6]. More inclusion is not just asking for more gender equality, or ethnic diversity, or addressing me-too issues, but it is really about the distinction of shareholders and those with a real stake in co-constituting the health and prospect of an organization.

A. Corporate Shared Value or Sharing Created Value?

Optimizing revenues and profits should not cause significant unpriced externalities that negatively affect stakeholders or even directly harm people and communities. This kind of organizational harmful behavior is not acceptable anymore in the current global economy where reputations – built over years – can be destroyed within minutes or days. Firms are increasingly scrutinized by concerned stakeholders these days.

Akin to the notion of "corporate shared value" (CSV) – a notion brought into the realm of business strategy by Professor Michael Porter and Michael Kramer – is what I believe can be described as *creating and sharing value*. Sharing created value can be seen as an "architectural innovation" that emphasizes the contributions from relationship between the components of a system or organism without necessarily changing the components themselves. Without loyal customers, managerial talent, employee productivity, or committed suppliers, an organization would not last too long. It requires an act of profound imagination and creativity, in the way we make decisions and judgements about a future we never are certain of. That is what this book aims to focus on: emphasizing the importance of relationships among members of teams, within the organization, between humans and AI technology, and even between organizations and those (stakeholders) in an eco-system. By looking at those relationships, organizations may start re-thinking the way all the pieces fit together – interpreting the organization as a nexus of relationships.

We believe that this is a more sensible approach for any business than just focusing on one of the stakeholders in the organization, more particularly the providers of capital who are indeed taking financial risks. Obviously, shareholders are the initiators or founders of the organization and therefore likely among, if not the most important stakeholders. However, we claim that high levels of employee satisfaction who are fully engaged to help materializing the firm's objectives, loyal customers who feel satisfied with the organizations' delivery of service and experience, and the presence of a purpose are all closely linked to strategic thinking and will ultimately improve the total shareholder value.

Much research indicates that quite a number of investors are often "long-term" thinkers, but their asset managers may not be. These asset managers or traders gain from each small number of trades made; in the worst scenario, even "churning" that only benefits the financial "traders", not the ultimate owner. Having said that, we need to shade that long-term thinking a little since the average time an investor holds stock in the USA used to be 5.6 years in 1976, but it has been reduced to 7.4 months on average in 2015[7]. Is the reduction mainly due to the asset managers and analysts trading on behalf of the financiers, or are the equity-owners becoming less patient as well? Again, these are aggregate average figures that do not reveal anything about the individual organization or its individual owners.

Free markets really work their magic only when everything is properly priced. Which of course it not always the case. As long as an organization and consumers can burn fossil fuels at no ecological cost, poison the oceans and discard their waste without penalty, they will continue to drive global warming and negatively impact our planet.

B. Reimagining Capitalism

The interplay and tension between self-interest and a shared sense of common good or "shared destiny" will provide the energy that is propelling us forward to a "reimagined capitalism", as Harvard Professor Henderson eloquently stated[8]. I may go a step further by emphasizing our interdependency in the eco-system and its relations or connectivity, and remind us about the (philosophically and spiritually) illusive nature of our self-interested needs.

Financial performance as expressed in the balance sheet and profit and loss report tells you how well the organization has done historically, but not whether it is making the right investments to create a prosperous future. If one only looks at the financial statements, there is an incredible amount of information that one does not see. Admittedly, that is why liquid stock prices and capitalization of aggregate stock incorporates the expectations of investors and the market. If a listed company such as *Tesla* or *Amazon* is expected to generate considerable (surplus) cash flow in the future, the stock price will likely rise. But at what socio-ecological cost? One of the attempts to broaden the view and take the future more into account is to look at non-financial data. The current trend is to reform accounting and to include audible ESG data, as in incorporating those non-financials in the disclosed information to the investors, and in case of public listed companies to the public at large.

1.2. ESG-Criteria and Impact?

Increasing external pressure by stakeholders like climate activists or stricter government regulations, or more conscious and demanding customers who want ecological, ethical and fair trade products ask for more openness on how products are manufactured. Equally demanding and mindful managers and aspiring employees see a built-in sustainability vision as a way to improve productivity and meaning in their job. Last, but not least, an increasing number of investors believe that sustainability – as expressed in ESG criteria[9] – should be part of the performance benchmarks beyond mere short-term profitability. It is clear that corporate leaders will soon be held accountable by shareholders for their non-financial ESG performance.

A. Businesses Warm Up for Sustainability

It is not a mere coincidence that early 2019 Blackrock's CEO, Larry Find – one of the biggest global investment funds based in New York with more than USD 6 trillion assets under its management, and making almost USD 5 billion profit on USD 12.5 billion earnings – urged his colleagues to link profit to purpose, and constructively engage with important stakeholders to integrate sustainability into their performance measures. It is obvious that these investors are not acting out of altruistic motives but believe that corporate responsible investments will reduce risks and create more value for their organizations both in the short and definitely over a longer period.

A recent research (2020) by Accenture and United Nations Global Compact (UNGC) confirmed that a majority of 93 percent of CEOs believe that sustainability will be critical to the future success of their businesses, and 91 percent report that their organization will employ new, more innovative technologies to address these sustainability challenges. Almost 67 percent of global CEOs strongly believe that sustainability has become crucial for their strategies, and more than 90 percent is convinced that collaboration between companies, government institutes and not-for-profit organizations is needed to materialize more sustainability strategies. A recent survey confirmed that investors want their organizations to become more sustainable. A 2016 PWC study of sustainability reporting by 470 companies in 17 countries found that 62 percent mentioned Sustainability Development Goals (SDGs), although less than a third (28 percent) provided precise quantitative targets that linked performance to social and environmental impact. More than half of global asset owners are currently implementing or evaluating ESG considerations in their investments[10].

Quite a number of cases and international studies reveal that "social responsible investments" (SRIs) which adhere to stricter ESG criteria are expected to lead to higher productivity and operational efficiency while complying to changing market expectations. The biggest barrier is the fact that most of ESG reporting – be it Global Reporting Initiative (GRI) or Sustainability Accounting Standards Board (SASB) reports – is catered not at other investors but directed at stakeholders such as NGOs. The reported numbers in these ESG reports are rarely subject to a rigorous audit[11]. Nonetheless, the quality of ESG data may not be perfect yet; these reports are rapidly improving, especially among big asset managers and institutional investors such as Blackrock, CalPERS and Vanguard. Today, the EU directive requires all European companies beyond a particular size to report non-financial information once a year. But still too many subjective interpretations remain possible – absence of a real generally accepted international standard[12], which can easily lead to greenwashing[13].

When ESG reporting is used to "greenwash" and hide the real intention of investors, nothing will really change for the better. On the contrary, fake and "false" – or deliberate ambiguous data to hide the facts – information is "devaluing" the potential real improvement in, or impact of, sustainability on society. Using ESG reports to allegedly "signal" (misleading) commitment to societal value in particular investments in organizations is akin to greenwashing and will ultimately undermine the credibility of those sustainability ESG reports[14].

The effect of alleged water drainage of Coca-Cola manufacturing in India, or Google's privacy infringement of confidential information channelled to Chinese authorities leading to the imprisonment of a Chinese activist years ago, has proven the importance of preserving the firm's corporate reputation. The answer to avoiding such reputation damage is to enhance the accountability of the organization and its executives. To do so, CEOs and boards need to design organizations that become more ethical and act beyond mere compliance. It starts with creating an ethical culture within organizations, not just in terms of beliefs and values, but also systemically designed to engage in more ethical behavior and making ethical principles foundational in strategies and policies. To succeed, boards need to hire the right CEOs and board members, to evaluate them according to those foundational principles and compensate these top executives accordingly. That's exactly the reason why I joined this global executive search company Amrop as an advisor to assess the future criteria to be considered for a "new kind of leadership".

B. Adhering to Horizontal Accountability?

Mainstream economists consider a firm as a "*nexus of contracts*" between the principal and the agent – labelled as the Principal-Agency Model. This traditional industrial society may need to be translated into another form of governance (in a changing post-industrial knowledge society). We argue that the firm defined as a *nexus of contracts* should be reinterpreted and broadened to interpret the organization as a *nexus of relationships (be it contractual or informal)* – or rather a *nexus of relational commitments* to a certain objective or even purpose. Such relational-oriented perspective can and will impact its value creation on the opportunities upside, and value preservation on the downside – as visualized in Figure 1.

Unfortunately, at the heart of most of enterprises' untrustworthy behavior to disrespect customers', employees' and communities' concerns is a nearly manic obsession of top executives with short-term financial results and disregard for longer-term financial and non-financial implications, partially due to misaligned incentive and price systems. Short-term oriented companies dismiss the long-term consequences of their actions in order to generate current-period profits – feeding the potential bonuses of executives, potentially pump up stock prices to meet the analyst's expectation.

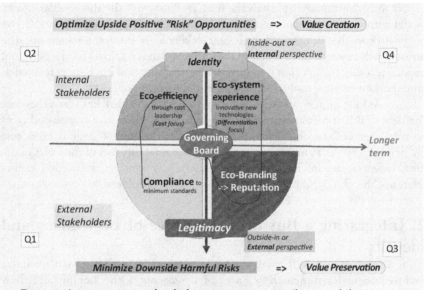

Figure 1: An eco-narrative that links steering strategy and sustainability

A good strategy that encapsulates responsible and more sustainable corporate behavior would enable to produce more value for society for every dollar spent or invested – analogous to charging a higher premium price. Otherwise it would produce as much value using fewer resources – the equivalent of lower costs. In both cases, the firm would obtain a competitive advantage as result of enhanced responsible behavior – even if it would only be in a particular niche. Although we deliberately distinguish accountability – underpinning its license to operate to secure its legitimacy – from responsibility that likely engrains a form of identity of such social and ethical behavior in most discussions, the two notions are used interchangeably.

Paradoxically, pursuing the creation of shared value[15] and improving skills of human talent while reining in extreme selfish corporate behaviors may help to improve the competitiveness or productivity of corporations[16]. Sharing value with stakeholders may become the corporate narrative of an enterprise, allowing them to be perceived not just as being trustworthy (i.e. honest) but also as trustable. Indeed, the notion of sustainability can be embedded in a strategy (1) to reduce potential organizational *reputation risks* or as a *social safety net* in cases of crises, (2) to enhance the *brand's reputation* of an enterprise, (3) to express and embed the *purpose* of a more responsible "vanguard" enterprise or (4) to align non-financial objectives (as in ESG reporting) to financial long-term planning.

Obviously, board members have a *fiduciary duty of both loyalty and care* to the organization. *Multi-market accountability* or *horizontal accountability*[17] requires boards to be accountable not just to capital providers (i.e. vertical accountability) but also to other "markets" (e.g. employees, customers, community and government) that expect some "sustainability" from the firm. By "merging" the shareholder theory model with some valuable aspects of the stakeholder and stewardship model, the argument goes that by taking the relevant stakeholders' interest into account, the firm will reduce potential conflicts in the future and thus retain its good reputation. In such a conflict-resolution hypothesis, sustainability and ESG are perceived as an important tactical tool to address potential reputational risks.

As long as greenwashing can be minimized or avoided, ESG could become the new standard measurement for proper accountability and responsibility of firms[18]. When ESG becomes *built-in* or baked in into the firm's strategic or economic financial objectives, to make socio-ecological sustainability part of the DNA of the firm, the enterprise and its board start to function as "syncretic stewards", serving reference shareholders and concerned involved stakeholders.

2. Integrating a Business Narrative of Legitimacy and Identity

Some organizations will focus on an identity that is aligned with a more socio-ecological vision such as *Puma* or *Pantagonia*. Others emphasize their legitimacy by incorporating ESG requirements in their annual reports to show their "goodwill" to do good to the public at large. *Nike* and *Adidas* are examples of companies legitimizing their existence by incorporating those ESG criteria.

2.1. Identity of Legitimacy?

Unilever, an example of a leader in sustainability and corporate shared value, is trying to find new ways of doing business by working with others to accelerate social transformation and to embed sustainability at the core of their corporate strategy, brand and company vision, and mission statements. Unilever's Compass Strategy, for example, aims to "double the size of the business, whilst reducing the environmental footprint and increasing its positive impact" and argues on its website that it "will lead for responsible growth, inspiring people to take small everyday actions that will add up to a big difference". Unilever definitely identifies itself with those socio-ecological objectives. Paul Potman, Unilever's former CEO and a major protagonist of more sustainable corporate behavior claims that at Unilever, "brands all have a social, economic and a product mission"[19]. Unfortunately, the financial market currently remains sceptical about Unilever's sustainability objectives and rather unconvinced as long as its stock-price lingers behind its main competitor Nestlé.

Pantagonia, an ecological US apparel manufacturer, is committed to ESG and has lobbied with partners and competitors – the Sustainable Apparel Coalition – to develop a rigorous value chain index that provides consumers a uniform rating mechanism to judge the socio-ecological impact of those firms. Its founder recently decided to take the exceptional step to give away the shares to "the planet". One cannot be more radical than that to embrace a stakeholders' perspective.

Marks & Spencer's latest advertising campaign seems to be committed to corporate responsibility goals by trying to persuade consumers to change consumer attitude and behavior choose something to recycle by conveniently "shwop drops" in its stores before purchasing a new item. They call it "shwopping" (a conflation of shopping and swapping). M&S's CEO is taking social responsibility very seriously since its practices have been under heavy scrutiny.

Puma, a sport lifestyle provider, adjusted their methods and work systems trying to live its ethics every day in every way by adhering to their "Puma.Safe". These internal guiding standards embrace eco-branding and seem to imply some form of eco-systemic vision, as in their "Social Accountability and Fundamental Environmental Standards".

These socio-ethical and ecological objectives or standards can be translated into a "sustainability-oriented" tactics or strategy that emphasizes identity and/or legitimacy (of intangibles) as visualized in Figure 1.

2.2. Integrating Sustainability into the Organization's Business Model

Today, intangible value constitutes the biggest part of the valuation of shares on any major stock exchange, whereas three to four decades ago, most value was derived from financial profitability. It is not too difficult to see that investors often incorporate the urgency of sustainability or CSV (or the lack thereof) into the stock price of listed companies[20]. Hence why ESG has become an albeit imperfect tool for measuring and reporting non-financial performance objectives.

A. *Visionary Responsible Leadership Integrates ESG into Its Strategy and Operations*

Ultimately, only the board can push and steer the organization to a more coherent and visionary ideal with a positive impact on the economy and society. Genuinely building sustainability objectives into the overall strategy of a firm takes time. Boards should be given ample time to go through different phases (1) to comply to more stringent (external) sustainability rules and regulations, (2) to invest into resources allowing to creatively innovate and achieve some eco-efficiency in the firm's operations, (3) to incorporate those sustainability objectives into the overall strategy of the firm while ensuring the reputation of the brand while minimizing potential risks and ultimately, (4) to envision an organization that oozes the philosophy of emphasizing the interdependence and linkages between financial business targets and the broader societal objectives – as visualized in Figure 2.[21]

In an initial phase, often regulations are driving organizations to adopt a more sustainable strategy to comply with some minimal requirements such as automotive car manufacturers trying to reduce the CO_2 footprint conform to the EU commission standards. Moreover, organizations adapt to a more sustainable strategy to obtain production and productivity efficiency gains, be it from less waste or recycling. Under external pressure, quite a number of companies build

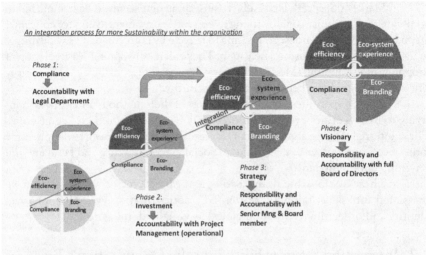

Figure 2: Integration process of sustainability (CSR/CSV) into strategy and the board's responsibility

in a more sustainable strategy to gain over customers and the community at large, often based on branding their products or services as part of being a trustworthy corporate citizen. Such reputation gains take quite some effort and time, but can be lost in a few minutes as *BP, Siemens* or *Volkswagen* have found out at their peril.

Ultimately, organizations continuously invest into the organization to materialize their sustainability vision. Such visions and missions are reflecting the eco-systemic experience that engages organizations attempt to achieve. Sustainability becomes the DNA of the organization with well-known examples as *Pantagonia* (a B-company), *Body Shop* (recently acquired by *Natura* from L'Oréal), *Ben & Jerry* (owned by Unilever) and a couple of other pioneers in creating more sustainable products and services.

B. The Reality of These Lofty Goals on the Ground?

Empirical data suggest that the positive stock market reaction by (institutional) investors to eco-friendly initiatives has decreased over time, while negative reactions to eco-harmful behavior have become more negative. The more that becoming green is institutionalized as the norm, the greater the negative effect of negative news on perceptions of a firm, because firms are punished for not following the norm. Similarly, the more that companies enact the institutional norm of going green, the less reactive shareholders are to the announcement of eco-friendly initiatives. The latter is called an internal perspective that states that environmental ESG is a resource with decreasing marginal returns. In addition, ESG seems to function as insurance, mitigating shareholders' negative reaction to the announcement of eco-harmful events. Moreover, firms with stronger environmental performance experience a smaller stock-price increase following the announcement of eco-friendly initiatives – as if the price has already incorporated "good responsible behavior" – and a smaller decrease following the announcement of eco-harmful behavior. Research cautious boards and managers to limit ESG investments. Especially, firms that already have a high corporate debt level may not financially justify investments in social commitments. Stock markets and capital providers apparently value socially responsible actions only if firms have good financial health. Yes, we believe that organizations may not be able to immediately achieve a holistic stakeholder perspective; it takes time. It is a work in progress where firms go through phases to achieve ESG objectives[22]. Investors who claim that ESG-associated firms or funds outperform traditional funds are dishonest or not precise[23].

When looking to the reality of "doing good as long as business is doing well", where economic rational prevails over ethical or ecological objectives, we could question the importance of "building in" sustainability into strategy rather than "bolting it on". It all boils down to the perspective of a board as the ultimate decision-maker, whether one sees the dichotomy between business reality and social objectives, or whether one envisages and values the interdependency of business objectives and social reality.

The central question we put forward requires an answer to why a company exists and whom it serves and what broader purpose each of the organizations is catering to. Obviously, each individual company will need to fill in the details to answer its shareholders and stakeholders what the company stands for, constituting its intangible assets that will be supported by its traditional tangible physical and pecuniary assets. A wise board will author a short but definitive document[24] with clear and persuasive language, setting forth the central idea of why the company exists and how strategy is translated to achieve the overall objectives. Corporate leadership – especially the ultimate channel of legal and actual power that is been given to the board members – cannot ignore its role in steering the organization to a more purposeful future. However, it is also true that leadership will occasionally face trade-offs and grey areas. Just emphasizing the ecological part at "all costs" could backfire and even jeopardize the (initial) idea of becoming more responsible.

C. Systemic Approach to Integrate Sustainability into Business

A more *systemic* approach to create corporate sustainable value will require a clear commitment to corporate purpose that entails some social and ecological goals. Any board will need to play a determining visionary role in directing the firm towards a more coherent and purposeful organization that is sensible to investors and other stakeholders. Such vision needs to be translated into a strategy that is a coherent, compact and memorable expression of what unique value proposition will be offered to which kind of customers. That vision then will need to be executed through tailored value chain activities with engaged human partners and capital that aims to create and capture value in the immediate future as well as over a longer-term perspective.

Today, most boards at bigger organizations have sub-committees to monitor, address and resolve these challenges. We quote three committees that function as the workhorse of a board's functioning: an audit committee (emphasizing the transparency and disclosure of the financials), a compensation committee (determining the rewards and remuneration of the top executives) and a leadership and governance committee (dealing with a number of other issues). In financial institutions, boards have included a risk committee (focusing on the future). However, it would not be a bad idea to have an additional sub-committee – as in a Sustainability Committee – where the above can and will be discussed and ultimately brought and engrained into that central idea or vision of the organization.

Some thoughts to take away:

- We explain why purpose-driven organization is crucial for responsible leadership – analyzing the reasons why shareholders' primacy is not the most adapted model for this changing context.

- We argue that boards need to adopt their traditional perspective of shareholder primacy towards *sharing* value. A broader socio-ethical perspective – as in an interconnected systemic view – allows leaders to make "more nuanced" decisions that benefits the organization over a longer period. Occasionally, the board will face grey zones or trade-offs between short-term profit and longer term value creation and economic profit.

- The debate is now moving towards including climate change risks into the investment strategy of organizations. The now-hyped but badly defined notion of ESG is just one of the tools that allows to create and share value in a more "fair" manner. To do so, the current paradigm of short-term profitability for its investors-owners needs to be expanded.

Chapter Four

Why Is Expanding Space- and Time-Vector Necessary?

"*A materialist is someone who knows the price of everything and the value of nothing*".

Oscar Wilde

"*Selfishness beats altruism within groups. Altruistic groups beat selfish groups*".

D.S. Wilson & E.O. Wilson, 2007

"*Rather than evolution being driven by competition, it turns out that cooperation has played a far more important role in producing the treat transition that led to Earth's current breathtaking state of diversity and beauty*".

J. Lent, 2021, The Web of Meaning

A more inclusive view will require the expansion of two important vectors in the decision-making process of boards and top executives: space and time. The "*space*" *aspect* refers to the interpretation that the stakeholder view is complementary to the primacy of the shareholder perspective. The "*time*" *aspect* implies to find a balance between the necessity of short-term cash flow generation to survive, and the long-term visionary investment necessary to explore new innovative technologies to become economic and ecological-social sustainable.

I emphasize the distinctive features of "*space and time*" in a board's wising up activities that are assumed to be both reasonable and responsible. By moving from smart to wise decision-making, business could become part of a solution to the global challenges, by embracing short-term cash flow generation and capturing long-term visionary investments. Let us call them features of "*time*". Such complex perspective is only possible by becoming a *learning organization* that imagines a meaningful stretching future[1] beyond our life time[2]. Focusing on results reflects a focus on short-term performance[3], but it may become a potential obstacle to long-term learning and exploring new business opportunities. The board should get continuously updated information and embrace certain risk-taking[4] by learning about and investing in new technological developments such as artificial intelligence and new trends[5] that could be beneficial for their organization. A broader perspective implies to expand the *"space"* focus from pure shareholders to a more inclusive stakeholders' perspective.

1. The Space Factor

Any organization that is serious about making wiser decisions should start with expanding their perspective or start using multiple metrics that are linked to the incentive systems of boards and top executives at companies. There is always an imminent danger of destructing instead of creating and sharing organizational value. However, this space- and time-vector are nothing but tools attempting to provide a method to inquire a new reality. This is exactly what science does: a methodology of inquiries through experimentation that allows progress in understanding. The latest theories in physics now even claim that space–time assumption may not be a reality after all and is even doomed[6] to disappear in its present form, potentially to be absorbed into a more coherent new universal model of physics. Obviously, that's a discussion beyond the scope of this book. I am using the space- and time vector as a metaphorical manner of speaking to indicate the importance of a broader, more holistic perspective that will allow smarter but above all wiser decisions to be made.

1.1. Sharing Created Value Aligned with Giving Stakeholders What Is Due?

In order to become economically, ecologically and socio-ethically more sustainable, executives and their boards aim at optimizing the *value capturing* by the company (as in Price x Quantity – Cost x Quantity) while *creating value* for the customers (Willingness to Pay – Price) and providing value for suppliers and employees (Cost – Willingness to supply).

Everyone with a real stake in the organization benefits from value creation that is somehow purposefully "shared". This *"sharing[7]" of created value* – or creating more *sustainable value* – is usually rooted in an socio-ethical (cultural) and thus "relational" context[8]. Business schools teach their participants the ability to both create **and** claim value. Negotiation between the organization and its stakeholders determines its relative success of the outcome. "While any trade negotiation should care about how much they gain themselves, wise leaders also focus on how to create the most value to be shared"[9]. Instead of focusing on beating the other side (as in a zero-sum game), wise leaders create a bigger pie that can be shared by all those who have a stake in the organization, as in mutual beneficial trade deal or exchange. In other words, a win-win solution.

That sharing of created value is also applicable (and implicitly agreed upon) to a particular community in which the organization operates and is connected to. What is peculiar about this socio-moral thinking is the fact that *passion* (as in "do what you love") linked to a particular *purpose* (as in "what can I or the organization give the world") usually evokes emotions that play a rather complementary but nonetheless crucial role in the cognitive rational argumentation to pursue a certain goal(s) that could determine a different future.

Having a sense of **meaningful purpose** is understood as making valuable contributions to others (individuals or organizations) or to society in the form of any value creation that you as a leader or a board member (or any employee) find personally meaningful. That also implies not to harm anyone[10]. Purpose is the organizing principle of, or an anchor for, a firm, shaping decision-making and binding stakeholders to one another. Purpose reflects an intention to accomplish something that is simultaneously meaningful to the self and consequential for the world beyond the self. Purpose in its deepest sense refers to (1) delineating an ambitious longer-term goal for the company, and (2) giving this goal a broader societal duty[11], as in an aspiring promising future.

Competent smart decision-making in business is allegedly assumed to effectively and efficiently contribute to capital allocation that optimizes the profitability among other financial objectives. Those decisions may not help to preserve cultural or ecological equilibria, or worse they may occur at a great expense. Trends are changing though. For instance, shareholder value maximization may be "smart" in the short term, but it is often a misguided fiduciary objective to claim to be the only goal of business[12]. *Wising up* is a profound reaction against short-termism and (speculative) equity-holding primacy. Wise decision-making is meant to take full accountability and responsibility for the firm's activities. Such attitude goes against the traditional myth that shareholder returns should be maximized even if that is at the expense of ethical and ecological concerns.

1.2. Fiduciary Duties Beyond Maximizing Profitability?

The fiduciary duty of directors is often misinterpreted as "shareholder primacy" – putting shareholders first and assuring short-term profitability. The paradigm of shareholder value is partially linked to influential scholars like Nobel laureate Milton Friedman from Chicago University and quite a number of his colleagues in the finance department at the Chicago Booth School who had immense influence on President Reagan's and Prime Minister Thatcher's policy making in the US and UK, respectively.

A. *Freedom of Individual Choice That Results in Maximizing Self-Interest*

Wasn't it the same Nobel laureate winner Milton Friedman who famously stated in 1972 that the only fiduciary duty of managers is to make money for their shareholders within the constraints of the rule of law. It became the paradigm of neo-classical economics and business. However, fundamental interdependent relations between those who are directly engaged with the organization need to be respectfully restored – especially if the "rule of law" is inadequate or lagging behind in addressing our current challenges.

Admittedly, Friedman's shareholders' primacy has definitely lost its lustre in recent years amid the increased scrutinized social media reports on illicit or outright unethical behavior in publicly listed companies – as argued in the previous chapter. This prevailing economic business paradigm – especially in the USA and UK and other Anglo-Saxon jurisdictions – has been fiercely contested by the growing expectations from activists and society alike, claiming that corporations are (co-)responsible for their negative (ecological and socio-ethical) consequences on communities and their physical environments.

Harvard Business School professor Michael Jensen's seminal papers on shareholder value and stock options[13] have had a significant impact on boards and their governance decision-making. Jensen's influential thoughts stood by the shareholder value but amended it with a nod to a form of enlightened stakeholder theory. These scholarly work is crucial in understanding the tension in this paradigm battle and ongoing shift. Our goal is not to ignore or annul the tension of the extremes in the space-vector, but rather emphasize the importance of not choosing a zero-sum game. Instead, one should dialectically embrace these extremes into a new more coherent model – as I will argue in Part V. Concretely, it means that a board should give due attention to the fiduciary duties vis-à-vis the organization and its owners or holders of shares. But it also implies to take the concerns seriously of those who have a real stake in the organization, such as employees, customers, suppliers and other partners.

These "new" broadened demands of socio-ecological progress – the "space" factor – are translated in the now popular "environment, social and governance" (ESG) agenda. Admittedly, there is some overlapping between the notion of purpose and ESG. Some would directly relate purpose with an ESG agenda, and even interpret ESG as a proxy for purpose[14]. I define purpose more broadly and define it slightly different.

However, not everyone at boards agree with this new development: the successful and revered investor Warren Buffett of Berkshire Hathaway has questioned the legitimacy of this moral quest by corporations which he believes falls under the responsibility of governments, not corporations[15] – clearly echoing Friedrich Hayek's and Milton Friedman's neoliberal economic philosophy. Reality though begs us to slightly differ: boards cannot omit or escape the growing pressure to embrace and adopt to these ESG demands.

B. Why Including ESG Demands Now, and Not Much Earlier?

In fact, executives have a fiduciary duty of care, loyalty and prudence to the organization and its long-term value. As far as the organization's objective is to create value, "there is no difference between shareholder and stakeholder capitalism[16]." *Creating and sharing value is simple good business practice.* It is the board's and leadership freedom to decide how to share the value the organization creates. There is no (legal) reason stipulated to believe that organizations need to be beholden to stockholders only.

The global (Western) institutional context in which firms operate is changing into a new reality that is less forgiving. External stakeholders such as customers, governments and communities, but also employees and investors who have "internal stakes" in the organization, have expressed concerns over neglected socio-ecological and governance aspects. Firms remain accountable and responsible for both financial and non-financial performance. Boardrooms and MBA programs are "programmed" to maximize profitability of the firm. It is seen as an evident truth in business. Other goals than aiming to optimize shareholders' net return on investment were till recently seen by managers and employees not only as betraying their fiduciary duty of care and loyalty, but also as a fast way of losing their job. Many business observers consider global challenges such as climate change and rising inequality and malfunctioning of institutions as external risks and thus "external" to the concerns of a boardroom. These risks have been assumed to be left to governments to deal with, although organizations may attempt to circumvent these external risks. It seems that shareholders and their private for-profit organizations have created an institutional context in which public goods are not their obligation.

C. The Invisible Power of Architectural Innovation or Systemic Design

Today, this mainstream economic paradigm is under scrutiny and may be changing: without good government policies and proper public governance, free capitalist markets will collapse under its own self-destructing behavior. Be it by ignoring the tensions of numerous stakeholders, or by degrading its own socio-economic and ecological environment in which it operates, or by contributing to an asocial and unethical disengagement which would disfranchise and alienate the most ardent stakeholder[17]. A good functioning public sector with fair governance need wealth-creating innovative private sector, and vice versa[18]. The economic and political institutions are meant to be inclusive and interdependent to remain sustainable[19]. The expanded space-vector embraces and transforms the tension between stakeholders and shareholders as a potential driving force of potential energy.

What is so different today, compared to two to three decades ago? An awareness about the need for more collaboration and thus relationship-building to resolve some of the pressing ecological and socio-relational sustainability challenges has seeped in at the boards of organizations. The CEO of the Danish Oil and Natural Gas company – now the rebranded as Ørsted – spearheaded a fundamental transformation of the company into the largest offshore wind developer in the world and one of the most coveted investment companies in renewable energy. What is remarkable is the statement that for a company's vision to be truly aspirational, the company has to make a bigger contribution beyond mere self-interest towards more sustainability. The power of the message is the simplicity or clarity of a vision, which gives focus that in turn will potentially lead to bold action.

The *wising up* at Boards sees this debate around *creating* and *sharing value* in the first instance as a way to innovate, more precisely as an *architectural innovation*[20]. The organizational system's architecture deepens and changes the relationships between the components of the system without changing the components themselves. Because this kind of architectural innovation is quite invisible, it is hard to react to this kind of innovation. Probably, clearly articulating an organization's purpose that strengthens the "emotional relations" beyond profit maximization may be key for preparing such stealth architectural innovation.

In vain, *General Motors*, for instance, attempted numerous times to copy *Toyota*'s manufacturing processes like "just-in-time" inventory systems in their new factories in the early 1980s. They got a good understanding of the continuous innovation processes of the Japanese, but they omitted the thought that Toyota's advantage lay in its relationship with its employees. Instead, GM focused on the tangible changes to the production process, overseeing the real relational component that constituted the architectural advantage of Toyota. That trust between the organization and the employees – its real flourishing human capital – functioned as the glue of the invisible trusting relations at Toyota factories in the 1980s. Goals were discussed, and a common consensus was reached through an invisible (bottom-up as well as top-down) communication process across multiple levels within Toyota. This "tacit" Toyota approach was completely different from GM's traditional command- and control management style, partially explaining why GM never was able to match Toyota's competitiveness. Mainly because GM didn't or could not incorporate Toyota's architectural innovation, its "invisible" strong relationship with stakeholders.

Admittedly, like in any transition from one theoretical paradigm to another[21], tensions, ambiguities and paradoxes will accumulate, and time is needed to make that transition in the most effective and peaceful manner.

2. The Time Factor

In principle, I do not necessarily object to short-term "short-trading" or other speculative motives – which could function as vultures in the financial world[22] – but we warn against investors and owners omitting long-term perspectives as if "anything goes", or worse, harming our ecological and socio-ethical communities.

2.1. A Broader Time Perspective Also Assumes a Multitude of Intelligences

Wise board members and top executives combine a short-term perspective that emphasizes exploitation of current assets, and a longer-term view focusing on exploring innovative solutions as well as "foreseeing" visionary very long-term horizons beyond the executives' life span. Figure 1 hereunder graphically represents this idea of broadened "space" and "time" factors in wise decision-making.

Although the idea of this visualization is to indicate the interconnectivity of the different kinds of variables that roughly contribute to a successful outcome of pragmatic wisdom, I humbly admit that this model has a number of shortfalls in explaining performance. My focus is on better decision-making, initiated by top management and boards. Smart and wise decision-making are obviously dependent on different kinds of intelligence as well as on a combination of different perspectives. Likewise, intelligence is not a one-dimensional notion that stands on itself, but covers

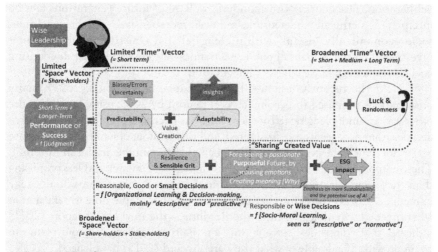

Figure 1: Wise decision-making (with broadened "*space*" and "*time*" factors) balancing profit optimization with engaged stakeholders

quite a number of epistemological perspectives. Generally speaking, **intelligence** is the ability to perceive or infer information, and to retain it as a form of knowledge applicable in the appropriate context *to achieve a set of goals or objectives* to resolve a concrete problem *sensu largo*. Hence, why different forms of intelligence can be distinguished[23].

2.2. How Much Can We (Economically) "Discount Away" Our Own Future?

Allow me to highlight one destructive particular characteristic in the "time" factor applied by executives: the habit of "discounting" future expected cash flow by most investors because one dollar today is worth more than an (expected) dollar tomorrow. This intuitive and rather plausible idea of discounting numbers in the future logically undermines any notion of intergenerational justice or long-term thinking because the further in the future, the more risky this potential revenue stream is being perceived.

Public philosopher Roman Krznaric believes that "discounting is a weapon of intergenerational oppression guided as a rational economic methodology[24]." One of the reasons why large-scale renewable energy projects, or any innovative but risky project, struggle to get government and financial backing is that their start-up investment (often mistakenly interpreted as a cost) is relatively high with the long-term economic benefits getting discounted away, and the ecological-social benefits often ignored or also "discounted"[25]. Discounting simply reflects our obvious preference for today's gratification rather than provisions for tomorrow.

One could argue with Nobel Prize-winning economist-philosopher Amartya Sen that value judgements like discounting should be a matter of public deliberation. Discounting the economic welfare of future generations can be interpreted as ethically indefensible and even reprehensive – though sometimes socio-economically "useful" within clear debated constraints for particular investments in the domain of public economics. We could add that discounting may also be a form of weakness of imagination.

At the recent Glasgow Climate Change Conference (2021), many organizations promised to become carbon neutral by 2050, using long term the other way around: pledging to hit those lofty but necessary targets in almost three decades from now seems too far-sighted, and this without committing immediate action for which they could and should be held accountable in the short term[26]. These corporate ecological pledges may be marketing gimmick and less promising than they seem because of the "discounting" factor. If corporations do not take immediate action – thinking that in 30 years one has ample time to take action when needed when closing in to the deadline – the new MSCI report (2021) indicates that companies' current emission plans are endangering our planet to warm up with 3C, double of what the Paris Accord (2015) has pledged.

Don't we really care for our grandchildren or for future generations? It sounds logic that we do have a responsibility to take action today to mitigate the future impact of today's actions. That is plain "ethical consequentialism". Boards should not hide behind mere short-term profit calculations as a justifiable way to fulfil their fiduciary obligations to "take care of the organization" – if these corporate actions would result in causing harm to communities and environment.

Some thoughts to take away:

- This fourth chapter describes this expansion by extending the "space- and time-vector" in the objectives of an organization that takes more responsible decisions.

- Both the concerns of different stakeholders and short- and long-term consequences need to be taken into account to benefit shareholders over a longer time frame. The space- and time-vector explain such broader and more expansive picture of what an organization could stand for.

- How does widening the space- and time-vector strengthen the organization? Because it makes the organization more futureproof. History has shown that focusing on one group of people at the expense of others leads to inequality and ultimately to revolution to change the regime. In this case, the dominance of shareholders at the expense of other engaged and committed stakeholders becomes quite an untenable situation over time.

Chapter Five

Wising Up: Harmonizing Different Intelligence Perspectives?

"There is a long-distance race between humanity's technological capability, which is like a stallion galloping across fields, and humanity's wisdom, which is more like a foal on unsteady legs".

Nick Bostrom, Oxford AI scientist philosopher (2018)

"When people say I changed the culture of Boeing, that was the intent, so that it's run like a business rather than a great engineering company".

Harry Stonecipher, former CEO McDonnell Douglas, and former CEO Boeing (2017)

"The more we know about our universe, the more difficult it becomes to believe in determinism".

Ilya Prigogine, Nobel laureate Chemistry (1996)

New realities are being continuously imposed on us. Two obvious ones come to the fore: one is the recent *digitization* that permeates our life. It also deeply affects the *"analog" relations* that carry life. Digitized assets will gain value through more connectivity; the same can be said about an organization that will gain from more "connectivity" to a higher level of potentially taking advantage of well-organized platforms and ultimately of a broader socio-economic realm. Such relations are expressed on different levels, including how we relate to ourselves, and others, and how we are embedded in an eco-system that encompasses our socio-ecological reality.

Although sustainability may be a buzzword these days that has lost some of its profound linguistic meaning: the fact that we are part of a liveable eco-system is undeniable. The visionary physicist Geoffrey West is a staunch believer in a notion of a higher form of sustainability[1]. The current behavior to achieve insatiable growth in business is clearly unsustainable because it requires a presumed unlimited, ever-increasing and eventually infinite supply of (carbon non-renewable) energy and resources. We better play safe than sorry, and acknowledge clear ecological and socio-ethical boundaries – Oxford academic Kate Raworth has aptly labelled them as "doughnut boundaries"[2] – to avoid a socio-ecological disaster. This non-linear thinking about a "higher form of sustainability"[3] will need to integrate an *analog* ecological-ethical-economic framework with cognitive abilities in which *digital* networks, particularly artificial intelligence, play a crucial role. We better integrate different perspectives into a more comprehensive eco-system. We can find the potential of such integrated perspective (on intelligence) in unusual places, with the underlying idea to increase the overall pie. (Business) Relationships often imply (implicit or even explicit) negotiations.

1. Wise Decisions Creating Value and Sharing Value Aligned with a Compelling Purpose

When negotiating a deal, ideally the two parties share information. However, in reality, they see little reason to share information, especially when the pie is fixed in size, they fear exploitation of that information by the other adversary side. But clearly, this often leads to suboptimal Nash equilibria. How to avoid such a suboptimal situation in negotiations?

1.1. Negotiations: Increasing the "Psychological Pie" Through Information Sharing

Real value creation in negotiation occurs when negotiators focus more on understanding each others' interests. Asking relevant questions and attentively listening to the other party usually help to create such value. If you provide or disclose useful information, you create a process of reciprocity that often enhances your odds to enter in a mutually beneficial agreement, more optimal than the Nash equilibrium. Strategically sharing information with the adversary or counterparty allows you and the other side to create value, allowing them to either use that information to discern mutually beneficial trades, or benefit from reciprocal process you started. Sharing information signals that you're interested in understanding the other side, but also that you're willing to compromise.

To take an open-minded approach often helps to find (hidden) opportunities in negotiating an agreement. When I was a negotiator – supported by my superb team of accountants, engineers and data analysts – for the Ministry of Finance in Indonesia – closely cooperating with IMF – I was privy to see how you can create "trust" and increase the (psychological) pie – even when the counterparty may have (the reputation of) been corrupt. Remember, that in 1997 in Southeast Asia, many Asian tycoons became extremely wealthy because of their close nepotistic relationship with the political elite[4] who granted them oligopolistic "deals". As a negotiator, you have to be pragmatic and listen to the other side what's really crucial for them. In that sense, negotiating is a subtle dance with two parties, trying to harmonize the demands of the two sides in a workable "fair" compromise. Usually, I offered a couple of "possible scenarios/deals" that allowed me to find out the sensitivities and priorities of the "adversary". Such understanding helped to adopt the offers and calibrate till something is close to mutual acceptance. People often quibble about sharing the pie while they often fail to realize that perhaps that pie can be jointly enlarged ... call it a post-settlement settlement[5]. Indeed, in very complex negotiations like the ones I led for a number of years during the "Asian flu" (i.e. the profound governance crisis that hit Asia in 1998–2001) but also recently in discussing a restructuring deal of a non-performing loan with a Singaporean bank, the pie is not fixed, and trade-offs are possible by creating opportunities in which the pie can be significantly expanded. That is also sharing value.

Similarly, "dysfunctional" companies may be able to be very innovative but not really increasing the pie. For example, Kodak's brilliant engineers were able to create a digital camera in 1975, but the old guard managers who reigned over Kodak's film product business over all these years did not give up their film-product empire. So instead of dramatically increasing the pie for Kodak, these entrenched managers' interest to safeguard their cash cow, film products, blocked the company from commercially exploring this new venue of digitization. The pie was kept intact instead of being expanded. Other tech companies ran away with the idea of increasing that pie by entering and integrating the digital camera, computer-internet apps and mobile phone business.

At the end, this value creation is boiling down to foresee the *interdependencies* and *relations* between the different players in the value chain but also between new potential stakeholders. Foreseeing new potential business opportunities is only possible when organizations and their leadership know how to "learn" from relationship-building and are able to really value interdependent values- and emotional-laden relations.

1.2. Learning: Cognition, Purpose and Values

Important is another distinction I make between (1) *cognitive learning* that is mostly descriptive or predictive – can be easier digitized since it follows a certain (formal) logic – and (2) *socio-moral learning* that is embedded in ethical normative or prescriptive values, and often "relational" oriented. One can also see two sides of the same coin: a *yin* and *yang* perspective. Such invisible fluid relations are hard to be fully "digitized"[6] and remain most often tacitly analog embedded and or entangled.

A. How Socio-Ethical Learning Does Complement Cognitive Learning

Socio-ethical learning is rooted in cooperative behavior that acknowledges the interdependent relationships within our eco-system, as well as the interpersonal relationships and dependencies between the stakeholders of an organization. Based on numerous data in bio-evolutionary research, socio-biology, biology, psychology and even bio-mathematics[7], it can be argued that cooperation and thus relations has been uncommonly important in our survival as a species.

Wise decision-making emphasizes these socio-moral learning abilities that broaden the cognitive focus on short-term profitability for shareholders

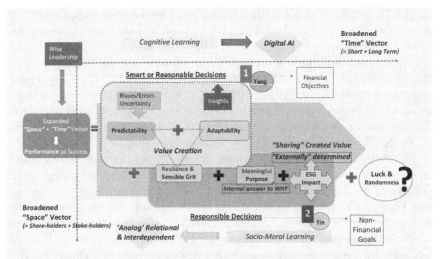

Figure 1: Wise decisions integrate cognitive and socio-moral learning = expanded "space" + "time" perspective

(see Figure 1). Indeed, smart leaders focus on making reasonable decisions that reduce risks and optimize innovative business opportunities. Short-termism seems to have become entrenched in current corporate behavior and financial "speculation", especially within the circles of efficient-market theorem in the Anglo-Saxon context. These international investors and institutional funds – often listed on Wall Street and the City of London – have expanded their (theoretical and practical) grip on overseas markets, in Europe, Asia and other emerging markets. It should not surprise us that anywhere in the world today, profit maximization has become the prevailing norm in investment.

Adding explicitly the wish to make responsible decisions that go beyond the mere focus on shareholder value maximization finds its roots in relational and interdependency of the different goals. As argued in the previous chapters, the critical factors of smart decision-making are related to more *predictability* that secures more alleged stability by reducing errors and uncertainty, *agility* and adaptability linked to innovative insights, and finally *resilience* and *sensible grit* that allows to "fight" and persevere against a constant stream of obstacles to reach their goals. I like to add the notion of a principle-driven or *purposeful future*[8] that inspires meaning and constitutes sense, linked to passion. Combining purpose with passion improves "smart working"[9] – more energy per hour work, and thus increased productivity.

An appealing narrative, a firm's big story, conveys the firm's values but does it in a more direct and emotional way. Tapping into the potential of a metaphorical elephant's power – our emotions and feelings – creates an atmosphere of abound energy to be materialized for "making the dream come true". Identity answers the question "who are we as an organization?" while purpose answers "why is our organization here?[10]" implicitly referring to the commitment of the organization to a "higher goal" that binds a moral community.

B. How to Determine the Relevance of the Purpose in an Organization?

It seems that Boeing, for instance, has lately lost some of its mojo. Since Boeing's inception in 1910, the company has been dedicated to scientific progress and technological achievement in aviation. This engineering perspective was entrenched at Boeing. This technological identity has made Boeing an engineering company with the ideal of building ever better, faster and bigger aircraft – with commercial success remaining a secondary goal. Since the merger of McDonnell Douglas and Boeing in 1997, the spirit at Boeing started to slowly change with more and more emphasis on efficiency and the creation of shareholder value. Many observers draw a direct line between Boeing's cultural erosion and the 737 Max debacle where profits are prioritized over engineering and safety goals. Even a company like Boeing that has operated "purposefully" for decades seems to have stumbled into the seduction of shareholder primacy.

At the other hand, Unilever Indonesia, for instance, has developed strong stakeholder collaboration within the Indonesian communities in which they operate, be it in palm oil or distribution of their products. When violent protests erupted in Indonesia in 1998, when rioters burned and looted a number of factories, they left Unilever's facilities alone. It became clear afterwards, that this was not a coincidence: Unilever had taken care of their employees and communities over all these years they have been operational in Indonesia. In such uncertain times of social unrest, the communities in return protected and took care of Unilever, protecting it from looting and destruction[11]. Consider it real symbolic and social capital, coming in handy in times of crises. People do not forget what you've done for them: it seems the principle of relational reciprocity in full motion[12]. Helping to build communities instead of merely extracting value from them. In the same vein, Unilever has a reputation not to apply aggressive accounting practices to (legally) minimize taxes – as many other reputable brands do such as Amazon or Starbucks that also use public roads (to deliver their products) like anyone else. Unilever even considers fully paying their taxes due without any attempt to apply assertive accounting practices and or tax negotiations in those emerging markets – as part of the "S" of (ESG) – as a validation for their social contract with society[13]. It is to be noted that aggressively avoiding paying taxes and forms of veiled corruption are often correlated. At reputable companies such as Unilever, the boards makes it crystal clear to all employees and management that (financial) success without integrity will be regarded a failure.

2. A Deep Organizational Purpose Aligned with a Moral Community

It is also notable that values in both successful business and well-known global brands seem to increasingly articulate a strong and purposeful meaning that can be reflected in their respective mission and vision statements. One which steers the organization to both profitability and purposeful meaning. A little bit like *Pepsi's* visionary slogan: "Profit with Purpose", recently rechristened by the new incoming CEO as "Winning with Purpose".

2.1. Purpose as an Appealing Narrative Linking Cognition with Morality

Purpose may touch the mind and heart of stakeholders. A deep purpose comes alive around that emotionally appealing story[14]. This meaningful purpose that incites passion can be (in)directly linked to ecological, socio-ethical and governance variables that emphasize the invisible trust in *relations* with those who carry a critical stake in the organization. This new broadened perspective critically includes (often tacit) *relational* variables that somehow distinguishes smart from wise decision-making. Purpose fulfils the desire to "make sense"; it's the prism through which one understands its place in the world, which in turn shapes one's actions and priorities. A deep purpose pushes the organization to a dedicated cause, implicitly evoking an image of a good society. In that sense, purpose, by providing longer-term "idealistic" goals, feeds the *"driver"* – our metaphor for rational and reasonable decision-maker – and by giving it a soul and a broader inspiring socio-ecological duty, it's nurturing the metaphorical *"elephant"* – or the emotions and passions which occasionally are far from rational. Harmonizing these different elements and goals constitute wise decision-making. Pursuing a purpose is consciously dedicating oneself and the organization to the "ongoing and imperfect navigation of trade-offs between stakeholders", recognizing that these potential win-win solutions are "imperfect apportioning of the mutual benefits[15]."

Despite the overwhelming evidence of the positive effects of creating a business narrative that gives purpose and meaning in a business, only 44 percent of family businesses had written values statements anno 2021[16]. What criteria should business apply in preparing for a promising future? We believe that an understanding of trends, keeping an open-mind and ensuring a dialogue with all engaged stakeholders is a first crucial step. Secondly, boards really have to catch up their game plan by expanding "space" and "time" horizons.

A. *Wise Decision-Making Links Purpose with ESG*

If some boards interpret ESG as a "tax" for doing business and are not emotionally linked to the purpose of the firm, there is a good chance that these firms (especially big ones who can afford it) will pay to continue to create negative externalities, an euphemism for (continuing) pollution.

In a very different context, research in an Israeli care centre faced a similar problem: more and more parents were coming late after closing time to pick up their babies. Since the day care centre could not leave this babies behind, the caretakers has to continuously work overtime without any incentive or reward for waiting for the errant parents. Finally, the day care company resorted to imposing a fine for being late. Surprisingly, the lateness immediately increased from

25 percent to 33 percent, and even went up to 40 percent after just six weeks. Why did the fines have this paradoxical effect? Many of the parents interpreted the fine as a price for an additional service. The parents did not feel "related" to their baby caretakers anymore. They didn't feel "morally" obliged to be in time (anymore) when paying USD 25 for an hour being late. Instead of interpreting it morally, they are economically calculating their "utilities". The pecuniary fine de-moralized what had previously been perceived as a moral act. Such subtle degradation – in which some kind of disrespect is conveyed to the relations with the caretakers – shows how monetised incentives can (unintentionally) harm. Once the moral and relational dimension is lost and crowded out (in economic thinking), it is hard to recover. Similarly, research has proven that extrinsic motivators such as bonus payments easily squeeze out intrinsic (often socio-ethical) motivations such as pride and autonomy[17].

After all, is *wising up* then another marketing gimmick to "greenwash" business? We don't think so. Admittedly, corporate social responsibility (CSR) and well-presented ESG reports, and their potential impact may not be a real proxy for actual progress with impact. ESG reporting may be oversold[18], and misleading: "sounding good", rather than actually "doing good"[19]. Nonetheless, *wising up* implies a fundamental shift of the prevailing paradigm to a more holistic systemic narrative with real progress.

Smarting out the potential naivety of (dis)engaged stakeholders won't do the job anymore. Making responsible and thus wise decisions are required to provide ammunition for the lost *legitimacy* of businesses. But it also creates opportunities for new products, reduces costs, impacts investors who grant lower cost of equity and debt, and results in higher productivity from engaged and proud employees in the organization. Wising up is an insurance policy for reducing reputational and legal risks when dealing with governmental institutions and regulators who overlook compliance to or envisage new stringent ecological and societal regulations[20]. In order to make decisions to act more socio-ecologically at boardrooms and for leadership to execute such decisions, *The Economist*[21] claims that ecological re-balancing and investments in renewables will require organizations to make changes in the current bottlenecks of the supply chain, the on-site land-use policy approvals as well as the financing of such renewable energy. We believe that technology such as AI may positively contribute to such re-balancing act. Integrating and harmonizing the different perspectives requires leadership to *wise up*.

B. Some Critical Pillars of (Potential) Wise Leadership

In a study by global survey, I collaborated with the executive search and consultancy Amrop in setting up this "wisdom" framework to assess the potential of wisdom in actual leadership[22]. We hypothesized – based on an extensive literature review on wise decision-making and some own empirical research – that individual-wise leadership is organized along three pillars, each with their own unique characteristics. (1) *Self-Leadership* refers to how leaders exercise self-governance;

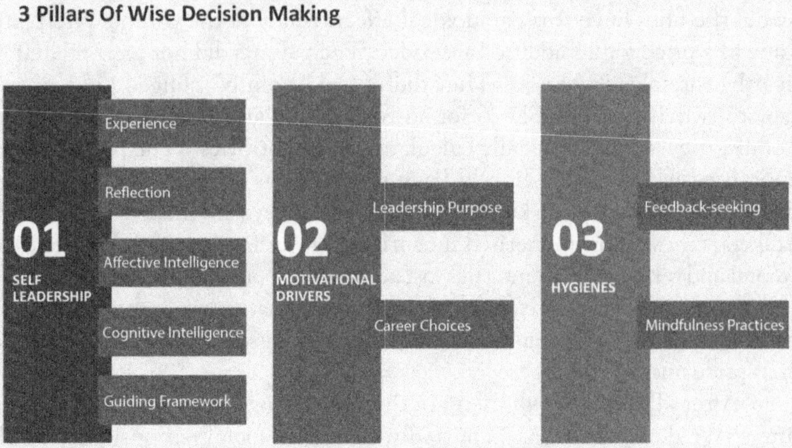

3 Pillars Of Wise Decision Making

Figure 2: Wise decision hypothetical framework

Source: Verhezen, P. & S. Gande (2018), *Wise Decision Framework*, Amrop Papers

(2) *Motivational Drivers* explains what actually really drive leaders' choice and (3) *Hygiene* factors refer to features of how leaders nourish their decision-making "health" – visualized in Figure 2.

The conclusions of this extensive published Amrop survey were quite revealing. When assessing *Self-Leadership* (with its different forms of intelligence), we found that quite a number of leaders who participated in the survey are on the path from smart to wise, but they are missing some vital steps and opportunities. Although they place a high premium on ethics, the notion is not properly understood in its nuances by most of these corporate leaders. Few reflect on their own experiences and how to learn from them – which was a lost opportunity, and indicating some lack of mindfulness. In their decision-making processes, they were prone to a number of biases as group think and commitment bias as could be expected from the vast research on biases in decision-making. Diversity and using humour to diffuse tension were hardly applied by those participating leaders, another lost opportunity to enhance better decision-making. Although most leaders were aware of the ESG factors, planet, people and profit, they sometimes were confused when under pressure, choosing for optimizing profitability, even if that meant that ethical behavior may have been in jeopardy.

Secondly, focusing on the *motivational drivers* of wise decision-making, it became clear that leaders are driven by service, virtue and entrepreneurship – but not to the point of self-sacrifice. When testing the key motivators, the "need for power" prevailed over prestige, social eminence and superiority. Only a small minority sees potential promotions to the C-Suite as a position to appeal to "wise values" that could demand personal sacrifice. The majority clearly avoided such choice. Moreover, most of the leaders interviewed could not really describe their personal mission or goals, indicating that there may be a lack of consciousness of a personal "North star" that could guide us as a beacon. The moral guiding light is in sight, but often lost in the (conceptual or actual) clouds.

Finally, for the "*hygiene*" of wise decision-making, we came to the conclusion that many leaders are habitually engaging in personal mindfulness practices, but only a small minority were engaged in some formal training of meditation. Mindfulness or reflective practices are important hygiene factors. They help to gain awareness and insight, and often bring about a state of "flow". Proactive feedback-seeking is vital for self-awareness and self-development, but is far from widespread. Indeed, when these leaders had the chance to ask for critical feedback – crucial for any decision process – from others (either peers, subordinates or board members) on the decisions to be made, hardly any took that advise, and such feedback was often skipped.

So far some empirical evidence about the status of potential wise leadership. Allow me to conclude by emphasizing the reason behind the need for wiser leaders: if all men were angels, no government or governance rules would be necessary. Fairly perceived laws[23] would minimize the need for "wise men". However, in reality, substituting rules for wisdom does not really work because life is too complex to bring the unfolding of human life within the compass of human powers. That is what practical wisdom is all about[24]. Knowing how to make life work sometimes implies to bend the rule to fit the circumstance. A business reality is most often not black and white[25]. We all behave in a less-than-consistent way. We are all more fragmented, less true to ourselves, more malleable[26], than we might wish. We are a tangled nexus of emotions, dispositions, desires and traits which pull and push us in different and occasionally contradictory ways. Executive leaders are no different. Figure 3 hereunder summarizes some of the facets of such wise decision-making.

Making wise decisions is connotated to broadening our perspectives, harmonizing our intelligences and enhancing our consciousness into more sentient beings who make decisions on behalf of the organization that synthesizes apparent opposing ideas – as in profitability for investors and caring for customers, efficiency and compassion. Consequently, continuous learning at organizations will be necessary to survive.

Having a deep purpose engrained in the DNA of the firm may help to energize the "soul" of that company, allowing engaged employees to compete and deliver to customers, turning durable profits for the shareholders. Purpose serves as the foundational narrative of long-term strategic thinking that is linked to enable the materialization of a more sustainable organization. Making decisions that are more holistic with more sustainable outcomes likely requires a compelling narrative in the organization that eloquently communicates a meaningful future to its engaged stakeholders. In a nutshell, a meaningful and authentically perceived purpose probably elevates transactional relationships into trusting partnerships – because it connects with an ineffable "soul".

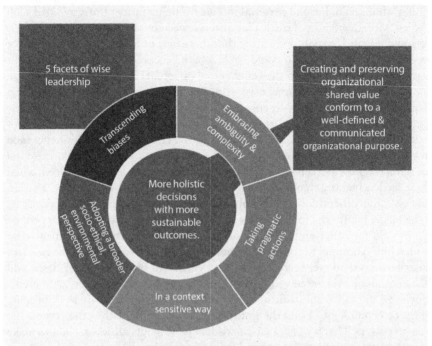

Figure 3: Wise leadership integrates and its decisions are likely more sustainable

Source: Verhezen, P. & S. Gande – Amrop (2018), *Wise Leadership and AI*

Some thoughts to take away:

- Wise decision-making is about creating value and share value aligned with a compelling purpose that gives meaning to engaged and committed stakeholders.

- Reasonable decisions are associated with cognitive intelligences (as in explicit knowledge) that eventually can be digitized (and focus on financial objectives).
  - However, responsible decisions are linked with a socio-ethical realm where the focus lies on social interaction and relations (hence why non-financial objectives).
  - In this socio-ethical realm, leaders will need to become more conscious and mindful to be able to become more "responsible". Practice gets you a long way.

- Purpose is an appealing narrative that links cognition and morality.

Chapter Six

How to Understand the Thick Notion of "Wising Up"?

"Strategy without tactics is the slowest route to victory. Tactics without strategy is the noise before defeat".

Sun Tzu, The Art of War

"Children must be taught how to think, not what to think".

Margaret Mead, 1928

Businesses have proven to be visionary, by coming up with innovative products and services that has benefitted the life of many. In short, wise leadership relies on the ability to imagine a more meaningful future, to "foresee" such a future, to plan and strive to fulfil worthy objectives. Doing so implies a balancing act between a short-term desire to survive – as in *exploiting* current assets to generate immediate cash flow – and long-term ideas that are usually dependent on innovation and R&D – allowing firms to *explore* new opportunities that likely will generate future cash flow. Exploring new business opportunities through trial and error requires a particular risk mindset that is rather more akin to a metaphorical fox than a hedgehog. People who think more like foxes are known to be cunning and smart. Can these pragmatic thinkers also become wise decision-makers? Let's attempt to briefly decipher this thick notion of wise decisions[1].

1. Understanding the "Thick" Notion of Wising Up

Once executives or directors are perceived as "smart", the next step is moving to some level of pragmatic wisdom. Wisdom is an "old" notion; it is a thick concept. Indeed, *philo-sophia* refers literally to its *love for wisdom*. In business terminology, wisdom is a way of strategizing about the future, and the highest wisdom is the art of dialectic balance. Balancing between the different relations that affect the organization, and the subsequent potential trade-offs or paradoxes. Leaders are under enormous pressure. Dealing effectively well with ambiguity, uncertainty, volatility and complexity constitutes good leadership, both from a strategic and risk perspective that prepares the organization for the future as well as from a governance point of view that steers the organization in a transparent, fair, accountable and responsible manner to regain trust from those directly involved, and by extension from the community at large.

1.1. The Fox's Love for "Wisdom"

Wise leaders do not shun complexity, nuances and ambiguity. Indeed, wise leaders think more like (metaphorical) foxes (pragmatic thinkers) than like hedgehogs (experts with one focused vision – paraphrasing Isaac Berlin's metaphor)[2]. Hedgehog experts burrow into one vision or idea. They believe that this vision captures the essence of everything. Such an attitude sometimes results in some form of proselytization, or glides off to an overwhelming ideology that consumes everything. Occasionally, especially in scientific contexts, such focus on one idea only, leads to breakthroughs and scientific discoveries.

A. Credible Experts as Wise Leaders?

The debate around the hyped machine learning and superhuman cyborg abilities sometimes feels like an ideology instead of facts, supported by "credible experts". Foxes, however, accept volatility, complexity and incalculability as a mere fact they have to deal with. Foxes either avoid bold predictions, or make safer and smarter predictions by constantly updating and adopting to the ever-changing reality. For the fox, the business of long-term predicting is almost foolhardily, because nobody really can (cognitively) foresee and tell what kind of contextual reality will emerge on the future crossroads of the dynamics of geopolitics, local politics, science, business and innovative technology. Business and boards are generally better off with foxes than hedgehogs. Is that also the view of philosophers who "love wisdom"? Obviously, I cannot give credit to the enormous cultural wealth of wisdom that exists and is beyond the scope of this work, or even single life time. I just want to provide a brief glimpse of some of the variety of this (thick) notion of wisdom.

Various cultures may have slightly different interpretations of what constitutes wisdom for their specific context. Living at about the same time 2500 years ago, each of those wise teachers has provided us with a slightly different emphasis or interpretation. Plato's *Phaedo* in which Socrates as his spokesperson describes that the pursuit of wisdom is the highest calling. Aristotle's *Nicomachean Ethics* emphasizes virtuous behavior as leading to *eudemonia* – as in a worthy flourishing and thriving life. This may sound slightly different from Buddha's teaching about compassionate awakening and mindfulness to reduce human suffering. It may even seem like the Hindu Upanishads that offer a more intuitive understanding of life and death. Confucius' teaching, whose *Analects* greatly influence the contemporary Chinese thinking about morality, focuses on the relationships within the family hierarchy and attempts the molding of personal moral behavior with a larger political order. Confucianism – committed to a form of moralism grounded in public virtue – emphasized the primacy of emotion over reason which may seem to be the opposite of Plato's thinking in rational Idea forms. Confucius' foundational principles that guide the good life refer, for instance, to *gen*[3]– translated in "goodness" or "the Way of Life" – as the most powerful beacon for illuminating human behavior in the history of civilization. In the Confucian hierarchy of virtue, even wisdom and courage were secondary to *gen*. But Confucius and his intellectual successors also understood that you cannot have goodness without wisdom and courage. Those virtues are likely more interdependent than we logically accept. Those incredible rich traditions resulted in a rich interpretation of "being good" and some of the ingredients to reach wisdom.

The Chinese philosophers Confucius and Mencius were convinced that a "good" person sets his heart on doing good – which can be found in practicing benevolence, being humane and yes, being altruistic. This emotional component (euphemistically referring to the heart) may be akin to the Western philosophical notion of "intent". It is definitely connotated to David Hume's astute analysis of the role of moral emotions, of what he labelled *"the moral sentiment"*[4]. Confucius' ancient version of the Golden Rule finds its obvious echoes also in Buddhism, in the teaching of Islam, in the Greek philosophy back to Thales of Miletus and of course in the Judea-Christian tradition.

B. Source of Wisdom Is Understanding Humans

However, since the Renaissance, the Western philosophical tradition has abandoned its function as a source of wisdom and has restricted itself to (cognitive) knowledge. The philosophical roots of wisdom allow leaders still to tap into an enormous source of useful recommendations, based on centuries of striving to understand, and to live a proper life, be it in our personal or in our professional reality. Wisdom extends knowledge to the understanding of our human nature that is profoundly social, ethical and relational while also being deeply personal, adaptive and intuitive. It operates on the reality of paradoxes, contradictions and change. In that sense, I recommend to retrieve the jewels of wisdom from a rich philosophical tradition, beyond just constituting the boundaries of cognitive learning.

Wise decision-making is discerning some form of truth and renders a fair yet meaningful judgement. It also remains a praxis in which action is pivotal. Wise decision-making encompasses various forms of intelligence combined with conscience. The Hebrew term for wisdom, *chokhmah*, suggests that the concept resides in both the mind and the heart. It fuses and melds cognition and emotion, consciousness and unconsciousness, mind and body. They are not necessarily distinct parts, but marbled together. This is exactly the core message what this books emphasizes: fusing cognition and feelings. As "the rational rider" (sitting on the back of the elephant) subtly and masterfully steers "the emotional elephant" into a certain direction.

Over the past couple of decades, a consensus emerged from various sources of research that cognitive, reflective and affective components are crucial to understand how to make wise decisions. The **cognitive** aspect includes the ability to understand, to perceive a situation clearly and to make decisions despite ambiguity and uncertainty. The **reflective** component of wisdom deals with a person's ability to examine an event from multiple perspectives which encompasses to step outside oneself and to understand a broader perspective that includes an "other-regarding" view. The emotional **affective** component of wisdom primarily involves the ability not only to remain positive and minimize negative feelings and emotions, but also relate ourselves to the other. Bringing those components harmoniously together allows someone to become more aware, to become more "mindful" of the (broader) surrounding.

1.2. Expanding a Perspective Implies an Attitude of Mindfulness

Mindfulness underpins both unconscious affect and conscious reasoning. Although there does not exist a firm consensus among psychologists and other researchers on the different dimensions of "intelligence", we refer to four forms of intelligence often encountered in business: *cognitive knowledge* (IQ), *risk-related intelligence* (RQ), *emotional sentience* or *intelligence* (EQ) and *moral consciousness* or *conscience* (MQ). Steering an organization goes beyond merely resolving problems; it implies to give a meaningful reason to exist, to give direction to the organization that fits an unfolding and evolving reality. In a very simplified modelling manner, I stipulate that the prevailing paradigm in business focuses on our cognitive abilities to maximize (short-term) profits. However, in the process, corporates have ignored the interpretation of another potential pathway that acknowledges the fact that business is entangled into a broader eco-system.

I have argued that stakeholders ("space" expansion) and long-term thinking ("time" expansion) should be brought into the "equation" of performance. Put differently and overly simplified, profit maximization is mainly rooted in the cognitive abilities of IQ and RQ: competent and risk-taking executives and board members who understand to take reasoned informed decisions that turn a problem into a commercial product and service – but who unfortunately have ignored or omitted the longer-term and often harmful consequences. Call it smart leaders who know how to generate cash flow. The result of this cognitive focus is to optimize the profitability for the shareholders, seen as the primary and to many, the only goal in managing and governing an (for-profit) organization[5].

My argument claims that smart leaders should go a step further and include other abilities that allow to see "further" and more holistically, caring for the people and environment in which the firm operates. The focus does not turn away from cognitive intelligence (improving *efficiency* and return on investment as in **IQ + RQ**), but it adds the important notion of *relationship-building* to survive over a longer period – by including Emotional Intelligence[6] (**EQ**) and Moral Consciousness (**MQ**) or even Spiritual Connectedness, not exactly notions in the vocabulary of business people.

Training and learning is required in order to gain a minimum level of intelligence, any form of intelligence. Underneath, the ability to express oneself intelligently, both through tacit and explicit knowledge, is necessary, underpinned by an unconscious "affect"[7] that stimulates the logic and consciousness when one explains solutions to problems. **Consciousness** is *the awareness and subjective feel of phenomenal experience*. In that sense, consciousness is paradoxically not only part of our "modelling" ability, but also constitutes the model we apply. A conscious mind is a mind that is aware of what is happening around us. As I will explain in Part III, a preconscious mind contains ordinary memory, which can be retrieved and shuttled to the conscious mind. An unconscious mind is home of all feelings, urges, memories and thoughts that are outside conscious awareness[8].

Interestingly, psychologist and neuroscientist Michael Tomasello argues in his excellent book *Becoming Human* that the *cognitive process* to intellectually understand something is to be supported and complemented by a *form of societal understanding*[9]. This is often seen in oscillation between forms of cooperation and competition in business. In evolutionary sense, cooperation is rooted in a collective intentionality and culture – as in language and social norms or morality. Humans can only really thrive in a moral community. The ontogeny of uniquely human cognition is fundamental *relational*. It is this relational component that has led to forms of collaboration and cooperation[10] without which humans would not have survived. Being mindful of those relational and cognitive components helps to improve our judgements.

The idea developed by Tomasello that two distinctive processes – cognition plus emotional and ethical understanding – drive the learning and development of any human has deeply influenced me in bringing "values" back into the core of economics that pretended to be free of values and focused on mere cognitive and scientific processes. Economists have been traditionally in awe for the mathematical precision and prediction power of (Newtonian) physics, attempting to (cognitively) replicate these insights into their own domain of economic modelling. My aim is to re-infuse or re-link values back into the model. To acknowledge that an economic business reality implies not one but two realities: an objective cognitive realm and a more subjective social-ethical realm.

2. Individual Judgement Requires Consciousness and Intent

Consciousness is not a thing; it is the word that we use to describe the subjective feelings of a number of instincts and perceptions and/or memories playing out in time in an organism. That is why consciousness is sometimes seen as a proxy for how a complex living organism operates. In order to understand how complex organisms work, we need to know how the brain's parts are organized to deliver conscious experience as we know it.

2.1. How Emotions (EQ) Relates Cognitive (IQ) with Moral Intelligence (MQ)

Emotional intelligence implies an ability to understand and regulate one's own feelings and desires[11]. In a nutshell, emotional intelligence implies the notion of empathy that often result in a form of caring for those involved in the business with you. EQ is rooted in the neuroscientific notion of "affect" that drives our cognitive thinking (as explained in Chapters 16, 17 and 18). Reading someone's mind in negotiations is another useful characteristic of EQ. Reason or IQ gives us the tools to cognitively think to make an informed decision, but it will be our emotions (EQ) that function as the barometer that most accurately predict our actions. Especially, three kinds of emotions in particular play a key role in ethical conflicts or dilemmas: anger, guilt and shame[12]. These are feelings that can serve as powerful motivations to act on our values[13].

Moral (and spiritual[14]) intelligence, however, refers to the way executives and top leadership (un)consciously deal with ethical values in a particular business context – that admittedly can change over time and space. Any judgement by a board member can be seen as the result of the interaction between the unconscious intuitive powers and our rational conscious mind. Indeed, any fair judgement is a balancing act: reason is a co-participant, not the only or final arbiter of good judgement[15].

A. *Lessons of the Art of War: Know Yourself, but Also Your Adversary*

Values, though powerful and often subconscious emotional motivators, can get lost in the rush of everyday life. Sun Tzu's teaching – in *the Art of War* – clearly advises strategists to know your enemy but also yourself so that "you will not be imperilled in one hundred battles". This self-reflection of knowing yourself and the others is quite similar to Socrates' philosophical teaching. By knowing yourself and the adversary, you will become very conscious to learn to recognize the enemies of our own values. These misleading forces of conformity, misguided authority, misplaced goals with omitting socio-ethical and ecological concerns, and systemic corruption will tempt us to go along with the "corporates" when we know it is ethically wrong to do so. By being conscious and becoming more mindful, we develop a more sensitive "conscience".

We hardly are sure how to behave and act morally in ambiguous and uncertain business contexts. Hence why business practitioners should have a deeper understanding of this moral uncertainty[16]. Morality becomes a core evolutionary advantage that fosters cooperation and innovative creativity. Humans share an intentionality with other humans which forms the basis for morality – or shall we say ethical behavior.

When one is approached with the assumption that you are a person of conscience, there is a probability that you will make the duty of this identity immediately salient. You likely will answer the direct call for (moral) assistance. This feeling being called upon by someone in need could strengthen your self-image[17] of someone who (sub)consciously possesses an "extensive" rather than "constricted" moral imagination[18].

B. *Moral Intelligence in a Socio-Ethical Realm*

We can interpret morality or *moral intelligence* (MQ) as (1) feeling concern for others, as well as (2) concern for justice and fairness. Evolutionary psychology informs us that humans – and organizations by extension – show multiple motives and intentions[19]. People are neither purely selfish nor purely altruistic; usually, behavior is a combination of both where one system can prevail over others. This chapter argues to "regulate" and harmonize those intentions in a way that benefits the organization over a longer period. However, following ethical values requires effort and energy, especially in ambiguous unclear situations. Wise executives and board members need to prepare themselves by focusing on improving the moral conscience and being conscious about it. The forces one will face when these ethical values are tested – forces that can trigger temptation, fear, uncertainty and anxiety, and lack of confidence – are often very powerful. Being prepared and trained to discern those tempting forces will help smart executives to become a person of conscience (with a relatively higher MQ) and this likely wiser as well.

In my terminology, smartness is linked to various forms of intelligence and knowledge. It is constituted by the cognitive element or IQ, as well as the ability to look forward and to see the often still fuzzy trends in the future, which I have labelled RQ (Risk Intelligence or quotient). To a certain extent, a smart leader will be emotionally attuned to have a minimal self-control and a positive affective attitude to the other members of the group. But as I will argue (in the next chapters of Part II), emotions or rather feelings and affect drive our ability to make decisions. In that sense, emotional regulation helps us to focus on what is important, essential in any smart judgement.

Wise decision-making also requires such an emotional, affective component, based on the notion of empathy. That "affect" of empathy is able to read in a social situation or another person, loosely labelled EQ. Instead of the ability to empathize, we rather speak of the ability to be compassionate which implies direct "detached" action towards the other and oneself[20]. Probably referring to some more subtle interpretation of a "virtuous" emotional intelligence that accepts some form of spiritual connectivity. Crucially, wise decision-makers have the ability to sense social norms and ethical values that underlie the foundation of any interdependent relationship, be it personal or in society at large. Such relationships assume a form of moral intelligence (MQ) – as I've attempted to visualize in Figure 1. Knowledge tells you how to do something, which can be subtly distinguished from wisdom that tells you whether you should do something or not. Not surprisingly, *should* or *ought* is referring to moral behavior, whereas scientific studies mainly focus on what *is*. Moral values and social norms constitute the possibility to cooperate, to create new possible relations and to constitute a different possible reality. This kind of cooperation or collaboration is, in fact, nothing else as our ability to social wisdom[21].

2.2. Making Wise Decision Requires Mindfulness

Ultimately, wisdom evokes questions on how to make fair judgements and pursue a particular course of action. Wisdom lies at the intersection of analysis, reflection, evaluation and choice. The difference between a wise choice and an unwise answer lies in a deep understanding of context which requires a form of flexibility in thinking, intelligence and consciousness[22].

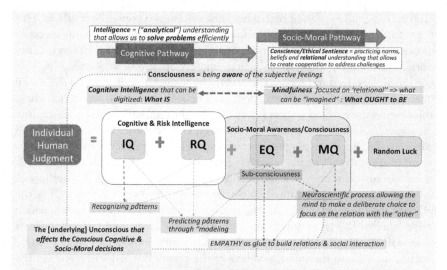

Figure 1: Cognitive and socio-moral learning abilities that result from the interaction between unconsciousness and consciousness

A. Looking for Wisdom ...

Researchers – known as the Berlin Wisdom Paradigm – defined **wisdom** as "an expert knowledge system concerning the fundamental pragmatics of life"[23]. The Berlin-related researchers saw the quality of wise decisions not only as a quality of an individual but also groups, institutions and even societies at large.

By its very nature, however, wisdom was a quite utopian concept and virtually unattainable, which explains why it lost relevance in management studies and in the public debate in general. Despite their idealistic and subjective nature, wisdom could still be perceived as a collectively anchored product[24] where individuals could be seen as weak carriers of wisdom, but able to occasionally make wise decisions nonetheless. Especially in times of crisis, good decision-making is crucial to survive. Indeed, the ability to deal with crises and adversity without getting overwhelmed might be a hallmark of wise individuals but also one of the pathways to wisdom[25].

If wisdom implies a high level of self-control and thus mindfulness, it can be seen as an awareness that what you do now likely predicts your (behavior in the) future. **Mindfulness** refers to the ability of an individual to be conscious about their attitudes, beliefs and behaviors. As with risk-taking, a board should balance taking risks to enable innovation and creativity while avoiding too high levels of unreasonable risk-taking. Similarly, as any entrepreneur understands the importance of open-mindedness, complete risk aversion will not be a right decision to create value since it never will result in any innovative product, unless by mere luck. Wisdom is indeed an art of *(dialogical) balance*, or rather *(dialectic) harmonizing*[26] of *different perspectives*. *Wisdom* is not simply a matter of knowing the "best" answer to a problem or a dilemma; it is a matter of knowing a good approach for finding an *appropriate judgement*. And seemingly strange or paradoxal, wisdom feels very comfortable with uncertainty. Wise decisions tolerate ambiguity and paradoxes. Wisdom[27] is practically applied fair decision-making, not in the Socratic sense of abstract ultimate truths, but in the more modest pragmatic Aristotelian or Confucian sense of doing the right thing in order to live a good and meaningful life.

I was quite fortunate myself to have been formally trained in Western philosophy at one of the best schools in that field in Europe and even beyond: The School of Philosophy at Louvain University (KUL). However, I am as grateful for the experience and studies I was able to undertake in Buddhism in the backyard of the Mangkunegaran court and the old Javanese traditions, and close to the fabulous magnificent Borobudur Buddhist temple in Central Java (Indonesia) – that traditionally have been culturally Buddhist, till traders converted the region into Islam. I studied meditation and Buddhism there for a couple of years, allowing me to make my first brief attempts to link mindful awareness to the present suggested management framework – to open up the perception of how boards could look at their business and impact on people and environment. The thoughts and practices I learned from Buddhist philosophy and psychology have been quite useful in my own career as an entrepreneur and advisor, being able to be more patient and looking at the intentions of people and oneself while being aware of your own feelings, emotions and thoughts when trying to make (important) decisions. Today, I live (part time) with my family in beautiful Bali[28] where we have learned to live peacefully and harmoniously with the local Balinese community in which the wisdom of Hindu norms and values steers the daily life of the farmers and surrounding.

B. ... Finding It in an Enlightened Soul with Cognitive Insights and Compassion

Indeed, we can tap in the wisdom of different cultures and see some similarities (and differences of course). An "enlightened soul" – let's describe such a person as a *wise savant* – seems to be able to tap into two major sources of energy: an *inner insight of who we are (or not are)* and a *deep compassion* for all organisms[29]. The primary energy currents of the psychic nervous system – as understood in the Buddhist tradition – that are united in advanced meditative attainments are always explicitly identified with the forces of wisdom and compassion[30]. How to describe those two energy sources of Buddhist wisdom? In a few pages of a chapter, I won't obviously be able to fully decipher the subtleties that Buddhist philosophy and psychology offer us in transcending some of our daily "concerns and mental suffering". But let me try to link some of these notions to our analysis on making wiser decisions. By giving attention – being very conscious about the reasons why we take a certain decision – we have taken a first step to broaden our perspective. Meditative practices may help to sharpen that process of conscious awareness. However, we also need to become aware of a sense of purposeful meaning[31].

First, elevating and reaching a deep inner understanding of ourself – or our internal *"cognitive" insights*, or briefly described as *wisdom* in the Tibetan Buddhist tradition – sees the ephemeral (non)reality and the "illusive" character of a "presumed but falsely perceived grounded" self. The spiritual or mental insight uncovers the transformation of our often rather "narcistic" tendencies as well as a misunderstanding of the desire for certainty and seeking to find a foundation for who we are. The self-awareness is not completely denying a "fluid" self, but it is denying a wrong perception of the self as a presumed "firm" objective existence, because it is a mere illusion, according to the Buddhist perspective.

Concretely, it means that any board member or executive should remain humble in pretending to "cognitively know" (themselves and their team members in an organization). So many reasons – beyond mere efficiency or profit optimization – may play a role in making particular decisions. But we'll be fine to use our cognitive abilities to push forward – as long as we are aware of the limitations of our own cognitive (conscious) thinking, hopefully allowing us to make wiser and thus more insightful decisions.

The second source of energy that leads to a form of "enlightenment" in a Buddhist tradition is referring to our deep *"socio-ethical" compassion* to living organisms. This compassion refers to a (upgraded) broader perspective vis-à-vis our own *interdependent relations*. This compassion transforms desire and anger and shows the destructiveness of trying to continuously satisfy a magic instant perceived gratification of fulfilling those desires, or attempting to find "certainty" in a reality that is by definition fluid and continuously changing. **Mindfulness** somehow may help us to steer our emotions a little, which then allows us to obtain a better understanding of ourselves and reality. Being able to broaden or change some of our narrow perspectives about ourselves and our organizations helps to become better, less judgemental and wiser decision-makers. In my analysis, I have used the rather fluffy notion of *purpose* – though we should always attempt to make our purpose very concrete and down to earth – as a link between smartness and making wiser decisions. Purpose provides the mental energy to feel a higher non-financial goal that allows stakeholders (employees, suppliers, customers) to find some intrinsic meaning. The more "conscious" stakeholders have become of their reasons to buy products, or to supply labor, skills or products, the more they may be able to tap into these energy levels of meaning. Yes, consciousness becomes crucial to make smart decisions and primordial for being able to make wise decisions.

Although this is not the place to get in detail, I suspect that the (philosophical) *hard problem around consciousness*[32]– the difficulty to scientifically pinpoint what consciousness is, exactly – is directly related to the Buddhist view that one should not focus on "founding" a self or conscious self. It does not mean either that we need to deny our personal individual experiences about which we are conscious. In that sense, Figure 1 above – in which I put *"consciousness"* as "being self-aware of individual experiences related to the other, or its relations" – is not completely faulty, but definitely not completely correct either. Let's call it a "working-definition-in-process". What is this "self", and what kind of (foundational) entity is it? It likely does not exist in that "form". The moment we try to define it, it seems already escaping us and make itself undefinable – making it a "hard problem" to understand, indeed. As a Westerner, we try to define and decipher "the self". We try to put names on phenomena as if there were *natural objects* or we may have *subjective experiences* – i.e. having conscious experiences – that can be grounded in a scientific framework. Easterners, especially Buddhists, never tried to pinpoint a notion; they let go. Buddhism would even deny the firm static existence of an identified "self[33]." Asians in general are much more pragmatic and accept the "floating" phenomena that cannot be grabbed in a description as a possible reality. They work with "it" as long as it functions. We may find some insights and thus better understanding of what this notion of self-awareness could mean, by studying the psychology presented by Buddhism. Succeeding in becoming more **aware** – through *mindfulness practices* and *mediation* – about some of our "illusionary" thoughts of ourselves, and the world is a good start to transform smartness into a form of wisdom.

Quite often, wise decision-making requires a level of experience well-digested. Experiential learning is well taken into account in the selection of any board member in most organizations. Wisdom is to think *dialogically* (taking an other-centred approach that attempts to understand multiple viewpoints of different stakeholders), and *dialectically* (understanding that a solution that is right at one time and place may well be wrong when circumstances change as they have in business over the past decade) – to be further explained in the last chapters.

Let us turn first to the debate on the benefits and limitations of artificial intelligence, and how machine intelligence differs from human intelligence, how digitization is profoundly impacting our own way of thinking and of course, decision-making within businesses. How should wise board members manoeuvre within such digitized AI world? And can AI help us to become smarter, or even wiser?

Some thoughts to take away:

- How to understand the old "thick" notion of wisdom in business. What it does mean, and what it does not mean. Despite the danger of adding another buzzword to the potentially sloganistic management theories, we argue that the philosophical underpinning of what meaning is all about – applied to business – may help to "wise up" boards and their executives.

- We distinguish two major realities in (business) life: a cognitive reality and a socio-ethical reality with each its characteristics.

- Wisdom is found in enlightened souls who share cognitive insights and show elevated levels of compassion for others. In other words, wise decision-making takes place at the intersection of an "objective" cognitive pathway and a more "subjective" socio-ethical realm.

PART II:
The *Future Is Digital*:
Smart Decisions in an Era of Artificial Intelligence

My interest in artificial intelligence (AI) is linked to the question whether AI will help executives to become smarter or even wiser in their decision-making. The short answer: yes, AI will augment the decision power of executives and individuals, likely making them and their environment a "*smarter*" *world*. But I will express serious doubts about AI's ability to make us wiser, unless in helping us to pinpoint measurable predictions around ecological or other social phenomena, and act upon these insights accordingly.

Early 21st century, business has embraced AI that created some extraordinary value for its investors. The owners of these algorithmic engines have amassed enormous wealth over the past three or four decades. During the corona crisis, the divide between e-commerce tech companies – fuelled by data, powerful engines and algorithmic "magic"[1] – and traditional "main street" companies has been incredibly powerful. The stratospheric capitalizations of those tech companies are extraordinary, almost insane – though recently slightly rectified by lower capitalizations but still "probably overrated" technology stock on Wall Street. Devices, machines and infrastructure will become smarter and smarter – energized by the latest specialized artificial intelligence ships and fabricated by a superhuman knowledge, with the efficiency of 5G or next generation to run the connectivity in the world. Admittedly, the actual benefits of current AI algorithms and machine learning are significant, and the potential opportunities are quite promising for a number of businesses. But the gap between those digital haves who successfully embraced AI and have-nots who are seriously lagging behind in applying innovative AI-technology is enormous.

This digital transformation of business processes could probably be quite disruptive. For instance, *Amazon* and *Amazon.Go* shops have proven that online commerce has been given a boost by the Covid-19 crisis. That is equally true for many other online e-commerce challengers. However, boards and top executives cannot and should not forget the potential dangers and limitations of artificial intelligence[2]. Boards are assumed to take reasonable but also responsible decisions. This second part describes the enormous business opportunities of digital platforms automating – the "good" of AI. However, boards should also be aware of the "bad" and the "ugly" of AI and how to curb or limit those AI-related risks. The next three chapters indicate the "good" of AI, and the subsequent last three chapters of Part II warn us for the "bad" and the "ugly" of AI.

Chapter Seven

A Digital Future: AI Contributing to Create Value in an "Industry 4.0"

"The gold rush in AI is coming for real ... the Earth will become one big computer".

Masaryoshi Son, founder of Softbank & Vision Fund

"Imagine how much harder physics would be if electrons had feelings".

Richard Feynman, Physicist, speech at CalTech Graduation ceremony

T he Covid pandemic has likely demolished any lingering doubt about the benefits of digital transformation in corporations. Those businesses with an established digital presence generally fared better during this recent crisis. The global e-commerce market is booming like never before and is expected to grow from USD 4.2 trillion in 2020 to USD 6.2 trillion in 2022. Companies with strong digital capabilities such as *Amazon, Uber, Netflix* and *Airbnb* have reshaped whole industries. Digital natives such as *Google, Facebook, Baidu, Alibaba, Tencent, Microsoft* and *Apple* have proven more competitive as their costs were kept under control while their flexibility proved to be extremely valuable. Smaller companies that have embedded e-commerce capabilities into their core strategy have gained as well. Data has allegedly become the new oil, especially when data is turned into information and knowledge that allows businesses to get a better understanding of trends or desired outcomes that can be automated or augmented through Artificial Intelligence.

1. Digital Transformation Through Artificial Intelligence?

The power of this "data-ficated" (or data-fied) reality, be it biotech, nanotechnology, robotics, cyber-technology or artificial intelligence systems, will have a huge impact on everyday life; it records all our movements, human interactions and financial transactions, all stored in the "cloud". This new reality of *Industry 4.0* will facilitate our life and possibly enhances it. These incredible AI opportunities sometimes evolve into messianistic statements[3]. The transactional improved efficiency may possibly help to predict better ways to use limited resources or reduce waste by optimizing raw material with maximum efficiency in output. All with the objective to create more sustainable solutions. But at the downside, this *Industry 4.0* will also be managed and possibly manipulated by a few multinational quasi-monopolies, and in the worst scenario, a global interconnectivity could also result in systemic failure, or misuse of power[4].

1.1. Human and Artificial Intelligence

Businesses need competent and smart employees and managers. Increasingly, business is also in need of wise leadership to deal with the ambiguities of the enormous global challenges. We strongly believe in the enormous benefits of digital innovative technologies, in particular, AI from which deep learning machines is a well-known example.

A. Will AI Be Able to Find New Solutions Faster and More Effectively Than Humans?

Universities and research centres around the world now use AI algorithms to find patterns and correlations in molecules from the hospital data sets available to attempt to develop new medicine for specific diseases. Initially started as the *Covid Moonshot project*, a close collaboration between USB in Belgium using Microsoft's supercomputers aims to crunch the huge available health data sets and aims to predict possible correlations that could result in a new medicine. Lengthy clinical trials are now aided by AI algorithms: what usually takes six months can now be achieved within three days. Evaluations are sped up, and the new medicine is possibly available much faster. AI will definitely help the health industry to come up with more innovative solutions.

Increasingly, our world is being dramatically influenced and driven by big data. In 2000, about 25 percent of all data were digitized; about 18 years later, 97 percent of all data are digitized in one form or another. In the future, data-rich markets will offer individual choices without the constraints of inescapable cognitive limitations. We could easily argue that we are moving from a *finance capitalist system* to a form of *data capitalism*, facilitated by the growing internet traffic or network effect, massive data sets and the enhanced processing data capacity or analytical power of a computer. One of the consequences of this data capitalism lies in the curious shift from *causation* – as scientists have looked for through appropriate statistical methodology – to *correlation* where data "speak for themselves", without necessarily understanding the why behind the correlation. Admittedly, unlike correlations, scientific experiments to infer causal connections are often not practical or raise challenging ethical questions. In comparison, non-causal analysis and mere correlations, however, are often fast and reasonably cheap. Unlike for causal links, data scientists now have the mathematical and statistical methods to analyze correlative relationships and the necessary digital tools to demonstrate the value of data with a high level of confidence.

B. Is AI Really Intelligent?

Are these digital tools intelligent? What is Artificial Intelligence (AI)? **Human intelligence** is the ability to achieve success according to one's personal and shared community standards, within one's socio-cultural context. **Artificial Intelligence** (AI) can be defined as the science and engineering of (automated or semi-automated) problem-solving: "The object is to generate solutions by using computers to mimic the cognitive functions associated with deliberative thought, including perception, reasoning and learning[5]."

Is artificial intelligence the branch of computer science that is concerned with the automation of intelligent behavior? We all can agree in principle that intelligence is the ability to deploy novel means to attain a goal – which are extraneous to the intelligence. In other words, *intelligence* is the ability to accomplish complex goals. The distinction between specialized intelligence and general intelligence helps clarify the difference between the specialized abilities of today's learning machines or AI and the more general abilities of a human. Artificial intelligent machines are "smarter" – faster and better – than humans in terms of certain kinds of specialized knowledge or intelligence. But it remains very specialized knowledge about a certain specific domain. IBM's Watson may have beaten the human champion at Jeopardy, but it can't play any chess game at all. A *Tesla* car may (sort of) drive autonomously, but that car cannot autonomously pick up a box at the near Carrefour centre. Nonetheless, AI applications are hugely promising in business. It is recommendable that one identifies a crucial slice of the business in terms of digitization and possibly rethink it completely. The focus should be on domains that allow major improvement in performance[6].

Organizations that have embraced all possible intelligence and technology will be better prepared for the next disruptive period. But as always, benefiting from AI requires not only a clear strategy and top management commitment, but also the willingness to transform key operational activities. Collaborating across internal company boundaries and between other companies that share the same platforms and technology allow these firms to potentially take advantage of such (new) ecosystem. Such an ecosystem is a cluster of vital industrial activities tied together through common digital connections and practices. Some of those organizations will excel in such an Industry 4.0 context; others will lag behind[7].

Since AI is becoming better than humans at predicting, the value of its complementary elements such as data will go up as well: "data is the new oil"[8]. Despite this trendy analogy – possibly even a myth – we emphasize that data is always application-specific. Having the data of the most mobile phone users does not automatically translate in effective AI-applications. Whether it is smart manufacturing or transportation or agricultural applications, or natural language processing, all of those will be expressed in distinctively different data sets and data demand.

1.2. Perception and Cognition in AI

Although AI may help humans to make better judgements through its predictive power within certain "stable" constraints, it is the smart corporate leader or engineer who know how to handle the more cost-effective and more precise prediction of AI technology. In the future, some AI researchers[9] believe that we will see more top-down systems that don't require as much data, which are faster, more flexible and likely more innately intelligent than humans – an idea that I don't share.

Despite the accuracy of AI predictions, they are worthless if business do not include them in their business processes to create more value. AI is as an efficiency-enhancing tool that can give a company a lift – possibly a 1 percent to 10 percent increase in EBITDA or some other measure of productivity[10]. However, despite the impressive achievements by AI, the applicability still remains quite narrow. One of the challenges is the fact that we know more than we can tell – call it tacit knowledge for now – which severely restricts our ability to endow machines with real intelligence. The latest applications by refined AI-algorithms, however, are now using learning from examples and using structured feedback to start solving problems that previously were considered as impossible to "automate" or allow executives to use for "augmenting" the ability to make smart decisions.

Today, the biggest advances by AI has been in two broad areas: *perception* and *cognition*[11]. In the area of improved perception, some of the most practical advances have been made in relation to speech and image recognition. The speed of improvement has been accelerated in recent years when one adopted the applications to "deep" neural nets, where the smart computer can now recognize faces or voices. The second type of improvement has been in cognition and problem-solving. Google's *Deep-Mind* has used ML systems, for example, to improve the cooling efficiency at data centres by more than 15 percent, even after they were first optimized by human experts. Similarly, intelligent cyber-agents are now being used by cybersecurity company Deep Instinct to detect malware, and by Paypal and other financial institutions to prevent money laundering. Several other examples exist today.

2. Augmentation and Automation by Artificial Intelligence

Building some form of intelligence out of pure information technology based on digital data without human components is what people normally refer to as "artificial intelligence". The IT researchers Davenport and Ronanki distinguish three types of **Artificial** Intelligence: (1) *Process Automation* with robotics and cognitive automation, (2) *Cognitive Insights* that allows better predictions which will be our focus and (3) *Cognitive Engagement* as in natural language processing chatbots and intelligent assistants – as made visual in Figure 1.

Artificial Intelligence is being perceived as transformative. AI can therefore be applied in supporting for three key business needs: (1) *automating business processes*, using robotic process automation technologies, (2) *gaining insights* through data analysis and enhanced, more precise and cost-effective prediction, based on algorithms that detect patterns in vast volumes of data and interpreting their meaning and (3) *engaging with customers and employees,*

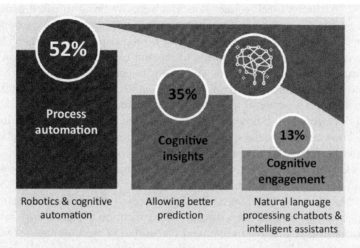

Figure 1: The applications of artificial intelligence in business

Source: Visual interpretation, based on Davenport, T.H. & R. Ronanki (2018), "Artificial Intelligence for the Real World. Don't start with moon shots", *Harvard Business Review*, January-February: 108–116

in which natural language processing chatbots, intelligent agents and machine learning play a crucial role[12].

It is becoming obvious that humans are not so good in predicting future outcomes since we are "noisy" thinkers with a lot of well-documented cognitive biases. Despite this inherent weakness, any executive knows the importance to be able to "predict" the next change in their industry, to know the next great product. Those changes are influenced by a number of factors, customer's taste or change in regulations such as a potential ban on plastic bags in retail, for instance. Knowing faster than your competitor may give you a temporary advantage.

2.1. Automatization and Robotization

Moreover, artificial intelligence can be seen as "automation on steroids". Indeed, AI is good at automating tasks rather than jobs[13]. Hence why boards and their executives need to question whether AI will (or not) help in creating value for the organization. AI can potentially (1) reduce costs by speeding up repetitive tasks in a more efficient way, (2) increase revenues whereby recommendation and prediction systems increase sales and efficiency and (3) launch new lines of business, enabling new projects that were not possible before.

A. The Prediction Power of AI ... Fueled by Reinforcement Learning

AI can help us in improving our innovative insights and reduce our biases in our presumed rational thinking, but AI can also improve our cognitive prediction abilities. "Artificial intelligence" does not actually bring us intelligence but instead a critical component of intelligence, namely *prediction* in a cost-efficient manner (i.e. AI will make prediction cheap). Prediction – i.e. "if-then" logical intelligence – is the process of filling in missing information. Prediction takes digital information you have, data, and uses it to generate information that you don't have. For instance, statistical regression minimizes prediction mistakes on average which is a powerful tool with relatively small data sets. With the vast amount of personal data, however, digital devices will learn more about us than we may know about ourselves, enabling us "to better predict" and thus allowing us to make better and smarter decisions by reducing uncertainty. Not surprisingly, Google's CEO Sundar Pichai sees a shift from "searching and organizing the world's information to AI and machine learning".

Machine Learning[14], as part of AI[15], refers to the ability of computers to detect patterns in large data sets through the application of algorithms[16], whereas **Deep Learning** is the most advanced technique of reinforcement learning for predictive modelling in which it connects software-based calculators to form a complex artificial "neural network"[17]. Indeed, within AI, deep learning technology – representing the area of greatest untapped potential – relies on complex neural networks that process information using various architectures comprised of layers and nodes, which approximate the functions of neurons in the brain.

Every time *Amazon*'s recommendation engine becomes more accurate by a couple points, the company will increase its bottom line. And the more Amazon benefits from analytics by "delivering the right insight of AI to the right people at the right time in a way that informs their decision making to drive better outcomes"[18], the more powerful Amazon will become. When the predictive power of its AI reaches a critical level of cost effectiveness and efficiency, a switch to a "shipping-then-shopping" approach may generate more sales than the current "shopping-then-shipping" framework. However, this is some way off. Due to the high costs of returning items, the Return on Investment for "shopping-then-shipping" is still higher than the AI-savvy aspiration of "Shipping-then-Shopping". Amazon is just one example.

Models can estimate whether a loan will be repaid but won't actually change the probability that payments will arrive on time. Executive leaders are not just concerned with predicting things that they cannot influence, but their primary duty is to get things done. It is to mobilize people to achieve a desired goal by inspiring their followers to reach demanding objectives. In other words, algorithms and artificial intelligence may be extremely effective in predicting things – we cannot control.

Netflix, for instance, captures rapid feedback to learn what programs have the greatest appeal and then uses these insights obtained through algorithms to adjust its offerings. And models can be updated through the instant use of feedback, enhancing their predictability power. However, we should also see their current limitations, especially in those contexts where leadership can shape the situation in the future, and not just predict particular outcomes (for which AI is extremely useful).

Intelligent technologies such as robotic process automation, machine learning and natural language processing systems offer companies new opportunities to improve performance and realize significant cost savings[19]. Businesses can, indeed, benefit from AI and machine- and deep-learning technology that relies on systems and algorithms that absorb and "learn" from data. This knowledge base is applied to make better predictions and decisions over time. The real value comes from embedding data analytics as a core capability in the organization and using it to detect pain points, design solutions and enable decision-making.

B. AI Robots: Immigrants from the Future

In automated business processes, using AI and machine learning algorithms, decisions are faster than human decision-makers and often at a fraction of the cost. You should have a look at how the team of *RoboVision* – a Belgian AI start-up founded by Jonathan Berthe – is able to apply AI algorithms to automate repetitive bandwork for precisely cutting roses, for instance, at an enormous speed, enhancing the productivity with a multifold: just impressive. RoboVision is now applying a similar AI algorithm that identifies waste – specifically plastic – after which an autonomous ship collects it[20]. The cleanup is fully automated and growing increasingly intelligent, a big plus for the environment and a huge win in efficiency for DEME, the dredging company who is responsible for reducing waste with their vessels in the Schelde river that passes the Antwer port to the North Sea, a major logistic seaway.

Everyone still remembers the introductory steps of *Asimo* (short for Advanced Step in Innovative Mobility), the humanoid robot developed by *Honda*, entering main stage in 2018 – after more than 30 years in the making. This robot can run at 15 km an hour, jump, walk up and down stairs, move its fingers like humans do and speak a few words in different languages. Asimo has also the ability to recognize faces, sound, moving objects, human gestures and the surrounding environment. Yes, Asimo is able to interact with humans and can respond to questions by nodding or providing simple verbal answers. It is expected by its Japanese developers that Asimo may become a good companion or a helping hand to have at home in the future, especially for those whose mobility has been impaired[21].

2.2. Augmenting Capabilities

Smart leaders will combine *human intelligence* with the use *artificial intelligence* as a very effective tool[22] where huge data needs to be churned with predictable (but difficult) outcomes and will use their creativity where they can make a difference by establishing a new solution over which they have influence[23]. Applying AI into the mass of complexity allows CEOs and executives to draw lessons of original and unexpected ideas[24]; it may even lead to more collaboration between teams of different departments – the well-known business silos – who use AI's predictions and analytics as trustworthy outcomes and the basis for a new dialogue.

A. Some Local Promising AI Start-Ups in My Hometown Antwerp

A young Belgian start-up *Toqua* uses an algorithm to map and improve the efficiency of the shipping industry: how to optimize shipping fuel costs by knowing when to speed up or to slow down dependent on the predictive power of salt percentage of the sea-routes that affects speed, to predict maintenance of the vessels, how to adopt to predicted heavy weather and optimize sea-routes accordingly. The AI algorithms of Toqua aim to reduce the fuel consumptions and thus CO_2 emissions of these huge ocean vessels. Today, shipping with its different players in the industry is played out as a zero-sum game. If AI enables to visualize and improve the financial margins of all stakeholders in the shipping supply chain, and even benefiting the climate cause, the interconnected shipping industry may become a win-win game. Partially thanks to the power of algorithms that map and optimize all those interconnected activities.

Around the same river giving access to the North Sea, the *Port of Antwerp* is developing a "digital twin" allowing the Antwerp port authority to augment and improve its decision-making. With the use of drones and artificial intelligence, the port authority understands real time what is going with respect to pollution, traffic, near-traffic accidents. It is able to continuously assess potential necessary dredging work aiming to secure enough depth of fairways for vessels in the harbour. The AI-driven digital tool to visualize the harbor infrastructure with real-time data would provide valuable information on the maintenance of the bridges, lock gates and quay walls of the harbor. In case of crisis, the harbor's infrastructure could be managed through this digital twin. The Port of Antwerp algorithms and sensors in the harbor are also designed to search for ecological pollution. Another important application of this "digital twin" is the potential efficiency improvement – especially in a port like Antwerp where the physical expansion of the harbor is very limited. If the port can improve its efficiency though better aligned bridges, lock gates and quay walls, it could manage to handle more than the current annual 15,000 sea vessels[25]. One estimates that this Advanced Port Information and Control Assistant (APICA) algorithm assessing and analyzing the sea traffic at the Port of Antwerp could be 30 percent more effective than humans. But it is the combination of human visionary and automated process that enhance decision-making and therefore could be quite promising in the future.

Like many phenomena, technology and AI follow an *S-curve*. Only a small fraction of 10 percent of companies have tried to diffuse AI across their enterprise, while a long tail of 65 percent of companies have yet to adopt any AI technology[26]. The use of big data analytics is often correlated with the use of core digital technologies. Virtual agents, natural-language generation and processing, image recognition, decision-making, robotic process automation, robotics and speech recognition are all powerful AI techniques implemented by a minority of companies. Nonetheless, early movers adapting those AI techniques can realize significant benefits and return advantages compared to followers and laggards, especially in energy, finance, automotive, tech and telecom industries.

B. How Real Is the AI-Driven Virtual Reality?

Although I may not be the biggest fan of *Facebook* (now rebranded as *Meta*), its approach to AI/ML teaches us a thing or two, especially since everyone talks about the latest AI-buzz and its promises in business: a virtual completely connected smart meta-world where uncertainty will significantly be reduced. At the end of the day, AI/ML is not about some magic formula in the algorithm that will change our life overnight, but rather to scale up the potential of AI/ML by building up an AI/ML factory-like capabilities[27]. Despite much of the conversation around AI filled with reverential descriptions of its power and near-magical capabilities, the real impact of AI is much more prosaic, depending on training and the use of data, alongside experimenting faster.

For instance, *Facebook*'s AI system allows for more than 6 million predictions a second. All of this is to increase the velocity of running experiments on the data and scale. At Facebook, the focus is on data and speed, less on improving the algorithms itself by making it more sophisticated. It does make sense to use a robust reliable AI/ML algorithm – possibly not the newest or most sophisticated – but feeding it with useful data that can be experimented on, allowing concrete answers to concrete questions like "where can I get a good bite around here?" or "can it recommend the right swimsuit if it notices them posting pictures on the beach?"[28] Let us not forget that ML is only as good as its training, with clearly definable categories.

Crucial to optimize the benefits of AI is to ask questions such as "What problem am I trying to solve? What is my goal? What are the trade-offs?" Indeed, AI is no magic. One needs to build a data science team that helps to think through a problem and apply the human litmus test. If one doesn't have an intuition (based on a model), if one can't build a very simple, rule-based system, it will be hard to achieve real substantial benefits from investments in AI. The major challenge in transitioning organizations into Industry 4.0 is not just AI technology, but understanding a business process or challenge that could be (semi)automated, contributing to strengthen the value proposition, and allowing the value chain activities to be resolved in a speedier and more accurate manner.

Some thoughts to take away:

- This chapter zooms in to this future that is fundamentally digitized and driven by smart machines. It attempts to deconstruct the contours of **opportunities and threats of an unfolding *digital* reality** that seem to **fuse with our *analog relational* reality**: our life is becoming more and more organized and dominated by AI algorithms that augment our decision power or automate some of our manufacturing processes, anywhere any time.

- Most progress by AI algorithms has occurred in **improved and cheaper prediction** (as in more precise recommendation engines) and **automation** (the ubiquity of AI robots – replacing or speeding up human tasks or making automation possible).

- The fusion of analog and virtual is already a reality. How long will it take before AI engines make **a virtual world** – a mega world – a reality?

Chapter Eight

The Potential Benefits of Artificial Intelligence in Business

"Nothing in life is to be feared. It is only to be understood. Now is the time to understand more, so that we may fear less".

Marie Curie, French Nobel Prize winner physicist

"Tel est le paradoxe de l'IA: extraordinairement puissante, extraordinairement spélialisée, et sans une once de sens common".

Yan Le Cun, 2019, AI pioneer and winner of Turing Price
(Nobel Prize equivalent for Mathematics & Computer Science)

Humans will never be able to compete with the fastness and calculating powers of computers and machine learning. Jack Ma – the owner and chairman of *Alibaba* – recently said that wise leaders should not compete with artificial intelligence, but they should optimally use the technology tools available. Machine learning ability may obtain an intelligence – here defined as the ability to solve problems with limited resources in which a key resource is time – that equals ours and likely exceed in calculative speed and accuracy. But do not expect a learning device *in silico* to make conscious or let alone responsible decisions. These digital machines possibly could become slightly less biased through mere statistical averaging and therefore quite reasonable in their outcomes, but cannot take a responsible contextual decision that is normative.

One thing is for sure: artificial intelligence and digital transformation in general will fundamentally change our society and transform the global economy[1]. Corporate leadership, on the other hand, can and should also take "responsible" decisions. Indeed, human leadership continues to outmanoeuvre computers in terms of creativity, unexpectedness and innovation, and their crucial ability to empathetically relate to other humans, within and beyond the organization.

1. AI-Driven Applications in Augmented Decision-Making

Having established this critical distinction between reasonable and responsible decision-making, executives and board members are advised to prepare and, where possible, to embrace AI to strengthen decision-making, and/or automate certain repetitive processes.

1.1. AI as Personal Assistant

Just consider the GPS lead systems that are behind guiding autonomous driving cars or virtual assistants such as *Apple's Siri* and *Amazon's Echo*. These tools are reflections of the way we have been thinking and talking. Artificial Intelligence, today, is functioning by brute force using millions of samples, using reinforcement learning based on little pieces to approximate a desired function. *Vanguard*, an investment service company, uses cognitive technology (or a form of AI tool) to provide customers with investment advice at a lower cost than their competitors. Its Personal Advisor Services system automates many traditional tasks of investment, while human advisors focus on higher-value activities.

A majority of people in the developed but increasingly in emerging markets now communicate via the prevailing channels of social media. *Facebook, Instagram, Snapchat, Twitter, LinkedIn* and *TikTok*, to name a few, are all powered by digital data and algorithms. A company such as *Amazon*, for instance, looks for unique patterns in the data they receive from customers, which reveal the preferences of these customers. Identifying such patterns enables Amazon to statistically deduce customers' wants and needs without having to ask them directly. The data approximately tell what you and I want. The data do not know why we prefer one thing over another; it just "sees" that we choose one over the other, indicating some hidden patterns of our preferences. But that is sufficient for Amazon to feed the preferences-matching algorithm and search for the products (potential) customers are most likely to purchase.

Artificial Intelligence seems to become a new functional tool that provides intelligence unavailable before. Or does it? Could it also be that Artificial Intelligence is only the newest fad in town: every organization is eager to put forward the enormous benefits of this newest digital technology, without really knowing how to turn this abundance of data in real changing business models. *Amazon* seems to know what it is doing: it just opened to the public, a physical grocery store, without check-out lanes or cashiers. You'll fill up your bag, walk out the front door and get a receipt minutes later for everything that is in your bag: no human interaction is involved in the transaction.

Quite a number of companies are already taking advantage of big data and its prediction power. *Aviva*, a private global insurance company, is now able to predict insurance claims not based anymore on a detailed report of the health of its subscribers – who may have given blood and urine samples, costing the company USD 125 per person for the analysis – but on credit reports and consumer marketing data, which cost only USD 5 per person on average. Those data on the life style of people taking an insurance now function as a proxy to predict the health of these customers.

Even sport gets excited about data analytics. Football club *Liverpool* got into an agreement with DeepMind, the London-based AI lab of Google, to help them decipher patterns in the different games they play in reaction to their opponents' strengths and weaknesses. In the same vein, *Manchester City* hooked up with astrophysicist Laurie Shaw to help them model the chaotic game to increase the expected goals. AI can help to determine – i.e. to predict accurately – from which angle one should shoot to have the highest expected goal outcome. AI algorithms seek to discern certain patterns which allows the club to optimize the chances of a gifted and informed player to improve his average effective score level.

1.2. AI Facilitates to Make Smarter Decisions

Banks can detect credit card fraud by looking at anomalies, and the best way to find them is to crunch all the data – big data – rather than a sample. The card network uses information or data about past fraudulent (and non-fraudulent) transactions to predict whether a particular recent transaction is *anormal* and possibly fraudulent, and stopping illegal transactions in its tracks.

Another interesting application is the combination of converging robotics and AI: for instance, drones may be a useful tool for mitigating a looming deforestation disaster. Today, we lose over seven billion trees a year to timber harvesting, agricultural expansion, wildfire, mining, road building and other human interventions. This deforestation may become a major cause of climate change and species extinction. Today, tree-planting drones are called in to "automatically" fire seedpods bullets into the ground, allowing a single drone to plant as many as 100,000 trees a day without the intervention of a human[2]. This device is AI-driven and automatically recognizes "patterns" where seeds are needed. Agricultural farms will highly benefit from the robotization of planning crop through the use of GPS-navigated tractors and/or drones. Precision agriculture uses the GPS- and AI-driven robots to assess the land that drastically improves the efficiency of the agricultural firm. The sensors on the tractor – drones or on the ground – measure the land characteristics, allowing subsequently to precisely determine the need for fertilizers, water, etc. The reduction of waste, better water usage and less fertilizers will also have a positive impact on climate change objectives, i.e. less CO_2. However, this improvement in efficiency won't fully resolve the negative (climate change) impact of agriculture on the eco-system. One still needs to think and explore solutions in a more circular and nature-inclusive manner.

When a mall operator uses advanced analytics to select tenants, optimize mall layout and determine rents, its revenues can rise by 20 percent, according to a McKinsey survey[3]. In general, the ability of AI to enable personalization and customization at scale makes it a powerful differentiator for consumer-facing businesses. It improves precision and speed-to-market and enhances interactions, engagement and purchases. Companies such as *Spotify* playlists; the *Facebook* newsfeed combines human and computer expertise to create new services and enables people to discover and engage with content and brands in new ways.

Few use AI for personalization better than the fashion ecommerce *Stitch Fix*[4] or the movie streaming giant *Netflix*. These organizations basically personalize their offers to individual customers by applying a sophisticated algorithm that is using continuous conditional probability calculations – which is the chance that one thing happens, given that some other thing has already happened. Conditional probability is how AI systems express judgements in a way that reflects their partial knowledge. Additionally, personalization algorithms run on conditional probabilities, all of which must be estimated from big data sets in which you as an individual are the conditioning event.

Other examples are governments that understand having sensors affixed to bridges and buildings to watch for signs of wear and tear that could prevent potential disasters to occur. The cost of collecting and analyzing the data that indicate when to take early action is lower than the cost of an outage. Note that these predictive analytics may not explain the cause of the problem (the why); it may only indicate that a problem exists (the what). *General Electric* and *Rolls Royce* both have implemented big data analytics into their commercial jet engine business to predict more accurately when to replace expensive parts or when to optimally start maintenance of the jet engines, allowing those firms to apply new business models by leasing or renting power to the airplanes instead of merely selling engines.

Today, businesses churn out "smart objects" using the blockchain technology – a distributed, mutable, permissible and transparent digital infrastructure ledger. These smart objects are digital objects with a blockchain layer sitting beneath it, which makes the object unique and provides them with authenticity and scarcity. Most of these smart objects are AI-enabled: they can learn and have "memories". The futurist Peter Diamandis and award-winning journalist Steven Kotter gave the intriguing example of purchasing a "digital suit". Upon buying this suit, you automatically get a digital version on your mobile phone that shows the entire history of every thread in the suit. The blockchain-backed digital suit version does not allow any potential marketing pampering, but it also guarantees that the initiated information reflects the actual fact that no part of your garment in the suit was constructed using child labor[5].

The progress in AI will, in many cases, be exponential rather than linear. Already the progress in a wide range of applications (e.g., vision, natural language, motion control) over the past 12 months was faster than in the 12 months prior, according to McKinsey and the Boston Consulting Group. The level of AI investment is rapidly increasing. The quality-adjusted cost of sensors is falling exponentially. Also, the amount of data being generated is increasing exponentially. In most cases, when AI algorithms are properly designed and deployed, they're better predictors than humans are. And yet, we're often still reluctant to hand over the reins of prediction to machines. For example, there have been studies comparing human recruiters to AI-powered recruiters that predict which candidates will perform best in a job. When performance was measured 12, 18 and 24 months later, the recruits selected by the AI outperformed those selected by the human recruiters, on average. Despite this evidence, human recruiters still often override the recommendations provided by AI algorithms when making real hiring decisions. Where Artificial Intelligence has demonstrated superior performance in prediction, companies must carefully consider the conditions under which to empower humans to exercise their discretion to override the AI. The organizations that will benefit most from AI will be the ones that are able to most clearly and accurately specify their objectives. Remember that today AI is at its best within very specific domain of expertise – within a stable situation.

2. Promising AI Applications to Create a Smart(er) World

The applications can vary from medical diagnosis where raw data come from patient imaging, to crediting bank loans where the raw data are made up of payment history, defaulted loans, credit score and some other risk or demographic information. The mechanical systems learn from processing all this data, and each layer of deep neural network learns to progressively recognize more complex features which then are captured in mathematical algorithms. Admittedly, the decision process itself is far from transparent. With sufficient training and adaptation by humans, the AI system may become highly accurate in prescribing or predicting certain behavior or patterns. In order to allow managers and organizations to trust these algorithms the machine learning models on which the systems are based must be made as transparent and explainable as in any scientific process, adding to the AI's justified model's interpretability. By enhancing transparency in the way AI algorithms function, one can avoid blind faith in the financial quants, for instance, who partially caused the global financial crisis in 2008 .... Let's focus on a couple of areas where AI has proven to be extremely useful: the healthcare and finance industry.

2.1. Healthcare: Diagnosing, Preventing and Predicting Diseases

An obvious terrain where artificial intelligence can make a huge difference is health. By analyzing scans of patients' brains made on admission in a hospital, machine learning – a form of artificial intelligence – will tell the administrators who needs urgent attention from those who may safely wait, especially in the case of imminent strokes. Another promising field is AI's assistance in oncology, especially in classifying skin lesions that may indicate skin cancer. Computers are now more accurate or competent in diagnostics of certain diseases than medical experts. AI systems were slightly superior in comparison with oncology experts. Computers were also able to misdiagnose fewer benign moles as malignancies[6]. DeepMind, a London-based subsidiary of Alphabet, Google's parent company, has an AI that screens retinal scans for conditions such as glaucoma, diabetic retinopathy and age-related macular degeneration. And the list goes on.

A. Artificial Intelligence Personalizes Medical Treatment

For instance, in Belgium, the *Athena project* helps to personalize the cancer treatments based on data that reveal more accurate predictive diagnoses. And to limit the ballooning costs of healthcare, smart applications that combine the enormous amount of (currently dispersed) data could help to prevent many diseases instead of waiting for a diagnosis when the disease had the chance and time to materialize.

What medical AI will not do is to make human experts redundant in the fields it invades. Machine learning systems work on a narrow range of tasks and will need close supervision and input for the coming years. Admittedly, medical doctors, for instance – just as any other leader – can be quite biased and opinionated, whereas machine learning will be able to screen patients for cancer or taken from the scene of a horrifying accident in an unbiased manner and indicate which patients need to be treated urgently and for what – quite similar to important strategy decisions boards need to make in business.

B. Artificial Intelligence Improves Medical Diagnostics

The convergence of sensors, networks and AI is fundamentally upending the future of medical diagnostics. If you add genomics and potentially quantum computing to the equation, we are talking about a potentially dramatic transformation in medical science. One sees a shift from a reactive generic sick care to a pro-active and personalized healthcare system. Data are crucial for healthcare and disease-prevention applications. Especially, preventing diseases to materialize through sophisticated data analytics may allow us to keep the increasingly expansive and expensive healthcare system manageable and payable. One of the major organizational challenges – next to the technical progress to use data to "predict" more accurately – in healthcare to effectively use medical data is caused by the enormous dispersion of medical data on one hand, and the legal and ethical implications of using this sensitive data, on the other. However, from a pure technical perspective, the AI algorithms increasingly are able to detect diseases early on and enough to make a difference to prevent diseases to take a full run on the human body. A possible solution is to create a "common data model" where privacy is respected and security enhanced.

C. Mobile Healthcare Facilitated by AI-Driven Wearables

The big tech companies are joining the fray, making "mobile health" a reality in the near future[7]. Apple's mobile devices will be able to gather and analyze real-life data and translate them in readable personalized charts. For instance, *Apple's* fourth generation iWatch includes an ECG scanner capable of real-time cardiac monitoring and issue warning signals if deemed necessary, preventing a potential cardiac arrest. Today, some wearables are measuring the physiological activities of your heartbeat and skin receptiveness which may indicate some form of stress. The applications claim to allow people to control their stress level, though the data do not make the distinction between a jolting energy hike as result from a surprise party or being harassed on the street. Data itself cannot make that distinction since an algorithm cannot interpret the context (yet). In other words, these wearables that may prevent some overstress to help people with a personalized way to prevent a breakdown or depression will need to be enhanced by experts or potentially other tools to interpret the importance of the context itself.

In essence, each person has their own "personalized algorithm", and any deviation from its personal normal may help to detect anomalies and possible underlying causes for getting sick. The faster one can detect such anomalies, the easier it may be to prevent a stress breakdown, for instance, such as the *Biorics* – a small spin-off of KULeuven in Belgium – that attempts to measure and detect acute and chronic stress levels that could potentially result in depression, which the app tries to prevent by being early enough to pick up the signals that could be addressed in a sensitive manner. However, diagnosing depression based on a wearable is not possible at this moment. Nonetheless, the German racing team *Getspeed* uses Biotrics' technology to detect stress peaks in lifetime to coach its riders during rally to keep the "correct" focus at the right time[8]. Today, some trucking companies are offering truck drivers to help them with these wearables to control their stress level that could avoid accidents. Again, stress may have benign or more worrisome causes; wearable applications today do no understand this subtle though crucial distinction.

D. Artificial Intelligence Speeds Up Finding New Pharma Medicine

Similarly, pharma companies want to speed up the process of finding new medicine for diseases or even better, finding clues in big data that may indicate potential diseases and take measurements to prevent such diseases to actually materialize. For instance, *Janssen Pharmaceutics* – now playing a crucial part in the Johnson & Johnson group's innovation and revenue stream – is participating in *Melloddy* (a European initiative) in which pharma companies share data in their development through machine learning platforms[9]. Relevant data – property of individual pharma companies or hospitals – are encrypted first and via a Blockchain ledger securely shared with the algorithm of Melloddy on the cloud. This allows pharma companies in Europe to analyze encrypted data – and not individual data sets which could jeopardize privacy law – that helps them to analyze this billion data points and to model the biological effects of molecules through this algorithm.

Early 2020, researchers at Massachusetts Institute of Technology (MIT) discovered a novel antibiotic able to kill strains of bacteria that have been resistant to all known antibiotics. In other words, quite an achievement in the field of medicine and pharmacy. Unique in the discovery of this antibiotic – named *halicin* after the 2001: A Space Odyssey science fiction movie – was the fact that artificial intelligence had discovered and identified this *halicin* molecule that proved to be effective in fighting those bacteria that so far had escaped the current pharma knowledge. AI "learned" the attributes of molecules predicted to be antibacterial, and "curiously, it identified attributes (of molecules) that had not specifically been encoded – indeed, attributes that had eluded human conception or categorization[10]." This MIT software identified structural patterns in molecules that proved effective in fighting those bacteria, and this in a more efficient, and less expensive manner. A triumph in the pharmaceutical field. It was remarkable that AI identified relationships in the chemical bonding that had escaped human detection – or even possibly defied human description. This neural network algorithm detected new molecular qualities. It captured the association between molecules (input) and their potential to inhibit bacterial growth (output). The

AI algorithm discovered relationships between the inputs and outputs through deep learning in which layers of a neural network were able to predict a desired output[11]. Even after the discovery, medical experts could not articulate precisely why this new antibiotic *halicin* worked. In other words, AI not only processed data more quickly than humans, but it also detected aspects of reality that humans have not detected or alluded human knowledge.

It is well documented that deep learning AI is increasingly good at image, voice and text recognition, and with the availability of massive data, they can be trained by pharmacological data sets in order to speed up drug discovery processes. For instance, the *Insilico Medicine*, a start up at the John Hopkins University – considered as one of the best universities and medical hospitals in the USA – is using this AI-driven recognition methodology to sift through millions of data samples to determine the unique biological characteristics of a specific disease, in the hope to identify the most promising treatment targets. This research is resulting in "an explosion in potential drug targets and a much more efficient testing process. AI allows to do with fifty people what a typical drug company does with five thousand[12]." The continuous development and convergence in artificial intelligence, machine learning, 3D technology and possibly quantum computing may make customized medicine a real possibility. Science fiction may then become the standard for (preventive) care in medicine.

E. Artificial Intelligence Supporting Surgery

Speaking to our imagination lies in the enormous potential of macrobots in the surgical rooms. This "autonomous" robo-surgeons driven by AI algorithms have the ability to perfectly execute routine procedures at a fraction of today's cost. Similarly, remote-controlled microscopic robots – so-called microbots – can be put in with minimally invasive surgery, and move in our body and can carry out specific tasks such as specialized diagnostics and targeted medicine delivery[13]. One hopes that this methodology may help fighting some cancers from the inside and reduce the overall invasive chemotherapy.

Neuroelectronics Research Flanders (NERF) – a collaboration between the KULeuven and the research centre IMEC, both located in North Belgium – has managed to develop mini-implants with powerful sensors (in rodents) to better comprehend the functioning of our brain memories. Specifically, the focus is how the brain processes information and how neurons record it, necessary to understand dementia. With an increasing aging population, Alzheimer and other diseases may find solace from this kind of AI-driven research in providing improved tools. Today, one already uses implants or brain probes to automatically stimulate brain activities in the case of Parkinson, or epilepsy[14].

2.2. FinTech Companies and the Unbanked

The Fintech companies are upending financial institutions because they focus on the real new needs of younger or unbanked customers – those people without a safe place to store their money, especially in emerging markets. At present, two billion people still lack bank accounts, but all have mobile phones. As I have been firsthand involved as a governance and risk expert with IFC in providing funding and advise to microfinance companies in Southeast Asia, I have seen the enormous positive impact these (investment) companies can have. You add new easy technology that run on these mobile phones, and you have a great potential market. Allowing those unbanked people to access credit online – based on a few easy verifiable personal variables – to start their own small venture can often be the difference between poverty and the start of a new promising life.

One of the most well-known and quoted examples was *M-Pesa* that was initially rolled out in Kenya in 2007. M-Pesa allowed their (poor) customers to send data and money via their mobile phone to other parties, allowing them to trade without having a traditional bank account. Today, M-Pesa provides banking services to more than 30 million people in 10 different (African) countries. The enormous success of this mobile banking application has inspired many other ventures in other emerging markets. Alipay – the ePayment system from Alibaba – serves just shy of a billion Chinese customers. The Indonesian Unicorn Gojek's GoPay allows anyone with a mobile phone to access credit points used to purchase food or taxi services or other perks that are featured on the application, all driven by smart algorithms gathering information on your preferences.

And some more technological disruption is coming. Blockchain technology – the underlying safe infrastructural ledger on which crypto-currency Bitcoin functions – may allow trading in stock, for instance, without the usual traditional clearing and settlement houses. Blockchain fueled by AI may remove everyone but the buyer and seller of the imminent stock trade. Blockchain technology companies will execute in the most secure and transparent way all the steps in between. They may even aim to replace the SWIFT banking network which today is the standard protocol overseeing international banking transactions. You clearly see how traditional banks are waking up by implementing AI applications at the expense of the traditional banking outlets. Both FinTech and banks are moving to "dematerialize" banking services.

In Financial Services, quant-driven funds got a serious beating during the global financial crisis of 2007–2008. This was a volatile time of the unexpected. So the historical data needed to find patterns were missing in action. Then, as now, these quant-based decisions were short-termist, taking advantage of the slightest fluctuation. To this day, these decisions rely on algorithms and assumptions, and these are often complex, ambiguous and poorly understood. So it is impossible to verify or falsify them until it is too late. The quants that delivered dazzling short-term profits within seconds of trading were actually one of the destabilizers of the global financial system, one burdened by huge, undercapitalized derivatives that were swiftly reduced from AAA to toxic assets. And that risk is still with us.

AI technology is also impacting on investment. Traditionally, specialized financial advisors had access to the best data which yielded these experts substantial influence in the funds they managed on behalf of their (often wealthy) clients. Now, AI algorithms have taken over. More than 60 percent of all stock trades at the NYSE today is made by robo-algorithms. When the market turns volatile, the autonomous trading volume can climb to more than 85 percent at the liquid NYSE. These "robo-advisors" have slashed the (human) costs of these trading.

The companies that are able to sharpen their visions the most will reap the most benefits from AI. Due to the methods used to train AIs, AI effectiveness is directly tied to goal-specification clarity. What makes AI so powerful is its ability to learn. Normally we think of labor as being learners and of capital as being fixed. Now, with *artificial intelligence*, we have *capital that learns*. Companies need to ensure that information flows into decisions, they follow decisions to an outcome, and then they learn from the outcome and feed that learning back into the system. Managing the learning loop will be more valuable than ever before.

Some thoughts to take away:

- Artificial intelligence hugely **contributes to particular domains** that remain **reasonably stable**, and where **huge amount of data** are available. More particularly in the field of *health-pharma-medicine, finance, agriculture, service industry* and some others.

- Most of those AI applications will help humans to either assist to make ***better and smarter decisions***, or to create a smarter world by enhancing the decision process or automating certain (repetitive) processes.

- Artificial Intelligence being able to learn independently from human operators – through a feedback system – will allow businesses to use this capital to invest in a **"smart world"**, be it smart (automated) decision-making, or smart cities, or anything that will enhance or replace human involvement, but with less errors and much faster and more efficient.

Chapter Nine

Datafication of Our Economy

"Computers make excellent and efficient servants, but I have no wish to serve under them".

Mr. Spock, Star Trek

"Unless humans merge with computers, homo sapiens are finished".

Yuval Harari, 2017, Historian-author

Digital technology drives the numerous changes in the Internet of Things, Artificial Intelligence and Robotics. It is improving efficiency in a number (manufacturing) of industries. In addition, bringing digital prowess and sustainable practices together should be at the forefront of any strategic thinker as a way to differentiate itself and to gain long-term viability among customers, regulators and the communities where businesses operate.

1. Datafication Using "Statistical Prediction" to Resolve "Wicked" Problems

Digital technology and especially the predictive power of AI can help organizations ease their pollution footprint and manage waste more effectively in the future. Be it optimized energy system forecasting, demand-response transportation infrastructure, analytics and automation for smart urban planning, "hyperlocal" weather forecasting for crop management, or supply chain monitoring and transparency, all can contribute to assist strategists and operational managers to deal with uncertainty and achieve some competitive advantage.

1.1. Stable Situations That Are Fully "Datafied"

AI is useful for some tasks, especially in relatively stable situations where ambiguity and volatility are rather limited. For face recognition, for instance, AI is extremely useful, especially for identifying an individual or to authenticate an individual. However, using face recognition technology for mass screening may be less effective, and politically a probable violation of privacy, infringing on individual freedom, and possibly also disrupting our social life in more or less subtle ways. Mass surveillance by governments should not be automatically trusted. My subsequent question begs whether the governing elite can be really trusted?

A. *Voice and Image Recognition and Business Model Innovation*

Technology is, indeed, excellent in fairly stable contexts such as unlocking your smartphone through image recognition, or for border control where your identity is checked automatically. But when screening our face in real-world conditions through mass identification, AI occasionally stumbles and causes false alarms, resulting in unnecessarily "harassing" innocent people[1].

The Dutch firm *Philips* is using digital technology to capture more information on the product life cycle in order to reduce waste. The company's analysis of the secondary market for components revealed that its customers had opportunities to reuse certain parts and thus extend the life of some existing equipment, such as X-ray machines. This integrated effort not only lengthened the life of the equipment customers had bought, but Philips could also develop an ongoing closer relationship with its customers that it had not had before[2]. Philips' lighting division drastically revamped its business model. Instead of selling bulbs or LED lamps to its clients, Philips has entered the circular economy by renting out light to the International Schiphol Airport in Amsterdam. The airport does not buy lamps anymore, but it rents light from Philips: a product turned into a service. Sensors are attached to these LED lamps, allowing Philips to know – through the Internet of Things where data are beamed to its cloud – when to replace or to execute a maintenance check on specific lamps. Most parts of those lamps are recycled which reduces the waste. In other words, sensors and AI allow this "product as a service" (PaaS) to become Philips' latest business model innovation.

B. *AI Driven "Social Physics" Predicting Behavior: A Dream or a Soon-to-Be-Reality?*

Now that everything becomes increasingly "datafied", it looks like we can measure most aspects of human life, and with those powerful machine-learning techniques, we now can build ecosystems. Well-known examples are weather- and traffic-prediction models which are being extended to predict the global climate and plan city growth and renewal.

Personalization can be interpreted as a euphemism that spearheads the generation of "prediction products" manufactured from the raw materials of the self. Personalization derives from the prediction power of these AI products and services. The latest field of behavioral surplus sought after by those AI firms is labelled affective computing, or sentiment analysis – based on specialized software to scour faces, voices, gestures, bodies and brains. All these emotional-related data are captured by biometric sensors, often in combination with imperfectibly small unobtrusive cameras. This new "emotion economy" has become one of the new frontiers of AI, potentially allowing these AI firms to expand from observation to modification. "Happiness as a service" may become within reach. We question the wisdom behind such hedonistic-oriented efforts.

It can be argued that the real aim of these AI firms may be ubiquitous intervention, action and control, allowing them to modify them in real time. It is therefore not too much a logical step to argue that conditioning at scale could become the news science of massively engineered human behavior that ultimately may undermine self-determination. In a more positive vein, one could also try to nudge citizens to become better citizens or to behave better for their own sake.

MIT professor Sandy Pentland and his team, for instance, researches to how human behavior and ecosystems interact; this *social physics* looks at the patterns of cultural behavior and develops mathematically accurate predictions how people make decisions. At present, organizations are trying to influence conscious processes and explicit knowledge. Pentland sees the potential for new predictive theories of human decision-making that leads or could nudge to "social efficiency", which means that participation must provide value not only to the individual but also to the system as a whole. Yet, Pentland's research indicates that sociometric data show that unconscious processes and tacit knowledge are potentially even more important in determining the behavior of organizations. One can describe how people socially interact, and assuming no expected change, one can calculate or predict how a group of people may react or behave in a certain situation in the future. However, those aggregates on social behavior – seen as certain patterns in a group of people – do not tell anything about the individual behavior (yet).

Value capturing of deep-learning will be initially found in the consumer sector such as digital voice assistants on mobile phones or autonomous cars. However, government (e.g. detecting potential cyberattacks, or traffic control systems, or the use of military drones using AI), banks (to detect suspicious behavior such as money laundering) or retail (theft detection, or enhancements to automated checkouts) will all benefit from the applications of AI[3].

C. Is AI Materializing an Expected Productivity Increase?

Despite the performance and productivity opportunities through artificial intelligence applications, hardly a fifth of the US economy and less than one in six European companies have been reached their digital potential[4]. Despite this enormous potential gap, some factors may drive a certain acceleration to adapt AI techniques in companies. The next wave opportunities will be rooted in machine-learning algorithm and reinforcement techniques based on neural networks, exponential increasing computing capacity and the Internet of Things that embed data and machine learning. These evolving technologies will unlock multiple benefits for companies beyond mere labor substitution. Yes, indeed, the next business growth opportunities will be fueled by productivity increases through automation (of physical activities in highly predicable and structured environments, as well as data collection and processing) and the use of AI techniques.

1.2. With Prediction Costs Falling, Are Autonomous Driving Cars a Reality Soon?

As the cost of prediction continues to drop, we'll use more of it for traditional prediction problems such as inventory management because we can predict faster, cheaper and better. At the same time, firms start using prediction to solve problems that have not historically been thought of as prediction problems. For example, we never thought of autonomous driving as a prediction problem. Traditionally, engineers programmed an autonomous vehicle to move around in a controlled environment, by telling it what to do in certain situations – *if* a human walks in front of the vehicle (*then* stop) or *if* a shelf is empty (*then* move to the next shelf). Useful applications can be found in factories and warehouses. That is exactly what *Amazon* does with automating much of their inventory system.

But we could never put those vehicles on a city street because there are too many *ifs* – *if* it's dark, *if* it's rainy, *if* a child runs into the street, *if* an oncoming vehicle has its blinker on. No matter how many lines of code we write, we couldn't cover all the potential *ifs*.

Today, we have reframed autonomous driving as a prediction problem. Then, an AI simply needs to predict the answer to one question: what would a good human driver do? There are a limited set of actions we can take when driving ("*thens*"). We can turn right or left, brake or accelerate – that's it. So, to teach an AI to drive, we put a human in a vehicle and tell the human to drive while the AI is figuratively sitting beside the human watching. Since the AI doesn't have eyes and ears like we do, we give it cameras, radar and light detection and ranging (LIDAR). In a way, machine learning may be seen as "inducing" theories from data. As autonomous cars drive, they gather information such as positions of traffic signs, road conditions and the like. The more information they get, the smarter the algorithm becomes, which equals safer cars, necessary to make these autonomous cars commercially viable.

That has been *Tesla*'s strategy to materialize its aim for autonomous driving cars. The AI takes the input data as it come in through its "eyes" and looks over to the human and tries to predict, "What will the human do next?" The AI makes a lot of mistakes at first. But it learns from its mistakes and updates its model every time it incorrectly predicts an action the human will take. Its predictions start getting better and better until it becomes so good at predicting what a human would do that we don't need the human to do it anymore. The AI can perform the action itself as long as the infrastructure is available which means that high-speed connectivity is continuous and of good quality – requiring a 5G network.

Having good reliable data is crucial in making AI algorithms work as expected. Tesla's competitive advantage is not just being an elegant and beautiful car, not its performing chips or even its algorithms steering the car. No, Tesla's advantage lies in the data that it controls. Indeed, every Tesla is equipped with eight cameras that operate and "see" continuously, capturing all these images, assess and evaluate them and then upload these in a compressed format to Tesla's own network. Multiplying the continuous data increase – resulted from all Tesla's camera equipment on the road – provides them with a unique set of data. This massive photographic data won't be easily matched by any competitor any time soon. All these data are gathered with the aim to succeed in making a self-driving car a reality – sooner than Tesla's competition[5].

Businesses are expecting that we are close to a tipping point in materializing this idea of automated cars and ships. Indeed, computers have significantly improved at image and voice recognition and speech synthesis. Computers can now detect tumours in radiographs earlier than most humans. Medical diagnosis and personalized medicine will improve substantially. Transportation by self-driving cars – where transportation is transformed into a prediction problem – will keep us safer, on average. And hopefully, we can sort out the ethical challenges regarding the use of this new kind of digitized intelligence. Hence why boards of car manufacturers around the world need to think differently about mobility in the future. Not just electrifying cars who can drive autonomously, but also a different view on cities and mobility.

And yes, AI is likely destined to become ubiquitous in our daily life; progress will be less homogenous because some technological and ethical challenges are more difficult to solve.

2. The Trade-Off Between *Accuracy* and *Explainability* in AI Algorithms

Machine learning algorithms are often called a *black box* because they resemble a closed system that takes input and produces an output, without any explanation as to why. Knowing why is important for many industries, particularly those with fiduciary obligations like customer finance, or in healthcare and education, where vulnerable lives are involved, or in military or government applications, where you need to be able to justify your decisions to the electorate[6]. This black box makes deep-learning platforms problematic in terms of *explainability*. And the appeal of machine learning lies in its ability to find patterns that defy logic or even intuition. However, the rationale behind (potential and actual) algorithmic regulation is *accountability*.

2.1. Making the World Smarter Through Datafication of Our Daily Life

Real problems are framed in terms of conditional probability (if-then logic) to solve them. Computers do not understand why you are watching a particular movie, but they are great at crunching data, i.e. tabulating vast databases of subscribers' movie-watching histories from a ratings matrix to estimate conditional probabilities of individual movies' preferences – discovered organically by AI. In other words, digital economy is about suggestions and thus conditional probability, translated into prediction, rather than search.

In AI, recognizing a pattern means fitting an equation to data. The big breakthrough in AI was the introduction of the use of neural networks for estimating prediction rules from data. The slightly misleading notion of "neural network" in algorithms is a complicated equation with a lot of parameters that is capable of describing very complicated patterns in data. These neural networks work incredibly well across a range of prediction tasks, from language to images to video.

But this progress of better "prediction" leaves us with a crucial question: who does own the data and how can these personal data be used by organizations?

Indeed, we should acknowledge the fact that today, more data means less privacy; more speed means less accuracy; and more autonomy means less control. More expected accuracy means less explainability. There are trade-offs to be decided upon. Let us not forget the simple heuristics that if "data or the application is free, then you are the product". The real customers are those who are willing to pay for access to knowledge about us (derived from these data), so that they can persuade us to purchase a product or influence us. Moreover, "datafication" is not value-neutral either, and using data still requires theory building on which they depend.

Managers make smarter decisions by reducing their biases and potential errors while probing creativity and enhancing environments where innovation can thrive. Our belief is that Deep Learning Machines and Artificial Intelligence as in improving cognitive insights can help humans to make better decisions by reducing errors and by enhancing innovative tools and economic efficiency. Uncertainty, errors and human biases (i.e. human irrationality[7]) could potentially be significantly reduced by having artificial intelligent machines using the availability of big data to improve predictions or to find hidden patterns. Similarly, the tools – be it digital automation or cognitive engagement – that originate from artificial intelligence can be easily incorporated in innovative products and services or employed in robotics to take over repetitive boring or extremely dangerous work.

And often there is a trade-off between performance and interpretability since a simpler model may be easier understood, but won't be able to process complex data or relationships. Nonetheless, implementing algorithms in the management's decision-making process in any organization will require that AI can be "determined" and interpreted by managers and employees of the organization. Data integrity and the possibility of unintentional biases should be a concern when integrating AI within an organization. In a 2017 PWC CEO Pulse survey, 76 percent of respondents said potential for biases and lack of transparency were impeding AI adoption in their enterprise, whereas 73 percent said the same about the need to ensure governance and rules to control AI[8].

2.2. Are Accurate but Unexplained AI Algorithms Justifiable?

For instance, someone from a certain less wealthy neighbourhood applies for a mortgage loan and is declined a loan based on such a data bias by the system. Business leaders facing such interpretability and consistent performance will need to ensure that data integrity is not compromised or "unconsciously" biased.

A. Should AI's Accuracy Be Aligned by Human Ability to Explain and Justify?

Developers and analysts under supervision of wise decision-makers are responsible for building machine-learning models using algorithms that can be verified and correctly built and adapted where necessary: "garbage in-garbage out". Make sure that one chooses the right data inputs. Because of the interpretability of data and learning machines, the system must get checked for biased data or results and "reasonably" calibrated and designed targeting a specific group of consumers in a campaign.

Artificial Intelligence systems and machine learning perform to particular standards. Any company needs to be able to justify these standards and their outcomes. The "soul" of any AI or machine learning system is still the human mind who has designed or is managing the system. One needs to be explicit about the goals when implementing AI because algorithms are extremely literal and do not necessarily allow of ambiguity. Algorithms do exactly what they are told to do – almost in a black and white fashion – and often ignore every other consideration.

B. What About AI's Accuracy That Doesn't Understand the Contextual Reality?

Algorithms are essential tools for planning or executing certain (mathematical or decision-process) tasks. These mathematical pattern churning machines are good at literal screening and processing huge volume of data, but they do not explain why they offer certain particular recommendations. Algorithms are extremely powerful tools to identify patterns often too subtle to be detected by human observation, and use those patterns to generate accurate insights aiming to make better and more informed decisions.

For the foreseeable future, artificial intelligence may be smart to a certain point, but still need humans to determine the goals and creative interpretation[9]. Mere human intelligence or, for that matter, artificial intelligence does not equal wisdom. Further, promises by AI vendors won't pay off unless a company's data systems are properly prepared for AI. When data are locked in silos, inaccessible, poorly structured and most importantly, not organized in such a way that it can be used as "the new fuel" that makes AI work, AI will disappoint. That is why a consistent representation of data and data relationships within the business is crucial, preparing a model of all the elements that go into and connect the various information systems[10]. Without such integrated information design, AI-powered application will fall short in fulfilling expectations.

Some thoughts to take away:

- The more data the organization will have access to, and the cheaper it will be to get these data, the easier it will be for algorithms to find patterns that can accurately **predict the future**, or future **behavior**.
  - ○ This methodology is used in autonomous driving cars like Tesla: with decreased cost of data access, and with enough data to have captured most of the realistic situations a camera of a self-driving car – following exactly what the driver "sees" – the more likely that self-driving cars may become a reality.
  - ○ Tesla's access to huge data on the road gives them a competitive advantage to other car manufacturers.

- The **datafication of our daily lives** will have a huge impact in the way we organize ourselves in the future. In a way, AI could become like energy, ubiquitous but **not necessarily visible**.

- The **accuracy of this algorithms** crunching huge amount of data comes *at a cost of less* **explainability**. The more accurate the AI, the less explainable the "black box" becomes.

Chapter Ten

The Darker Side of Artificial Intelligence

"To know the world is to exercise power over it, and to exercise power is to control it – to examine its features and characteristics, to sort it into categories and norms, to render it legible and observable".

Jathan Sadowski, 2019, "When data is capital",
Big & Data Society

"AI's abilities were somewhat overhyped ... by certain companies with an interest in doing so ..."

Yoshua Bengio, 2020, AI pioneer

The challenge for many boards is to use artificial intelligence in an appropriate manner. Using technology in such a manner requires wisdom, not just smartness. No doubt that artificial intelligence and other new technologies have contributed to more innovative business models that translated in better welfare of quite a number of people. But that does not preclude boards from questioning the overall promises of tech culture. In some instance, people have hit a point at which they are so enthusiastic about using the latest fad in technology for about everything – hiring, driving, paying bills, choosing dates, predictive policing in unsafe areas, etc. – that they have stopped being critical about these new forms of technology. Our collective enthusiasm for applying computer technology to every aspect of our life has resulted in ignoring a much darker side. And not all technology has been well designed. We have reached a point where we use a hammer and developed an attitude that everything around us looks like a nail. We need to take a more reflective stance and stop rushing blindly into the digital future.

Techno-chauvinism may not be the answer to our challenges[1]. Blind optimism about technology and a lack of critical thinking about the limitations of these technologies and how these are used and implemented are all characteristics of this current techno-chauvism. "It seems that efficient code is prioritized above human interactions[2]," when you describe AI machines as "intelligent", whereas they are inherently "unintelligent computing machines". *Amazon's* Alexa and other voice-response interfaces do not really understand language: they simply express computerized sequences in response to sonic sequences, which we describe as verbal commands. Customers need to be able to trust AI products and the algorithms or systems behind these products. Previous chapter provided a brief assessment on the potential benefits and the "good" of artificial intelligence. Let's turn our focus now to the "bad" and the "ugly" of artificial intelligence.

1. Can the "Bad" and the "Ugly" of AI Be Accounted for?

AI is built on the foundation of code, data, binary and electric impulses. The discipline of AI includes not only knowledge representation, reasoning, formal (inductive and deductive) logic, machine and deep learning, natural language processing (NLP), search, planning, mechanics but also digital ethics. So far, we have focused on how AI can help organizations to create value that empower their stakeholders. However, let us not forget that computers are artificially "unintelligent" because it executes commands but has no sentience and no soul or consciousness. The creators of AI, however, are intelligent, but can be blind to the faults of computational decision-making, or want to use computers for everything. In extremis, AI can turn into something quite "bad" and "ugly". Hence why it is crucial that boards are aware of not only the benefits but also the possible faults, limitations and dangers of AI in business. The darker side of AI cannot be omitted if we want to optimize the use of AI.

Obviously, data-driven markets offer compelling advantages, and innovation and progress should not be stifled by irrational emotional fears or too stringent regulations. But the shortcomings and ethical challenges should not be ignored, especially the concentration of data in the hands of a few and the possible systemic failure. The current AI systems have nothing remotely like common sense[3], yet we increasingly rely on them. The real risk is not superintelligence[4], but AI that acts like idiots savants with power – such as autonomous weapons that could target people with no values to constrain them, or AI-driven newsfeeds that, lacking superintelligence, prioritize short-term sales without evaluating their impact on long-term values[5].

1.1. Innovation Versus Accountability and Control

How to hold the architects of this AI-digital technology to account? AI is reshaping our world, but hardly anybody call the owners of those AI algorithms to be responsible, as you would for other products and services. Some may argue that enforced accountability would stifle innovation, or potentially harm our bright digital future, and likely delay inventions which could change our life for the better. Not really true: technology and innovation won't be stopped. But "we" need to be in control. The question begs who are "we"? Politicians, corporate leadership and their boards, or do citizens at large have any say in this?

Internet has opened many opportunities: we have used it as a virtual digital space to imagine and to create without too many constraints, almost with the promise of a limitless potential. However, without limits and rules, the current digital space and the corporations using it seem to create distortion and possible dangers, legally, politically and especially ethically. AI systems do not always make ethical or even accurate choices, because often the AI decisions are based on probabilities, they may be "taken by surprise" by unanticipated rare events and data, and their complexity precludes management to determine whether or not the system is making a logic mistake. Boards therefore need to understand, manage and monitor the risks of AI. It is their duty to monitor the potential downside of this advanced AI technology.

Facebook's algorithm decides what information to show us on the basis of the choices we already have made. This filter algorithm used by Facebook may create a filter bubble or echo chambers, even for initially unbiased people. The filter model picks up small initial differences and exaggerates them until the other side of the argument is lost. And we do not mention even the spreading of untrue rumors that become fake news which has become a source of constant entertainment. As in a kind of post-truth world. Do these AI-driven recommendation engines carry significant risks or not? Let's try to analyze and find out.

1.2. Is AI Causing an Imminent Danger to Us?

In most cases, the aim to use data and algorithms can be a force of progress and good use. Algorithms are used to help us better understand the world. Algorithms underlying artificial intelligence are only as good as the big data input. Indeed, algorithms are programmed to collect and categorize a vast amount of data points in order to identify patterns in a user's online behavior that could allow recommendations and more precise predictions. The algorithmic identity in any application gets more complex with every social media interaction, the clicking or likewise ignoring of advertisements. Huge amounts of digitized data are now available. The more people share their personal information and preferences on social media – and people feel empowered to do so – smart entrepreneurs will definitely take advantage and initiate new algorithms that embrace the enormous amount of data in cyberspace, and commercialize them in one form or another, or in best scenario initiate new insightful patterns that could help common good.

Computers are not necessarily more objective than us humans. We need to make more thoughtful decisions about when, why and how to use technology that is appropriate and the right tool for a task. Indeed, understanding the current outer limits of what technology can and cannot do will help business and consumers alike to be realistic about the implementation of technologies, and more importantly, to make wiser choices. Understanding the limits and darker side of technology may help us to have a more "collective conversation" as a society about what kind of technology we want – and what it ought to do – to improve the "welfare" and well-being of us as consumers, as citizen and as producers. Is it not the fiduciary duty of a board and their management to assess the positive but also negative impact of artificial intelligence (AI) on the organization and on society? Often, embracing the hype around AI and the transformative digitization in organizations clouds our judgement to distinguish the upside and downside of AI technology.

Would it be too farsighted to put the argument forward that the intentional accumulation of "like it" on *Facebook* is nothing else as the product of an algorithm that rewards attention-seeking and shock value? What could undermine the benefits of AI? Some high-profile entrepreneurs like Elon Musk, the CEO of *Tesla* and *SpaceX*, or the late Cambridge physicist Stephen Hawking claim that general AI and smart machines may become "our biggest existential threat" as a species. We discuss a few of those risks that is mostly inherent to big data analytics and AI.

2. Why Is Machine Learning Risky to Us?

Machine learning promises to improve the quality of decisions, due to the purported absence of human biases. Despite the enormous unique capabilities of leaders, their decisions are prone to be giving extra weight to their personal experiences, and it is well documented that this anchoring bias can affect business. However, if machine learning is designed to emulate the mechanisms of the human brain, such as deep learning with its artificial neural networks, then they can also be quite biased. Relying on historical criteria, machine learning predicting behavioral outcomes may reinforce past biases, including stability bias. In other words, AI has the tendency to discount the possibility of significant change[6].

2.1. The Inaccuracy or Biasedness of Artificial Intelligence

The major difference between machine learning and other digital technology is the ability of AI to make independently complex decisions, ranging from financial products to trade and how vehicles react to obstacles, to whether or not a certain patient is recommended to undergo a surgical operation. Their learning abilities are not only impressive, but also contain some serious limitations and risks[7], which could result in either *inaccurate* (as in "noisy" and or *biased* decisions[8]) or even outright *unethical* choices. Both potentially damage the reputation of the organization.

A. The Use of Big Data Does Not Exclude Bias

Algorithmic predictions are built on historic data that are always a social construct. Data of past decisions made by humans are likely also *biased*[9]. The data, however, mirror structural dynamics in our society and therefore remain incomplete. Mathematics and models in AI are systems of symbols created by smart scientists, which allow computers to perform millions, if not billions, of mathematical calculations. However, these calculations do not churn out some (alleged) absolute objective truthful outcome.

Artificial intelligence needs data, and data are not neutral as they merely reflect the bias in society. However, when this same data are used by governments and local authorities, banks and hiring companies, and the health sector to make decisions and to perform tasks on our behalf, the structural power imbalances in the society may escalate. In reproducing and re-structuring these same data without little or no scrutiny, local authorities and other organizations may (unconsciously) aggravate certain dynamics of society. For instance, alongside education, housing is one of the biggest opportunities for people to create welfare. So what happens when algorithms make decisions about assigning credit or homes to individuals or families? Automated systems have the alluring prospect of high efficiency and cost-effectiveness. However, the use of these algorithms – embedded in the fabric of our "techno-chauvinistic societies"[10] – remains for the most part unaccountable and unchallenged.

We should not overestimate the human capability to be "objective" or its capacity to absorb and process information effectively. For instance, people with rather static or dogmatic tendencies may not be willing to rationally review their perceptions after new information has been revealed. Recent scientific research indicates that dogmatism – often engrained in some form of inaccurate or even fake news – is correlated with the slower absorption of new scientific proof and with impulsive reactions[11] or even emotional outbursts, a characteristic dogmatic people seem to share with extremists of all sorts. Reasonableness is not exactly a compelling argument for extremists or dogmatic ideological[12] people. Their brain does not process information as effectively as more reasonable humans, which does not make them less morally responsible[13]. This data and information on the social media are often not accurately or sincerely falsified against the prevailing scientific insights or knowledge available, as traditional journalists used to function. Data on social media can be quite gibberish and often unreliable.

B. "Smart Computers Will Find Your Love for You"! How?

Let's rethink this ad: "AI finds your love". The popular *Parship* – a rather serious agency seeking a partner for life – or the more popular *Tinder* application, for instance – using algorithms to romantically link people together – is an example of what can be described as "amplified biasedness" by the machine learning. Tinder is one of the fastest growing social networking apps on a global scale with users in 190 countries swiping 1.6 billion pictures and generating around 20 billion matches every day. This location-based dating application plays a game-changing role in the dating world. However, we should not ignore how the biases of Tinder algorithms are a reflection of our society and how we analyze and perceive humans. Despite the personal swiping choices we make in finding a romantic partner, this online dating application seems to be reinforcing racial prejudices. Depending on how an algorithm is programmed – and Tinder's "magic" black box is not revealing how it functions – the users' online behavior and the set of data it is given to process the intended matching process, certain cultural aspects will be highlighted, visualized and prioritized, while others are left out or rendered invisible. These algorithms are not value-free: they reflect the cultural and individual preferences and human biases as in a darker shadow; not exactly what is expected from a cold, presumably objectively calculating machine.

It should not surprise us that the specific workings of algorithms remain rather elusive, as developers and data scientists rarely provide the coding of the underlying programs in the name of technological neutrality and objectivity and in order to preclude unnecessary competition. But we can derive some basic features of the Tinder application: since each user expresses individual preferences, the system provides personalized recommendations that are obtained through collaborative filtering and algorithmic calculations. Tinder's "algorithm of desire" all boils down to ranking people according to their desirability – based on "skill levels". Nobody wants to be rejected. Tinder complied with this psychological insight by keeping the left swipes unknown to the users. Similarly, the right swipes are kept secret as well, and sometimes matches are not shown to slow down the very desirable people – the "winner should not take all" (desirable …) – to give people with lower raking a chance, and thus keep Tinder in the game. Not exactly neutral, is it. But psychologically, you could describe it as smart but not necessarily wise business thinking.

With respect to the online agency *Parship*, for example, you may pay a monthly fee to find the love of your life; the algorithms of these agencies are actually not that successful as they claim: in 1,500 evaluations of online dating sites that Germans use, including *Parship*, none received a good rating. Only 7.7 percent replied that their research has been successful[14]. On average, someone joining and paying up the fee at a dating site has a chance of max 5 percent per year to find someone suitable and "fall in love". Getting access and enabling communication may be the true feat of online dating – clarifying *Tinder*'s and *Parship*'s popularity. But the chances of finding true love online may remain slim. "Unlike chess, finding true love is a game riddled with uncertainty, and that is where algorithms run into problems[15]."

Humans are now constantly bombarded with personalized recommendations based on our online behavior and data sharing on social networks as *Facebook*, *Twitter*, *Amazon*, *Spotify* and *Netflix*. The AI system does not know why it is recommending a particular match, but it has strategically learned to develop a "thinking" (i.e. finding correlating patterns) that could resemble human intuition. The system identifies languages and words that share a common context which could potentially indicate similarities, potentially resulting in swipes that are clustered together reflecting perceived preferences through these embedded vectors of the participants' likes. Unfortunately, such algorithms also reflect the darker side of our culture: embedded biasedness. Apparently, studies reveal that Black women and Asian men are potentially marginalized and possibly discriminated in such online dating environments. If initially several Caucasian matches were "successful", for instance, the algorithm will continue on the same biased trajectory. Confirming a "statistical commonality" according to gender, class or race in supplying a meaning for those categories will be "learned, analyzed" and conceptualized by the algorithm. Not exactly the most neutral manner to advertise your "assets". Admittedly, the data points remain hidden in the black box and cannot be overridden by any external critical remark or research, but it reinforces our suspicion against presumed cold speedy machines and its algorithm that are advertised to be neutral and objective. The opposite is often true.

C. How Objective Are AI's Recommendations?

Specific biases in the used criteria and variables in these algorithms are either unexamined or remain unconscious and unaware by the data designers, enhancing our point that we should be worried to blindly trust these algorithms. And here we face a paradox: machine learning AI pretends to be neutral and provides better decision-making options, whereas in reality, the underlying criteria and variables of these algorithms – often based on detecting personal preferences through behavioral patterns to come up with recommendations – are nothing else as a mirror to our societal practices, potentially even reinforcing existing biases. Indeed, *societal biased garbage in, biased garbage out*. The game of speedy and more precise predictions is not so objective as being proclaimed by the owners of these apps. Even if we or those owners have the best intentions, those intentions too could be easily (socially or personally) biased.

Sometimes, AI-driven business can take advantage of such biases: an example of such de-biasing is applied in improving the performance in the field of asset-management decisions. In investment decisions, assumed universal principles of actual self-interest and a sure grasp of dynamic inputs such as time and probability often give way to irrational and unpredictable actions based on narrow or flawed data and personal experiences. Fund managers who deploy machine learning, guided by hypothesis testing (about possible biases that negatively affect investment decisions) – and continuous feedback that is looped back in the algorithm – were able to significantly improve their return on investment between 100 and 300 points[16]. The fund learned that sales often took place in an emotional environment defined by pride and optimism, resulting in lower than optimal performance. So, smart executives were able to de-bias their decisions by using algorithms and machine learning techniques which are "emotion-neutral" and without conscious or heart – just like one can expect from machines.

And every machine-learning algorithm operates within the world defined by the data that were used to calibrate it, resulting in limitations of data that is translated in bias outcomes. This reinforces the recommendation of professionals trying to understand the "black box" through de-biasing these algorithms. In other words, the very real limitations to AI and more particularly machine learning must be constantly addressed and monitored by responsible leadership.

2.2. The Amorality of Artificial Intelligence: The Potential of Unethical of Data

Data sets could easily be turned into unethical use as *Facebook* has shown during the US elections in 2016. *Cambridge Analytica* used a personality model – based on the big five personality traits test[17] – in its promotional material to send specific political tailored messages and ads catered to people and undecided voters with a specific profile to influence the US elections. What about Google's possible decision to drop "do not evil" in its mission statement mid-2018, allowing the possible road to be opened for a watered-down version of a Google search engine – aptly labelled Dragonfly which blocks or self-censures sensitive topics regarding human rights, for instance – to consider a re-entry into China's huge consumer market. Moreover, artificial intelligence is more like advertising intelligence where big corporations have got better at collecting consumer data, filter and package them and sell them back to these consumers in the form of recommendations.

A. *Bringing Values into Digits: Difficult or Impossible?*

Even if a data set is accurately reflecting historical facts, it does not mean that these data are fair, especially if it can be proven that history itself was not necessarily fair. We should question whether an algorithm is fair, whether AI is doing things that humans believe are ethical. Bringing ethics into AI, one needs a human-in-the-loop approach as in an "open algorithm", not a black box.

At best, algorithms may match the accuracy of humans in this exercise, but just much faster. So while these models are far from perfect, they can be useful speedy tools. Admittedly, studies by Professor Philip Tetlock from the Wharton School found out that the average "experts", who were able to continuously include new info/data in their probabilistic reasoning, created bell-shaped curves in their head and drastically improved their predictions[18]. But still it is hard for an individual to beat the collective wisdom or the "wisdom of the crowd". And here algorithms basically reflect the power of collective data that smart decisions could be derived from.

Does there exist a fairness equation that allows us to think more accurately about responsible and fair use of data? Some philosophers may argue that there is[19]. What is fair sounds like a real normative statement. These ethical argumentations take us to David Hume's **naturalistic fallacy** theorem which states that a normative notion cannot be fully derived from descriptive logic. This *is-ought* problem stipulates that there is a deep gap between *what is* as in a scientific objective reality, and *what ought to be*, which refers to an ethical question of how we want to live and what kind of society do we want. Hume's dichotomy between "is" and "ought" implies that aspiring ideals cannot really be bridged by algorithms. On the contrary, algorithms may reinforce "old ethical habits and norms"[20]. There still remains a gap between these two kinds of logic – despite the many attempts by eminent philosophers to overcome it[21].

Only conscious and mindful humans can put forward what kind of society we want to live in, what kind of life we want to strive for. Research by Ernest Fehr and others with the *Ultimatum tests*, for instance, indicates that the notion of fairness seems to be inherent to human thinking. What society we would like, what we consider as "fair", our aspirations are (human) norms set to make it a better world. It seems that evolution has enabled (only) humans to make the distinction of what is and what one hopes for or believes to be an (socio-ethical) ideal. Using the factual data of what is in the world does not make AI a good "prescriber", only a good "recommendation engine in perpetuity". No change should be expected from such (commercial) thinking, unless we explicitly bring in these values and norms that aspire for a better and different future. Science does not provide the answers to normative (ethical) questions.

However, whatever the logic behind algorithms, privacy and ethics should be explicit requirements from the start of any tech project. Individuals should not tolerate that their right to privacy – as in property ownership – would be violated. Privacy is not only a legal but also an ethical right for good reasons that needs to be protected and defended.

B. The Fairness Debate: Probability and Punishment

An example of unfair use of data here is the case of "predictive policing or profiling". Commercial software that is widely used to predict recidivism is no more accurate or fair than the predictions of people with little to no criminal justice experience[22].

Big data threatens to imprison us – perhaps literally – in probabilities. For instances, the use of big data to conduct "predictive policing" may seem to be sensible, but it also stigmatizes certain socio-racial groups further. This predictive policing uses big data analysis to select what streets, groups and individuals to subject to extra scrutiny, simply because an algorithm pointed them as more likely to commit a crime. For instance, US Homeland security's FAST (future, attribute screening technology) and other foreign Western government agencies try to identify potential terrorists by monitoring individual vital signs, body language and other psychological patterns. If these data and analyses are misused, it can lead not only to discrimination against certain groups but also to "guilt" by association. Punishing people before they do something bad negates the very idea of the presumption of innocence – the principle upon which our legal system as well as our sense of fairness is based. We should acknowledge that thinking bad things is not illegal; doing them is. Guilt is only possible when someone actually committed an (illegal) act or crime, not thought of it, or may have a higher probability to potentially commit a crime because of a specific social-economic background.

Predictive analytics predicated on mechanical presumed objectivity comes at a price. Indeed, in the courtroom, objectivity, trade secrets and judicial transparency may pull in opposite directions. Mechanical objectivity is not the same as ethical thinking. Nor is such objectivity necessarily reflecting the essence of scientific thinking or discovery. This predictive policing deprives citizens from a free will and erodes the fundamental notion of human dignity.

Business will need to determine what is fair to their (potential) customers and focus which attributes should be protected (for example, gender and race). Assume a credit card company that is implementing an algorithm using historical data to predict whether individuals applying for a certain credit offer are "good" or "bad" risks. Corporate leadership needs to determine which protected variables to consider in achieving a fair outcome – and who is accountable and responsible within the corporation.

Now, as any AI developer will know, how to distinguish true positives from false positives. True positives are instances in which the model correctly predicts an application to be a good risk, whereas false positives occur when bad-risk customers are interpreted as low risk. Negative false indicate good customers who are wrongly rejected as too risky: an obvious unfair outcome.

Although fairness remains a social construct, determining what is unfair and fair requires engagement and active discussion among teams to decide what constitutes fairness in particular scenarios. Marketing teams may want to issue as many cards as possible to increase the company's market share and boost the brand, while the risk team's goal is to minimize potential losses incurred when high-risk customers who should not be given a card do not pay their credit bills. Striking a fine balance between both and supporting the ethical standards of the organization require truthful and serious deliberation[23]. Not something AI machines are good at, are they.

We urgently need some guidelines to avoid those AI-related risks[24]. Boards monitor and coach top leadership to make the right decisions for a sustainable future of the organization. That duty of care, loyalty and prudence[25] also includes the necessity to continuously monitor how environments evolve and how technology adopts or not. Often it makes sense for a board to be pro-active and preempt any liability to focusing on the legal, technical and socio-moral impact of the technology. Maybe institutionalizing some procedures, structures and procedures could be a start to limit those AI risks – both at the organizational and nation-state level.

Some thoughts to take away:

- Despite the numerous benefits of AI, there exists a much **darker side of AI** that should be acknowledged:
  - Inaccuracy of AI because of biases in data
  - Amorality of AI applications
  - Unfairness of AI algorithms when decisions are based on probabilities only (completely ignoring the socio-ethical sphere)
  - Privacy and unethical use of data by AI

- The innovative power of AI hype neglects the **lack of control,** or **lack of accountability of AI black boxes.**

- Behavioral patterns that result in **AI recommendations** are nothing but a **mirror of our (societal) practices** – inclusive of its existing norms and inherent biases.

Chapter Eleven

Surveillance in Exchange for Convenience? Data Governance?

"Personal data shall be processed lawfully, fairly, and in a transparent manner in relation to the data subject".

Article 5 (1a), EU General Data Protection Regulation

"The greatest danger in times of turbulence is not the turbulence; it is to act with yesterday's logic".

Peter Drucker

Can humans still compete with fast computers, or are we losing the battle with powerful machines? Should we trust computers? How should one address the numerous risks and address the darker side related to Big Data and AI while still be able to benefit from the speed and potential accuracy of AI (be it cognitive insights, cognitive engagement or digital automation)?

Human society is a network just like the neural nets trained for deep learning, but currently, the "neurons" in human society are still a lot smarter. Some artists have described the current form of AI as "artificial stupidity". But we should not underestimate the enhancing "creativity" by AI either. Nonetheless, boards imposing some proper governance on data usage and having a clear idea on digital ethics may be a good start to reduce the darker side of AI.

1. The Power of Data in AI and Our Desire for Convenience

The numerous "free" services offered by tech companies such as Facebook and Google make us the product. Our data are the source of their power[1]. We users have accepted what we thought was a bargain without realizing that we were given up our private data and potentially our autonomy[2]. Our data are not sold: both Facebook and Google sell the power to influence us, they sell the power to show us ads, and the power to predict and ultimately to manipulate our behavior. This "power to forecast and influence derived from personal data is the quintessential kind of power in the digital age[3]."

We can easily fall into the trap of the fetish of quantification and data. However, the quality of underlying data can be poor or even biased. It can be misanalyzed or used in a misleading manner. Or worse, data can also fail to capture what it purports to quantify. Consequently, we may attribute a degree of truth to the data which it does not deserve. Many thinkers have argued that creative brilliance does not depend on data[4].

1.1. Surveillance and Nudging

The increasing reliance on data may also lead to the risks of a "tyranny of algorithms" where unelected data scientists and data experts are running the world. The incredible power of *Google, Amazon, Facebook, Apple, Microsoft, Baidu, Alibaba, Tencent* and others cannot be overstated. They currently control the data, and thus they control AI. Can we trust these organizations that they do the right thing, always? Not quite.

We have entered a form of *"mass surveillance"* today. Data collection points pick up information about the way we drive, the way we talk, the shops we visit and the lifestyle we lead. If a citizen behaves "appropriately" and according to the agreed norms, the Chinese Credit System rewards them with lower insurance premiums or easier access to housing. That is the social contract between the Chinese authorities and the Chinese citizen: for proper and loyal behavior, you will be rewarded. Clearly within such a strict "surveillance capitalist" system[5], one better complies. Another interpretation could be that persuasive and seductive authoritarianism keeps a lid on its citizen to secure law and order.

Digital technologies went from being perceived a beacon of democracy, able to offer a space and voice for dissent[6], to becoming a tool of oppression and discord by powerful political elite[7]. This form of surveillance is not just a practice in China and other authoritarian regimes, but Western organizations have also become the masters of data gatherers and predictors. Those tech companies provide the collected data to be fed into advanced manufacturing processes whose algorithms learn to become more efficient by the minute. These processes result in *prediction products* that attempt to anticipate what you are doing now, will do soon, and likely will do at a much later stage. The ideal for organizations is to anticipate the potential behavior of customers, clients or just citizens and to nudge them to the expected or desired direction.

Similarly, some companies hugely benefit from their predictive recommendation engines. Amazon is not just known for its powerful recommendation algorithm, but with their face recognition software sold to police agencies in the USA, the company could be seen as potentially facilitating authoritarian surveillance. There are rumors that Federal Agencies in the USA are planning to monitor "neuro-behavioral" predictors of violence by collecting data from smart devices – derived from Apple Watches, Fitbits, Amazon Echoes, Google Homes – with the purpose of identifying the signs of someone headed towards a violent, explosive act[8]. It looks like another tool of social control with the aim to predict the unpredictable.

Unfortunately, tech companies such as Amazon and Facebook, for instance, are in the business of completely immersing us in a digital present that distracts us from pursuing goals and objectives of our own individual choosing. Such policies implicitly undermine our ability to think long term. It all boils down to "instant gratification" instead of resisting our ancient "Marshmallow" brain that craves for dopamine to feel satisfied now[9]. We prohibit ourselves to explore new ways with our neo-cortical "Acorn" brain, attempting (or not) to postpone gratification. Facebook's intentional objectives reflect their desire to hijack out attention by focusing to answer the question "how do we consume as much of your time and conscious attention as possible". Our smartphones electronically offer us infotainment, advertising and fake news alike. Facebook sees us as Pavlov dogs, capturing our attention and selling our attention spans for profit. How to understand *wising up* as a potential anti-potent against such instant and often selfish fulfilment of gratification?

The internet has made tracking easier, cheaper and more useful. However, the internet and big data also threatens our privacy. The *Cambridge Analytica* debacle – which used data from Facebook to influence the US elections and possibly the Brexit vote – shows that through access of personal data, companies and individuals (having access to these data) can influence human behavior by personalized messages and advertising in a way never seen before. We believe that individuals should own and control access to their personal data, instead of the application providers. Instead of self-awareness and making conscious political choices, we are influenced by recommendation engines who are masters in tapping in our revealed preferences and emotions. Moreover, in non-democratic states, or even in nominally democratic ones, governments know things about their citizens that was considered fiction during Orwell's *1984* time. And obviously, the prospect of AI for malicious military purposes remains frightening[10].

Moreover, research demonstrates that rating just six obscure movies (out of the top 500) could identify a Netflix customer 84 percent of the time. If one also knew the date on which a person rated the movies, the accuracy rate apparently increased to an incredible 98 percent. Hence why in an era of big data, the three core strategies long used to ensure privacy – (1) individual notice and consent, (2) opting out and (3) anonymization – have lost much of their effectiveness. It is obvious that *privacy* is under attack from all sides. To what extent should the power of the internet and AI firms be clipped and constrained to secure the privacy of the individual?

1.2. More Accuracy of Data at the Expense of Loss of Privacy?

Algorithms underlying artificial intelligence are only as good as the big data input. Indeed, algorithms are programmed to collect and categorize a vast amount of data points in order to identify patterns in a user's online behavior that could allow recommendations and more precise predictions. The algorithmic identity in any application gets more complex with every social media interaction, the clicking or likewise ignoring of advertisements, and the financial status as derived from online payments. Huge amounts of digitized data are now available. And with the enormous potential, we also need to acknowledge some serious darker sides of using artificial intelligence in business and our personal life – be it the biases that are engrained in the data used, or unethical use of data, privacy concerns or the fear of Big Brother.

Albert Einstein agreed that theories are simplifications of reality, but we should be wary not to simplify too much. Hence why narrow AI suits well for solving particular problems[11]. But we have no choice but to embrace complexity, volatility and uncertainty to make proper valuable judgements (about the uncertain future). If we rely on an elegant but too simplistic theory, we will be misled by "the effectiveness of data that were unreasonable"[12]. Indeed, a data-driven approach – however useful and efficient – may ignore a number of factors that matter a great deal for decision-makers. In other words, data-driven decisions may not always fit the complex sets of rules that people apply when taking (smart) decisions. To add to the complexity and ambiguity, judging social challenges usually requires more than just calculations. This kind of "socio-moral" relations almost always involve social norms and ethical values that are hard to "code in binary data". It requires "sentience" and consciousness about (often invisible) relations.

However, boards may like to focus on the potential trade-off between accuracy and ethics. As I'll explain in Chapter 25 till the final 30th chapter, wise leadership paradoxically embraces a "synthesis" between this trade-off. As the Penn University professors Kearns and Roth argue, the tension between fairness, accuracy, transparency and ethics may always exist[13], but organizations need to find a balance in minimizing unfairness, inaccuracy, non-transparency and unethical biases in preparing AI algorithms for commercial use. A credit card company attempts to refine its algorithms to optimize its desired outcome, i.e. minimizing to accept those individuals who may default on their debt. The better the algorithm, the more profitable the organization. The amoral AI will always try to "encroach" on consumer privacy, and possibly may be quite biased and even unethical in the way it interprets the data of these individuals. Only by deliberate restraining the algorithms in a legal or clear moral manner can we reduce the possible harm.

Obviously, data-driven markets offer compelling advantages, and innovation and progress should not be stifled by irrational emotional fears or too stringent regulations. Data are not just a resource as "the new oil", but rather a form of capital that constitutes power. Data accumulation is a double-edged sword since "data extractivism[14]" – and thus online manipulation – can easily turn into a geopolitical weapon, as well as an incredible source for strategic advantage in organizations. But the shortcomings and ethical challenges should not be ignored either, especially the concentration of data and the possible systemic failure. And in case real artificial general intelligence would become a reality, a "matrix"-like intelligence, we really should be concerned about the malicious consequences of such super powerful machine-related intelligence. What interests us here is the importance of transparency of information and its algorithms to reduce potential information asymmetry. In other words, can data governance control artificial intelligence?

2. Data Governance Requiring More Accountability from "Data Users"

In order to reduce the risks of the darker side of AI, we suggest a more stringent data governance for those who use data provided by people who often have been unaware of the potential misuse of their privacy. We therefore suggest to enhance the accountability of organizations using these data to their commercial benefit. Secondly, we believe that recommendations in sensitive areas as justice or the medical field should not undermine the basic principle of human dignity and the principle that people should not be judged unless strong factual proof is available. And finally, we also believe that more transparency is needed to reduce the risks related to these AI "black boxes", by having gatekeeping third-party certification that could enhance the trust in AI and its use of big data.

We always should be wary of data fetishism and surveillance capitalism[15]. Especially when we give up privacy for convenience. Indeed, we may move from "Big Brother is watching you" – our current surveillance capitalist system – to the reality of a "Big Brother is guiding you". What does interest us here is the importance of transparency of information and its algorithms to reduce potential information asymmetry. In other words, can data governance control artificial intelligence and reduce this information asymmetry?

Transparency functions as one of the four corporate governance pillars in any domain. However, it sometimes can be double-edged, as research shows that humans place greater trust in transparent models, even when those models are wrong and should not be trusted at all. Apparently, there is great power – and often great benefit – in being able to offer persuasive explanations for one's behavior whether or not they are true. The danger and opportunity in demanding more transparency in AI algorithms to open up black boxes require some caution[16]. We do not want to create (AI) systems optimized for the appearance of (enabling on) explaining or to convince us only. This could be quite deceptive. It would be better to make sure that AI systems are aligned to our value systems. Admittedly, we want those AI systems to be truthful, i.e. being accurate and sincere in being transparent, and willing to share the details "under the hood".

We here focus on some *governance solutions* and *smart decision-making* that are related to (1) privacy concerns, biases in predictive recommendations, (2) the audit of black box algorithms and finally, (3) enhancing cybersecurity as more and more devices, systems and apps are inter-connected to the internet and intranet. Deepfakes are not on the list of the latest concern – for the sake of creative innovation argument. But is there an "escape" from being completely incapsulated by unreliable data, including deepfakes?

2.1. From Personal Privacy to Firm's Accountability

Traditionally, antitrust regulations were imposed for companies that became very powerful – oligopolies of monopolies distorting competition. Firms being able to raise prices without losing customers deserved antitrust attention. Given that *Facebook* and *Google* do not charge the customers – because they provide "free" services – that heuristic fails. Hence why antitrust regulation needs to be adapted to this new digital era and apply it to any company that can do damage to its customers without losing them. There is a very high chance that this firm might be a monopoly or oligopoly. When tech companies take our data without asking for it, their methods can become quite "authoritarian". Our data privacy should be taken more seriously[17].

A. Is Personal Consent for Data Use Sufficient?

Although consumers and individuals should provide their consent in the use of their personal data, we suggest to be less focused on consent as such, but make the data users – i.e. the organizations using or selling those data – accountable for what they do with the data by default. It concretely means that the burden of responsibility is shifted from the public (and the aggregation of individuals who may have consented on the use of their data) to the effective users of data who actually benefit most of these secondary data use.

Another method is "differential privacy" which implies that the data are deliberately blurred so that a query of large data set only reveal approximate and not real results. The EU's General Data Protection Regulation (GDPR) has imposed strict rules to protect privacy. These privacy principles have been copied by many countries across the world. In addition, EU regulation is convinced that digital firms cannot lock out competition, such as *Microsoft*, *IBM*, and lately *Google* and *Facebook* have attempted to do for which they all were fined. We do not even focus on the Chinese AI-related organizations which are less bridled by privacy regulations; since the Chinese communist party here play a role that is questioned in the West.

The rule in Western democracies imposes equal treatment of anyone, including rivals, who may use their platforms. The weekly *Economist* claims that that European regulations want consumers to control their privacy and how their data are monetized. The ability of European consumers to "switch creates competition that should boost choice and raise standards". The challenge is to make GDPR less clunky, and to avoid Europe from becoming a tech enclave, cutting off from the mainstream, and allowing the (geopolitical) rivalry between US and China to create tech giants who will continue to act in an oligopolistic fashion.

B. Can Nudging Help to "Opting-In" Instead of "Opting-Out"?

People should have to opt in to data collection, rather than opt out as tech companies organize their default settings today. Although GDPR is a step in the right direction, this piece of legislation has addressed the use of data, not its collection. Despite GDPR's inclusion of a principle of data minimization, according to which companies should collect only adequate, relevant and necessary data, many organizations take a very broad interpretation of what are "legitimate interests". More stringent legislation on data collection is required.

Boards should take their fiduciary duty of care and loyalty seriously. The Latin verb "*fidere*", to trust, refers to a relationship between a trustee and a trustor. To trust someone means that you expect the other not take advantage of your vulnerable position. The board's fiduciary duty to the shareholder and the customer also implies to take "care" of the data they gather, which means that the individuals must be protected and their data not to be misused by professionals who are supposed to be trustworthy but who may serve conflicting interests. The reason we have fiduciary duties translated in best governance practices is rooted in the idea of asymmetric power and knowledge of some professional agents, managers, who could harm the shareholder and or the customer. Hence why fiduciaries, including the supervising board, must act in the best interest of their customers and ultimately in the best interest of the organization.

2.2. Improving Algorithm Design

So far, most AI proponents have emphasized the positive practical consequences of artificial intelligence. However, the real danger lies in the fact that scientists do not really understand the "black box" behind the machine learning algorithm. The new machine learning programs may have recognized patterns via deep neural networks and subsequent practical useful conclusions. But we have no idea how the computer or algorithm came up with an inference or a conclusion. And the larger the data set, the more difficult it will become to understand and to analyze – even with the help of computers – these predictive conclusions. Does this mean that we will become completely dependent on the computer? It reminds me to the incredible and in hindsight misplaced faith in the practical wisdom of mathematical quants when calculating the "exact" value of these collateralized debt obligations – securitized risk tools – which partially caused the global financial crisis in 2008, bringing us to the brink of a real and complete global disastrous meltdown.

A. Deciphering AI-Black Boxes to Create Safety, Accountability and Credibility?

Allowing governments to take predictive action because certain big data analysis suspecting someone is not good enough since it undermines the human dignity and the foundations that one is innocent till proven guilty. Not the other way around.

Indeed, the more we may switch to holding people accountable for their possible actions based on data-driven interventions and predictions with the intention to reduce the risk in society, the more we categorize or stigmatize certain groups, and the more we devalue the ideal of individual responsibility which we believe remains a fundamental human right.

Moreover, by pushing people to take certain decisions based on recommendations basically denies people's responsibility for their actions since it destroys their fundamental freedom to choose their own behavior, though admittedly often (unconsciously) influenced by peers and social pressure.

Relying on the accuracy and "objectivity" of the conclusions prepared by black box algorithms does not provide any explanation on why or how this inference was reached. There is a strong argument to bring back the notion of *explainability*, the why beyond the mere what. Explainability should not be sacrificed as the mimetic lamb in the name of more accuracy. In other words, we suggest that trust in AI can only be achieved by increasing more disclosure about the algorithm and the underlying prediction system. This is even more important in sensitive industries such as health and finance where AI's autonomous conclusions can have serious ramifications for the individual affected.

Hence why the possible introduction of an "*algorithmist*"[18] who acts as a reviewer of big data analysis and predictions in an impartial and purely confidential manner could be sensible. Similar to the function of independent external auditors in relationship of verifying the annual or quarterly firm's accounting and financial results. In other words, a form of external certification may be needed to create trust by a third party endorsing the reliability, replicability and accuracy of the AI algorithm. For instance, in the case of AI driving cars, AI diagnosing patients and in AI "robo" investing, some form of certification should become mandatory. I admit that this attempt to clarify these black boxes may be futile. The owners of tech companies will certainly lobby against any form of legislation to "open up the boot" of their AI-black boxes since nobody may be able to explain thse complex layered neural networks – though I suspect they may use the argument of secrecy protection of their "patented" competitive advantage. Although ideation, creativity and innovation are often described as thinking outside the box, it does not justify secretive black boxes for nobody seems to be accountable.

Developing some form of professional certification, compliance monitoring and oversight programs for AI and neural networks will be crucial for further development in AI[19]. Similarly, developing auditing expertise in AI to execute these tasks will become as important as safeguarding some minimal level of accountability in the field of AI. Let's not forget that an expected failure can be either quite harmful or challenging, especially if society cannot mitigate these risks if it did not foresee them. Again emphasizing proper risk management and prudence with respect of AI implementation and the execution of AI apps won't be a luxury anymore, but rather a necessity.

B. *Improving Cybersecurity Standards*

As hacks, cyberattacks and data leaks proliferate, we need a more holistic and enterprise-wide approach to curb cyber breaches. About three quarter of international global board members of private organizations believe that their companies would respond effectively in a crisis; yet, fewer than half of these companies have taken steps to be truly "crisis-ready". Incidents from cyberattack vary from critical data lost, business interruptions and customers lost, property damage, theft, adverse media coverage, regulatory actions, profits impeached, loss of trade secrets or confidential information, extortion, breach of contract, product recall, to network security liability and other liabilities. We believe that risks posing a potential threat – and especially those related to the security of our data and networks – cannot be ignored anymore; all business executives should be prepared to take measures to prevent, prepare or cure in case of a cyberattack.

A recent research revealed that 64 percent of companies surveyed had experienced a ransomware attack in the last 12 months and a staggering 83 percent of those paid the demanded ransom, from whom only 8 percent fully recovered all data[20]. Organizations that were caught unprepared, without a reliable backup, end up with reputational and or financial losses. The General Data Protection Regulation from the EU includes cyber-incident reporting obligations – allowing cyberattacks to be investigated[21].

Indeed, cybersecurity has become a priority at boards since core processes, jewel assets and sensitive data need to be properly protected. Moreover, regulators increasingly are applying their own pressure to guarantee the privacy of data, and these privacy demands are also on the mind of clients. Strengthening the **hardware, software and network procedure aspects** may be important, but addressing the **managerial, organizational, people and strategic aspects** is even more crucial. About 70 percent of data breaches and cyber-intrusions are due to human lapses and error to safeguard the organizational digital network[22]. The unauthorised disclosure of personal data and system outage events are other key elements that contribute to cyber-risk. The flow of data and information from internal points to points external to the company can be quite substantial and part of a business model.

Overall, the cybersecurity is not adequate in a majority of organizations. Often, executives have no clear sense of the overall magnitude of the risk of cyberattacks, malware and data breaches. Neither do they have a concrete plan to improve protection of their key assets against the biggest threats. We need more cyber-risk reporting that helps executives to increase corporate resilience; more transparency on cyber-risks allows companies to integrate these risks in their reporting. Corporations need an integrated decision-support system that creates clear visibility of all relevant assets to be protected, and that embodies the principles of good cyber-risk governance.

Our data privacy is directly linked to cybersecurity standards within the organization. Data are too easy to steal. Business has much to gain from investing in good cybersecurity, and a lot to lose when things go wrong. Cybersecurity is a collective and an organizational action problem.

And yes, generally speaking, most AI scientists agree that the current technology should aim for some common good and avoid killer robots, political advertising, the use of data that reinforce discrimination, and the shadow of Big Brother.

C. Fake News and Deepfakes: Unavoidable Side Effects of Our "Data Capitalism"?

A last increasing concern is how to deal with fake news or fake information and deepfakes. The way one can make individuals and groups smarter, the way one can make a more "humanized AI", will work only if feedback is truthful. In other words, data must be grounded on truth. However, manipulative advertising, propaganda and "fake news" destroy the usefulness of social sampling and data in general. In fact, "what is real and what is fake" has always been difficult over human history. Putting that distinction in the hands of a company like *Facebook* (or *Google* or any other social media firm) would be very unwise. A third more independent party verifying facts, like Wikipedia does, may be more appropriate but a more energy-absorbing solution. However, companies such as Facebook benefit from exploiting the emotional desires or fuzzy statements that stir social media buzz and consequently potential advertising: the business model is almost created to embrace emotions that keep us glued on the screen, irrespective of whether they feed us with facts, fake news, dreams or illusion.

Most digital natives are woefully unprepared in telling facts from fakes, or real from deepfakes[23], and news from hidden ads[24]. If one cannot make the distinction between truth and falsehood, then one should not expect either an accurate or truthful description of the "real facts". We need data that can be trusted and we also need fair, data-driven assessment of public norms, policy and government based on trusted data about current conditions. Only under those circumstances, the individual and especially societies' overall fitness and intelligence can improve or can be "trusted".

Some thoughts to take away:

- A potential trade-off: **From privacy to convenience**.
  - Data capitalism encroaches on the privacy of our personal data in return for us to conveniently benefit from their AI apps.
  - We have moved from "Big Brother Is Watching You" (already a reality) to "Big Brother Will Guide You" where AI apps determine the choice we will make.

- How to make AI firms using "big data" more accountable? A better **Data Governance** is necessary:
  - To minimize privacy violations
  - To enhance cybersecurity
  - To audit AI-Black Boxes

- How to address **fake news** and **deepfakes**? Is a post-truth society unavoidable?

Chapter Twelve

Ethics Legitimizing Artificial Intelligence?

> *"We may not be cultivating the right kind of leaders. What a novel, dynamic and unstable world needs are "wise" leaders who can act as thinking agents of change. [...] They must see what is good, right, and just for society while being grounded in the details of the ever changing front lines of business".*

Nonaka & Takeuchi (2019: 5), The Wise Company

To what extent should and can we trust AI algorithms? Technically, algorithms do not really understand the data describing any phenomenon they "decipher and analyze". At the moment, good AI seems to be narrated by the PR departments of big companies, and bad AI by the whistleblowers.

Boards should take ethics, and especially digital ethics seriously, and aim to prevent "bad AI" in the first place. Talking about computer or digital ethics, we immediately think about computer hacking, software property issues and piracy versus privacy. Above all, we infer the incapability of AI to make (ethical) judgements; humans are needed to do that for them. Only wise decision-making can establish "responsible artificial intelligence".

1. Digital Ethics Demanding More Responsibility and Transparency

Are workers really "quantifiable" and reduced to a series of data points that can be sold? It were *Amazon* workers who rebelled for the lack of privacy when they found out their company was selling facial-recognition software to *Palantir*, a data-analytics company that closely and often secretly collaborates with the US Federal Law Enforcement agencies (such as FBI and US Immigration). Is this an example of the tyranny of convenience – where data and algorithms are sold by big tech companies at any "profitable" price?

Another example is *Facebook*'s unethical behavior that ranges from data privacy issues to propagations of fake news, to enabling Russian interference in the 2016 presidential elections – all rooted in its business model. Obviously, CEO Zuckerberg and his team at Facebook have a deep understanding of the technical platform. Yet, till recently, the team neglected to consider the broader ethical implications of actions that platforms make possible. Yes, the digital world and its platforms facilitate relationships through technology, but ethical issues seem to be ignored. Not surprisingly, digital technology presents us with ethical dilemmas like any other situation where social relations play a role.

1.1. Digital and Ethical Literacy => Digital Ethics Is Part of MQ

It's obvious now that the debate within AI has veered to make it more "responsible" and aligned with human objectives, and rightfully so. Hence why both *digital literacy* and *ethical literacy* are required to understand *digital ethics*[1]. Organizations involving digital technology cannot omit the epistemic concerns[2] (about the things and ways we know) coupled with the ethical concerns (about the things and ways we value). Digital ethics is embedded in a knowledge economy in which digital information technology plays its crucial role. *Ethical literacy* combines *ethical sensitivity* and *ethical reasoning*. This sensitivity is a blend of affective and rational processes that form a synthesis of moral imagination and the recognition of ethical issues at stake. Such ethical sensitivity helps to understand the larger context of norms and values and the relative merit of individual beliefs in them. Ethical reasoning refers to the traditional normative theories such as deontology, utilitarianism, ethics of care, virtue ethics or other possible paths[3]. This ethical reasoning gives leadership the ability to assess what is held to be valuable in a particular context. The ethical sensitivity allows leadership to assess and reason about those ethical issues, resulting in a moral judgement that prescribes a certain action (in our socio-ethical sphere).

Ethics in the field of artificial intelligence requires a minimal level of moral and digital literacy. Moral and digital literacy allows board members and corporate leaders to move beyond legal rules, policies and procedures, and to evaluate such structures and the situations in which ethical normative decisions defy or confirm certain corporate policies and beliefs. In the context of board decision-making, that is what this book is about: **how to make wise decisions in a smart world**? Or *how to make responsible judgements in a presumed reasonable world in which automating and intelligence machines gain ground?*

The moral sensitivity and reasoning skills – summarized as **MQ** – include the ability to determine the relevance of an issue to ethics, the ability to weight competing values and to reach a dialectic synthesis, and the ability to identify mistakes and possible biases in value assessments. It should not surprise anyone that algorithms reflect the values of their human designers. There is nothing "values-free" about it. "Algorithms may be evaluated as moral if authored in an ethically responsible fashion and evaluated according to an ethical framework, or immoral if designed in a less thoughtful way[4]."

More problematic are the "black-box" models of computational processing since their outcomes are "trusted" without understanding the how and the possible amoral, if not immoral, thought processes within or behind the data processing in machine learning. No accountability is foreseen which obviously is unacceptable, especially for important decisions that have a normative content. With these black-box procedures, there does not seem to be a central moral authority or agency making moral judgements. Or is there?

1.2. Can AI Be(come) a Moral Agent with Moral Intentions?

To what extent might one consider a machine becoming a full ethical agent, or having moral reasoning capabilities, similar to a human being? Since AI and smart computers or robots lack intentionality, consciousness and free will – as explained in the subsequent chapters – AI becoming or autonomously being ethical is very unlikely, if not entirely impossible. However, the designer and owners of the AI – the tech companies – are agents and thus morally responsible. Agency assumes a minimal autonomy, or having the capacity and the (intentional) freedom to act. AI does not have either.

An estimated 90 percent of car crashes are due to human factors such as speeding well above the speed limit, using handheld electronic devices, ignoring fatigue and driving while drunk. No artificial intelligence network would fail because it's tired or distracted – although running out of power could have a similar effect. The conspicuous differences in errors made by smart machines and humans, respectively – similar for object recognition – show how fundamentally distinctive human intelligence is from artificial intelligence.

Nonetheless, too few tech companies take full responsibility for their business models underpinned by algorithms fueled by big data. Too often, ethical theories are presented and governed as rules that make ethics a mere compliance exercise. Legality and ethics should be clearly distinguished. Failing to comply to a checklist may have legal consequences. Complying to minimal legal conditions does not necessarily exonerate them from potential unethical behavior. Indeed, regulatory compliance is definitely not enough.

The responsible use and adoption of AI systems transcends legitimate concerns around minimizing biases (in product design, promotion and customer service). It goes beyond manipulation of customer pricing and other business practices. Instead, AI can become a managerial and board tool to align certain organizational behavior with broader related goals that include societal related purpose, equity in the workforce or more inclusivity.

Mastercard, for instance, worked hard on their ethical AI process, centred on minimizing biases as well as building a more inclusive future at the organization[5]. Managers at Mastercard are very mindful of what's inherent in the data set: what's there and what's missing. It helps the company to better articulate values around which the organization wants to align. The value of ethics is not just to focus on narrow particulars and tweaking around the ethical edges of the specific AI technology or implementation, but rather to take a step back and have a real dialogue about values in the organization: what are these values, and how to align those values with what it is that the organization is working on from a technology standpoint. These conversations may cause some serious discomfort, but without them, we may forgo to be really responsible for what technology can and cannot do, and how AI can cause collateral damage. The aim should be to create "responsible artificial intelligence", not autonomous moral AI agency.

We can easily argue that the code of algorithms is not value-neutral – it contains many judgements about who we are, who we should become and how we should live. In case we would be asked to choose a software solution, will we be subtly influenced to buy from a particular online vendor and will we be affected by the vendor's (subconscious) prescriptive norms and values? What if these values are less than benevolent? During one of the conversations I had with Darden business ethicist Professor Edward Freeman at the Melbourne Business School – where we were both teaching – he highlighted this ethical conundrum by asking what will happen when a self-driving car under certain unfortunate circumstances – where an accident cannot be avoided – will need to make a (algorithmic) decision by making a choice about whether to sacrifice its occupants or risk (possibly fatally) harming passengers in other cars or pedestrians. Sounds like the trolley problem.

2. Of Trolleys and Ethical Thinking in an Era of AI

The trolley problem is a thought experiment where participants are asked to imagine a runaway trolley moving towards five people, incapacitated and lying on a track. What happens when a self-driving car, meeting an unavoidable collision, has to algorithmically choose whether to sacrifice its occupants or risk fatally harming other passengers or pedestrians? How should the algorithm deal with such situations? How to guide developers to write such "ethical" code? Facts are distinct from values, but from an evolutionary perspective, our genes attempt to survive. If we attempt to bring ethics into machine learning, it leads to a whole series of **trolley problems**.

2.1. How to Resolve the Trolley Problems?

Most of the assumptions in these moral thought experiments assume a world of high level of certainty, shying away from the fundamental uncertainty and ambiguities of real life. When this hypothetical certainty is replaced by a more realistic uncertainty, moral judgements become even more permissive and less stringent, and likely also more random. It should be noted that moral psychology has a long tradition of posing moral dilemmas that somehow ignore this fundamental aspect of uncertainty[6]. For that reason, the trolley thought experiment does probably not pose too much of a (real)problem, but in real traffic, the presumed certainty becomes an illusion. Ambiguity thrives in real uncertain situations, making it even harder to resolve this problem rationally. In such real-life cases, both human intelligence and artificial intelligence are forced to make swift decisions, often without exactly knowing what the consequences will be. Moreover, most engineers have discarded the illusory certainty of the trolley problem as a guide to ethics, because there is no prefect prediction possible of what will happen after an actual collision. Setting these critical remarks aside, let's analyze this famous trolley problem.

The trolley problem refers to a "runaway tram" as made visual in Figure 1 – first coined as a thought experiment by the Oxford philosopher Philippa Foot[7]. The trolley dilemma has inspired numerous books and articles about this thought experiment that reflects the following generic problem: "Peter is the driver of a trolley, whose brakes have just failed. On the track ahead of him are five people; the banks are so steep that they will not be able to get off the track in time. The track has a spur leading off to the right, and Peter can turn the trolley

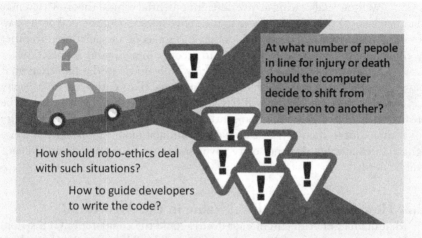

At what number of pepole in line for injury or death should the computer decide to shift from one person to another?

How should robo-ethics deal with such situations?

How to guide developers to write the code?

Figure 1: Ethical dilemmas in the trolley problem

Source: Verhezen, P. & S. Gande (2019), *Artificial Intelligence*, Amrop publications

onto it. Unfortunately, there is one person on the right-hand track. Peter can turn the trolley, killing the one; or he can refrain from turning the trolley, killing the five". What should Peter do? Many people have the intuition that she should turn, so that four more people will survive.

Consider now, an updated revised version of the trolley problem, related to a transplant case. "David is a great transplant surgeon. Five of his patients need new parts. One needs a heart, the others need, respectively, liver, stomach spleen, and spinal cord – but all are of the same, relatively rare, blood-type. By chance, David learns of a reasonably healthy person with that blood-type who is under observation for a kidney stone operation. David can take the healthy person's parts by killing him, and install them in his patients, saving them all five. Or he can refrain from taking the reasonably healthy person's parts, letting his five patients die". What should David do? Here, the common intuition is that David should not remove the organs from this reasonably healthy person. This is all about ethical choices: what things should we do, morally speaking? What things shouldn't we do and why?

Most people think we should turn the trolley in the trolley case with minimized consequences, whereas we all seem to agree that we shouldn't cut up the healthy person who has kidney stones or the patient in the transplant case. The question is "why"?

Will a comprehensive moral theory be able to guide us? Note that in real life, it is likely our "subconscious elephant" – the affect and emotions providing data for our information processing and rational thinking in our brain – that will make a (unconscious) decision in a split second without the chance of a deliberative ethical interpreter to intervene.

Without elaborating all the different potential ethical theories[8] that may (but maybe not) provide an answer to the above question, at the end of the day, we should ask what moral status do we give to someone or something. In other words, whose welfare we need to take into account in our moral deliberations.

Ultimately, ethical reasoning likely boils down to the fact that what bestows moral status is being able to be **conscious**. If an entity has no capacity for consciousness, and never will have, then it has no moral status. It can be treated as an object, or lifeless non-sentient person. If an entity has the capacity for consciousness, then it has at least some minimal moral status. AI can cause ethical dilemmas but does not carry any moral status to resolve them. Humans will be needed.

2.2. How to Program Ethical Value in the Algorithm?

At what number of people in line for death should the computer or GPS system decide to shift a moving trolley to one person, or should the computer decide to shift an autonomous driving car from one person to another? Or differently put, how to implement *robo-ethics* or address ethical challenges with respect to AI?

A. The Trolley Dilemma: How to Resolve This Real Wicked Problem?

"How to guide developers to write this code", Darden business ethicist Edward Freeman is asking. Keeping in mind that facts are distinct from values, we can conjecture that from an evolutionary perspective, our genes and memes attempt to survive. It remains an extremely difficult ethical challenge for most humans to make a fair and just decision. Obviously, we could also turn the whole trolley problem by questioning who has given pedestrians access to the rails. These kind of judgements about moral and ethical choices are just as important as they always have been.

How can we make sure that autonomous driving cars "behave ethically" in a crisis? Most computer scientists believe in a technical engineering solution by finding a good-enough rule that tells the vehicle when something is ethically "correct" or not – also in alignment with the *Asimov Laws of Robotics*[9]. This won't be enough to make smart robots wise decision-makers. A technical coding solutions won't be very helpful. Humans might.

When discussing ethics in artificial intelligence, we often end up with the inescapable and extremely difficult ethical dilemma of the trolley problem[10]. This dilemma has profound consequences for the plausibility of autonomous driving cars, fed by AI algorithms, sensors and big data. How to make amoral algorithms ethical – as humans would? Working out how to build ethical algorithms or robots is one of the thorniest challenges in artificial intelligence. A conundrum that may be impossible to resolve.

Assume the following: what if an autonomous car swerves to avoid a child, bit risks hitting someone else nearby? Unfortunately, even ethical theory may not fully provide a satisfying answer. The principles that emerge in a crisis situation are difficult to be written into the computer code. Creating programs with explicitly formulated rules, rather than asking a robot to derive its own, is wishful thinking. A lot of the principles and "knowledge" behind wise decisions are quite tacit, not all following a rigorous "preprogrammed" logic (in coding terms). "Logic is how we reason and come up with our ethical choices" is an often heard statement: we disagree. Wisdom is usually the result of a combination of many factors, including affect and emotions[11], which are (sub)consciously processed in crisis to emerge.

Trying to code the "doctrine of double effect" in a computer will be extremely hard if not possible. This doctrine tells us that deliberately inflicting harm is wrong, even if it leads to good. Human emotions usually block people to deliberately sacrifice and harm innocents' life even if that would save more lives. Despite claims that scientists have successfully written code to make decisions that are based on the doctrine of double effect[12], I remain very sceptical. Maybe some coding and learning from many cases is possible, and this doctrine of double effect may satisfice some utilitarian ethicists. But this consequentialist ethical perspective is not necessarily acceptable by deontologists or virtue ethicists. There is no clear answer in this dilemma, despite the efforts of scientists. When facing with ethical dilemmas – such as the trolley problem – robots may get into a helpless dither and let humans perish[13]. Ambiguity is not the strength of algorithmic robots. This is food for thought for ethical development and mindfulness of human leadership when attempting to commercialize robots and other (semi-)autonomous devices.

Admittedly, AI may be much more accurate in driving autonomous cars than human drivers; it does not make them infallible. In most cases, autonomous cars are safer and cause less accidents than human devices. But the risk in the tail – unforeseen circumstances and values interpretation – cannot and should not be ignored or omitted. Judgements about moral or ethical choices are as important and difficult as they ever were. How can an AI algorithm graciously fail? There is no answer to this question yet? Let us remember that algorithms are basing themselves on past actions to make predictions. But just because data may accurately reflect historical facts does not make them ethical or fair, especially if history itself was not. Bringing ethics into AI will need a human-in-the-loop approach. An open algorithm, not a black box. And even then, some challenges remain extremely difficult to solve, even for wise sentient leaders, who try to steer mechanical robots away from causing harm.

B. Reinterpreting and Re-Engineering the Unresolvable Trolley Problem

Instead of emphasizing (the technology of) self-driving cars with the conundrum around ethical trolley problems, maybe it might be worth exploring the potential of having access (not ownership) to public and private mobility that reduces congestion and pollution, trying to create a socio-ecological context that improves the quality of life, allowing people to flourish. The focus switches from "having" to "being". Different infrastructure and a totally different perspective on mobility solutions may make autonomous cars more viable instead of trying to replace humans with software under current ambiguous circumstances of increased traffic congestion. The absorption of roads is only so much, be it for human-driven or robot-driven cars.

The software of a large commercial airplane is less complex than that of a self-driving car[14]. The software of a self-driving autonomous car will need to deal with much more uncertainty, like other crossing cars, cyclists and pedestrians or animals. Their proximity and the algorithmic decisions dealing with it will determine life or death, to put it dramatically. Berlin-based risk researcher Gigerenzer eloquently convinces us that "there will be no self-driving cars (Level 5 Automation). Rather a fundamental change will happen: our cities and roads will be redesigned to create the stable and predictable environment that algorithms need (Level 4 Automation), such as wired highways from which human drivers are banned, and cities where human driving is illegal[15]." One could call it the "adapt-to-AI principle", which basically means that to improve the real performance of AI, one needs to make the physical environment more stable and people's behavior more predictable. Indeed, to benefit from the AI efficiency, humans will learn to adopt – both changing their behavior and operating environment.

The bottleneck for autonomous driving cars may be government regulation[16]. Where robotaxis and robo-shuttles will be available in particular areas of cities, one needs regulatory constraints to make sure that insurance can be applied. Early robo-taxis will be more expensive, comparable to ride-hailing costs, but costs will decline quickly. Indeed, the cost of autonomous vehicles is very diverse and depends on the use case, vehicle type, region and operating area.

C. How to Make AI More Trustworthy?

Even if AI is a better predictor than humans, we are still often reluctant to hand AI the full reins. Understandably so. Where AI outperforms people, companies must carefully consider its operating conditions – including when to empower humans to exercise their discretion and override them. Indeed, AI is not that "smart" as many think. Montreal professor Yoshua Bengio, a pioneer in the field of deep learning, paradoxically warns us against using AI to make important, life-changing decisions, such as how long a convicted felon should go to prison. "People have to understand that current AI – and the AI that we can foresee in the reasonable future – does not and will not have a moral sense or moral understanding of what is right and wrong. [...] It's crazy to put these decisions into the hands of machines[17]."

At the end of the day, AI should address a few concerns that are the pillars of responsible AI to create trust among customers and to be considered aligned, appropriate and reasonably safe to implement in devices we use every day. We like to suggest to delicately answer the following questions prior to rolling out any envisaged AI application:

1. **Is the AI unbiased and fair?** AI learns from data, so that data must be representative of the real world. To ensure that AI models are fair, organizations must be able to identify data or algorithmic biases to understand what influences a model's decision.

2. **Is the AI interpretable?** AI offers little insight into how it reaches its outcomes, because many algorithms are beyond human comprehension. Organizations must create AI systems that are explainable, transparent and provable so human users will be able to understand and trust decisions.

3. **Is the AI robust and secure?** The best AI system cannot operate independently, and as with other technologies, cyber-attacks can penetrate, slow and fool it. Ongoing cybersecurity is needed to both stop attacks and monitor performance.

4. **Is the AI appropriately governed?** Just as businesses auditing and operating practices, they must also be able to audit their AI systems. AI is currently developed and maintained in silos, creating confusion and uncertainty around inspections and assessments. Enterprise-wide accountability is required.

5. **Is the AI legal and moral?** Organizations must use AI in a way that aligns with their mission and social responsibilities, be able to evaluate the technology's impact on employees and customers, and operate within the boundaries of regulation, both enacted and in discussion.

AI cannot "understand" context, nor can it reflect. Humans, therefore, must regulate, put boundaries and monitor technology. The robustness of AI auditing and compliance remains poor. Developing some form of professional certification, compliance monitoring and oversight programs for AI – however limited they may be – will be a crucial board responsibility but even more so a societal project. Our concern here reflects the possibility that society cannot mitigate what it does not foresee. Hence the importance of boards not only to foresee, but also to reflect upon the fundamental difference between artificial and human intelligence, not to speak of the importance of moral consciousness in the matter of dealing with AI-projects.

Some thoughts to take away:

- Only wise decision-makers have moral agency; **artificial intelligence is not conscious** and thus **unable to have moral intentions**.

- Only by reinterpreting and reengineering the **wicked Trolley Problem** – an ethical unresolved dilemma – can one find a resolution that is sensible and make common sense.
  - Keep in mind that these (trolley) ethical dilemmas are often thought experiments under unrealistic assumptions of certainty.
  - In real life, the situation is even more ambiguous and therefore almost impossible to predict, making AI dangerous or useless under those unstable, contingent and complex conditions.

- Human decision-makers need to acquire digital and ethical literacy to make "**responsible artificial intelligence**" a possibility, and not just a desired or expected dream. Not making AI more responsible will potentially cause enormous harm.

PART III:
Learning: Artificial Intelligence Versus Human Intelligence

Part III rebuffs the claim that artificial intelligence (AI) might surpass the ability of human intelligence and possibly replace human employees and even managers. Obviously, AI and other innovative technology will (1) *augment* the ability of leaders to make better decisions and gauge them to make more precise forecasts than their competitors, and/or (2) enable to *automate* repetitive and familiar activities and decisions. But, I am rather sceptic that we will see any form of artificial general intelligence (or superintelligence) any time soon. Yes, AI – and machine learning in particular – has done a great job in improving our abilities to find hidden and/ or invisible patterns to predict diseases or a new market trend, but that does not mean that smart computers will replace human decision-makers any time soon.

Deciphering how our brain functions will probably help to become aware and to rectify some of these misperceptions, and also help understand how executives make decisions despite being distorted by numerous biases. The choice between the emphasis of unconscious behavior (the "automatic" short road) versus the openness to conscious deliberate social collaborative behavior (the "deliberative" long road) probably results in either competent and smart decisions or potentially more profound wise decisions. As mentioned before, consciousness can be interpreted as our subjective sense of experience or knowing – like being aware that I am writing this book now. Consciousness includes both the knowing and the known[1]. When we try to *expand our consciousness*, we are then *strengthening the experience of knowing, becoming more open to our capacity to be fully aware of the now*.

With the progress of computer science and information technology networks, AI is increasingly standing out as a transformational technology. As a matter of fact, AI systems are based on simulating connected "neural units" loosely modelling the way that neurons interact in the brain. These neural networks are able to resolve problems, to find patterns that allow organizations to predict faster and cheaper, and make the future a little less uncertain. We should heed the *"stable-world principle"*[2]: complex algorithms work best in well-defined and stable situations where large amounts of data are available. Human intelligence has evolved to deal with uncertainty, with or without data, to fit best in the environment, in order to survive and thrive.

Of course, it's important to highlight the socio-economic advantages of AI techniques, and contemplate, assess and act upon the disadvantages. Nonetheless, neuro-marketing and other practices also teach us that the scientific insights can be "(mis)used" to manipulate unconscious consumers' behavior. Again, organizations require the board and top executives to make the right decisions to optimize the organizational long-term profitability within the constraints of accepted ethical norms and socio-ecological sensitivities. Such broader perspective is associated with wise decision-makers.

Smart computers cannot think or feel in terms of empathy-based relations. They only "see" patterns, and correlations. As long as computers cannot consciously think or make causal connections, a general form of intelligence will remain beyond their scope and ability. Machine learning, in particular, is great in resolving specific narrow problems, and they do it much faster and better than any human can. However, humans have at their disposal *imagination, creativity* and *flexibility* in addressing any sort of challenge.

Humans usually don't say irrelevant things since they pay attention to how their interlocutors are affected and to the specific context in which the conversation takes place: this requires consciousness (and intelligence). As long as this form of consciousness – part of a theory of mind – is absent in AI, "smart robots" will remain highly asocial and amoral, as in a kind of non-adapted heavily autistic entity, good at churning data into information within a very limited scope and scale.

Chapters 13, 14 and 15 explain how machine learning computers have succeeded in partially mimicking the human brain. We'll also indicate the inherent limitations of artificial intelligence in copying the human brain. Artificial intelligence has made incredible progress over the past two decades. But it still faces profound limitations in "competing" with or fully mimicking the human intelligence. Neuroscience has taught us that human learning is far superior to that of artificial intelligence. In the near future, it is unlikely if not impossible that computers will fully replace creative CEOs and C-suite executives. In Chapters 16 and 17, we argue that human leaders think more holistically than any artificial form of intelligence. Neuroscience and social humanities studies reveal that on top of human cognitive and creative abilities, human have also learnt to cooperate in groups and teams because of relational understanding through a socio-moral learning process.

Smart computers do not have the ability to understand or "relate" to other people or situations. Indeed, machine learning devices are meant to resolve a (narrow cognitive) challenge in an incredibly fast and accurate manner. These alleged smart computers remain "idiot savants", speedy and reliable, but not really able to understand, let alone interpret different contexts or ambiguous situations. Therefore, boards embracing new technology such as AI should be aware of the enormous potential abilities as well as their "ontological" and "epistemological" limitations. Chapter 18 explains the importance of mindful leadership to see the different variables and interdependencies in their appropriate perspective. Only then, wise decision-making is possible.

Chapter Thirteen

Inside the CEO's Brain

"We humans are neural nets. What we can do, machines can do".

Geoffrey Hinton, Computer scientist and AI expert

"Live is good. If there are gods and they are just, then they will not care how devout you have been, but will welcome you based on the virtues you have lived by. If there gods, but unjust, then you should not want to worship them. If there are no gods, then you will be gone, but you will have lived a noble life that will live on in the memories of your loved one".

Marcus Aurelius, Roman Stoicist emperor

Our brain seems to function as an algorithm where unconscious and subconscious processes gather enormous amount of data and perceptions, which subsequently are ordered and structured by our conscious reflective mode into a meaningful and linguistically communicated sentence or knowledge. A deeper understanding of the neural processes reveals how unconscious intuitive and subsequently conscious rational reflective mode of cognition "collaborate" to enable decision-making. In our learning process and conscious deliberation, it is intriguing to see how emotions and rationality jointly affect and drive the way smart executives make decisions.

This small detour into neuroscience attempts to make the point that conscious and mindful decisions by wise leadership are quite distinctive from "smart" but also "soulless" artificial intelligence – despite some similarities of computer neural networks attempting in mimicking the human brain structure. Indeed, *l'essentiel est invisible pour les yeux*, "le petit prince" famously said. The sensors on AI may capture some reality but won't see the "invisible (meaning)" that we humans can "see" or sense. Nonetheless, I believe that we need to continue to attempt to explore and understand that what remains invisible ...

1. Artificial Intelligence Mimicking Human Intelligence ...

It is true that scientists in the field of Artificial Intelligence – especially in the AI-subdomain of machine learning[3] – are mimicking the ways of our layered neural network constructs ideas, the way we see, hear and think.

1.1. How Smart Machines Mimic Our Human Brain

These mimicking networks *in silico* promote the alleged incredible abilities of, for instance, self-driving cars or translators and personal assistants Siri and Alexa. To a certain extent, algorithms and their basic architecture try to copy the brain's functioning of human intelligence[4].

Most recent breakthroughs in machine learning that get the front pages of newspapers and journals can be ascribed as successful leaps in the way enormous amount of *data*, *algorithms* and *huge processing power of computers* converge. Despite these laudable achievements, humans remain superior decision-makers. Why?

Neuroscientific insights on decision-making allow us to argue that smart people are far superior learners in comparison with the smartest computer (AI fuelled by big data). Despite the intellectual superiority of the *Homo Sapiens* over the *Machina Sapiens*, every business leader and executive is aware of the enormous potential but also challenges of digitization and artificial intelligence in an Industry 4.0 context. The question is not just whether or not artificial intelligence will ever match human intelligence, but rather **why** human intelligence is so distinctive from AI's objective to be efficient. Let's review some notions first. **Intelligence** is defined as *the ability to deploy novel means to attain a goal* – which are extraneous to the intelligence. It is a sophisticated and flexible goal-oriented behavior to achieve those goals or objectives. Figuring out something, knowing some "facts" much faster is still very different from deeply understanding these facts.

Some recent neuroscientific insights may highlight the importance of cognitive and non-cognitive capabilities[5] – constituting intelligence. Let us try to get inside the brain of a CEO. The extraordinary resilience and plasticity of the human brain[6] – to change itself and to adapt – allows us to overcome massive difficulties and make decisions that provide real solutions. Could AI scientists draw inspiration from this extraordinary power of our brain to build more efficient machines and "copy" our human intelligence? Yes, they do. Can boards and their decision-makers benefit from some basic understanding of the difference between human and artificial intelligence? Yes, indeed.

Let's briefly summarize the notion of hierarchical pattern recognition through a set of layered neural nets, how learning unfolds, and why we are biased and prone to errors.

1.2. The Future Will Be (Fully) Digital

Harari's *Homo Deus* – seeming to indicate a rather mechanistic or "material"[7] perspective of the human mind[8] – assumes that organic algorithms such as the *homo sapiens* will melt together with digital platforms. Could the *homo deus* replace us?

A. The Future Human Will Be a Cyborg or Transhuman?

In Davos (2018), Harari gave a lecture on *"Will the future be human?"* to which he negatively answered the question. He and other AI enthusiasts like Ray Kurzweil at

MIT believe that a new "transhuman" will emerge, rooted in data-, bio- and brain engineering. In that sense, one cold convincingly argue that *the future will be digital.*

Organisms could be interpreted as bio-chemical algorithms whose code we are about to crack, according to Harari. A new *homo deus* may arise who "possesses" and uses data that may well rule the market and likely the world. This *homo deus* – a "cyborg" – will be more effective and efficient than the *homo sapiens* – who may become the new serf of the former.

Will this new envisaged *Homo Deus* – a combination of human, strengthened by artificial intelligence devices (fueled by the availability of big data) and implants – replace the current human executive?

Today, scientists have already managed to create an artificial interface between the brain and the spinal cord which enables paralyzed animals to move their affected limbs by replacing spinal neurotransmission with radio signals[9]. First attempts to apply robotics to paralyzed humans are now taking place. One uses radio waves to transmit the very same information via an artificial medium, to produce the intended movement. In other words, the function that the radio waves performed artificially was an information-processing function that is normally performed naturally by cortico-spiral pyramidal neurons. Despite some of these extraordinary successes, well-regarded scientists claim that the aspiration of AI or "human-cyborgs" taking over human intelligence may be a little premature.

B. Intelligence Is Information Processing Leading to a Desirable Outcome

Nature and nurture seem to have found an incredible form of "collaboration" in its evolutionary sense. Deterministic devices such as smart computers work well in clearly defined and relatively stable contexts. The idea behind the "stable-world principle" is that the better defined and more stable (less uncertain) the situation is, the higher the chance that "uncertainty" becomes quantifiable and thus a "risk" that can be measured and controlled. In such stable well-defined situations, machine learning will likely outperform humans.

Admittedly, natural selection – plausibly a remarkably efficient "algorithm" – can certainly succeed in adapting organisms to its ecological niche, but at an appallingly slow rate. However, organisms do not necessarily function as algorithms in spite of the partial similarities in terms of *information processing.* Artificial intelligence, in contrast to human intelligence, is unable to recognize what constitutes the essence of an object. However, animals and humans have the "innate" ability to learn that allows them to adapt to unpredictable conditions as quickly as possible. Similarly, corporate leaders and their organizations – a form of artificial organism in which group collaboration is crucial – need to strategically but also tactically adapt to an ever-changing different business context. How is that different from AI's ability to effectively and efficiently get things calculated and done?

2. ... but (AI) Still Be Fundamentally Different (from Human Intelligence)

Wise leaders are aware of the potential benefits and dangers of AI – especially if the applied algorithmic robots are not in line anymore with human objectives. Computers and AI need to be aligned to human values, at any time, at any place, as AI expert Russell and AI journalist Christian powerfully argue[10]. That is exactly what wise leadership is expected to do: thinking, understanding and envisioning a desired world or strategy in terms of beliefs and values, and not just in terms of short-term profitability opportunities.

2.1. The Intelligence of Deep Neural Networks *In Silico*

Computers cannot envision anything; they can accurately and swiftly predict the next move or pattern in the immediate future.

A. Machine "Intelligence"

The intelligence of a deep neural network trying to recognize a face (or a voice) consists of finding statistical associations between pixels and assigning probabilities to pixels. The stronger the association, the more certain the network *in silico* is. However, the AI network does not "know" that a picture represents something in the real world, because it has no fundamental or even superficial understanding or concept of things. Indeed, AI can make inferential errors that are totally non-intuitive for humans[11].

AI machines basically mimic human intelligence. Instead of talking about intelligence, machine learning could be seen as human-task simulations[12]. However, if intelligence is defined as an action-oriented cognitive ability to achieve a certain goal, computers can be endowed a minimal form of intelligence.

It should not surprise us that AI simulation – as well as virtual worlds – can be (perceived as quite) real and appealing[13]. Crucially, AI does not evolve, but its computational capability[14] is devolved from computer engineering smartness. Facial recognition technology, virtual assistants, machine translation systems and stock trading bots are all built upon perceptron-like algorithms[15] – as visualized in Figure 1. The breakthroughs in machine learning can be ascribed to enormous leaps in the amount of data available and the processing power (in the cloud) through the technique of hierarchical pattern recognition[16] that turns data into a clear (expected) output or pattern[17]. Although these smart machines may "know" an object (as in an "output"), it is not the same as a deep understanding or full comprehension of this object. Admittedly, achieving a particular goal or "output" can be interpreted as a form of intelligence.

B. Human Intelligence

If a system is good at only one sort of goal – say, winning a game of chess – then, we talk about narrow intelligence. If a system attempts to achieving a wide range of distinctively different goals, we talk about general intelligence. What matters

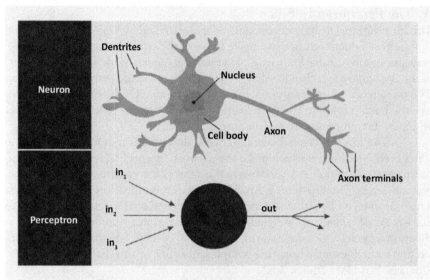

Figure 1: An artificial perceptron mimicking the functioning of human neurons

are the objective processes in the system and the behavior they produce to achieve one or more goals.

Leaders are able to imagine, "see" and create a (new) future – as we will explain in subsequent and especially in the final chapters. These leaders can and should deliberate for a better future, which obviously is not completely dependent on patterns found in historical data, but rather created in the novel combination of new insights, beliefs or warranted arguments.

Algorithms capable of making predictions do not eliminate the need for human understanding and interpretation when drawing connections between cause and effect. Pattern recognition is not a replacement for controlled scientific experiments. But what they can do is extremely useful and powerful. They can identify patterns too subtle to be detected by human observation, and using those findings to generate accurate insights and inform better decision-making[18]. The challenge for us is to understand the risks and limitations associated with AI, and through effective and ethical management, unlock their remarkable potential for business applications.

2.2. Inside the Brain *In Vivo et In Silico*

The "perceptron"[19] visualized in Figure 1 – simulating the human neurons in our brain – is able to learn, which inspired AI scientist and NYU Professor Yann Le Cun, now CTO at Facebook, to develop an algorithm to be able to recognize pictures[20]. This algorithm was a crucial breakthrough that allowed AI to apply this *neural network* – or deep learning – to concrete applications such as face recognition and pattern recognition in general. Algorithms in machine learning use building blocks for the convolutional[21] neural networks that characterizes deep learning processes in "smart computers"[22].

A. *The Perceptron* In Silico

The convolutional neural networks are modelling and mimicking our visual system that help us understand how we make sense of the world by turning in-coming perceptions into useable knowledge. Hierarchical hidden Markov models are part of the data-analytic technique that are applied to recognize patterns in big data. The more recent deep-learning networks are structured in hierarchies of layers, like the human brain[23]. The deep neural networks consists of three major parts: an input, its transformation and an output.

The input of layered neural network algorithm is transformed through a series of (hidden) layers which make the network "deeper"[24]. Hence the name of "deep neural networks". A layer down in the network can contribute to refining the previous layers. This fine-tuning through these layers is called deep neural learning. This learning can be either supervised, unsupervised or through reinforcement. Further AI developments are guided more by experimentation than based on a theory or a model. Once the network is trained to execute a desired task or output, we don't know exactly how this complex network of internal nodes actually function. It is like a "Black Box".

B. *The Human Brain's Power*

The conventional deep learning algorithms currently mimic only a small part of our brain's functioning, i.e. the first stages of sensory rather fast processing (about 200th of a second) which operates in a mainly unconscious manner in the brain. The subsequent conscious slower and reflective part of the human learning process allows us to deploy the abilities of reasoning, inference and flexibility – features that today's machines cannot copy (yet). It is not an exaggeration that even the most advanced computer architectures fall short of any human infant's ability to build abstract models of the world. Let alone the aspirational power of corporate (or political) leaders who can guide organizations and countries towards a "better future". Machines may be able to make us more efficient and effective, or "see" unnoticed patterns in existing (historical) data that improve our predictive power. Applications abound in medicine development, pharma industry, finance trading, planning in general, autonomous cars, search engines, etc. But these smart computers don't change the context itself, or create a potentially new and better future, for instance.

Algorithms or deep learning machines use statistical techniques that provide an approximate meaning, but they never capture the real thing, *das Ding an Sich*[25]. If they can't capture individual words with precision, they certainly aren't going to "understand" complex thoughts (or the sentences that describe them) with adequate precision in all circumstances[26].

C. *The Complementary Component of Nature and Nurture in Our Brain*

Looking inside the CEO's (or any executive's) brain allows us to appreciate the enormous human capabilities to *adapt* to changing environments. From a

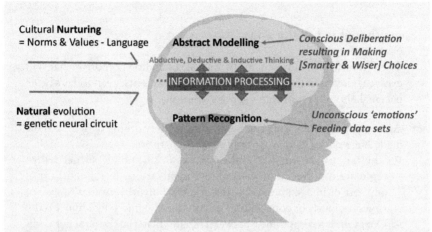

Figure 2: Brain as an information processing algorithm, comprised by innate neural circuits and cultural nurturing

neuroscientific perspective, the leader's brain is the result of a compromise: every human inherit a great deal of innate circuitry but also a highly sophisticated learning algorithm that can refine those early skills according to our education and our own individual experience[27].

Our brain is a compromise – a made visual in Figure 2 – of an innate *natural* highway of predetermined neural networks that allow newborn babies to learn fast, and to embed them through the linguistic *nurturing* of our environment (with the important parental guiding role) into a socio-cultural and moral context of norms and values, focusing on how to fit and to act "appropriately" within a group or organization. Evolution literally wired our brain for efficient prediction, while cultural influence, personal experiences and enhanced awareness allowed us to construct "new realities"[28] – rooted in increasingly more sophisticated mental maps through which we "see" the world now and in the future.

Our brain is molded with assumptions of all kinds. Indeed, babies are already organized and knowledgeable; their brains are full of innate constraints, and only specific parameters from different contexts remain to be acquired. *Natural evolution* and *cultural nurturing* are intertwined and not opposed. There is apparently some innate knowledge that constitute our human cortex that the human species has internalized as it evolved over (evolutionary) time. Human learning is not just setting of a pattern-recognition filter, but also involves the forming of an abstract model of the world. Learning is improving performance based on experience. Deep learning machines attempt a similar objective. They increasingly succeed to "autonomously" perform certain narrow tasks. But they still fail to pass the Turing test[29] or to beat the human brain's plasticity and versality.

Some thoughts to take away:

- The future will be fundamentally digital, including "cyborgs" that will evolve (humans with mechanic digital enhancements; even today's heart pacemakers are part of that cyborg evolution).

- AI researchers mimicking the human brain's networking of neurals have made huge progress in voice and image recognition.
  - These convolutional neural networks *in silico* have succeeded to replicate quite accurately concrete applications in recognition of any sort of image and voice. But these AI algorithms don't "see" or (unconsciously or consciously) understand the image like humans do.
  - Our brain is a compromise between innate (material) natural networks that allow us to learn a language and imagine or construct models and allow us a linguistic subjective "nurturing" and interpretation of our environment.

- The Turing test allows to verify whether an intelligence machine may be able to fool a human by making the latter think that he or she talks with another human fellow.

Chapter Fourteen

Why Human Learning Is Superior to Machine Learning?

"Realistically, deep learning is only part of the larger challenge of building intelligent machines. Such techniques lack ways of representing causal relationships (such as between diseases and their symptoms), and are likely to face challenges in acquiring abstract ideas like 'sibling' or 'identical to.' They have no obvious ways of performing logical inferences, and they are also still a long way from integrating abstract knowledge".

Gary Marcus, an AI-scientist and entrepreneur (2012), in *The New Yorker*

"Staying smart means understanding the potentials and risks of digital technologies, and the determination to stay in charge in a world populated by algorithms".

Gerd Gigerenzer, a risk expert (2022), *How to Stay Smart in a Smart World*

One of the reasons that the executive's brain is superior to machines is that the brain functions as a statistician constantly attending hypotheses to probabilities and uncertainties, expressing cognition in an extremely flexible manner. Humanity strength is its ability to mentally diversify and to explore completely new opportunities. When confronted with a problem, human ingenuity hypothesizes numerous possibilities that increases the odds of cracking the problem. In *automated* behavior, error is a failure, whereas in *creative* thinking, trial and error is a necessity to find new functioning models, abilities or products. "Instead of running set algorithms, the (human) brain bends, breaks and blends its storehouse of experiences, imagining what-ifs[1]." When our brain proliferates different options, it gets off the path of easy solutions and reaches more widely into its internal network. Like so many other human endeavours, creativity is strengthened with practice. Similarly, astute companies continuously adapt and sprinkle seeds broadly to find the swaths of fertile ground for finding functioning solutions, mainly because the landscape is continuously changing.

1. The Human Learning Brain Is Superior to That of AI[2] (The Cognitive Pathway)

Our brain also optimizes its ability to learn, especially in changing contexts. The intrinsic brain activity represents millions and millions of nonstop predictions to give meaning to the perceived external environment. Through prediction, our brain constructs the world we experience. Our "experience" resulting in perception is a creation of our brain's modelling ability. Human perception is a rolling process of continuously adopting our view with more data and subsequent feedback process. In that sense, it is a process of human prediction of minimizing errors based on modelling and hypothetical thinking. Human learning is in essence predictive processing[3] or active inferring based on generative modelling – an ability which current AI lacks.

1.1. Flexibility of Human Intelligence Versus Extremely Fast Artificial Intelligence

During its evolution, our brain seems to have acquired sophisticated algorithms that constantly keep track of the uncertainty associated with what it has learnt. Evolution literally wired our brain for efficient prediction. Through prediction and correction[4], our brain continually creates and revises our mental model of the world. It is a huge, ongoing simulation that constructs everything one perceives while determining how to act. Even babies seem to understand probabilities, that are deeply embedded in their brain circuits. Admittedly, *humans are very good to make decisions with limited data, but not with an overload of data. Computational learning algorithms, on the other hand, are very good at finding patterns in big data.*

We admit though that the *Internet of Things* creates distributed cognition and a form of "intelligence" by connecting "smart devices". We are entering in an epoch of *Internet of Bodies* – cyborgs or human hybrids – that creates some level of smart interactive distributed bodies, as in an *"intervolution"*, as Columbia professor Mark Taylor argues[5]. Our body is an information-processing neural network. But in contrast to AI, our brain is a kind of Bayesian neural network of incredibly high plasticity[6] that learns through "causal modelling". Learning is a kind of problem-solving. Learning systems as AI, however, is known as just narrow problem-solving systems. Human learning, on the contrary, encompasses both, narrow and general problem-solving, rooted in "modelling". AI remains within very narrowly defined boundaries to solve particular problems[7]. We do not know yet how to mechanically translate narrow into a broad perspective, teach a mechanical digital device to learn in general.

Human learning[8] is grounded on the foundational principles of emphasizing *focused attention, active engagement, positive feedback on errors* and *consolidation*. In that sense, learning also implies enormous patience and grit, crucial systematicity and a necessary tolerance to error. The possibilities of learning of humans are almost infinite, and this human capability is no match (yet) for the current learning abilities of smart machines.

What is hardwired in the *homo sapiens* is not so much language itself as the ability to acquire it – as Noam Chomsky postulated that our species is born with a language acquisition device, a specialized system[9]. The innate "highways of our brain" is automatically triggered in the first years of life. What is innate in us is the instinct to learn any language which obviously is partially culturally triggered and influenced[10]. Baby brains run a detailed mental simulation of the situation and the associated probabilities. The human brain is endowed with an intuitive logic since birth, allowing infants to

> *Humans learn extremely effectively from a small amount of data. Most likely there is an architecture in the human brain that serves all the tasks that humans have to deal with, and can skillfully transfer general abilities and skills from one path to the other. These transferrable skills and ways of learning are something that AI researchers have not yet been able to give artificial agents – and AI needs a great deal of data to learn.*

constantly experiment. Children are curious about everything, and their favorite word is often **why**, never stopping to experiment on the world, and their "scientist" brain ceaselessly accumulate the conclusions of their research. As we age, the brain plasticity decreases, and learning, while no completely frozen, becomes more and more difficult[11]. Babies are real "learning machines during their first years because their brains are the seat of an ebullient synaptic plasticity. The dentrites of their pyramidal neurons multiply at an impressive speed"[12]. Enriching the environment of a young child helps her build a better brain. Hence why it is plausible that executives also can enrich their learning abilities to broaden their perspective and embrace different and unusual views, enabling them to better resolve paradoxes and other business challenges in general.

1.2. A Wondering "Human Consciousness" Versus AI Seeking Patterns-Associations

The major force of the *homo sapiens* over the *machina sapiens* lies in (1) *the capability to make a (causal) representation of our world and even of a future that does not yet exist*, and (2) *the ability to share our ideas with others through communication, as linguistically*[13] *expressed* (in a language). Humans can even *"faire de l'infini avec du fini"*; they can imagine something unimaginable. The human brain's unique capabilities reside in the human ability to conceptually represent the world – i.e. the human ability to model a complex reality with causal relationships[14] – and the ability to share notions and ideas through our incredibly advanced communication linguistic skills and writing. It is this capacity of **imagining** and **linguistic** sharing or communicating unlimited combinations of possibilities – as if creating an infinite potential of futures – that makes us so powerful and special. This ability allows us to create, to be "creative" and artistic. Let us get back to the comparison between a smart machine and an executive's brain.

Most artificial neural networks[15] implement only the operations that our human brain performs unconsciously, in a few hundreds of a second, when it perceives an image, recognizes it, categorizes it and accesses its meaning. However, the human brain goes much further: it is able to explore the image consciously, able to formulate symbolic representations and explicit (model-like) theories of the world that we can share with others through language. AI fueled by big data cannot do this yet. Our brain is much more flexible than the strongest computer today[16]. However, computer scientists, such as MIT professor John Tenenbaum and his team, are attempting to incorporate this type of self-organization into AI as well. In the same vein, the South-African neuroscientist Dr. Marc Solms argues that our self-organizing and very plastic brain "embed" *consciousness* that paradoxally aims to find an existential balance of "satisfied fulfillment" (that allegedly may be similar to a "Nirwanic state") and the need to continuously neutralize the uncertainty of new perceptions we encounter in our world. Hence the foundational human (philosophical) characteristic to "wonder" and being eager to understand new contexts. Wondering urges our want to learn about new phenomena and understand them.

Despite all these neuroscientific efforts to determine "consciousness" in our brain, the "hard problem" of why consciousness exists still remains. We may need to revisit this Cartesian dualism again, but in a more nuanced form. We still seem to distinguish an objective material (bodily) reality and a more subjective immaterial sphere of consciousness. You can call it an attributive dualism in which two inherently distinct and incommensurable kinds or attributes co-exist: understanding the physical properties of the "body" reality and the "mental" properties of giving meaning; a cognitive sphere of understanding and a steering our life in a socio-ethical sphere. René Descartes conspicuously succeeded in alerting us about a vital human part that necessarily alluded to a qualitative understanding and more mechanistic categories of scientific explanations.

2. Machine Learning Differs from Human Learning

The cognitive pathway of learning can be partially digitized and thus using some form of "intelligence" in resolving problems. However, the crucial importance of emotions – or affect – in driving conscious behavior is remarkable. Smart machines may "learn" some frequent repeatable emotional behavior from big data, but have no clue what emotions really mean.

As we will see, the emotion "sympathy" being transformed into a feeling of "empathy"[17] is the link to our unique human ability to relate to each other and take an ethical "*relational*" stance[18]. Computers are unable to really understand "emotions" or "feelings". They just "mimic" them in an effective and a fast way. Emotions evolved as behavioral and physiological specializations. They are bodily responses controlled by the brain, that allowed ancestral organisms to survive in hostile environments and procreate. Programming a computer to be conscious would be an essential first step towards programming to have a full-blown emotional experience[19], and potentially even general intelligence (or IQ). I remain quite sceptical about such an ability of AI to become conscious.

2.1. Abstraction and Models Resulting in Common Sense

What is AI missing in comparison with the human ability to learn? Contemporary neural networks in AI are unable to recognize what constitutes the essence of an (abstract) object. Unlike a computer, humans possess the ability to question our beliefs and refocus our attention to those aspects of an image that do not fit with our first impression. Human learning is not just the setting of a pattern-recognition filter – as artificial neural networks function – but the forming of an abstract model of the world. This model simulation lets your brain impose meaning on the statistical noise, selecting what is relevant and ignoring the rest. In every waking moment, the human brain uses past experience (stored in the human memory), organized as concepts, to guide human actions and give specific sensations meaning.

The brilliant UCLA mathematician Judea Pearl revolutionized the study of causation and constructed a formal scientific language for expressing causal relationships. Any human intuitively knows that the sunrise causes a rooster to crow, rather than vice versa. The most powerful deep neural network would likely fail to achieve a similar insight[20]. Causation cannot be achieved simply by analyzing data.

A. Common Sense Facilitates the Possibility of Morality

Human intelligence evolved to deal with uncertainty. Those emerged skillset involves causal thinking according to conceptual modelling, able to make fast decisions based on intuition. Children implicitly and "intuitively" understand the use of the basics of time and space – as result of an in-built sociality. Children learn from a young age to develop and defend moral standards[21]. All those skills can be described as "**common sense**" – shared in common with most normal people across cultures. Common sense is *shared knowledge about people and the physical world as experienced by humans*. Morality is a specific form of common sense, reflecting the prevailing value, beliefs and norms in a particular community or societal context. This ability to sense those norms can be described as moral intelligence (MQ).

This common sense is enabled by a biological brain and hardly requires a lot of practice or experience; children learn it from early on through their built-in capability to grasp quite rapidly how to deal with uncertainty. Till now, we have not succeeded in programming common sense into computers. To a limited extent, smart computers may have succeeded in mimicking some of the outcomes of common sense, but without understanding it. Hence why a good AI translation system remains an *idiot savant*.

For instance, in contrast to logical languages, natural languages have multiple sources of uncertainty such as the same word having several meanings. A related kind of uncertainty that is hard to resolve for a translating computer is a sentence whose meaning cannot be inferred from the individual words, but can only be derived from understanding and interpreting "common sense". Another source of uncertainty lies in the different grammars of languages. In German and French, for example, the words for male and female professionals such as a nurse or a doctor differ, whereas in English, they are the same. Furthermore, although we may be impressed with the remarkable ability of computers to find correlations, they actually don't grasp the argument. And as long as a smart computer does not "recognize" the essence of an object, higher level cognitive abilities such as abstraction, thought and complex decision-making will remain extremely difficult. This is in contrast to human learning where there is immense flexibility of the brain to rely on changing cues. This vicarious functioning[22] on a few cues only – without much data – can be found in most biological systems that evolved through evolution.

B. Human's Abstract and Abductive Reasoning

Humans deploy an unmasked knack for (causal) abstraction. Today's AI neural networks need billions of data points to develop an "intuition" of a particular domain. In the field of learning, the effectiveness of the human brain remains unmatched. Machines are data hungry and extremely fast, whereas humans are data efficient but rather slow. Human learning makes the most from the least amount of data. And the extraordinary efficiency with which humans share their knowledge with others using a minimum number of words remains unequalled.

To learn is also to succeed in inserting new knowledge into an existing network. Indeed, the human brain manages to extract very abstract principles, systematic rules that it can reapply in many different contexts. Humans can draw inferences of extraordinary generality. Deep learning is almost entirely incapable of any profound new theoretical insight[23]: currently, the *machina sapiens* is largely unable to represent the range of abstract phrases, formulas, rules and theories with which the *homo sapiens* brain models the world. Call it abductive inferences, if you like. Reasoning with probabilities is a form of **abductive** *reasoning*[24] which is nothing but to infer the most likely cause for the observed data, or a form of reasoning backward.

2.2. Understanding Requires Intelligence and Consciousness

Today's AI – be it **symbolic AI** or **neural networks AI**[25]– solves only extremely narrow problems. In the human brain, however, learning almost always means rendering knowledge explicit, so that it can be reused, recombined, explained to others or transferred into useful and reusable tacit knowledge.

A. The Predictive Power of AI Cannot Be Conscious

The current *machina sapiens* is not able to initiate predictive models of our world that proves some form of causality. People are masters in seeing causal relationships and thus be able to use models that allow them (un)consciously to continuously predict what will happen[26]. Admittedly, the human tendency to "see" everywhere causal relations (even when there are none) sometimes distorts reality. And yes, "noise"[27] in the (abundant) data very often clouds the executive's decisions. Sure enough, neutralizing this noise and biases remains difficult[28].

What are the limitations of AI? Smart machines are able to copy certain behavior and allow autonomous cars to automate this behavior without really understanding it. Such deeper understanding requires to have a causal model as a representation of this world – as said earlier we seem to be born with that incredible ability as part of our human evolution. Understanding contexts is possible because we see (causal) relationships and subtleties that machines cannot.

Can we assume that our mental life is mathematically tractable? Our information-processing brain circuits literally do compute prior probability distributions and then sends predictive messages to sensory neurons, in an endless effort to dampen the incoming signals; and perception literally does involve comparisons between the predicted and actual distributions, resulting in computations of posterior probability. It's our conscious embodied mind that imposes "meaning" in the squatted and messy data, keeping what is relevant and ignoring the rest: that is a unique and almost magic human ability. The resultant (unconscious) inferences are what (human) perception actually is. The puzzling observation that perception and cognition are mostly unconscious and that we are unconscious of our psychological acts most of the time has profound consequences of how we relate emotions, feelings or affect and rationality.

B. *Human Consciousness*

A sentient subject[29] would be literally constituted by **affect**. In other words, any form of consciousness is based on affect, and thus *cognitive intelligence is almost completely dependent on "affect" or emotional intelligence*. These two forms of intelligence are closer related than one would admit: IQ ⇔ EQ?

However, that inference still triggers the question what **"consciousness"** really means, and how this definition of consciousness may differ from what the "cognitive" power of AI is and can be. If our brain is indeed a Bayesian brain that through a hypothesis-updating method makes inferences, the brain plausibly can transfer information.

A subjective perception[30] proceeds from inside outwards, always from the viewpoint of the subject. It really is **apperception**, an inferential process, a matter of Bayesian hypothesis-testing[31]. What you see and perceive is your own best guesses as to what is actually out there. The brain's task is to use (sensory) signals to create a probabilistic model if the regularities that exist in the real world (or rather between itself and the world) which it then uses to generate inferences that guide its actions – actions that must ensure its survival in that world. Our brain is an extraordinary tool that is unusually equipped to learn from experiences that allow "prediction errors" to be used through feedback to upgrade and update the model or hypothesis.

Human intelligence is basically conjectural or "abductive" and is dependent on a conceptual framework that assumes a form of consciousness, which AI completely lacks. Paraphrasing Erik Larson, we could say that **"deduction"** proves that something must be – *logically* speaking; that **"induction"** (*empirically*) shows that something may be, while **"abduction"** suggests that something may be true – based on a *hunch*. Abduction sparks innovative and creative thinking since it enables human researchers to conjecture and hypothesize, fundamental in the way we use our innate ability to understand[32]. Machine learning relies on inductive logic of data observations, and it learns statistic regularities or patterns in a data set. However, machine learning does not understand high-level abstract concepts that humans use in modelling[33]. Artificial intelligence remains characterized by impressive computer science and statistics, but not by any form of general intelligence, let alone (self)consciousness. AI remains "dumb machines on steroids" for the time being.

The human brain is constituted by a layered architecture, which allows the option of adding supplementary layers. This layering offers a framework to explain how brains became increasingly complex through the process of natural selection whole conserving successful basic features[34]. And consciousness – not located in any region in the brain, but probably being engrained in all the organism – is part of organismic life.

Some thoughts to take away:

- Human intelligence is conscious and aware of the perceptions they experience. Artificial intelligence only correlates or associates "Bayesian" probabilities that result in predictions, or are able to find correlations that occasionally contribute to interesting useful patterns.

- Human learning is flexible and is linguistically communicated, in contrast to machine learning that is extremely fast but very narrowly defined in finding particular solutions (or predictions).

- Until now, nobody succeeded to program self-learning "common sense" in computers. Common sense is also the notion of shared norms and values that makes socio-ethical learning and thinking possible. Without common sense, without causal abstract modelling, without counterintuitive argumentation and imagination and without consciousness, artificial intelligence will never be able to match the human ability to learn and to really understand.

Chapter Fifteen

Learning: Multifaceted Intelligence and Consciousness

"Belonging is a call to integrity and creativity".

John O'Donohue, 1998, *Eternal Echoes. Exploring our hunger to belong*

"The ability to learn faster than your competitors may be the only sustainable competitive advantage".

Arie De Geus, 1997, The Living Company

Learning has the same root as apprehending, or *"apprendre"* in French. In that sense, be it an executive or a child, learning is grasping a fragment of reality, catching it and bringing it inside our brain which then forms an internal model of the world. Through learning, raw data that strike our five senses turn into refined ideas, abstract enough to be reused (through our memory) in a new context that the neuroscientist Dehaene labels as "smaller-scale models of reality"[1]. Learning is a way for the brain to internalize a new aspect of reality by adjusting its innate neural circuits to appropriate a domain that it had not mastered before. The human brain breaks down the problem of learning by creating a hierarchical multilevel model. From this hierarchical organization of the human cortex as in a pyramid of successive layers emerges the ability to detect increasingly complex objects or concepts.

1. Learning: *Quid Cognitum Habere In Vivo Et In Silico*

Human learning always starts from a set of *apriori hypotheses* which are projected onto the incoming data and from which the system elects those that are best suited to the current context. A complementary combination of a strict form of innate structuralism in the human brain and a pure empirical state of continuous subtle form of fluctuating impressions. This idea of complementary structures resonates to John Dewey's interpretation of intelligence as an intermediary between *apriori* and *aposteriori*, which allows experiences to be understood. The activities of intelligence in that sense are interpreted as "instrumental" – to resolve problems, a way to an end. Intelligence reacts to a challenge and creatively explores solutions. Being intelligent implies to be able to look at a problem from different angles at the same time and "provides an automatism" to resolve the problem.

1.1. The Human Bayesian Brain Able to Be (Self)Conscious

Our brain learns much better and more flexibly than machines, so far. Indeed, humans combine two levels of insights: (1) the *innate knowledge*[2] of our species (what Bayesian statisticians[3] would describe as "priors", the sets of *plausible hypotheses* inherent throughout evolution) and (2) our *personal experience* (the posterior or revision of those hypotheses, based on all the inferences we have been able to gather throughout our life). For that reason, neuroscientists argue that all (human) knowledge is based on two components: a set of *innate apriori assumptions*, prior to any interaction with the environment[4], and second, the capacity to sort them out according to *aposteriori plausibility*, once we have encountered some real data that we "experience" and have nurtured.

A. Multifaceted Human Intelligence and Human Consciousness

The mechanisms of **intelligence** indicates a complementary balance between *apriori structure without genesis* (transcendental metaphysics or biologically evolution-driven engrained structures) and *aposteriori genesis without predetermined structures* ("individual" experimentation or an empirical epistemology)[5].

As argued in the previous chapter, the final result of "learning" is **a compromise**, a selection of the best internal model from those that our prior organization makes available, that contains the "*complementary* forces" in it. For instance, a (young unexperienced) person "knows" what a face (a conceptual output) looks like. A human can easily recognize and thus predict a specific face of someone. A computer, however, does not have this innate pre-understanding. Through layering and backpropagation (feedback), the input of an "object face" turns it finally to see "the face of x". And a human can be self-confident and show confidence in others, and therefore distinguish truthful scientific statements from mere opinions or even false statements that can be falsified[6].

The functioning of the brains of young children clearly includes built-in capacity that helps to jump-start any form of learning. Almost from birth onwards, babies are able to recognize human faces. In the animal kingdom, the presence of such actionable innate intelligence – not relying on learning – to immediately survive in an often hostile environment is even more pronounced[7].

Intelligence and *consciousness* are two notions with profound different meaning. Once more, **intelligence** aims to find concrete solutions for achieving a certain objective, whereas **consciousness** refers to the awareness of our streaming thoughts, longings, emotions and feelings about the world, others and ourselves. Consciousness defines the experience of living[8]. The conscious self seems to ride above the physical brain and all its layers and modules. *Consciousness* is associated with awareness and mindfulness; intelligence with mind-logic and mindset. If *intelligence* is about exploring insightful solutions to resolve a problem, we infer that smartness is therefore related to intelligence. Intelligence is form of efficacity, based on "learned (past) experiences that allow knowledge to take hold and cognitively predict the future"[9]. Intelligence is a constant re-configuration of past models, which makes it constructive and, to a certain extent, also creative.

A French proverb claims that *être intelligent, c'est regarder de plusieurs côtés à la fois*, taking plural views in perspective to resolve ... Professor Howard Gardner speaks about *multifactual intelligences*[10]. However, when managers "value" a problem, looking for its social and moral implications on others, they normatively imagine – as in moral imagination – what the consequences could be of such a decision, or what the moral duty could be in certain circumstances. Managers then "prescribe" and thus create a future-based reality.

B. Morality Is Derived from Consciousness, Not from Mere Cognition

Morally valuing is never solipsistic and always depends on norms and values within a certain community and its relations within that (moral) community. Morality makes this kind of "collective intelligence" a function of relations between members of such a community, organization, team or family. *Wising up* taps into that *collective intelligence*, which we sometimes also describe as *"conscience"*. This conscience is infused consciousness – a form of subjective experiences and mindful awareness of those experiences. Aggregated "normal" individual intelligence – or collective intelligence – may *unfold* in a form of moral conscience that is shared within a community. How is (human) learning related to consciousness and/or intelligence?

That learning ability of our brain formulates hypotheses and select those that fit with our environment[11]. If the intention is focused on resolving a certain problem or more precisely achieving a certain *objective (measurable) goal* – for instance, predicting certain behavior that allows business to optimize investments catering those expected behavior in an uncertain future – we can talk about **intelligence**. Being aware and having a certain *subjective feeling or reflection* about that attempt to achieve a certain (monetized) goal is defined as **being conscious**. Because it can be stipulated that only the notion of (self)consciousness can carry moral agency, we therefore infer that machine intelligence (or any form of cognitive intelligence only) cannot comprehend moral reasoning. In other words, moral agency without consciousness and conscience is an impossibility *in terminis*.

1.2. Learning as Thinking in Probabilities

Reasoning with probabilities is deeply inscribed in the logic of our learning, though in a largely sub- or unconscious manner. Learning progressively forms our internal model of the outside world. Be it tacit knowledge like (internalized) bike riding through implicit practice or explicit knowledge that we easily can communicate with others. As an adult, we are predicting and explaining the meaning of sensations and perceptions based on probability and experience, often processed in a subconscious manner. Similarly, a computer algorithm learning to recognize faces, for example, is acquiring template models of the various possible shapes of eyes, noses, mouths and their combinations.

Algorithms use large data sets as inputs to learn patterns in data, inducing a simple binary hierarchical model that can be decoded on big data. In other words, our sensatory tools capture data, turned into information and interpreted by our brain through modelling in a coherent "perception". In a same manner, smart computers are trained to recognize and thus "know" a sentence. The most recent GPT-3 open AI program has shown us its capabilities in autonomously writing a novel. Apparently quite smoothly done with even a narrative plot but also with quirky almost unreasonable sentences.

> *Today's neural networks or deep learning machines are currently more about finding statistical regularities in complex patterns than organizing these in a way that allows them to detect how one phenomenon can affect another. To do this, Artificial General Intelligence would need to be contextualized, situationally aware, nuanced, multifaceted and multidimensional. But above all, it should be able to think in causal terms beyond mere correlations.*

A. *Learning* In Silico *Through Deep Neural Network Aiming to Find Correlations*

Learning in both brains and machines thus requires searching for an optimal combination of parameters that define together the mental model in every detail. In that sense, learning, *in silico* or *in vivo*, is a massive statistical search problem. Learning then becomes making predictions that are acquired and nuanced over time from incoming error signals. The better predictions we make – through experience and feedback – the higher our confidence level becomes.

Machine learning (ML) is nothing more as computational treatment of induction, or acquiring certain knowledge from (past) experience. ML is basically automated induction logic, using a multilayered neural network that recognizes patterns in big data. In deep learning (a specific type of ML), you give the computer a set of training data. If you are teaching a computer to tell the difference between drawings of cats and dogs, you use cat and dog pictures, as visualized in Figure 1. You also give the computer a set of labels for the training data that you know to be objectively correct. In this example, the learning algorithm might teach a neural network to distinguish cats from dogs. Once the computer has been trained, you can use the new program to label unfamiliar data, the test data. Once the algorithm in the computer program functions, one does not necessarily need to understand the precise layered working of the program. Hence the **black box** notion. To make sensible decisions, business people usually need to focus only on the data rather than on the inside of the algorithm that has proven its value[12].

However, AI is cursed by "dimensionality": if one adds enough variables into the "black box" of algorithms that underpin machine learning, one will eventually find a combination of variables that perform well together – but one

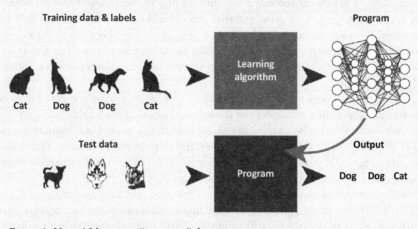

Figure 1: How AI learns to "interpret" data

does not know whether the correlation is merely random luck, let alone explains some form of causality. It is this causality in models what makes executives really understand a particular reality or context. Indeed, as one increases the number of variables one uses to make predictions, one needs exponentially more data to distinguish true predictive capacity from mere luck. In the latter case, the prediction success is the result of a chance "coincidental" alignment in the data – nothing more. This kind of data dredging can result in funny or nonsensical correlations that are merely coincidental: for example, the clear "observable" correlation parallel of deaths caused by anticoagulants on one hand and sociology doctorates awarded in the USA between 1998 and 2009 on the other hand, which of course is without any real meaning[13]. Or a "visible" correlation between ice-cream consumption and death through drowning in summer time: this is a senseless random correlation because the confounding factor is "the summer season" during which people swim more and have therefore a higher probability of drowning, independently from the fact that people eat more ice-cream with hot temperatures in summertime.

B. The Theory of Error Backpropagation

Computer algorithms and their artificial neural networks are called deep networks where each layer is capable of discovering only an extremely simple part of the external reality. In algorithms, on each trial, the network gives a tentative answer, and is told whether it made an error, and adjusts its parameters to try to reduce its error on the next trial. Every wrong answer provides valuable information and feedback. In machine learning, it is called supervised learning (because a supervisor knows the correct answer that the system must give) using "error backpropagation"[14] – because error signals are sent back into the network in order to modify its parameters. This clever feedback system remains at the heart of many current AI applications. It is this principle that lies behind our smartphone's ability to recognize your voice. But believe it or not, it is likely also the way our brain uses one version or another of it. The artificial network can correct itself only by calculating the difference between its response and the correct answer, hence why "supervised".

The theory of *error backpropagation*[15] predicts: every unexpected events leads to corresponding adjustment of the internal model of the world. The learning by error correction is also universally widespread in the animal and human world. In that sense, the brain is a massive hierarchy of predictive systems. The brain is a fundamentally **prospective** organ that is designed to use information from the past and the present to generate predictions about the future[16]. Quite similar to what current AI algorithms are doing. One may add that neural networks – algorithms that are programmed to turn inputs such as senses and perceptions into outputs as in decisions or judgements – and its backpropagation feedback system is often superior (in terms of speed and accuracy) to humans since it will learn from mistakes. Not always a guaranteed human ability since we often fall to hubristic tendencies. However, an error feedback system can also be found in our own *self-reflection* and *mindfulness* (as we will explain in the chapters 29 and 30).

Well-known and respected computer scientist and AI pioneer Geoffrey Hinton is convinced that we humans are neural nets, and what we can do, machines can do. However, at this point and the foreseeable future, that seems very improbable. A smart computer or AI does not have a pre-understanding of what is a human face, for instance. Through layering and backpropagation, a smart computer will manage to accurately recognize faces, but it would not understand in any meaningful way. The *machina sapiens* is extremely fast and effective for narrow tasks, whereas the *homo sapiens* are extremely versatile for many (infinite) tasks but is much slower. Smart machines today are not able to put forward – or to learn – "models" that essentially are predictive tools for our world. These machines incorporate the mass-made programmed algorithms and predict more "accurately" through the use of big data some narrowly aimed outcomes in a non-volatile or well data-fied context.

2. How to Diminish the (Negative Effect of) Unconscious Biases?

These days, one can take an image of your brain through functional magnetic resonance imaging[17] (fMRI) or electroencephalography[18] (EEG) and determine enhanced activities in the different parts of the brain[19]. This technology allows practitioners and academic scholars to better understand the functioning of the brain. It may bridge the enormous gap between the physical brain activities and how our mind determines our decisions[20]. However, mainstream media reports vastly oversimplify neuroscience research – and fuel a burgeoning industry of neuro-consultants who suggest to have unlocked the secrets of leadership and marketing from the brain functioning. More cynically, neuro-marketeers and big tech companies have found a way to take advantage of these human biases and oversimplifications. We aim to establish a more sophisticated and more nuanced perspective (but likely less over-promising as well) on how leaders' decisions are unconsciously affected by neural networks in the brain[21].

2.1. The "Rider" Steering the "Elephant"

When we make decisions, we are not always in charge since we can be too impulsively driven by unconscious emotions or too paralyzed by uncertainty. Our civilization is like a veneer of our neocortex on top of a mammal's limbic and very old reptile brain[22]. This human cortex is the latest evolutionary stage that influences our choices for better or for worse.

A. How a Reasonable "Rider" Needs to Tap into (Biased) Emotions (of the Metaphorical "Elephant")

In trying to predict and reduce uncertainty in our decisions, we all are influenced and "misguided" by often unconscious (biased) emotions; be it board members – who are assumed to coach and to supervise management to prevent unreasonable, unfair and unethical decisions – or top executives who are paid to make informed rational and reasonable decisions in the interest of the organization, or loyal and engaged employees who have all signed an agreement to optimize their activities and decisions to be aligned with the organization's goals and purpose. Indeed, we all succumb to (biased) emotions, because that is how our brain functions facing a complex and uncertain world. We learn through modelling.

Pattern recognition helps us to swiftly recognize alleged patterns and assumed causal relationships (even if that is not objectively the case). We use patterns we have previously experienced "to shape our understanding of a complex reality"[23] now. Pattern recognition allows us to simplify a complex reality and make it more coherent and easier to deal with than it actually is. Generating a prediction, recognizing patterns, detecting one's error and correcting oneself are the very foundations of effective learning. Our biases are a by-product of heuristics, or intuitive shortcuts[24] we use as a powerful fast and effective method to make most of our daily decisions. Admittedly, for the vast majority of our decisions, our heuristics give excellent results. In some instances, however, they can be very biased and even disastrous[25]. Metaphorically speaking, the rational or reasonable conscious "rider" attempts to steer the often emotional (un)conscious and sometimes irrational but powerful intuitive "elephant". The rider refers to our analytical ability, while the elephant is a symbol of the (often) intuitive "affect" in our brain. They symbiotically collaborate to come up with sensible decisions.

2.2. The Conscious Human, Being Aware of Personal Experiences

The brain is a decision-making device gathering information from all sorts of sources to make decisions from moment to moment. Information is gathered and computed, a decision is made and then you get the sensation of conscious experience[26]. However, the way how we think, how our brain functions may be another contributing factor to bad decisions. Indeed, the brain is not the rational calculating machine we often imagine. It is also true that business remains littered with examples of bad strategies[27], mainly because flawed analysis, excessive ambition, greed and or other corporate biases and vices.

A. *From Unconscious Emotions to Conscious Decisions*

Being smart and reasonable is an attempt of a "de-biasing", of emphasizing our rational and analytical logic thinking, and not merely relying on our gut feelings or basic habits or biases, or even some heuristics that has served us well in our evolution and in contexts without a lot of data and information. Somehow, our brain's inadequacies may be part of this not-so-optimal decision-making: overconfidence, some mental accounting, a status quo bias, anchoring, sunk-cost effect, the herding instinct, misestimating future hedonistic states, false consensus are all forms of biased decision-making[28]. Being aware of the brain's flaws is a first step to help executives and strategists to steer around them.

It is this unconscious bias that has been studied at a number of Leadership NeuroLabs[29] with the aim to mitigate some of those gaps between unreasonable and reasonable decision-making. The more we are aware and conscious of our brain activities and its subsequent inaccuracies and unconscious biases, the more the executives may be able to rectify and become better and thus smarter decision-makers. Understanding how our brain works may allow us to get a better idea of why attempting to address so many biases remain ineffective because it may not necessarily change behavior itself. We argue with many philosophers, psychologists and neuroscientists that being aware is a necessary but not sufficient condition to improve decision-making. Indeed, providing information alone to people does not necessarily change their behavior.

Unconscious biases occur as a result of brain processes that are not consciously accessible[30], so thinking about them in a conscious manner is not changing the behavior yet. Hence, why trying to help executives to become less biased is extremely difficult. Awareness about potential biases needs to be aligned with the need to have collaborative teams who take less biased decisions and actions based on *"hygienic" architectural foundations*[31] – as we will explain in the last chapter.

Conscious perception[32] transforms incoming (unconscious) information into an internal code that allows it to be processed in unique ways. Our brain uses a division of labor, between an army of unconscious statisticians and a single decision-maker. This "interpreter"[33] creates order out of chaos, it creates a narrative of and explanation for our actions, emotions, thoughts, memories and even dreams. A strict logic governs the brain's unconscious circuits – they appear ideally organized to perform statistically accurate inferences concerning our sensory inputs. Our unconscious vision computes a landscape of probabilities, and our consciousness samples from it. Our unconscious perception works out the probabilities – and then our consciousness samples from them at random.

Consciousness acts as a discrete measurement device that grants us a single glimpse of the vast underlying sea of unconscious computations.

The mighty unconscious (emotional) 'affect' in the brain – the metaphorical 'elephant' – generates sophisticated hunches, but only a conscious mind – the 'rider' – can rationally think through a problem. Language (and memory[34]) provide(s) a categorical and syntactic formulation of conscious thoughts that jointly allows us to structure our mental world and share it with other human minds. Neuroscientific research suggests that the initial bit of induced activity is unconscious; only if the activation spreads to distant regions of parietal and prefrontal cortex does conscious experience occur. This conscious access corresponds to the sudden transition towards a higher state of synchronized brain activity. From an epistemological perspective, one could argue that most of what we know is implicit or tacit. We bring our knowledge into consciousness – or making it explicit – when the context or situation urges us to do so. Or when the agent deliberately analyzes and deliberates about a certain problem or challenge.

The power of prospection and better (hypothetical) foresight – while acknowledging the inherent future uncertainty that we all face – is what makes us smarter and potentially also wise(r). And this foresight or ability to contemplate the future may be the defining attribute of human intelligence. Looking into the future, or predicting through both our "innate" and learned (cultural and personal) beliefs and concepts, is a central function of our large brain.

Only in groups who actively can take decisions together, one can reduce one's own (un)conscious bias[35]. An architectural decision system in an organization and institutionalized standard operating procedures and specific rules, for instance, will help executives to become more effective in making smart decisions. Although education and awareness campaigns may be useful to become individually smarter, it is in the action through governance mechanisms and concrete rules at boards or through team diversity that makes executives better and thus smarter decision-makers. These dynamics can improve the decision-making processes and generate a more open culture in an organization.

Good decision architecture aims to reduce errors and uncertainty while improving the potential of coming up with new insights. Such architectural decision design also stimulates bias-reducing dynamics, open-dialogue and real divergence and diversity[36]. A sound decision architecture that evaluates decisions on their merits, and not (only) on their outcomes, will likely produce more optimal results where smart judgement and skills are rewarded – instead of relying on mere lucky decisions rooted in randomness[37]. Moreover, in unstable conditions of high uncertainty, it's not a bad idea to "keep it simple", and to rely on sensible heuristics rather than trying to get all possibly variables into a complex algorithm.

B. AI Does Not Have a Hard Problem, Only Humans Do

Organizations want their leaders to be as conscious as possible to provide insights that lead to decisions positively affecting the organizational prospects and its bottom line. Till now no (neuro)scientist, however, has completely deciphered the physical element of *consciousness* itself which remains both a scientific mystery – despite the attempts to find the neural correlative of consciousness[38]. Explaining consciousness remains a fundamental philosophical **"hard problem"** as the influential Australian philosopher David Chalmers quipped it[39]. Indeed, how does matter become mind[40]? Till today, this epistemological knowledge gap has not been resolved[41]. Even if the brain would function as a quantum computer, it does not explain the hard problem of consciousness. And let us not confuse *consciousness* with *cognition* either[42]. Extremely cognitive intelligent beings are not necessarily always very (self)conscious. Smart machines or even supercomputers are unlikely to become conscious any time soon. Scientists question whether Artificial Intelligence could evolve into consciousness[43] – but so far, that remains nothing but speculation. That is why AI can be potentially "intelligent" (within narrowly defined boundaries) but not conscious, let alone show any form of *wisdom* or some form of compassionate *conscience*[44].

Some thoughts to take away:

- Human intelligence = innate *apriori* assumptions + empirical *aposteriori* plausibility. The human brain and its **learning abilities** is the result of a **compromise** between **natural innate structures** and **nurturing ability to comprehend (subjective individual) experiences.**

- From unconscious (often biased) emotions to conscious deliberate reasoning, both along the path of cognition and socio-ethical thinking. AI cannot be bothered about the "hard problem" (of consciousness), simply because it does not have (a real clue of) consciousness. AI remains a mechanic non-sentient device. Only humans face a "**hard problem**" of *explaining consciousness.*

- When dealing with ethical dilemmas, we have long assumed that the rational person could conceptually resolve this and act upon this reasoning. However, neuroscientific insights have taught us that **emotions (or "affect") constitute our reasonable thoughts**. Our emotions in the brain gather all data and info, and the more analytical (and conscious) mind selects what's useful and meaningful. In other words, the rational "rider" on the "elephant" may make the decision, but the "energetic" emotions underneath determine whether one acts upon it or not.

Chapter Sixteen

Moral Community Versus Amoral Artificial Intelligence

"The most beautiful and most profound emotions we can experience is the sensation of the mystical. It is the source of all true science. He to whom this emotion is a stranger, who can no longer wonder and stand rapt in owe, is as good as dead".

Albert Einstein

"It is not so much our judgments as it is our prejudices that constitute our being".

Hans-Georg Gadamer, 1976, *Philosophical Hermeneutics*

How leadership makes decisions helps us to explain our ability to make wise and, thus, ethical decisions, something a smart but soulless and consciousnessless computer cannot[1]. Most probably, the hype around AI has overestimated its capabilities within the near foreseeable future. From a neuroscientific perspective, it is fair to conjecture that we are hardwired to survive and thrive in a (moral) community where relations form the foundational governance stones. Let's explain this.

1. A Theory of Mind: Socio-Moral Thinking Beyond Cognitive Reasoning

Because of the brain's neuroplasticity[2], executives can learn through practices of **mentalizing** and **mindfulness** to become more attuned to a more holistic perspective[3].

1.1. Is Moral Ability Engrained in Our Brain?

Activating the dorsal part of the lateral prefrontal cortex of the brain allows us to pay attention to our "wise advocate", or by self-directing from the easier low road of tactics (similar to Kahneman's *system 1 thinking*) to the reflective high road of strategy (as in Kahneman's *system 2 thinking*) but in a very particular "focused" manner. Invoking the high road of moral deliberative reflection is not a miracle practice, but it will help executives to strengthen their wise decision-making, acknowledging the fact that organizations and their leaders are embedded in a broader community.

A. Morality: Consciousness and Conscience

It seems that humans are admonished to act in accordance with their "constituted" conscience, as in a fundamental moral obligation taught by their parents and tribal community. Cognitive sciences do not tell us what is right or wrong. However, neuroscience indicates human (but to a certain extent also mammalian) brains are wired to make us social. To create order in such social groups, certain community standards are needed. Humans internalize those standards and boundaries resulting in human (ethical) *conscience* that constitutes a community of teams. That conscience reflects the moral right that provides us fuzzy boundaries. They allow us to apply some ordinary prudence to make appropriate (moral) decisions within a moral community. Often, we have been "admitted" as a child into such relational community. This conscience is strongly embedded in a social community and its collective "intelligence". The subjective experience of phenomena within an integrated web of connectedness can potentially give us some meaning. Meaning is therefore "found" in the connectedness and relations of an individual, not in a mere individual solipsistic attempt to be completely cut off from community connectedness and any interdependent relations.

Previous chapters explained how human *cognitive pathway of learning* tries to decipher the current reality, describes *what is*. A *socio-moral pathway*, however, refers to intentions of humans to build and *prescribe* a new *collaborative* context, necessary for any team and/or organization to thrive. Such collaboration almost always contains a value-laden or socio-moral component. In examining how executives deal with social, ethical[4] and environmental challenges on the one hand and with uncertainties, opposing ideas and paradoxes on the other hand, we can learn quite a bit by understanding the underlying brain mechanisms of those decision-makers. Ethicists focus on "*should be*" and "*ought to*" that aim to provide clues on how to live a good (executive) life, whereas scientists describe *what is* and what can be expected according to the predictive force of causal thinking and modelling. However, the gap between what is and what should be – as in the (Humean) *naturalistic fallacy*[5] – is never far away.

If we assume that nature has provided some natural ability to think in terms of moral dilemmas and paradoxes on the one hand, and on probabilities on the other hand, neuroscience may help us to indicate some form of ethical thinking built into our brains that differs from say more egocentric thinking (for mere objective optimization or individual survival). Someone who thinks more consciously, his or her brain functions slightly different from someone who runs on "automatic pilot". Similarly, in ethics, the notion of intention plays an important role. We can ask whether this guiding principle of intention in ethics is also hardwired in our brains? Research on the "theory of mind" suggests that it is indeed: intention may be one of the defining characteristics of the human consciousness. Intention is context-dependent. Only the human brain allows us to analyze, reason, form theories and adapt to different contexts, something that a machine cannot do (yet).

B. Emotions Facilitate Moral Thinking

From a neuroscientific perspective, *emotional intelligence* is about getting the brain to construct the most useful instance of fine-grained emotion concept tailored to fit a given specific situation. These fine-grained emotions[6] allow us to make moral decisions. Emotions are a social reality[7]. Emotional intelligence – or rather emotional sentience – constitutes a crucial neuroscientific link with moral "sentience" or ethical (sub)conscious conscience, an apparent innate ability in our brain structure. It can be argued that EQ is a prerequisite to attain reasonable and even "responsible decisions". The latter represents a fair level of *consciousness* resulting in moral *conscience* (MQ). This **human socio-moral pathway** that focuses on the social and moral interaction of people within a certain context can hardly be "copied" (understood) by a soulless or non-conscious artificial "intelligence". What is prescribed and created as a socio-political ideal – be it optimizing profit or sharing created value – always implies the weighting of certain moral values. Of course, such judgement and choice are purely normative. Here again, the natural fallacy trying to create a moral world out of scientific facts is rather hard and has been well documented – and beyond the scope of this book.

Reasonable or smart decisions to maximize or optimize shareholder value, for instance, require a cognitive pathway, whereas responsible or wise decisions are rooted in a broader "relational" perspective. We claim that boards need to exercise these different forms of intelligence in transforming organizations to competitive thriving entities, that increasingly will also require some form of collaboration between both spheres.

1.2. Cognitive Thinking Versus Socio-Moral Reasoning

Neuro-scientifically, the brain allows us to develop a number of different kind of intelligences, be it cognitive, emotional or socio-moral[8]. **Cognitive thinking** is based on both *cognitive competence* (or IQ) and *risk intelligence* (RQ) that aim to reduce uncertainty or to accurately predict. In addition, the combined forces of IQ and RQ could possibly come up with great new insights and innovative ideas. The cognitive skills require an intentional agent (or individual intentionality), but also a form of joint agency that allows groups and teams to form cognitive representations[9]. However, to create a broader and more holistic perspective – that we argued for in the first part – is only possible when a form of **socio-moral thinking** is acknowledged and further developed.

A. Human Collaboration Based on EQ and MQ [...]

This form of sociality and moral thinking is based on strong cooperative motives to survive. Social bonding occurs via the sharing of emotions, attention, actions and attitudes where team members share experiences with each other. Important for any well-functioning organization is the ability of this foundational human cooperation and shared intentionality[10] to build cooperation between groups or teams – based on a combination of *emotional intelligence* (EQ) and *moral consciousness and conscience* (MQ) – or should we define it as human *conscience*[11].

More specifically, morality and its moral intelligence – expressed in our conscience – is a set of shared attitudes and practices that regulate individual behavior to facilitate cohesion and well-being among individuals in the group[12]. Morality is therefore a human interpretation of resolving practical solutions to common problems within organizations, groups or teams. Conscience refers to feelings of "oughtness" (positive valence) or "ought-not-ness" (negative valence) that typically accompany social behavior and social habits that emerge from reinforcement learning and imitation.

Today, cognitive sciences do not explicitly oppose emotion from ratio anymore: each emotion has its own reason to exist because it is useful in the survival of the species. Indeed, humans have this incredible desire to explore the unknown, to seek to understand the unknown. Emotions such as exploring and playing are two intrinsically rewarding activities. But in case of crisis and thus stress, when we perceive a threat, these emotions are suppressed. Hence creating a safe working environment[13] in which comfort and well-being can evolve are crucial conditions for being creative and thus insightful – one of the necessary conditions to make reasonable smart conditions. There seems to be a close link between competence – and risk attitude – and emotional intelligence. This emotional desire is linked to a brain circuit that is fed by dopamine which compensates us for learning and understanding something new[14].

An intriguing question may be whether conscious experiences could bubble out of a computer simulation. Prof. David Chalmers sees this as a possibility in the future[15], but so far no scientific theory can explain how. And what does awareness and consciousness add to information processing? Some neuroscientists go that far by inferring that consciousness[16] is about comprehending feelings (or affect)[17]. Unconscious cognition or autonomic reflex, or even *unconscious emotions*, needs to be distinguished from *conscious feelings*[18]. The quest to understand the genesis of a conscious experience remains an enigma shrouded in some perceived magic ... where explanation (so far) stops.

B. ... While EQ Also Makes IQ Possible

The voluntary action or conscious cognition is less certain and therefore requires more time. This process that delays automatized action tendencies and enables them to be held in mind (as in the short-term or working memory of the human brain). This working memory entails inhibition of automatic action tendencies and the stabilizing of intentionality while the system feels its way through unpredicted problems – which is the main function of the cortex. In that sense, the cortex or *cortical cognitive consciousness specializes in uncertainty*.

Subconscious emotions drive our ability to rationally think: EQ => IQ. Emotional intelligence (EQ) in an almost subconscious manner constitutes[19] intellectual intelligence or competence (in brief, IQ)[20]. In short, emotions construct our (intellectual) thinking. These emotions capture data through our senses. Both competence (IQ) and Risk Intelligence (RQ) create trust. Similarly unconsciously but definitely also intentionally and thus consciously, EQ constitutes moral consciousness: IQ <= EQ => MQ. *Emotions and feelings are the engines of our moral appraisal and action* in what we are calling the "intuitive track" of **moral cognition**. But equally, affect (EQ) steers competence (or IQ). Emotions are our on-the-ground responses to our mostly non-conscious assessment of the situations in which we find ourselves. *Unconscious emotions can turn into conscious feelings* that play a crucial role in the reasoning involved in our reflective deliberations. This reflection assesses competing alternative courses of action and comes to grips with competing values. These process of imaginative moral deliberation are cases of genuine ethical consideration of what one **ought to do** in a certain complex uncertain situation where we have the opportunity to reflectively assess our options for action.

2. Learning a Socio-Moral Pathway Beyond Our Cognitive Abilities

When executives make wise(r) decisions, we could argue that this requires a certain **mindsight** – closely related to a form of compassionate mindfulness and awareness – which here is seen as the result of a combination of mind[21], embodied physical brain and relational self-organizing processes[22] of the brain. The mindsight embraces three capabilities of executives: the capacity to cultivate (innovative) insights, able to feel empathy, and having the capacity to integrate different elements into a coherent whole[23]. In that sense, this integration therefore implies kindness and compassion. If building on integration might help us to relate to common humanity, maybe this capability allows us to follow a socio-moral pathway beyond our more ego-centred "cognitive" perspective. Only with such an astute mindfulness one can make wise decisions. Wisdom is an attitude and not the property of an individual.

2.1. "Affect" Constituting Wise Decision-Making?

Any manager or employee – with the necessary supervised training – can learn to become more aware of the way he/she or the team makes decisions. Alert awareness is based on three pillars – cultivating *focused attention, open awareness* and *kind attention* – that needs to be brought into a daily routine to become effective in decision-making[24]. These are likely the ingredients necessary for making wise decisions.

Wise decisions unfold in the relationship with others. Wisdom (as a moral virtue) arises within each of us and is to be shared by all. Similarly, the notions of "meaning" and "purpose" in decision-making are not about you and me, but about what relates us together, what can be integrated into a whole that makes sense. It is when we are tuned in into a mindful awareness and non-judgemental presence of what is going on, and what we need to do to harmonize and integrate the different components that we possibly are able to create something "worth striving for".

Empathy and attention are enablers to channel energy and information flows – through the activation of neural firing in our embodied brain – that shapes our understanding and therefore our decision-making. The "affect" enables cognitive and socio-ethical reasoning. Affect is the result of prediction, or its processes to make predictions possible[25]. The affect allows to channel the "feeling felt"[26] into energy and information that flows and is consciously captured by our mind and translated into a deeper understanding[27].

A. The Physical Brain and the Embodied Mind

The *physical brain* can then be neuro-scientifically seen as an *embodied mechanism of energy*[28] *and information flows*, whereas the *mind* is both *embodied and relational*. And the shared element of this complex system of your mind is energy and information flows.

When referring to the notion of consciousness, we use a form of "phenomenal consciousness"[29]. The (embodied) mind[30] itself is interpreted as containing consciousness, having "subjective" experiences and creating meaning of the information processing and the energy flowing through the embodied brain. The embodied brain is also a self-organizing or self-regulating system of this information and energy flows[31].

Bringing our understanding of the human brain together – constituted by two complementary forces, nature and nurture – we can visualize the brain in a slightly different perspective as modelled in Figure 1.

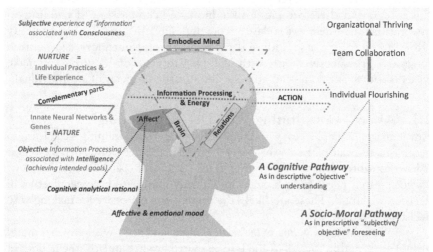

Figure 1: Cognitive reasoning and socio-moral flourishing + organizational thriving

B. Why Do I Refute a Materialistic View of a Conscious Mind?

Trying to understand the mind–brain problem, we assume two separated but intertwined spheres of realities: an objective reality of nature and the subjective experiences as a result of cultural nurturing. This innate natural ability to causal thinking or modelling and our subjective capability to experience phenomena within the constraints of contextual nurturing or culture are complementary properties of our brain power. Each of these two realities function through distinctively separate irreducible layers, each with their own protocols but somehow linked to each other. However, a detailed objective model of a measuring device cannot produce a subjective measurement[32]. A materialist view cannot explain the phenomenon of human consciousness that seems to escape the boundaries of its physical realm. Unfortunately, we are not much closer to really understanding the notion of consciousness itself, despite the enormous progress of neuroscience in the past century. Philosophers have tried to crack the dilemma of immaterial subjective mind versus objective material reality for centuries. However, most agree that cognition, consciousness and its related notion of (moral) conscience are distinctive notions which have enabled humans to become more intelligent, socio-ethical and collaborative in their respective organizations and communities.

In order to solve **the hard problem of consciousness**, science needs to discern the laws governing the mental function of "feeling"[33]. For us today, despite the breakthroughs of neuroscience, the source of consciousness, sentience and conscience remain just as surely (scientifically[34]) unfathomable as it has been for a while now …

I may not go that far as a Buddhist thesis that reality is consciousness only, or the ancient Vedas of Hindu philosophy in which the ultimate reality is held to be Brahman, a sort of universal consciousness. In the Western philosophical cultural tradition, the classical metaphysical theories of dualism evolved in which the idea is conjectured that both matter and mind are fundamental, but also "ontologically" different. Whatever inclination we may have in this well-trodden metaphysical landscape, there is no satisficing overall explanatory model yet. Nor do we adhere to the idea that reality is reduced to information and bits[35], though we agree that the brain processes "interprets" information that then becomes an experience. However, there seems to exist a fundamental epistemic gap between subjective and objective reality, that we don't seem to be able to resolve any time soon if we stick to the prevailing but outdated "Western" paradigm of presumed objective factuality only[36]. We probably need to "holistically balance" the prevailing cognitive realm with a more "subjective" socio-moral sphere.

C. Wise Decision-Making and Meditation Can Bring Order in Our Socio-Ethical Reality

Wise decision-making is transforming potential chaos and rigidity into an integrated consciousness[37] and awareness of a whole in which relations could reach a form of eco-systemic harmony. What we are really saying is that our conscious mind is *relational*; it constitutes the essence of what we are. Hence why the socio-moral "consciousness" and moral conscience – I prefer to talk about compassionate detached mindfulness – likely implies a deeper level of understanding than mere achieving cognitive competence.

Interestingly, from a neuroscientific viewpoint, researchers observe electric energy patterns during compassion practice – e.g. meditation. Moreover, a high degree of gamma waves are activated when engaging our minds to focus on care for and connection with others, which relates to the experience of *belonging*. It is as if the mind within the embodied brain is in a state of integration, being fully entangled into an interconnected reality of coupled forms of energy. Those gamma waves were found to be the highest with the non-referential sense of compassion, kindness and love[38].

Smart decisions are crucial, but wise decisions will likely make a more profound difference. It is this open and mindful awareness, a receptive state of presence, that offers us the possibility to embrace the reality of now, which is also a state of acceptance. In that sense, consciousness catalyzes choice and change[39].

We are inherently collaborative and social species: we are neuro-scientifically built to *connect*, to perceive actual interdependencies and seek to be embedded or entangled[40] in social-moral relations. Concretely, we can interpret that this connectivity with other stakeholders and giving meaning to what we do emerges in an integrative life. This entangled connectivity of life is considered at both at a personal level, but equally at an organizational level. We seek more communities in which we feel comfortable.

2.2. The Amorality of AI and a Leader's Moral Responsibility

Although computer networks and algorithms (machine learning) have been designed to make judgements about ethically appropriate sales strategies and tactics in an e-commerce setting, this AI does not have any "real" (conscious) sense of emotional or moral "sentience".

A. The Impossibility for AI to Establish Consciousness

Technology is neutral; it doesn't think itself nor is it aware of anything. Hence why I claim that AI is "**amoral**"[41] without agency, able to put humans at risk but without any conscious intention to do so: that varies from smart robots to autonomous cars. AI algorithms only describe and statistically use past human moral experiences to find (data) patterns. With "experience" through trial and error practice and feedback, the program learned that withholding information, misrepresenting what products can do, hiding costs from customers were all seen as unethical according to the current prevailing norms. The AI "learned" these ethical principles by being exposed to examples – big data – making judgements, and getting feedback about those judgements. Having learned, for example, that it is unethical to withhold information about limited battery life of a laptop computer. These trained algorithmic networks behave *as if* they are following a set of (moral) rules that they have been given by their designers. These "rules" are embodied in the connections among the elements of the network themselves. The algorithm learns to recognize patterns as people do, but do not "understand" morality, or sense the meaning behind our numerous socio-moral relations.

B. Can a Mechanical Brain Be Responsible?

With recent better neuroscientific understanding of the human brain (clarifying the function of how we learn and make decisions in a bio-physical and bio-phenomenal manner), should we abandon the notion of personal **moral responsibility**? No, we should not. In most instances, people remain free and therefore responsible for their actions. Brains are not responsible for human actions. *Our (ir)responsible choices cannot be reduced to a pure brain functioning.*

We must realize that even if the cause of an act – criminal or otherwise – is explainable in terms of brain function, this does not mean that the person who carries out the act is exculpable. According to the renowned neuroscientist Gazzaniga, brains have a high form of plasticity; they are automatic, rule-governed, determined devices, while humans are personally responsible agents, free to make their own decisions. Prescribing a theory of mind or entertaining the subtleties of the analysis of a free mind and free will is beyond the scope of this book. But I do argue that the prevalence of mechanistic descriptions of how the physical brain carries out behavior adds fuel to the general idea of determinism. However, philosophers like Daniel Dennett and scientists like Anil Seth have argued that the notion of *free will* can exist, even if one stipulates that the brain is as mechanical as clockwork. Responsibility may be a moral value we demand our fellow rule-following human beings.

The issue of *responsibility* is above all a *social* and *ethical* choice based on a presumed and "desired" *relation* (or not) with *the other* (as found in a moral community). This social construct exists in the rules of a society. Such a social construct – often politically evolving in a *social contract*[42] which can vary depending on the historical context – does not pre-exist in the neuronal structures of the brain. But "responsibility" would mean that we make deliberate choices that can change our concepts and models applied in the human brain.

We usually are able to make (free) choices. For instance, in any conflict situation, the individual does bear the responsibility for continuing (an assumedly unnecessary) conflict instead of deflating it. No particular conflict is predetermined by evolution. Conflicts persist due to social circumstances that wire the brains of the individuals that participate. Someone must take responsibility to change the circumstances and concepts[43]. That is what can be expected from a wise leader who is expected to take full responsibility for his/her action[44].

Some thoughts to take away:

- Emotions of sympathy and feelings of empathy constitute the possibility of facilitating moral thinking. Morality – a socio-ethical construct – is engrained in our (self)consciousness and conscience. Without the metaphorical "elephant" – the unconscious emotions – we likely won't be able to take moral and thus wise decisions. It's the metaphorical rational "rider" who selects the relevant data and makes the deliberate conscious choice.

- We fundamentally distinguish two different spheres of human reality: a natural objective sphere and a subjective nurtured realm. Humans can learn to become more intelligent by fine-tuning their cognitive learning abilities. But to make judgements about a desired future that doesn't exist yet within a socio-ethical realm, only humans can make that wise decision or not. We are always free to take our responsibility or not.

- Only humans who are conscious can make wise decisions, whereas AI (without the ability of self-consciousness or moral sentience) cannot take such decisions.

Chapter Seventeen

The Ethical Brain

"The effort to rewire our brains through mindfulness is the true moral act ... we bear the responsibility of choosing our habits before they choose us".

J.M. Schwartz & S. Begley (2002:325), *The Mind and the Brain*

"All spiritual experience is participatory".

Jorge Ferrer, 2001, *Revisioning Transpersonal Theory*

The human brain is constituted by three major functional "components": the rudimentary spinal cord that we share with reptiles and fishes, the ancient limbic brain that we share with mammals and finally, the more modern uniquely human cortex. Using scanning devices that measure the brain's activity, neuroscientists can glimpse how the different parts of our brain allow humans to coordinate and to compete when we make informed decisions. Thus, the more we understand how we make decisions, the better we likely will be able to manage them.

1. Can Responsibility Be Found in the Brain?

In the *Ultimatum game* – that tests our sense of fairness to make a decision to accept or reject an offer – researchers have shown that we often struggle between emotion and rationality when making that decision[1]. When being challenged with a perceived "inferior" offer – the disgusted anterior insula area (part of the animal limbic brain) was more active than the rational goal-oriented prefrontal cortex – the players rejected the offer. When the prefrontal cortex dominated, the players accepted the offer[2]. The relationship between reasons and emotions is complex[3], and much of the traffic between the primitive and modern parts of our brains is devolved to the conscious calculation of risks and rewards in our decisions we make, often boiling down to a choice between immediate and some future gratification (as part of RQ). The reward circuits depend on a mélange of chemicals or neurotransmitters to communicate (and compete).

Our prefrontal cortex is the steering wheel that directs rewards seeking towards specific goals, driven by the emotional intelligence fueled through our powerful limbic brain areas[4]. Our decisions are influenced by biases we are not aware of, which are driven unconsciously by emotions. As Sigmund Freud claimed, humans need to free themselves from the power of the unconsciousness[5]; business leaders need to become more aware of the way they make decisions[6]. Admittedly, like our reward-seeking circuitry, loss-avoiding circuits involving the amygdala and anterior insula have served us well in our evolutionary survival. What then could be the distinctive neuroscientific difference between making smart and making wise decisions? Let us briefly decipher this from a neuroscientific perspective.

1.1. The Individual Responsibility of Any Executive

If neuroscience can teach us to find out how their brains work, can boards then use these neuroscientific insights and rectify those potential aberrations? Likely not something we can expect in the immediate future. But executives are taught to methodically frame problems to question their and others' beliefs[7], consider alternatives, collect data and information, weigh the different options presented, and then decide being self-aware and open up to a broader mindset.

In other words, as one has learned in *meditation* and *mindfulness* practices, business leaders should *cultivate emotional self-awareness* and pay close attention to feelings of excitement (a heightened expression of reward seeking) and fear (an intense expression of loss-aversion) and ask where these feelings come from or what causes them[8]. Should we completely rely on a mechanistic approach of brain functioning to determine whether a leader is ethical or not – all assuming we understand the meaning of ethical leadership, or that there is universal definition on ethical leadership across organizational borders? No, not really.

A. Choosing the High Road or the Low Road?

Let us try to decipher the process of individual responsibility in the brain of a CEO, which is triggered in the interaction between the brains of people as we established in the previous chapter. Neuroscientists distinguish the high- from the low-road perspective. The ethical "**high road**" in our brain focuses on the others which also implies a strategic broader and longer view. The other "**low road**" in our brain emphasizes the subjective valuation of the (egocentric) self – not necessarily selfish – looking to "what is in for me?" or "how much is it worth?"[9]

Choosing either the low or high road is a moral deliberate choice, and not mechanically predetermined by the brain[10]. Interestingly though, the difference in this choice can be visually seen in the activation of the respective different areas of the brain involved. However, executives can train and practice to focus attention on (1) taking either an easier tactic perspective that activates the Reactive Self-referencing Centre in our brain or Low Road – comparable to Kahneman's automatic "intuitive" fast system 1 thinking[11], or (2) a more reflexive strategic view connecting to a function that neuroscientists label as the Deliberative Self-Referencing Centre that is associated with the dorsal (upper) medial prefrontal cortex or High Road, or Kahneman's analytical slow system 2 thinking. The latter is often also perceived as being more ethical because it deliberately reflects about others' perspectives and focuses on the interdependent *relations* with others. Such reflective perspective also takes literally and figuratively more energy and time.

B. Why Is the High Road Associated with Consciousness and Moral Reasoning?

The Low Road in the Affect Network is an expressway that bypasses brain areas that support conscious reasoning. Information travelling via the low road evokes a visceral response before the high road has time to finish processing the information. The Low Road – associated with the ventral medial prefrontal cortex (vmPFC) – is mostly concerned with subjective and self-centred valuation: What is in for me? How much is it worth? What might others want? The same Low Road is also functioning as the warning centre that generate feelings of fear, gut-level responses and the sense that something is worth pursuing or avoiding. Finally, another function of the Low Road is the habit centre – associated with the basal ganglia that is manifested in most animal evolution – that manages automatic thoughts and habits. However useful the Low Road functioning may be, it also can be deceptive or biased.

The high road, on the other hand, is the local road that runs through other brain regions to the Affect Network allowing to think rationally which always is slightly slower because of the bigger "distance" it travels. The mental activity of the High Road, however, also connects different brain regions. Similarly, as the counter of the Low Road, the centre function of the High Road is associated with the amygdala, the insula and orbital frontal cortex that channels feelings of urgency. And the dorsal (upper) medial prefrontal cortex (dmPFC) – above the vmPFC – is the deliberative self-referencing centre that considers what others are thinking and evaluate of what future actions might perform. In addition, the High Road is also the executive centre associated with the lateral prefrontal cortex that functions as the working memory, reflecting about meaningful aspirations. It is the centre of cognitive flexibility that sees a situation from different angles, and it is the same centre of the brain that self-regulate or inhibit particular behaviors[12].

2. Claiming the High Road in Our Brain That Results in Wise Decision-Making

The High Road requires a particular form of effort that results in a higher form of consciousness, being aware of the situation of others in a particular context. Philosophers may describe those ethical actions – resulting from conscious or deliberative responsible decisions – as *virtuous*, or *deontological*, or *utilitarian* good actions. Any top executive who sincerely thinks about the consequence of the decisions made will empathetically understand that the indirect impact, either positive or negative, cannot be omitted anymore. In exploring new business opportunities, investment decisions are made to produce innovative products and services that result in high(er) returns on invested capital – but without harming community or people. The value proposition creates value for the customer, and indirectly to the employee and suppliers.

2.1. Compassionate Behavior Is the Result of a Conscious Deliberative *Choice*

However, ignoring the potential negative consequences – for instance, strengthening child labor in producing cheap clothes or accessories, or the negatively ecological impact in the form of huge wastes of fast fashion today – are symptoms of the Low Road travelled, unconsciously or deliberate ignoring the impactful consequences of a board's decision to focus on profitability only. Only by taking into account the long-ignored externalities, a board will be able to take responsible decisions. It will require a deliberate effort to be really mindful of what one is doing. Call it the High Road of our brain's information processing or compassionate behavior.

It is definitely a way to take a wiser decision. Wise decisions[13] take into account a broader perspective; it may be less "profitable" short term, but will have (positive) strategic ramifications over a longer period – as visualized in Figure 1. The easy solution of maximizing profitability at the expense of others should be questioned. A more holistic – and thus broader perspective in terms of "space" and "time" – could be advised. And yes, that can be quite challenging, requiring virtue, courage, and thus "pushing" in the direction of the High Road.

In essence, neuroscience indicates that the Low Road is concerned with subjective ego-centred value, whereas the High Road is concerned with genuine worth. Hence why I argue that a "wise advocate", paraphrasing the compassionate version of a Devil's Advocate, is not just a metaphor but represent a real recurring mental process of our mind in a particular area in our brain. By managing our

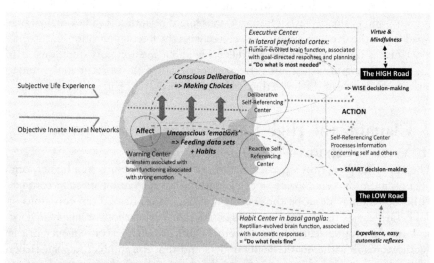

Figure 1: The high versus the low road in the brain

Source: my own personal amended interpretation of Schwartz, J., Thomson, J. & A. Kleiner (2016), "The Neuroscience of Strategic Leadership. Research shows how leaders can take the high road less traveled", *Strategy + Business*, December

attention to achieve more significant goals, we move our mind activity more frequently onto the High Road, and strengthen our internal wise advocate accordingly.

Although brain activity is not the same as mental experience, making up one's mind – a mental activity – is associated with a physical circuit in the brain[14]. The more frequently a pattern of mental activity occurs in the mind, the more entrenched the associated neural pathway becomes in the brain, and the easier it becomes to repeat or to follow that particular neural pathway – making it a habit and therefore automatic when practiced enough. Ethical thinking[15] can be "trained" by actively making those decisions over and over again – the High Road – and abstaining from instant gratification as indicated in the Low Road circuit – as seen in Figure 2. Such training may allow individual executives to tap into a collective intelligence. That collective intelligence is the expression of an aggregate of the values that prevail in a moral community and can be "felt" in the individual behavior of moral conscience.

2.2. Wise Decision-Making and Spiritual Wisdom Beyond Smart Decision-Making

Indeed, at first, the Low Road is more comfortable, because the High Road is less travelled or used. But as one learns to make the hard choices – which are often about "the other(s)", as in a socio-ethical and ecological sphere – it likely results in a more sustainable situation. Those more difficult choices (to broaden the perspective in "time" and "space") strengthen the related circuits in our brain, as physical muscles

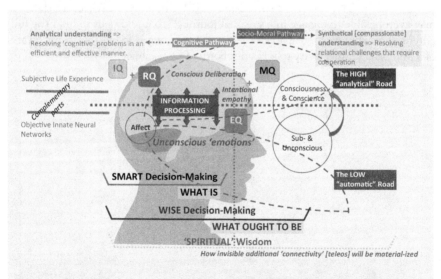

Figure 2: Elevating executive learning: A cognitive pathway + socio-moral pathway + spiritual awareness

strengthen with actual training. Such training can be in the form of mindfulness practices or meditation or yoga, or any practice to be "in the present"[16].

The Low Road is focusing on what is, trying to come to grip with a reality around us and taking advantage to fit in as much as possible. In business terminology, it means that business embraces an opportunity by creating value for its customers, and other stakeholders, but making sure that the biggest portion goes to the investor, even if that implies ecological and social-moral damage. Call it "collateral damage" of doing business in a competitive environment. That may be cognitively sound and smart. But from a socio-moral perspective, extremely self-oriented and likely not very sustainable over a longer period. If we assume that trusting relations are fundamental in any community, or group, and especially in highly performing teams, then a social-moral pathway comes to the fore. That is definitely true in the light of a surviving group of people that fits the current context in evolutionary terms. A socio-moral theory prescribes what we like to become, what ought to be.

Our brain seems to have embedded that ability as well, part of the evolution of our humankind to be fit to the changing contexts and to survive the onslaught of fierce competition. I would advise my strategy students to focus on being unique and create a niche to increase the overall pie, instead of emphasizing a (current) fixed pie which you try to slice up in the for you most advantageous manner. Better to broaden the pie by segmenting the customer base and to potentially create a win-win situation, rather than dwelling in an existing situation of fierce zero-sum competition. Moreover, in the short term we have higher chances to survive when we collaborate together against a potential intruder or adversary. However, that line between foe and friend may be more blurred than we usually assume in business[17]. The brain activities as expressed in the High Road provide us the tools to prepare us for such a journey. Ultimately, I conjecture that we may even be able to engage in a spiritual journey[18] that allows us to fulfil the full potential of what we are capable of, beyond "what ought to be", but being aware of a potential connectivity to a Higher Form of Conscience.

Some thoughts to take away:

- Neuroscientific research seems to suggest that there are **two distinctive areas** that are **activated** in our **brain** when it takes either a selfish-oriented decision – the *Low Road* – or a more other-oriented decision – the *High Road*. In that sense, morality can be "found" in the brain and its embodied mind.

- The **High Road** can be associated with **consciousness** and **moral reasoning**. The Low Road is a more "intuitive" fast and easy manner to pursue and focuses on preservation and "self-efficacy" and efficiency.

- Choosing the **High Road** can result in **wise decision-making**, expressed in a compassionate behavior.

Chapter Eighteen

Mindfulness and Wise Decision-Making

"Human beings are a species splendid in their array of moral equipment, tragic in their propensity to misuse it, and pathetic in their constitutional ignorance of the misuse".

Robert Wright, 1994, The Moral Animal

"What we are today comes from our thoughts of yesterday, and our present thoughts build our life of tomorrow: our life is the creation of our mind".

Buddha, *Dhammapada,* Verse 1, Mascaro, 1973

"Not everything worth expressing can or should be expressed scientifically".

Owen Flanagan (2002: 268), The Problem of the Soul

Overwhelming research indicates, for instance, that mindfulness can help to improve our decision-making, to reduce tension and stress that negatively affect our choices. If mindfulness is the awareness that arises through paying attention, on purpose, in the present moment, non-judgementally[1], then it can be assumed that this open and accepting attitude changes the person's relationship with the experience itself, by being more detached and slightly less reactive. **Mindfulness,** a characteristic of wise decision-makers, implies to take a step back, to reflect, to pay attention to the way others respond and follow-up, trying to become a compassionate detached observer. Such a "wise advocate" takes a broader ("space" and "time") perspective that could help to make better (i.e. more socio-ethical) decisions.

1. Mindfulness and Wise Decision-Making

It seems that we do not act completely randomly. We seem to be guided by moral values that guide our behavior. An internal (intentional) core – our self-consciousness – functions as a barometer of what is more right than wrong. We seem to appeal to this internal core, which influences the final course of our action. In addition, our brain is adapted to extreme efficiency. For that reason, the brain and its memory[2] distort incoming information to fit in with our current assumptions and beliefs about the world. In order to make sense and to understand, the brain seeks to confirm incoming information to our mental, culturally influenced models. Hence why memory is also very "subjective" to help us to find meaning. Consequently, morality, in spite of seeking common sense and normative norms accepted in a community, remains "subjective", as being part of a "prescriptive" realm.

1.1. A Structured Brain That Facilitates Wise Decision-Making

Do humans have an ethical brain that incorporates an innate human moral sense? There seem to be some universal impulses because they are so common. This commonality is related to a form of collective intelligence[3]. Those impulses scarcely need to be stated in the form of a rule. Murder and incest are such common moral "obligations". If the human brain is to make decisions, then assuming a universal moral compass inherent in humans is not too far sought[4]. However, this moral compass "device" needs to be contextualized historically and geographically.

A. Moral Feelings Motivating (Ethical) Behavior

Moreover, moral feelings – those that motivate behavior – are driven mostly by the brain stem and limbic axis, which regulate basic drives. The mirror neurons, the orbital frontal cortex, the medial structures of the amygdala and the superior temporal sulcus are believed to be responsible for conscious theory-of-mind processes. Abstract moral reasoning, as brain imaging is showing us, uses many brain systems. Neuroscientists have concluded that the neural processes responsible for searching patterns in events are housed in the left hemisphere of the brain. This part of the brain engages in the human tendency to find order in chaos, that tries to fit everything into a story and put it into context. It seems that the human brain is driven to hypothesize about the structure of the world even in the face of evidence that no pattern exists.

Interesting is the argument that there seem to be common subconscious mechanisms that are activated in the human brain – irrespective of sex, age and culture – in response to moral challenges. These moral judgements are initially perceived as intuitive. In other words, it is almost an automatic reaction to a situation – a brain-derived response. It looks like our brain generates an innate *"interpreter"* process[5] (presumably in the left hemisphere of our brain) to translate this situation into (ethical) choices[6] – which could explain this pro-social behavior we humans engage in. However, the respected neuroscientist Gazzaniga also argues that the interpreter in the human brain is only as good as the information it gets – quite similar as garbage in, garbage out of the *machina sapiens*.

B. Empathetic Feelings, Meditation and Mindfulness

Some neuroscientists interpret these mirror neutron networks – that "fire together" and therefore "wire together" – as the building blocks for morality. An intention of another person can be anticipated by the activation of the mirror neurons, allowing empathy[7] or to feel with as a possible outcome. It is this empathetic feeling that can be seen as the ground for collaboration with others as the glue for any form of collaboration and productive team work, and possibly for morality itself – akin to Adam Smith's moral insights that functions as the glue of our socio-economic relations and overall system[8]?

Equally interesting is, for instance, that meditation positively affects our functioning, and in particular also how we improve our creative innovation skills as in an Eureka moment. Meditation[9] – as one of the crucial hygiene factors to become wise decision-makers[10] – allows someone to engage in processes such as simulating another person's thoughts, envisioning another time and place, or allowing free-associating[11].

Becoming aware or be mindful is a mentalizing process that allows the decision-maker to rise to higher levels of responsibility and authority as one could expect from a wise leader. These leaders can eloquently articulate what other people are thinking and why it is important. But they also can be mindful of the consequences of the decision for many other persons within or outside the organization – a typical mental neural activity within centre of the Higher Road.

An aspiring wise leader needs to practice this focused attention and mindfulness that can be linked to stress reduction and increased emotional intelligence. Although some are more prone to use particular neural networks in our brain, we all can learn to develop an inner dialogue that makes us aware of beneficial opportunities in how we can improve our decisions. Assuming that leaders succeed to become more innovative, accountable and responsible, they likely could be labelled wise leaders who are not just smart and competent but also able to provide a bigger and more sustainable picture for their organizations.

1.2. Creating Trust, Following Purpose and the Human Brain

Wise leaders are able to create trust among their followers. Such trust is often rooted in organizations and their leaders who have created a clear communicated purpose[12]. Interestingly, neuroscience has indicated that experiments show that having a sense of higher purpose stimulates oxytocin production, as does trust – whereby trust and purpose mutually reinforce each other. The mechanism of extended oxytocin release also produces a feeling of happiness: people at high-trust organization report 74 percent less stress, 50 percent higher productivity, 76 percent more engaged, 29 percent more satisfied with their life, 13 percent fewer sick days and 40 percent less burnout compared to low-trust companies[13].

A. Born to Be Social

High-trust organizations are often the result of intentional activities by corporate leadership who took responsible decisions to deliberately create such type. Hence why we perceive "responsibility" as a *social process*. Social interaction in organizations and moral norms in society and organizations is a "social dance" where ethical choices are made and moral systems initiated. Individual (ir)responsible choices – a crucial notion in our wising up – arise out of social interaction and therefore individual minds will likely also be constrained by social processes.

We are born to be social: even children as young as 14 months old will act altruistically to help others. Oxford anthropologist Robin Dunbar found that the brain size[14] correlates with social group size in primates and apes: the bigger the neocortex, the larger the social group. The most advanced social group among the great apes, the chimpanzee, compromises about 55 individuals on average. The size of the human brain typically correlates with a group of about 150 individuals. And guess what: even in our social networking, it appears to be no different. Although we may have hundreds of "friends", we typically interact with a limited number of them; an inner circle of about 150 people on average. Similarly, research has shown that 150 to 200 people are the number of people that can be controlled without an organizational hierarchy[15]. In order to develop a level of cooperation that is necessary for humans to live in larger groups, humans had to become less aggressive and less competitive. Call it a self-domestication process. Over time, the gene pool was modified, which resulted in the selection of systems that controlled (even inhibited) emotional reactivity such as aggression. The social group constrained the behavior and eventually affected the human genome.

B. Mindfulness and Self-Awareness

Developing the brain's capacity to "broaden" one's perspective can be labelled as "**mentalizing**". Instead of focusing on the desires and problems around you as an individual, you also could consider people and environment around you more dispassionately, trying to figure out their point of view. Such mentalizing helps executives to develop a more nuanced, sophisticated understanding of other people and see a socio-ethical contact that often helps manage others more effectively. Such mentalizing executives – who are also **sentient, mindful** and **self-aware** – can easier articulate what other people are thinking, and why it is important. Stanford psychologist Carol Dweck has called it a *growth mindset* capable of infinite progress, versus a fixed mindset that limits its growth (of learning and human development)[16]. Good judgement depends on having the skill and the will (and thus persistent intention) to be open-minded, willing to learn and rethink our beliefs and assumptions[17]. How does this practice of mentalizing and mindfulness allow executives to become more responsible and train the *ethical brain* to make wiser decisions in the process?

2. Wise Decision-Making Emerges in the Interaction of Mindful Choices

Ethical choices and moral systems are interlocking sets of values, virtues, norms, institutions, practices and evolved psychological mechanisms that work together to suppress or regulate pure selfishness and make social life possible. Respected researchers like Michael Gazzaniga, Jonathan Haidt, Joshua Green, Marc Hauser and others conclude that moral responsibility reflects a rule that emerges out of one or more agents interacting in a social context, and the hope humans share that each person will follow certain rules. This is not entirely a new idea: Aristoteles already claimed in his Nicomachean Ethics that a virtuous person is fully alive: his consciousness always reflects "*synaisthanestai*" – which means that being virtuous and thus morality is hardly possible outside a community with other persons[18]. Even more pointedly, the basis for friendship, according to Aristotle, consists in "*synaisthanestai*" as in feeling together. The old French verb "*consentir*" can be translated into feeling sympathy or sharing of emotional passions[19]. Only by living and communicating their thoughts together, a person becomes aware and develops a conscience.

An "abnormal brain" of a narcissistic CEO, for example, does not mean that this CEO cannot or should not follow these (social) rules. Every normally functioning executive or employee is accountable and responsible for his or her own actions; whether you're more narcistic or authentic.

2.1. Moral Responsibility Is Not Found in the Brain

(Ethical) Responsibility arises out of each person's interaction with the social layer that person is embedded in. "Responsibility is not found in the brain[20]." Intriguingly, professor Gazzaniga – like to many neuroscientists – holds a rather deterministic view on the functioning of the body and its brain, but maintains that humans remain personally responsible for their actions. Responsibility evolves by participation in a social network, not in the brain *per se*. As what is true at the individual level, is also true for an organization that is embedded in a social network or moral community. "Responsibility is a property of social groups of many brains interacting[21]," not forgetting to play the (individual often ego-centric) interest in its (socio-moral) context, instead of treating it a solitary individual affair. Being personally responsible is a social relational rule of a group or community, not a mechanism of a single brain[22]. The participants of a human social network or a moral community have to be held accountable for their participative and collaborative actions. Only within such intertwined relations – as in a socio-moral community – these rules of responsibility function. Without those relations, nothing would work.

Neuroscience has shown us that when non-financial variables are considered, two different areas in the brain are activated. The first one is closely related to taking decisions that are focused on other-centredness which is the more difficult and slightly longer cognitive road to take. The second one emphasizes the self-centeredness and is more associated with our basic emotions to survive. The more responsible a choice is, the more our brains have taken into account different claims of competing habits and impulses. It also means that our "brain" was able to overcome and "cooperate" those often opposing notions.

Mindfulness meditation, just one type of many, teaches us to stay alert and be present in the moment, but also to observe sensations as they come and go, non-judgementally. One can use meditation to prioritize categorizations. Meditation has a potent effect on the brain structure and function – and it helps to distance from your (often selfish) self or ego. We only can hope that some practice may direct to wiser decisions that usually imply a more holistic perspective that goes beyond mere self-centeredness. The higher moral road in our brain then prevails over the lower self-centered road in the brain. Wise decision-making is not the result of miraculous decision-making by moral heroes. Rather, it is the result of continuous practice of mentalizing. Indeed, mindful awareness intends to make the "right" responsible decision.

2.2. Biases Undermine Responsibility, and Thus MQ

Biases – nonconscious drivers in decisions – easily sap into our way we make decisions. But they also can blind a person to new information or inhibit for considering valuable options when making an important decision[23]. In a hyper-connected world, poor decisions can have dramatic consequences, and avoiding unhelpful biases becomes a priority for business leaders. Neuroscience helps to identify those quite universal biases and why we act in certain ways. However, individual cognitive effort – even from wise leaders – needs to be complemented with certain procedures and governance mechanisms that institutionalize certain desired behavior. Critical self-awareness is a necessary first step; institutionalized procedures and governance mechanisms is the subsequent step to help leadership and their teams to act smarter and more responsibly (cf. Chapters 29 and 30).

CEOs and executives are more than brains. The brain may be our major biological-physical vehicle to think intelligently (or cognitively) and consciously (with a more enlightened conscience). It allows us to make decisions that attempt to create and share value despite the numerous pitfalls of (unconscious) biases and emotions. At the end, a mindful executive can broaden his/her perspective, and thus potentially expanding the brain's neural networks that may result in wiser decisions, something that AI is incapable of.

Some thoughts to take away:

- An internal core – our **self-consciousness** or **conscience** – functions as the **barometer of moral behavior**. In that sense, humans have an innate sense of determining morality – driven by our evolutionary older limbic emotions. It can be subsequently argued that we have inherited an ethical brain with an **innate "interpretator" process**.

- **Meditation** and practices to increase **mindfulness** have a *positive (hygiene) effect* on our abilty to *make wise decisions*. We all can learn to become more mindful and enhance our (self)awareness.

- We are *born to be social* and by extension **to be morally sensitive** to the concerns of other stakeholders. Wise decision-making emerges *in the social interaction* and exchange between people and organization and is usually the result of intentional mindful choices. Responsibility does not happen in the brain *per se*, but in the social interaction with others. As Aristotle argued: we only can become fully conscious and express moral conscience in the development of sharing passions or becoming virtuous in a community.

PART IV
Artificial Intelligence as the New Delphi Oracle in Uncertain Times?

Artificial intelligence stirs up quite some emotions today. There seems to be a lot at stake. We could ask whether AI will become the new Oracle of Delphi[1] – this time based on correlations instead of mythological prophetic powers of the Greek Goddess Pythia[2]? The short answer: in some particular cases in which the situation is comparatively stable, a probable "yes"; but in more ambiguous, complex, volatile times under high uncertainty, a sound "no".

Yes, artificial intelligence helps to shed light in the darkness of the future, especially where big data can help to find patterns that escape the sharp eye of the conscious human observer. But no, in case of volatility and change, AI is less accurate when using historical data input that focuses on a specific object where it confidently predicts an outcome. However, that outcome is most probably completely wrong because of a significantly changed context. Mundane AI algorithms will not be a good replacement of the "divine" Oracle of Delphi. Knowing that AI can only be useful in stable situations, smart robots cannot replace humans. But smart robots will indeed most likely replace repetitive tasks that don't require ambidextrous skillsets.

For a long time, intelligent behaviors was only attributed to humans. With the progress of computer science and IT networks, artificial intelligence (AI) is increasingly standing out as a transformational technology. In this digital age – *Industry 4.0 – human* and *artificial intelligence* will continue to compete for jobs. But, they equally will collaborate and complement each other. However, humans will stay in areas that require complex negotiations, future thinking, creativity and coming up with profoundly new theories and ideas. Machines cannot offer an adequate solution where human relationships are vital. Only smart and wise people are able to perform such complex tasks. Human's creativity and innovative ability will benefit from the speed and power of AI algorithms. AI, in collaboration with humans, *augment* the predictive power and accurateness of decisions while also *automating* repetitive tasks in organizations.

Despite the hype around AI, computers could provide useful insights, but inductive and or deductive formal logic applied in artificial intelligence does not provide the desired output in unstable uncertain situations. Relying too much on AI and data-driven analytics for getting answers may be the wrong move – especially in the socio-ethical sphere. Real new insights and innovation usually transcend mere inductive power of computer logic. Better to focus on asking the right questions – highlighting the importance of managerial judgement[3].

Today, not only business but also politics has grasped the importance of AI as a transformational technology. It now seems probable that a geopolitical battle for AI supremacy between the two superpowers USA and China is evolving and may become inevitable. The winner may allegedly determine how the future of us will look like. A more sensitive geopolitical leadership is needed to defuse unnecessary political tension when pushing forward for good AI applications.

Chapter Nineteen

Is Artificial Intelligence Replacing Human Jobs?

"Computers are useless. They can only give you answers".

Pablo Picasso

"The machine's danger to society is not from the machine itself but from what man makes of it".

Norbert Wiener

Digital tools and artificial intelligence in particular enable humans to make better decisions when properly applied. We may not fully understand or control our destiny, but at least we have a chance to bend it in the direction of our own values which we feel are worth living for. Despite a certain randomness imposing "fate" upon us, I argue that the future (in the socio-ethical sphere) is not just something that happens to us, but it is likely something that we can build.

The emerging impact of "machine learning" on our mental wellbeing and welfare is mixed and unclear at the moment. Our job "security" seems to be wavering in the sight of evasive-looking "smart computers and robots" who, we have been told, will take over most of our tasks. In other words, the traditional interpretation of value creation is fast losing ground.

The AI revolution that we can expect will be on scale of a real industrial revolution, hence why the notion of "*Industry 4.0*" was quipped. There will be beneficiaries but unfortunately also some losers in the automatization process. Those jobs that need social interaction won't disappear immediately, but those that are repetitive and can be optimized using data will be replaced by smart computers.

Even low-cost workers can't compete with the efficiency and scale of low-cost algorithms, unless they rethink the value that they can bring. Humans are vital resources, even in a highly automated back office, but their role has to shift from working cheaply, doing things that rule-based machines can't do – namely, handling exceptions to the rules. This also includes doing things quickly. However, jobs that require insight, such as knowing when to intervene (setting new credit limits for a big customer, for example), or those that require inspiration (galvanizing the organization to respond quickly, work in new ways or do something novel, for example), will need creative people and innovative managers[4]. Creativity and innovation of the *homo sapiens* trumps fast and effective *machina sapiens*. Humans excel at managing exceptions and understanding the context of a problem, especially when there is a scarcity of data, significant ambiguity or high level of volatility.

1. Should We Be Afraid of AI-Learning Machines? Will AI Replace Human Jobs?

The overhyped artificial intelligence expectations and the ongoing (ecological) degradation of our economy post a real existential challenge. But unfortunately, there is no integrated theory or model yet to replace these old "management practices". Obviously, the huge *challenge of digitization* of the internal business processes, combined with the external relentless *ecological degradation* and *deteriorating relations* with stakeholders, forces corporate leadership to think carefully about its future.

There still exists a yawning gap between digital hype of AI taking over the world and the strategic business reality of digitization. Today, digitization remains operationally focused. Only 29 percent of executives surveyed agree that their board fully understands the potential and scope of artificial intelligence[5].

Yet, digital leaders are fully and even painfully aware that the relationships between humans and AI are tainted by a number of myths and fears. Whether via automation by AI-driven robots, or by augmenting human capabilities via deep learning machines, getting it right will mean that we can optimize the synergies between humans and AI better. Figure 1 visualizes those two main benefits of automation and augmenting power from implementing AI algorithms.

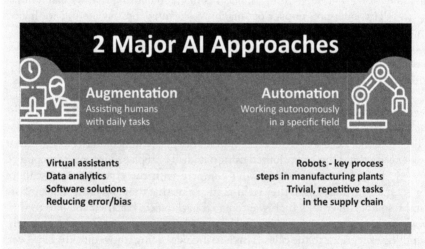

Figure 1: The use of AI in business: automation and augmentation

Source: Verhezen, P. & S. Gande (2018) "Can we trust smart computers?" Amrop Paper no 3

The most valuable AI applications don't displace humans, rather they accumulate more and better capital investments per worker, such as machine algorithms used by Amazon or Google to offer product recommendations and ads to users.

1.1. Automation Endangering Human Jobs?

Automation comes in different sorts and shapes. Good automation usually generates large productivity increases, creating a number of new jobs in its transformative process. Other less satisfactory automation, however, displaces workers with only meagre strategic or operational benefits.

A. Which Human Tasks Will Be Automated?

Automation that eliminates a human from a task does not necessarily eliminate them from a job. One cannot deny that computerization, robotization and digitization have been responsible for considerable losses in blue-collar jobs in the past two decades. The physical labor that is at risk of being replaced by computers include tellers, cashiers, garment factory workers, fruit harvesters, assembly line inspectors and labor. Receptionists, bartenders and caterers may survive in the medium term, but over a longer period, their jobs also will be at risk for being replaced by very smart machines. Presumably, elderly home caretakers, hair stylists and physical therapists will be able to keep their jobs that require a high level of dexterity within an unstructured environment. For the time being, also aerospace mechanics, taxi drivers, plumbers and house cleaners may sustain their job for a little while longer – as visualized in Figure 2.

However, lately, the white-collar jobs are also under siege. Accountants, many legal and medical professionals, insurance adjusters, financial analysts and stockbrokers, travel agents, personal tax preparer, basic translators and telemarketers all may disappear within years as result of ever more sophisticated machine-learning programs. Criminal defense attorneys, CEOs, psychiatrist, PR directors and social workers will likely keep their job because of the required social interaction and creativity or strategy-based cognitive work required. Scientists, medical researchers and artists likely will sustain their job as well in the medium term.

Automation also tends to disproportionally affect people in low-income occupations and exacerbate existing gender and ethnic or racial disparities. A 2019 McKinsey report projected that Black men in the USA would be easier displaced by automation at a significantly higher rate than White or Asian men, partially because they are overrepresented in occupations that could be automated, such as truck operators, food service workers and office clerks[6].

Despite all the pessimistic forecasts of what jobs would be technically possible to do with machines, the actual job losses or resulting unemployment levels will be likely much smaller. Some estimates forecast about 9 percent of jobs in the USA and Europe are at risk for being automated. PWC researchers find instead that 38 percent of jobs in the US *could* be at risk of automation by the early 2030s. The actual replacement is likely much lower, around 10 to 15 percent.

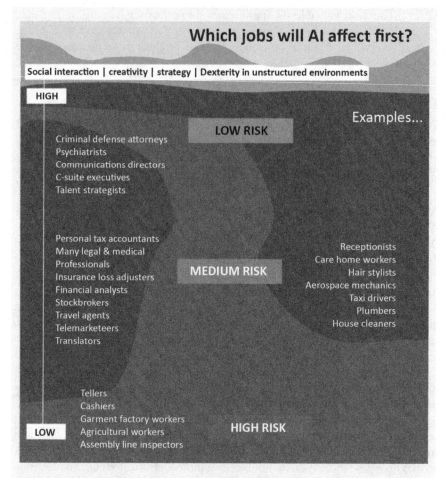

Figure 2: Tasks lost to AI, while new tasks will be gained

Source: Verhezen, P. & S. Gande (2018) "Can we trust smart computers?" Amrop Papers

B. Automation Negatively Affects Human Relations and Creativity

But automation by AI also affects human relations. Transformation through AI makes it possible for companies to squeeze out all inefficiencies and downtime. However, this automating process possibly and paradoxally may also kill creativity. Why? Creative power on the job often emerges during the time humans talk to each other, occasionally resulting in new ideas. By eliminating – for efficiency reasons – this "unnecessary" time-outs, or by fully automating this process, one undermines the potential crucial relations on the job that allowed innovative ideas to take place. If fact one creates fragility in the name of efficiency – as option trader and mathematician Nassim Taleb eloquently argues in his *The Antifragile*, or as the recent corona pandemic has shown us with the shortages as result of just-in-time-supply chain optimization. Moreover, technological change hasn't always resulted in better material conditions of blue and even white labor force. Inevitably, some laborers fall through the cracks.

Indeed, as this book argues, only emphasizing the positive effects of AI that leads to better cognitive outcomes and potentially better decision-making does not absolve organizations to ignore their responsibility vis-à-vis the socio-ethical consequences on stakeholders in implementing these technologies. We are especially concerned when efforts are made to replace "compassion" jobs such as nursing by AI.

Admittedly, in Japan, there is shortage of nurse personnel. These "carebots" are being developed in Japan to help older people remember to take their medicines, help them move and feed themselves and provide them with a minimal sense of companionship. These robots are not yet capable to relate to these elderly people. But, a subdiscipline in AI, "affective computing", uses AI to analyze speech and facial micro-expressions to determine people's emotional states. All promising stuff in AI, but can those smart machines really replace human interaction? We have serious doubts. And the reason is rather simple: what we do – as described in the job description – may not be as important than *how* we do certain tasks or jobs. A really caring person can hardly be replaced by an effective emotional-sniffing smart robot, because the latter fundamentally lacks the ability to understand socio-ethical and thus sensitive subtleties, including preparing someone for the ultimate act, to consciously prepare – beyond cognitive intellectual understanding – for passing on.

Yes, some tasks will be automated by smart robots, and those tasks will be "lost". Yes, routine jobs may be disappearing. But that is not necessarily a bad thing. Although 85 million "jobs" may disappear by 2030 as result of automation by artificial intelligence such as smart robots, we should not forget that about 97 million new jobs might be created. Jobs of the future with an emphasis on big data analytics and engineers, robotics engineers, virtual meta-world experts of all kind, process automation specialists, digital transformation specialists, database and network professionals, experts in cybersecurity and IoT, e-commerce experts and engineers. Indeed, the more the smart computers are trained to conduct high-repetitive tasks, the more roles focused on complex tasks with competitive salaries will arise in their place[7]. These jobs of tomorrow emphasize the abilities of human intelligence – easily outplaying smart computers – in the field of care economy, engineering, marketing, people and culture, product development, data and AI, business development and sales … And new types of roles will be created; jobs that did not exist before with young people being pioneers.

C. Rectifying Misaligned Objectives and Push for More Reasonable Automation

In the long run, the biggest effect of automation and robots driven by algorithms is likely to be on workers in developing nations that currently rely on low-cost labor for their competitive advantage. *Foxconn* is taking a lead in automating and replacing blue workers in China. The question then becomes whether these

Chinese factories in the global supply chain remain low cost and competitive. Probably, the low-cost advantage may disappear.

Let's have a look how *Amazon* automated work while putting its people at better use. Amazon's goal was never to completely eliminate tasks, but to reassign people to build new products – to do more creative things with the staff than doing the same with few people. Its "Hands Off the Wheel" has kept Amazon's competitors on their toes because Amazon, operating efficiently and nimbly, propelled it ahead of its competitors and has shown that automating in order to fire staff can mean missing big opportunities[8]. Amazon focuses where staff is the most productive, by being creative in R&D and developing new product, whereas AI robots do the repetitive boring work more speedy and accurately than people ever could. If Amazon can be any indication, businesses that reassign their human assets to more creative and development-oriented jobs, after automating their more manual work, will likely thrive.

Focusing on the idea of automation as replacing humans may not be the smartest or wisest decision. On the contrary, I argued to widen up the "space- and time-vector" to improve the way decisions are made. This automation and focus on AI robotization often stem from a misaligned fixation on near-term economic efficiency and desired financial outcomes. When a company only look at a traditional "lift and shift" equation that measures success according to the reflection in labor costs resulting from having fewer workers, these organizations may lose our reinventing jobs to optimize the work between humans and automation.

The reinvention of work in the gas and oil industry indicates how a more nuanced approach to optimize work automation may result in an array of benefits. For instance, *Willis Towers Watson* – an oil drilling company specialized in off-shore rigs – adopted an inventive strategy by refocusing their strategy to provide a more comprehensive extraction solution and to optimize their human talent, instead of fixating on eliminating human labor[9]. This work reinvention on the oil and gas rig into a platform of multiple oil field solutions and optimizing the core drilling performance produced a 45 percent increase in profitability and a significant reduction in performance variance between rigs. This substantial increase in overall rig profitability easily offsets the increased labor costs, while at the same time, the company could better compete for attracting and retaining top talent while also increasing the workforce diversity[10]. Those who fire their people after automating their tasks and thus having replaced them with smart robots may risk falling strategically behind. In difficult times, it is very tempting to cost-cut and let go your people, replacing them with machines who never complain, never ask a raise. However, that may not be the smartest let alone wisest decision you'll make.

1.2. How Important Is AI-Augmentation for Business?

Next to automation, AI will also augment our predictive power. Humans and AI are collaborating to improve five elements of business processes: (1) *Flexibility* as in robotics in auto-manufacturing, software to improve product design, software development estimates, (2) *Speed* as in fraud detection, aggregate patient data assisting in cancer treatment, video analytics that enhance public safety, (3) *Scale* as in automated applicant screening in recruitment, the use of bots in improving customer service, or monitoring systems, (4) *Decision-Making* as in diagnostic applications in equipment maintenance, real-time robo-advisors in financial services, disease prediction and (5) *Personalization* as in wearable AI devices that improves the guest experience, wearable sensors to improve healthcare and AI analytics in retail fashion. It seems that human–machine collaboration enables organizations to interact with employees and customers in new more effective ways.

A. How AI Generates Recommendations

These numerous AI applications allow executives and managers to *augment* their decision-making, either by making more accurate predictions, or by reducing possible biases, and by increasing the possibilities of new products and services in certain industries. AI could even assist management to improve ESG-related objectives.

However, augmentation of making decisions can also be much more subtle and subsequently more manipulative. Today's tech companies have access to huge amounts of computing power that allows them to have a pretty good idea about our preferences and our user behavior. Machines learning techniques can discover patterns in the enormous data sets, be it our online shopping behavior multiplied by millions of similar other consumers. Consequently, today, the world runs on recommendation engines powered by social media platforms such as Facebook, Twitter, YouTube, Netflix, Spotify and many others, all of which rely on algorithms to tell us which voices matter, which stories are important, and what deserves our attention. Even our culture, our interpersonal relationships now are bound up in the recommendations these systems make.

B. Augmenting Decision-Making Power

Nonetheless, AI will help us to augment our decision-making as visualized in Figure 3. Artificial intelligence algorithms will be to many white-collar workers what tractors were to farmhands: a tool that significantly increases the productivity of each worker and thus shrinking the total number of employees required. Algorithms already exist; those ambidextrous robots still need to be invented.

Artificial intelligence will reduce uncertainty, definitely within relatively stable situations such as health and finance, but likely in other domains as well. Data-driven analytics may potentially limit obvious biases, often committed in human decision-making – such as in overconfidence, sunk cost bias, confirmation bias. Although the bias in big data itself can be partially limited by (statistically) "averaging" away the extremes, AI cannot eliminate the socio-ethical bias in the data itself. Potentially reducing uncertainty and bias constitute my first variable in the "intelligence equation" associated with successful performance. Secondly, innovative processes may benefit from the predictive power of data analytics. Moreover, companies addressing ecological challenges may be able to use AI to

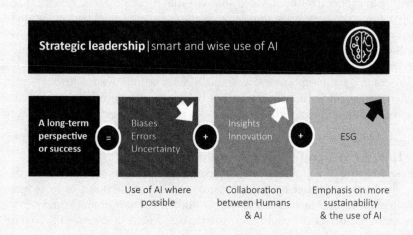

Figure 3: How AI can help augment improving management decisions

Source: Verhezen, P. & S. Gande (2018) "Why new technology will need a new type of leadership", Amrop Papers

optimize certain more sustainable solutions, or help with more accurate predictions of such complex calculations of what will happen with our environment under certain assumptions.

And let us not forget that some of the largest companies are now platform businesses. Large, scalable ecosystems such as Uber, Dixi, Airbnb, Netflix, Amazon, Alibaba, GoTo and Grab are connecting suppliers and customers through enormous networks. These provide access to exponentially more data and legacy organizations, enabling rapid experimentation and expansion. Ecosystems such as these are pulsating with life. They allow forward-thinking companies to draw on information and capabilities of a diverse pool of resources, to better explore existing markets and identify new ones. So new offers can quickly be developed.

2. The Future of Jobs: What Do Humans Best?

Artificial intelligence is becoming good at many "human" jobs – diagnosing disease, translating languages, providing customer service – and it is improving fast. Will this tendency of "automation" replace human workers throughout the economy? Not necessarily and not even likely. Cognitive systems such as AI and its derivative deep learning machines perform specific tasks – and admittedly through their feedback loops become more intelligent by the minute – but not really replacing entire jobs: automation and outsourcing will definitely change labor but "upgraded" more intelligent humans or executives will still be in charge.

2.1. Promised (Disruptive) Collaboration Between AI and Humans

For the near foreseeable future, AI may radically alter how work gets done, but AI will not replace human, rather complement and augment human capabilities. Human intelligence collaborating with artificial intelligence enables companies to interact with employees and customers in novel and often more effective ways. At *Mercedes-Benz*, for instance, cobot arms (i.e. smart context-aware robots) guided by human workers pick up and place heavy parts, becoming an extension of the worker's body[11]. In this sense, AI may instigate a need for new roles and talent that requires more than the implementation of AI technology. Indeed, human skills will benefit from collaborating with smart machines. Productivity growth can be achieved through digitization processes that encompass data analytics, as well as AI, robotics and automation.

Innovation and progress can be disruptive for some. What cannot be ignored is the need for wise leadership to acknowledge the enormous opportunities and prowess of computer learning abilities – enlightened by insights from evolving and progressing neuroscience. But should not even attempt to compete with computers, Jack Ma (Founder and Chairman of Alibaba) warned. We should focus on developing our creative and human collaborative skills. Managerial wisdom hopefully is able to address the enormous current challenges and to help create a better "conscious-" and purpose-driven future, something machines cannot do by themselves. A meaningful future requires that corporate leadership takes responsibility which is a dimension of life that only comes from social exchange requiring more than one brain. Responsibility – only a conscious mind can perform such a social-economic phenomenon – is *not* located *in* the brain, but it is a *social contract* between humans. Responsibility evolves in the interaction between people and their organization. In any job that requires the development of relations, humans should take the lead.

2.2. What Kind of Collaboration?

The future cognitive company will look very different from the current one. Data are just a bunch of numbers that without context are meaningless. Hence why smart leaders should facilitate innovation[12] and therefore will need to embrace collaboration between human and artificial intelligence, transforming the company's operations, markets and even industries and the workforce with new skills. Wise leaders infuse responsibility vis-à-vis other people and communities.

A. Speedy Robots Assisting Creative Humans

What are humans superb at and in which fields may AI do better? It is clear from Figure 4 that AI may be very good at taking over particular tasks that are repetitive – which often implies that a multitude of data are available. AI can easily scale and speed up those repetitive or familiar processes, doing it more efficiently and

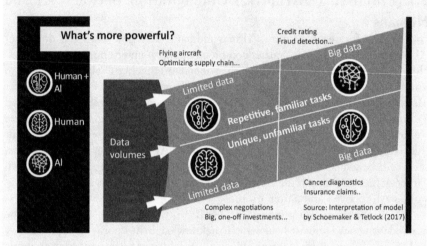

Figure 4: Superb abilities of humans versus machines

Source: Verhezen, P. & S. Gande (2018) "Why new technology will need a new type of leadership", Amrop Papers *that was an Interpretation of the model by Schoemaker & Tetlock (2017)*

effectively than any human. For instances, credit rating for individual mortgages are dependent on a few variables only, and non-emotional AI-bots are superior in predicting which customers are relatively risk-free to pay back the loan and who are likely not. Similarly, AI is superbly good at detecting unusual patterns in financial data transactions which could indicate some potential fraudulent behavior. Additionally, we all are familiar now with AI scanning your iris and impeccably allow you (or not) access to protected data or area.

However, the opposite is also true: in cases where data are hardly available because the situation is so unique and unfamiliar, or in situations that are highly ambiguous and volatile, the human flexibility and ambidexterity will always be superior to any AI machine. This is the case in intelligence briefings, complex negotiations and when boards need to make one-off decisions on particular investments that will significantly impact the organization in the future. And then there are situations where humans and AI collaborate very well, in augmenting and improving the decision-making process. The often-quoted example is healthcare diagnostics where AI "skillfully" detects patterns of possible diseases, allowing radiologists and physicians to make more precise decision on particular medication – as explained in Chapters 7 and 8.

We all are familiar with "automatic piloting" of airplanes once taken off. However, we still demand – for psychologically and thus subjectively safeguarding reasons – that the pilot is in charge with taking off and landing. There is also a data-related reason for that since the exact situation (an infinite combination of wind, sun and rain) at an airport is hardly the same and people still want an experienced pilot with ambidexterity to land them safely. So yes, the famous landing of US Airways flight 1549 – the "miracle on the Hudson" – is such an example of incredible human dexterity where the military-trained pilot, Mr. Sullenberg, safely landed this Boeing on the Hudson river near Manhattan. We presume that only an incredible versatile and highly experienced pilot who was very confident[13] can pull off such a fiat.

B. Which Jobs Are Safest?

Predicting which human jobs are the safest from the probable onslaught from smart robots, we need to look at what makes us unique and different from smart machines. Basically, one should avoid jobs that tend to be fundamentally routine and predicable in nature – because these will be the first ones to be automated by smart robots. Plainly said, avoid jobs that are rather boring.

Choose for a career trajectory that looks at the following jobs[14]:

1. Jobs that are genuinely **creative** in nature. Artificial intelligence will be used to amplify, rather than replace human creativity.
2. Jobs that put a premium on building **meaningful** and **complex relationships** with other people. Empathetic caring nurses and consultants with sophisticated advice to the clients will remain safe from automation.
3. Occupations that require significant **mobility, dexterity** and **problem-solving skills** in an *unpredictable environment*.

Some thoughts to take away:

- In its efforts to augment the decision power of people, and to automate certain human tasks, is it reasonable that people fear for their jobs? The picture is mixed: *repetitive ("boring") jobs will disappear*; the *most creative and dexterous jobs will remain*.

- Automation by AI may provide opportunities to **reengineer business processes** and become *more competitive by using AI–Human collaboration* – optimally to create better "experience" value to its customers and other stakeholders.

- The AI–Human collaboration focuses on **what AI does well** (*fast calculations with predictive power*) and **what humans do best** (*giving meaning, be creative and dexterous*).

Chapter Twenty

"Singularity":
Progressing Science or Science Fiction?

"Many of the dangers we face indeed arise from science and technology – but more fundamentally, because we have become powerful without becoming commensurately wise. The world-altering powers that technology has delivered into our hands now require a degree of consideration and foresight that has never before been asked of us".

Carl Sagan (1994: 316–317), *Pale Blue Dot: A Vision of the Human Future in Space*, NY, Random

"While the science-fiction discussions about AI and super intelligence are fun, they are a distraction. There's not been enough focus on the real problem, which is building planetary-scale machine learning-based systems that actually work, deliver value to humans, and do not amplify inequities".

Michael I. Jordan, Machine-learning pioneer

How smart is artificial intelligence, really? The arrival of neural networks made computer even more intelligent. Neural nets, whose basic design was directly inspired by our brain's architecture, have scored some spectacular successes in game playing, and patter recognition. Face recognition in *Apple*'s latest iPhone uses neural networks to uniquely identify its owner's face. Convolutional neural networks, a form of regression model used to predict, is used for face and voice recognition. This principal component analysis uses the data to classify people, rather than relying on our preconceptions. Their mathematical approaches underlie most of the algorithm used to classify behavior. Machine-learning, or self-learning or deep learning, attempts mimicking our human brain[1] – learning by itself – enabling the computer device and algorithm to learn "automatically" without us telling them what to do, or what patterns to pay attention to. Computers seem to become smarter by the day. Will AI outsmart us[2]? Does AI remain nothing but a "digital idiot servant"? Artificial intelligence is developing fast, and some researchers really foresee smart machines equalling the intelligence of humans within decades. I personally doubt this. No doubt that

General Artificial Intelligence is nothing but a dream at present. Let's decipher this philosophical but above all a technological conundrum of claiming to potentially realize "artificial general intelligence".

1. Artificial General Intelligence: From Science-Fiction to Science-Facts?

Whether AI will make humans subservient or obsolete, or whether AI will become a beneficial enhancement of our abilities to enrich our lives, the effective outcome of these different scenarios remains hard to predict at this point, but I remain modestly optimistic that the benefits outweigh this darker side.

1.1. Intelligent Computers? Not Really

Tesla uses neural networks in its car vision system to warn about potential collisions and is safer than most human drivers. *Google* has made great progress in the quality of its translations. The structure of these neural networks means that the algorithms are good at identifying objects in picture, putting together sounds to make up words and recognizing what to do in a game, but not yet beyond those tasks. When *IBM's DeepBlue* was able to defeat the world Chess champion Kasparov in 1997, it was considered a considerable step to the computer becoming "intelligent"[3]. However, while a computer could win a high-profile chess game, and 20 years later, *IBM's Watson* won from the champion in a more complicated Go game, which was an impressive engineering feat. This kind of "intelligence" focuses on a highly specialized problem-solving. IBM's Watson is never tired and remains emotionally unfazed, beating the Jeopardy! Champion by giving the question with the highest probability of being correct. David Ferrucci, IBM's team leader of the Watson project, commented provocatively, "can a submarine swim?" "Of course, a submarine swims, not like a fish, but better". Although Watson's intelligence is impressive, but it is very "narrow", and definitely not like a human.

It took AI less than three years to find solutions to beat the human champion in Go because human brains don't have the processing power to consider so many moves ahead. *DeepMind's* Alpha Zero – bought by Google – works by playing hundreds of millions of games itself, pruning mistakes that led to losses and elaborating on strategies that lead to wins[4]. However, on the other hand, let us not ignore the fact that it is still proving difficult to get a robot arm to pick up a cup of water. These "smart" machines are smart only in their specific domains. Present-day data engineering is still far away from matching the power and versatility of neurons and their synapses of our brain. Artificial intelligence cannot yet make their own plan – as a conscious being can.

Current AI machine-learning algorithms are, at their core, rather simple and straightforward. Some may even describe these computers as *dumb fast machines on steroids*, using "stupid little neurons" as basis. Those algorithms are based on *inductive logic* with all its known epistemological limitations. At this point, AI is doing descriptive statistics in a way that is not science and would be almost impossible to make into science. At their core, the current algorithms are "dead simple stupid"; they work by brute computing force correlating data – "if you use reinforcement learning of credit-assignment feedback, you can get those little pieces to approximate whatever arbitrary function one wants", according to MIT social physicist Sandy Pentland[5].

1.2. Misplaced Hype Around Superintelligent Machines

Despite the remarkable advances in computing, the hype about Artificial General Intelligence (AGI) – i.e. a general intelligence computer that will think like a human and possibly develop consciousness – smacks to science fiction, according to Venki Ramakrishnan, the 2009 Nobel Laureate for Chemistry, an idea that is supported by many other internationally reputable researchers. He is not the only sceptical scientist regarding AGI. We do not have sufficient neuroscientific knowledge yet to understand what exactly consciousness[6] is, or how we remember a phone number, or the reasons why we suddenly loose memory, how exactly neurons interact. Deep learning machines and AI cannot answer the "why" question yet. We have no idea which parts of the brain – if "the brain" at all – are responsible for human consciousness. It seems that we tend to underestimate the complexity and creativity of the human brain and how amazingly general it is, compared to any digital device we have developed so far.

Putting the "G" into "AI" is being announced a few times. True Artificial "General" Intelligence (AGI) would mean computers getting the grips with most of what human can do. Some thinkers like Kurzweil are optimistic about the timeframe and estimate that AGI is only a decade or two away. At that point, "singularity" is achieved.

A. The Notion of Singularity

Indeed, futurist and AI expert Ray Kurzweil coined this idea of "**singularity**"[7]. The notion of singularity is the point at which computers become as intelligent as humans – based on expected exponential improvements over the next 20 to 30 years. In his 2005 publication, he declared that computers will become as intelligent as humans by 2035 – based on the power of exponential improvements as we have seen over the past 30 years – the spirit was out of the Pandora box[8]. At singularity, then, computers will be at least as powerful as human intelligence.

Max Tegmark at MIT refers to the view among AI experts that AI systems will probably (more than 50 percent) reach overall human ability (AGI) by 2045, and very likely (with 90 percent probability) by 2075. From reaching human ability – singularity – it will move on to superintelligence in 2100 (75 percent)[9]. Again, there is no scientific proof for these inferences. It remains speculative and informed guesses at best. At such a point of singularity, computers will become as and likely more powerful than human intelligence. This would mean that humans may need to evolve apace. Humans therefore should logically progress to a stage of becoming "trans-human" – a cyber-human (electronically enhanced) or neuro-augmented (biological-genetically enhanced or bio-engineered) human.

A *homo deus* in other words. Such a superhuman may stay relevant in a world where we may compete with Artificial Generally Intelligent machines. To some, singularity is seen as an opportunity, whereas others emphasize the dangers. It is true that most discussions around AI are focused on a narrow weak interpretation of AI (as in machines controlled by humans) and limited attention on the potential dramatic transformations that AGI may bring.

B. The Possibility of Superintelligence or AGI?

Oxford philosopher Nick Bostrom coined the notion of "**superintelligence**" where supercomputers may see humankind as a potential threat[10] and react accordingly – possibly annihilating or enslaving humankind. Rather speculative I would think.

However, as MIT Prof Brynjolfsson expressed it, any future depends on the choices we make[11]. The near or further future is not different: "We can reap unprecedented bounty and freedom, or greater disaster than humanity has ever seen before". The future, however, will be an ever more demanding struggle against the limitations of our brain and intelligence. Singularity, on the other hand, is the point at which computers becomes as smart as us. With a rapidly changing ecology of intelligence and rapid evolution of machine-learning, we may need to consider the probability and advantages of an evolution towards cyborgs and superminds, above and beyond the *homo sapiens*.

I am much less optimistic – for philosophical reasons: humans are *intelligent* and *conscious*; AI may show a form of limited intelligence, but definitely lacks consciousness (as explained in previous chapters and potentially falsified once more in Chapter 20). In that context, I believe that realizing the notion of singularity (or superintelligence) is not impossible, but quite unlikely. Honestly, I am sympathetic to the argument of Larson who claims that singularity is not really plausible, and therefore improbable[12], mainly because AI lacks any form of consciousness – contrary to what researchers as Bostrom and Kurzweil believe.

According to these AI enthusiasts, the real risk with AGI is not malice but competence. Admittedly, a superintelligent machine should be extremely good at accomplishing its goals. As long as these goals are aligned with ours, no problem. In case they are not, big trouble can be expected. Hence why the importance of bringing the "ought" or ethical dimension in the equation without further due. Postponing ethical critical thinking on AI until after goal-aligned AGI is built would be irresponsible and potentially disastrous. A super-AI machine lacking a moral compass would be like an unguarded projectile on steroids – that could seriously harm us. Safety engineering and ethical thinking is more than needed. We would not send humans to the moon without all precautions that safety engineering could think of. Similarly, we should not build supercomputers without in-built safety mechanisms to guide actions in an appropriate manner.

Intelligence tests of AI should build on Alan Turing famous "*imitation game*" test, or an upgraded version of it. A computer passes the Turing test if it can fool a human, during a question and answer session, into believing that it is, in fact, a human being[13]. We are a long way from achieving this feat. Humans are very good and creative in connecting the dots of different frameworks, which can result in new innovative thinking or inventions. Our current algorithms are not yet very good at doing so.

Current machine learning systems operate almost exclusively in a statistical or even model-blind mode. In that sense, current systems remain rather opaque and focus on the what (if) question to execute a specific task. The Oxford quantum physicist, David Deutch – who conceptualized the notion of quantum computing – believes with the late London School of Economics philosopher Karl Popper that human-level intelligence and thinking *tout court* lie in the ability of creative criticism, interleaved with creative conjectures, allowing humans to learn one another's behaviors, including language and extracting meaning from one another's utterances[14]. The power of AI may be impressive, but the G of AGI still remains elusive. It is that aspect of general creativity which leads to innovation that is a truly human characteristic. Add the ability to ask relational, normative and thus ethical questions and to feel empathy and compassion (a form of emotional and moral intelligence), and humans still have some distinctive competitiveness over "intelligent" machines – at least in our perceived world that we currently "master".

Even the assumed but never corroborated idea that consciousness consists (from a neural point of view) in high-level information integration does not explain why it occurs, still less why it feels a certain way for that "integration" to take place, or how consciousness occurs physiologically. So far the idea of the brain as a computational biological organ is implicit in quite a number of theories. Unfortunately, this computer metaphor does not clarify to what extent or even whether the brain could be compared to a digital device. One could plausibly argue that brains operate in way that is both and neither merely binary[15] – using binary logic or arithmetic calculations – and analogue. However, if one rejects the brain as a computational model – as Nobel laureate Roger Penrose does – then even the most sophisticated computational model cannot simulate consciousness[16]. Penrose is using Kurt Gödel's impossibility theorem that makes the point that no set of rules for proving propositions in some formal system can ever be sufficient to establish all the true propositions of that assumption or system. Explaining consciousness and the development of a real (artificial) intelligence that is self-aware and is a computational device therefore does not seem to be really viable. We could even argue that interpreting the brain as a computational neural "device"[17] may fall in the same trap of ignoring the distinction between descriptive (trying to explain to objectively describe a reality) and prescriptive normative sphere (that can be associated with consciousness that is aware – related to an *intentional* character of consciousness and able to *feel* like to be in pain or be tranquil). The latter is the experience of qualia and is called "phenomenal consciousness"[18]. The brain as a computer metaphor is not persuasive anymore: the idea of mental and social relational phenomena – products of consciousness – as being reduced to billions of neural processes and events provokes real skepticism. Trying to reduce "meaning for a person" – as part of consciousness and its associated notion of conscience – to mere neurological processes is less than satisfactory. Ignoring the reality of normativity to be distinguished from a sphere of factual descriptions results in fallacies. A mind cannot be solely described in terms of brain activity alone since meaning – as a product of a conscious mind – is likely a relationship between that activity and the social and physical context external to it. The mind is not wholly explicable in terms of brain physiology, they are more than (physical biological) brains because it is the "product" of relational interactions between the brain and other brains and the physical environment. One cannot just put a "ghost in the machine"[19]. The mind assumes "agency" with moral capabilities to change. Even the most sophisticated and smart computers cannot simulate consciousness or a mind that is aware.

2. Big Data Do Not Speak for Themselves; Humans Interpret Data

Those intelligent machines are able to undermine trust at the factory level or in situations where employees work with or "for" algorithms, as the *Uber* drivers, for instance. This is a slightly more subtle argument about the efficiency dictatorship of the Uber algorithms with respect to its employees. Today, more than three million workers are using and working for the Uber algorithm to instruct drivers which passengers to pick up and which routes to take. Despite the enormous proven advantages for the customers of Uber, among Uber drivers, there has been three consistent complaints about working "for" the algorithm: (1) constant surveillance since the algorithm constantly watches and scrutinize the Uber drivers, (2) little transparency of the underlying logic of the complex "black box" of the Uber algorithm and (3) dehumanization as in Uber drivers feeling equally lonely, isolated and unable to socialize with colleagues[20]. They lack the opportunity to build personal relationships with a supervisor. All these three reasons behind those complaints to work for an algorithm are felt as "unfair" and make those Uber drivers disempowered and unable to be creative, reducing them to human "robots" executing the orders by the Uber app.

Even in the cognitive process of human vision, we do not just directly see an object, we always see it as because we always "interpret" the object from a particular contextual perspective. Even the shapes and colours detected by the successive neural stages of the process have meanings well beyond the basic content[21]. Despite the suggestion by researchers to mitigate such risks, by sharing information, inviting feedback, building in some human contact and building trust, it often remains quite PR-oriented. The reason is unfortunately significant: there is a darker side behind AI that cannot easily rectified. In a human world, we should definitely focus on what's important for us: *human relationships* – and not just emphasize efficiency that occasionally makes the system quite fragile[22].

What makes us different from AI is our unique personal history which gives us our notions of personal purpose and goals. There is no meaningful sense in which there is an abstract notion of purpose. It is likely embedded within our own history and traditions. Although there may not be a genuine demarcation line between intelligence and mere computation, we still see different kinds of intelligence beyond the brute force of rational computational logic thinking, including making sense and giving meaning on an experience, which is akin to a form of consciousness – to be clearly distinguished from intelligence. Finding a purposeful meaning to one's life – while humans collaborate with smart AI-robots – is the best scenario we should strive for. Such collaboration should be based on human values and human insights, requiring consciousness more than intelligence (MQ). Hence why wise beyond smart decision-making is not just a luxury but a necessity. Wisdom provides us with breadth and a broader and often longer-term framing.

At this point, deep learning machines are not achieving any form of general artificial intelligence but have become good at predicting based on big data. The key question is not whether AI will bring benefits, but how those benefits will be distributed and how we can limit the dark side of AI. Will some companies and countries have a huge competitive advantage? And will this advantage be translated in a vicious or rather virtuous stream of decisions? To answer that question, one will need a level of consciousness and sentience that AI cannot provide. Only humans have that level of awareness allowing to make those decisions. Let us not forget that all (moral) value arises, one way or another, from consciousness and human conscious social interaction. Indeed, what bestows moral status is consciousness[23].

Although some psychologists have accepted the view of the mind as a computer processing data into information and knowledge, the old Enlightenment link between intelligence and calculation seems to reemerge lately. However, cognition (in the mind) is more than computational calculations. The strong optimism in computer power has likely contributed to the idea morphed into the AI-beats-human argument, the vision of an artificial superintelligence that soon will match human intelligence in all respects. Let us be clear, computational power and big data (reflected in the power of AI algorithms) are of very limited use when ambiguity and high volatility reign.

Some thoughts to take away:

- Singularity – i.e. computers are as "intelligent" as humans – has been around a few times:
  - **Artificial General Intelligence** (AGI) with consciousness – and thus reach a status of singularity – is a **plausible** idea but **very improbable** *to realize*, because how do you bring "the ghost in the machine"? Nobody has an idea; it remains a philosophical problem that has not been resolved until today.
  - **AGI** is rather science fiction and **speculation** or thought experimental than it is hard scientific thinking.

- AI cannot answer the why behind associative patterns and correlations. **Artificial Intelligence doesn't understand causality** or modelling and is thus unable to be really "smart" in its broadest meaning, though the world may become "smarter" as result of a lot of automation without human involvement. AI can probably never shake off the "A", however smart it becomes, nor can the smartest AI computer simulate consciousness.

- **Big data cannot speak for themselves** – as some AI researchers claim. In a human world, human meaningful relations are as important as data efficiency. Ask the Uber drivers. Efficiency and meaning belong to two different spheres.

Chapter Twenty One

The Myth of Conscious Machines

"My chief proposition is simple: there are no moral phenomena, there is only a moral interpretation of these phenomena. This interpretation itself is of extra-moral origin".

Friedrich Nietzsche, *The Will of Power* (1901)

"No explanation purely in terms of brain processes will be such that we can deduce the existence of consciousness from it ... someone would know all the physical facts about the world and still not know about consciousness".

David Chalmers, philosopher, *Reality+* (2022)

"I imagine what it would be like if Galileo were to time travel to the present day. If a neuroscientist were to ask him, 'Do you think we'll able to explain consciousness in terms of physical science alone?', he'd take one look at them, hit them on the head with his telescope and say, 'Of course not. I designed physical science to deal with the quantitative, not the qualitative!'".

Philip Goff, philosopher, *Galileo's Error* (2019)

Understanding intelligence is easier than explaining consciousness, known as "the hard problem"[1]. Conceptually, as mentioned before, **intelligence** can be interpreted as a matter of objective behavior with particular desired outcomes or goals to be achieved. The notion of **consciousness**, however, is related to a conscious subject who is having a subjective experience. As philosopher Thomas Nagel famously said, consciousness is what is like to be a system, or as he puts it: how can we know what it's like to be a bat or to be another person?[2] Consciousness can be manifested even in a simple state, like feeling pain. And although some brain processes and consciousness seem to be correlated, there is so far no real theoretical model or compelling causal explanation for consciousness itself[3]. As a starter: till now, nobody has convincingly pinpointed down of why consciousness is like it is ...

1. Can AI Become Conscious, Ever?

Machines remain idiot savants for the time being. These smart robots are not really "intelligent", and definitely not conscious or sentient. Indeed, we should also "stop calling everything AI", machine-learning pioneer Michael I. Jordan claims, because artificial intelligence isn't actually intelligent at all. Those algorithms or smart robots are not conscious in any way that could indicate that they resemble to think or feel like humans.

1.1. Conscious Humans Versus Non-Conscious Robots

Quite a number of researchers consider the modern mind as the result of various neural pathways that were integrated in the brain, probably thanks to the evolution of a general-purpose language. Hence why computer and AI scientists see the enormous possibilities of machine learning that is based on a similar mathematic universal language based on neural networks.

A. *The Turing Machine*

The Turing machine, for instance, was seen as one of the first artificial intelligent machines that performed a mathematical computation equivalent to an algorithm (i.e. a series of logical steps that processed a statement and arrived at a conclusion). However, despite the strong arguments of AI researchers, **consciousness** is not yet been "coded" in an algorithm – and most probably never will. So far, human consciousness and its unique self-aware creative and subjective experiences and abilities are still very distinguishable from what artificial intelligence and machine learning are able to perform today.

Business leaders know that creativity of their business partners and subordinates goes way beyond computer power, especially because abstract symbolic reasoning cannot (yet) produce meaning on its own. Maybe neuromorphic computers[4] may succeed such a fiat in the distant future. However, reasonable and responsible leaders need to make decisions today.

Admittedly, we do not fully understand yet the neural architecture of the human brain that through evolution was trained to run well. But evolution goes slow, and we start to understand the constraints and limitations of our brain power. However, to achieve general intelligence, or human-level intelligence, learning machines need to ask normative questions that are guided by a kind of blueprint of reality, a model of society in which we aspire to live in. At this point, no learning machine is able yet to answer causal "*what if*" questions. A "smart machine" does not have any "purpose" *in se*, nor does it have any form of consciousness. Artificial intelligence only aims to achieve some specific objectives, not the design of those objectives or purpose.

Data science only facilitates the interpretation of data and connect them with, and to, reality. No matter how big the data get and how skillfully they are manipulated by data scientists, such machine learning and AI remain quite opaque in their learning. AI research has so far focused on systems that are better and much faster at making decisions, but not necessarily at making better decisions (which would require a normative or value-laden stance). Machine's decisions may be ineffably stupid in the eyes of humans if the objective or utility function of the machine is not appropriately aligned with our human aspirations and values. Unless, an artificial general intelligence would emerge that has its own conscious to make their own related goals, utilities and values to be followed – almost completely independent of ours. However, if a weak or strong AI is meant to serve humankind, then we need to think about AI and its purpose in relationship to how we see a fairer and more just world, which is an ethical question. Addressing such enormous challenges will require top-notch engineering, computer science, legislation and likely above all, moral and wise leadership to guide us through.

Any business should embrace technology where it could help to become more innovative in creating value propositions for customers. But we should not embrace technology for the sake of it. Basically, we strongly believe that the technological AI development should always be aligned to human objectives (as in intelligence) and values (as bestowed by consciousness).

B. Presumed "Sentient" Intelligent Robot Machines?

It will be an interesting but also challenging question how autonomous car will share the road with pedestrians, human-driven vehicles and other autonomous cars. How to combine the human values when they might be in conflict with the navigation system of autonomous cars? We need to think about this "robo-ethics" and make sure that these AI vehicles take our human nature into account, so that they are well coordinated and well aligned with our desires and values system to increase our quality of life.

When it comes to physical dexterity, there is a long road ahead. Robots are very good at performing sets of pre-programmed restricted motions, precision welding on assembly lines, for example, or calculating ideal distances in self-driving cars through a smart GPS system. But it's still proving challenging to build a robot that can perform multiple tasks fluidly and fast – tasks that come naturally to humans. Stacking shelves, tying shoelaces and pouring a drink, for instance. Despite what we might intuitively think, high-level reasoning requires very little computation, compared to lower-level sensorimotor skills. This paradox of AI-driven robotics progress is known as the *Moravec's paradox*[5].

Robots and their AI behind are great at performing dirty, dull, monotonous and dangerous jobs that no one else wants to do. In terms of risk management, artificial intelligence outmaneuvers human intelligence in the field of *known knowns* such as fraud detection, medical diagnosis and bail decisions. In contrast to machines, humans are sometimes extremely good at prediction with little data. Cognitive superiority of humans, however, is still very valid in the area of ideation, large frame pattern recognition and complex forms of communication. *Apple's Siri* and *Amazon's Alexa* can answer questions and control devices around your home, but can they appreciate a joke? Not (yet) at this time.

As executives, making decisions, one needs to focus on the consequences (which one is able to know) rather than the probability (which one likely does not know). This is the idea of making executive decisions under uncertainty. AI deep learning machines may be able to assist (smart) decision-makers to provide some clue in terms of conditional probabilities and reduce this fundamental uncertainty. Computers may be able to provide some lacking information (based on finding or revealing for humans hidden patterns) to improve decision-making. Unfortunately, with big data analytics, the fundamental uncertainty may seem to vanish under (statistical) averaging, but randomness may therefore not have completely disappeared, despite the feeling that we are better informed through big data. However, in practice, this may be good enough (*knowing how* or practical *technè* versus the more elusive *knowing that* or *epistemè*) to provide functioning AI-driven tools.

Narrow AI may have contributed to better and decentralized matching processes, but it has occasionally also created new forms of *information asymmetries* through centralized data in the hands of a few tech giants. Any information asymmetry draws the attention of a governance practitioner or researcher like myself. Hence why some forms of transparency of the (use of) data and information (by algorithms) is necessary, but likely difficult to achieve. So, the alternative is specific regulations wanting to ensure competitive markets that mandate the (progressive) sharing of data. The future of our economy lies in the clever exploitation of our informational surplus which we can achieve in our data-rich markets. AI and big data can enable better human coordination in the market which makes us more sustainable. The old adage of "trust but verify" is still valid. However, we cannot and should not ignore the darker side of artificial intelligence that could easily undermine the trust in this new technology. The future lies in a beneficial collaboration between human general intelligence with artificial specific intelligence and deep learning machines. The human advantage lies in the ability to ask (metaphysical why) questions and address ethical concerns. Only humans can feel empathy and mindful compassion towards other beings – which seem to constitute ourselves as social beings (based on emotions inherent to most higher-level mammals). In addition, our neocortex allows us to think rationally and make links between unexpected patterns that result in innovative and insightful improvements of tools.

However, we cannot fully lie our lives in the hands of soulless machines. Humans naturally strive to have a meaningful life, meaning for a particular person or business or family. Meaning in itself is much harder to characterise, definitely from a mental view. We believe that this is mainly due to the mind not solely describable in terms of brain activity alone, but as a relationship between that neurological activity and the social and physical environment external to it. As mentioned in Chapter 20, the mind is a product of relational interactions. As social animals, people are nodes in complex analogue networks from which their mental lives and meaning is derived[6]. These mental lives and their characteristics are not really found in the science of the brain, but likely more in the qualities of wisdom, philosophy, literature and history. The characteristics of descriptive science and neuroscience are somehow distinctive from normative moral mental lives with an envisioned meaning. In that sense, a mind is a brain plugged into two kinds of environment, a social moral sphere and a physical reality. Does the mind imply – as John Locke referred to when talking about personal identity, focusing upon the notion of an identifiable person – a self-aware agent bearing moral responsibilities and legal rights? Philosophically, it can be presumed selfhood and personhood – a soul? – are based on the experience of phenomenologically "being in the world" that is a key dimension of a conscious mental life. Such "contextual" experiences of the "self" are associated with personal intentionality, individual perception and proprioception (the awareness of oneself, one's physicality, one's mind). Neuroscientist Michael Gazzaniga interprets this self as an "interpreter"[7], whereas Antonio Damasio considers the feeling of being a self as the source of consciousness[8]. The notion of the self plays a role in the theory of both reputable neuroscientists. Moreover, deficits of consciousness in brain-damaged patients are always accompanied by deficits in emotional capabilities[9].

Let us get back to the moral status in the trolley problem. I established – like to many other ethicists – that the ethical theory of utilitarianism, and even deontology, was not very "useful" in deciding to kill (or not) the least amount of people in the interest of keeping a bigger number of people alive. One of the reasons it is so difficult to address the Trolley Paradox is the fact that one talks about sentient beings who can feel anxiety, fear and pain. Philosopher Peter Singer argues that *sentience* is what matter for giving moral status, which he used to expand that status to animals because they can feel[10].

However, there is likely more to consciousness than the experience of suffering or happiness. If we agree that in English the notion of sentience is roughly equivalent to the notion of consciousness, then the fundamental question to bestow values and thus moral status is: are they conscious? And so far, only humans and some mammals could be seen as conscious. Not artificial intelligence. Thus deciding about killing someone for the sake of more people in the revised trolley problem is extremely hard and almost impossible to make a "rational" choice. How then allowing AI-driven autonomous cars – non sentient or conscious machines – to take that decision for us? We strongly oppose this on the basis of moral values.

That *the myth of conscious machines* continue to emerge among smart people surprises us a little. A Google engineer who claims that AI seems to be sentient is attributable to non-definition or not being accurate in the use of notions[11]. Even more surprising is the discussion around the abilities of Machine Translation. Hence why I write this rather critical chapter about AI capabilities to explain why this is utter nonsense.

It is well known that a statistical machine learning approach constitutes the basis of computer translation today, often in combination with a rule-based approach. Semantics – the meaning of words – and pragmatics – what a person intends to do – hardly play a role in those automated translation programs. These are basically extremely powerful prediction systems that suggest the next word or phrase to your sentence as you type them. The AI system "sees" the words that users enter on their smartphones and predicts those that might follow based on those millions of articles, without a clue what these phrases actually mean. The result can be quite impressive, without any understanding of what these words are about.

Ray Kurzweil, who was hired by Google to bring language understanding into their algorithms, argued that statistical analysis is the epitome of understanding: "if understanding language and other phenomena through statistical analysis does not count as true understanding, then humans have no understanding either"[12]. I will debunk this statement as not accurate. It is a confusing statement that mixes outcome and process. It is one of those expressions coming out of the head of an extremely confident computer engineer without any subtlety or feeling for nuances. It likely also confirms that hybris and overconfidence are antipodes of wise thinking. Even if a program translates a sentence correctly, based on the proper use of statistics, that does not mean that it comprehends its content. Nor that it would be sentient or conscious.

These automated fast translation algorithms will function well for well-defined topics that feature logical structures with limited or no ambiguity, such as news and describing business facts. It may also work well for military purposes where massive amount of intercepted foreign language communication needs to be "filtered" in terms of relevance. Unlike a competent Chinese translator, an automated translation algorithm can work around the clock and does not need security checks and clearance or breaks ... But one still need human translators who understand what the texts actually means – to read in "between the lines" and understand the subtle omissions in a sentence.

1.2. Causal Determination in Nature Versus Indeterministic Human Causation

When comparing artificial intelligence and human intelligence, we also need to have a rough idea about the conception of being human: what does it mean to be a person, and not to be a robot? In essence, today, we claim that human beings are possessed of consciousness, with capacities for self-knowledge and the ability to live rationally, morally and meaningfully. No scientific formula has yet made an adequate effort to explain this definition of human being. Science currently limits itself to what is, to the material side of the matter. Cognitive neuroscientists come the closest in trying. Neuroscience describes the anatomy of the human brain and how it functions in concert with the rest of the body and the environment.

A. Human Consciousness and Conscience and Causal (Ethical) Thinking

Consciousness, cognition, volition and even conscience are perfectly natural capacities of fully embodied creatures, neuroscientists claim, engaged in complex interaction with the natural and social environments. It is widely agreed that humans can be pictured as rational social animals with a mind, morals and able to give meaning to life. All foreign to the smartest computer. Only humans really create something entirely new – whereby "creation" is understood as a synthesis of "being in trance" affected by "emotions", awareness of the self or consciousness, and logic rationality[13]. Probably, creation (of art or making progress in science) could be interpreted and seen as something "mysterious" since not all elements can be fully explained in descriptive or objective scientific terms. Somehow, creativity escapes the (explanatory) process of control by humans, be it in business or in a scientific process. Ask any accomplished human or expert in art, science or even business: creative beauty definitely escapes our scientific logic.

The assumption in neuroscience of the ubiquity of causation – or the principle of causal determination – does not warrant to discover strict (biochemical) causal laws of complete generality, fully explaining the functioning of our mind–brain interactions. The Cartesian dualistic picture is not yet fully resolved; the dichotomy between the inquiring of all greatest religions and the philosophical attempts versus the objective scientific methods, studying natural facts, still remains[14]. We postulate that human behavior (with a possible free will) cannot be fully explained in deterministic terms – presumably according to certain laws as does physics, although even contemporary quantum physics employs (objective ontological) indeterminacy[15]. Any credible account of a free agency will claim some of form of self-control, self-expression, individuality, reasons for sensitivity, rational deliberation, moral accountability, the capacity to do otherwise and some unpredictability.

If some events taking place are random – it means that they cannot be predicted in advance – the idea of complete predictability vanishes. Let's have a look how to treat a number of different scenarios of uncertainty. There is a lot of uncertainty in the world that can't be resolved or reduced to something knowable. A lot remains unknowable. Like when you roll a die, you don't know what number is going to come up until it happens in a random manner. A lot of that type of aleatory uncertainty is determining outcomes in the real world. Algorithms can't explain that. Randomness will remain to incite knowable unknowns or even unknown unknowns.

B. A Possible Typology to Address Uncertainty and Randomness

In the case of **known unknowns** (rare events such as predicting earthquakes), humans make better decisions than machines. When it comes to **unknown knowns**, prediction machines appear to provide a very precise answer that could be very wrong.

Scenario building can help imagining possibilities and actions to consider – as attempted to visualize in Figure 1. In case of **unknown unknowns**, the black swans, Nassim Taleb convincingly argues that we cannot predict truly new events from the past data. Most likely both humans and machines fail. Nonetheless, in some exceptional instances, AI is able to uncover unknown unknowns as *GNS Healthcare* applies machine-learning AI to find overlooked relationships among data in patients' health records, enabling GNS to uncover a new drug interaction hidden in unstructured patient notes. Again, randomness and "fate" can make us "lucky" winners.

Figure 1: How to address uncertainty, randomness and the unknowns?

Source: Verhezen & Gande (2018), Collaboration between Humans and Artificial Intelligence, Amrop Paper No 6

Whatever the case, machine learning and prediction enhance human decision-making by providing an initial prediction that humans can combine with their own assessments. Checking the creditworthiness of loan applicants, for example. It can provide second opinion, or facilitate monitoring of patients in hospitals, for instance. Thanks to reliable diagnosis from an image, patients can avoid an invasive biopsy. Advances in AI and machine learning mean less need to "satisficing" and more "*if-s*" and more "*then-s*". In other words, AI allows for more complexity with less risk, transforming decision-making by expanding options. Machine-learning techniques are increasingly good at predicting missing information, including identification and recognition of items in images. This kind of pattern recognition to predict disease is what radiologists do. Prediction machines may be able to reduce that kind of uncertainty, but they won't always eliminate it.

Intelligent machines driven by AI use their specialized intelligence to solve parts of the problem; humans use their general intelligence to do the rest. In that sense, smart AI machines can help engage and coordinate large groups of people to become more effective and efficient. Most likely, AI will shift human resources management towards the relational and away from the transactional. More crucially, the arrival of AI will lead to an increasing importance of human judgement (supported by AI predictions). Prediction by AI and judgement by humans are complements: *as the use of prediction increases, the value of judgement (or decision) rises*. The (human) judgement may use (AI) predictions to make a smarter decision. Thinking about a network – as our brain functions – is analogous to thinking about entire ecosystems. How would you guide ecosystems to grow in a good direction? Artificial intelligence use methods to "learn" from large quantities of data where computers can recognize patterns and derive conclusions from these "insights". Big data is of no use if one does not turn it into knowledge that can be applied in concrete cases. However, human learning and curiosity does not occur in isolation, but is always embedded in traditions, theoretical paradigms and accumulated wisdom of the past generations. Until scientists will have solved the basic paradox of learning, the best AI will be unable to compete with a four- or five-year old.

2. The Hard Problem Solved by a Potential Conscious Virtual Reality?

Allow me to briefly recapitulate the definition of consciousness. The notion of consciousness is experience, and by extension, having consciousness is intimately tied up with being an ethical subject[16]. Similarly, the movement to recognize a moral status of animals is built on the recognition that they are conscious. One can argue to expand the space of accountability and responsibility to all those who have a conscious stake in the organization. One could hypothetically expand the sphere of moral concern to include other creatures and life – our ecological environment.

2.1. The Hard Problem and Conscious Machines: A Non-sensical Myth?

Consciousness is the source of meaning and value, but we don't know why it exists. What makes us conscious beings, rather than zombies? This is the "hard problem" of consciousness. However, it is even harder than initially thought, because there is no firm agreement among philosophers of mind or even neuroscientists about what is consciousness.

A. What Is Consciousness, Actually ...?

The closest we come to defining consciousness starts with Thomas Nagel's thought experiment "What is it like to be a bat?"[17] You cannot really know *what it is like* to be a bat. But if hypothetically, if there is *something it is like* to be a bat, then that is what we mean by "being conscious". But we have no concrete idea what is exactly consciousness. Is it "being (self)aware of"? Only when we are mindful is there this sense of an experiencing self. Maybe consciousness refers to a story we tell ourselves the way our minds work. But that story is likely wrong[18]. Moreover, there is no constant self[19]: we are not the same person as that little baby that was given your name all those years ago ... And limiting consciousness to just sensory consciousness may be too restrictive to capture the rich variety of experiences that we have, to "what it's like-ness of an experience" as in (cognitive) phenomenology[20]. Maybe we should widen the scope of sensory experiences to the full scope of experiences.

Today, most mental states are associated with computer programs that carry information. However, that information is only "present" in the computer programs in relation to conscious programmers who created them. While you may be playing a game with computer Deep Blue, you may consciously think about your next chess move, while Deep Blue "soullessly" calculates its next move in terms of probabilities. In other words, everything Deep Blue does is understood in terms of mathematical algorithms without any reference to the slightest form of consciousness. Deep Blue – and for that matter any machine learning device – does not "consciously" understands the game (of chess) at all; it is able to simulate behavior and even emotions that could correspond to conscious human mental activity. And no, we are not machines in any sense, whatever convinced AI experts may try to tell you[21].

The presumably "objective" scientific approach has either denied the existence of a soul, or *une force vitale*[22] – a vital energy – or has tried to "determine" it as a neuroscientific process, whatever this means. However, plausibly ignoring the existence of an *élan vital* or soul – for such vital energy has never been detected in a scientific laboratory – is an absurd inference itself. It's similar to the idea of radical behaviorists of the 1950s who denied the existence of subjective mental states because they could not measure it "scientifically". Neuroscience has an overwhelming tendency to embody a strong form of reductionism to the effect that all mental phenomena are ultimately interpreted in (and reduced to) neurological (biological neural deterministic) terms.

Buddhist studies and phenomenology, however, have shown us how absurd this idea is, which nowadays has been acknowledged by quite a number of neuroscientists. Scientists though are still far from really understanding the neural correlates of subjective mental states and their behavioral expressions, to grasp the meaning and ramifications of such a "life force", or *force vitale*[23]. Despite the efforts of a number of prominent neuroscientists to directly link consciousness to the brain's neural network functioning, there is no consensus about the nature of consciousness. Consciousness itself – like "the vital force" that is "fully aware"[24] – can be detected only in terms of one's own subjective experience[25].

B. ... It Remains a Very Hard Problem

It remains a kind of mystery. Hence why it has been labelled *a hard problem*, by the Australian philosopher David Chalmers. This hard problem of consciousness is defined as the problem of how subjective experience arises from objective events inside the brain. Or in essence, the hard problem is the difficulty to explain consciousness. The easier problems of consciousness involve explaining behaviors and capacities: what we say, what we do and how we respond objectively to stimuli. The easy problems are the "objective" problems, and the hard problem is the "subjective" problem (of personal experience)[26]. This is essentially a modern version of the ancient body–mind problem, the Cartesian dualist problem. The question is whether we can escape from this duality. Evolution alone does not seem to be able to explain consciousness. We likely need to bring something more into the equation.

C. ... Though Consciousness Likely Entails Responsibility

I am inclined to think that without consciousness there would be no ethical value and no well-being. In other words, consciousness gives a living creature moral status; if a being isn't conscious, it probably has no moral status[27]. Consciousness alone seems to give moral agency. Consciousness then can allow moral thinking, and development of conscience. Consciousness and conscience lead to responsibility. Without consciousness, there is no responsibility.

Now, I admit that I don't believe the argument to the effect that silicon could replace carbon in order to develop conscious artificial intelligence. But I also admit that as long as the hard problem is not resolved, we should not exclude *apriori* the implausible and improbable but nonetheless (theoretical) possibility of consciousness in AI. However, at this point, evolutionary biology and neuroscience are not much closer to illuminate us about the "hard problem". Solving it will require some better understanding about the empirical facts around consciousness and a better theoretical model. Second, resolving the hard problem will entail to our ability to give meaning and purpose to life, and to our ability to have values and moral prescriptions.

2.2. Can a Virtual Reality Be as Real and (Potentially) as Conscious as a Physical Reality?

I concur the thesis that only living creatures are able to become conscious of themselves and others, and thus, an artefact like a smart robot does not have that ability. The main reason is that consciousness assumes a causal understanding of phenomena, quite different from association-found-patterns that imply correlations, but not necessarily causal relations.

A. A Conscious Simulated Brain?

However, David Chalmers provocatively suggests that in theory a simulated brain can be conscious – by gradually downloading the brain into a simulated brain (or computer) so that there is a strong case for consciousness being retained at the end of the process. And if a system with a biological brain is conscious, a system with a perfect simulation of that brain will be conscious, too, with the same sort of conscious experiences[28]. In his new intriguing book *Reality+*, an ode to a metaverse reality, Chalmers puts forward the argument that support the prospects for artificial consciousness more generally, whether or not the artificial system involves a simulated brain. It remains very speculative and not-yet-applicable.

B. An Extended (Virtual) Mind

The notion of an extended mind could be the result of an augmented reality technology that eventually becomes part of our "exocortex" – the brain outside our brain. Or an "extended mind" – inspired by Richard Dawkins's 1982 book *The Extended Phenotype* – which argues that evolved biological organism can extend into the environment. Chalmers argues that the same is true of the mind. One way to materialize this "notion of an extended mind" is using upcoming AI technology that could enable humans to augment reality and be better informed about reality. For instance, augmented reality glasses promise to be seamless, making information instantly available whenever we need it. In that sense, those augmented reality glasses could become part of our extended mind. The mind is not so much extended as embedded in an environmental web that greatly enlarges its capacities. The digital memory in his glasses is part of his knowledge, so it's part of his mind. Our knowledge of something doesn't go away when we stop thinking about it. Most of our knowledge is outside our consciousness, but it's still part of our minds.

The extended-mind hypothesis may also reconfigure how we think of morality and the self. If someone steals my smartphone, we typically think of this as theft. But if extended-mind hypothesis is right, it's more akin to assault. If the phone is part of me, then interfering with the phone is interfering with my person. According to David Chalmers, at some point, our social and legal norms may need to change to acknowledge the extension of our minds.

C. Living a Good Life in a Virtual Reality?

The discussion of augmented reality touches upon the philosophical but also practical question of what is value, and what makes for a good life? What makes one life better than another? Questions like this are part of value theory, the philosophical study of values. Values include moral values (right versus wrong) and aesthetic values (beauty versus ugliness). Here, we question what makes something better or worse for oneself? Which option would be best for me? Moral values and personal values are related. Many of us believe that, morally speaking, one should avoid harming other people whenever possible. That was my tenure in the first part when arguing for expanding our space and the time factor in order to minimize harm to a number of stakeholders and all those potentially affected. It seems that there may exist a connection between whether an act is right and the personal value it produces in others. Therefore, leading a personally good life requires also leading a morally good life[29].

The next question then follows whether we humans can lead a good life in a virtual reality. We don't need to answer yet whether our virtual avatar itself carries a moral status. The philosopher Robert Nozick states that in virtual reality, we won't have autonomy or free will in the experience of the machine because the machine programs every action in advance. David Chalmers seems to disagree: if we can have free will in ordinary physical reality, then we can equally have free will in virtual reality. We typically carry our virtual actions by performing physical actions. If the physical actions are freely chosen, the virtual actions are freely chosen, too. Many will point to relationships as something that would be missing in virtual reality. Where relationships are concerned, the range of options in virtual reality is roughly analogous to the range of options available when you move to another country.

D. What Is the Likely Source of Ethical Values?

What is the source of value, in particular ethical value? Again, it can be agreed that almost all value arises, one way or another, from consciousness. Conscious states (say, happiness and pleasure) are valuable. What is valued by conscious creatures (say, knowledge and freedom) is valuable. And relations among conscious creatures (say, communication and friendship) are valuable. One might say that conscious has value, and relations to consciousness add value.

That brings us then to the most difficult question: can artificial intelligence create real consciousness? Physicalists assume that fundamental particulars are not conscious, but some conjecture that an object can generate consciousness if its internal dynamics instantiates the right complexity. Some – and I don't belong to that group – argue that a sophisticated AI can ignite real consciousness. Physics Professor Hoffman, for instance, thinks that AI can open new portals into consciousness, just as microscopes and telescopes open new vistas within our interface[30]. I still opt for distinguishing both consciousness and (experience in) mind from an objective scientifically studied reality – admittedly not transcending (yet) this Cartesian duality.

Some thoughts to take away:

- As long as AI didn't pass the Turing test, AI won't be able to match human intelligence.

- Since AI does not have self-awareness or consciousness, it does not have moral agency. Therefore, it cannot make wise decisions.
  - Only humans with moral agency can make wise decisions.
  - And human creativity – sustained by an enhanced form of consciousness – somehow escapes the strict rational logic of induction and deduction.

- Whether a virtual reality is as "real" (with consciousness and sentience and thus potentially moral status) as the current physical reality in which we live remains speculative. With the upcoming metaverse, people may start to think of two separated though intertwined worlds that could influence each other. My position remains that these are two completely different realms, though I admit that one can morally act within a metaverse, and it is also clear that bullying – an (un)ethical act – can have dramatic consequences in our real physical world (as in suicidal behavior).

Chapter Twenty Two

What Sensible Collaboration Between Humans and AI Machines?

"I consider that the leaders of the present trend from industrialist research to controlled industrial research are dominated or at least seriously touched by a distrust of the individual which often amounts to a distrust in the human".

MIT computer scientist **Robert Wiener, 1950,** *Invention*

"We have taken science for a realist painting, imagining that it is made an exact copy of the world. The sciences do something else entirely – paintings too, for that matter. Through successive stages they link us to an aligned, transformed, constructed world".

Bruno Latour, 1999, *Pandora's Hope*

Human collaboration with smart AI-driven robots or machines should be based on "values alignment" in the interest of our community. Some have labelled it *"responsible artificial intelligence"*. We should not enable rogue robots to jeopardize the civil functioning of our community. And although some may argue that these values are contingent, that does not make them irrelevant or unimportant for our communities.

We as humanity do not always agree on common values, and even part of these values we have agreed on may change over time – *panthei rei*, everything changes – they still constitute our civilization (or community) *hic et nunc*.

This also implies that we should be wary of the destructive effects of social media algorithms, which entraps quite a number of users in ideological echo chambers that can nudge them towards extreme beliefs. In addition, smart machines or AI could not offer an adequate substitute for human connection and personal development. However, Here, I like to emphasize the net positive effects of collaboration between humans and smart computers, improving our personal life and adding value to the way organizations operate.

1. Optimizing Collaboration Between Humans and Smart Machines

Are humans and AI machines a match in heaven, combining the strengths of both, creativity and speed? Who would complain that some repetitive and boring tasks in administration or manufacturing would be taken over by fast machines or robots. Automation will allow the workers to free time for more interesting and fulfilling jobs.

Currently, there exists an inverse correlation between a machine's success in learning one thing and its success in learning some other thing. A computer system that learns to play championship-level GO won't also learn to help care for handicapped elderly humans at a nursing home. Despite the lack of flexibility, AI could definitely help businesses to become more efficient and more competitive by automation, augmentation of decision power and enormously improve the prediction power.

1.1. A Smart Robot Beating Champion Kasparov: Now What?

With ever more powerful AI machines, and in an economy where data are changing how companies create value and compete, experts predict that using AI at a large scale will add USD 15 trillion to the global economy by 2030. Quite a number of experts argue that much of today's AI is designed to work with humans, rather than substituting for them. AI should therefore be considered an opportunity, rather than a competitive threat[1]. Chess champion Kasparov, after being beaten by IBM's Deep Blue Computer in 1997, realized that human chess players and computers would be better off if they worked together. These human–computer teams, he figured out, would be "overwhelming" when pitted against computers alone.

A. How to Turn a Threatening Robot into an Ally of Humans

We cannot deny that AI may still pose a threat that requires our attention, despite the fact that our worst fears about AI may not play out. Intelligent artificial systems are already displacing humans in manufacturing, service delivery, recruitment and the financial industry. That begs the question whether humans and machines are really competing with each other for the same jobs? History has shown that since the Industrial Revolution, people have outsourced their labor to machines. While that started with rote, repetitive physical tasks such as weaving, today machines have evolved. Machines seem to be ready to replicate the work of our minds now, not just our physical bodies. This rather pessimistic vision of the future of work where AI is replacing many tasks from humans has taken a rather zero-sum configuration.

Humans, however, are often "emotional" or culturally (in)sensitive; they are also intuitive and creative; they can imagine, anticipate, feel and judge changing situations which allows them to shift from short-term to long-term concerns; all abilities that make humans quite effective. Taking full advantage of the complementary abilities of Artificial Intelligence and Human Intelligence will make the organization more efficient and accurate, but at the same time also more creative and proactive. It is also clear that the human capabilities are much more expansive. And humans do not require a steady flow of externally provided data to work, as in the case of artificial intelligence.

Competing seems to assume that both humans and smart computers have the same qualities and abilities. In reality, of course, they don't. AI-based machines are speedy and fast, more accurate and consistently rational within a relatively stable situation. Figure 1 visualizes and summarizes again the reasons why business should take advantage of AI.

B. Jobs Replaced by Smart Robots: Today and in the Future?

The evidence that current AI automation is inducing high unemployment seems to be scant. A "new view" of robots seems to emerge: research reveals that there exists a strong positive association between investment in automation and increase in employment. The opposite of the gloomy automation-induced unemployment

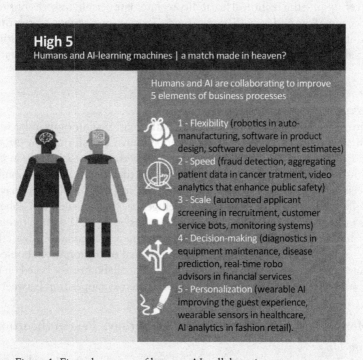

Figure 1: Five advantages of human–AI collaboration

Source: Verhezen, P. & S. Gande (2017), "AI and Wise Decision-Making", Amrop papers

scenario. Admittedly, the correlation between more automation through ever-cheaper robots and more jobs may be rather skewed towards the top tech companies[2]. These tech companies that swiftly adopt to a changing environment may move in new related areas, requiring more automation but also highly qualified human skills. Hence the reason of the positive correlation between automation and increases in highly skilled and dexterous lower paid employment. Firms on a hiring spree also happen to buy robots when their prices fall[3].

Almost half of the American workforce is engaged in one way or another in predictable activities, which therefore could be potentially automated by smart machines[4]. Predictable intellectual work is at risk of automation because AI software could take over those repetitive and/or predictable tasks. Manual labor, however, will require an expensive dexterous robot, and replacement is plausible but unlikely.

In the future, therefore, it is estimated that almost one-fifth of the US workplaces involves performing physical activities or operating machinery in a predictable environment in which workers carry out specific actions in well-known settings where changes are relatively easy to anticipate. In such a context, some estimations indicate that AI could automate 75 percent of those activities, and about 60 percent in manufacturing activities, given technological considerations[5]. However, despite the technical feasibility to automate certain tasks, a considerable variance is masked underneath. For instance, for customer-service representatives, the feasibility to automate is well below 30 percent, whereas in manufacturing, the potential of automation is much higher. The potential varies among companies as well.

1.2. Augmented Intelligence

Humans should cooperate or collaborate with smart machines in order to reach a form of *augmented intelligence*[6]. In open systems, transformation efforts are continuously at work, and effective management of that process requires individual "authentic" intelligence, complementary with artificial intelligence. Combining this personal human authentic intelligence with artificial intelligence may resort to a collaborative form of augmented intelligence. Clearly, such a collaboration stands in stark contrast with zero-sum predictions or what AI will do to our jobs, our society and organizations. But it will require a real collaborative effort in service of humans though, aligned with individual or organizational objectives. The sum of both human and machines – a proper collaboration – based on proper processes well governed is definitely superior to fierce competition between both.

A. More AI May Result in More Accuracy, Personalization and Scaling Up

The collaboration between humans and AI is based on the fact that humans could add flexibility to the rigidness of AI robots; the enormous *speed* by AI is crucial for business applications; the *accuracy* of AI seeing patterns in diagnostic application has enormous advantages; AI can easily *scale up* by having access to digitized data that are applicable anytime anywhere; AI is *more refined in diagnostics* than humans today; and finally, AI apps allow the *personalization* of products and services or product-as-a-service (*servitization*). Artificial intelligence has shown to be a valuable productivity tool; it brings tangible benefits in processing speed, accuracy, consistency and personalization.

It is clear that the dooms-scenario of smart robots replacing human labor does not have to be that negative. It is equally true to ask why would humans be needed when machines can do a better job. Instead of replacing humans with AI – the subject of Chapter 19 – there are better ways to onboard AI, using AI to help people. *Accenture,* for instance, has found that when companies make it clear that they are using AI to help people rather than to replace, they significantly outperform companies that don't set that objective along the usual objectives, notably speed, accuracy, scalability and effectiveness of decision-making. The idea behind the transparent communication of the objectives to use AI is meant to facilitate trust. Without that trust, technology may not realize the potential benefits it promises.

B. Embedding AI in Human-Aligned Objectives

Embedding AI in a human-aligned objective – instead of threatening human employees – allows to improve productivity and better decision-making processes, instead of undermining the trust at the job floor (by introducing new threatening innovative technology).

In the first stage, successful companies have learned to teach employees of the usefulness of AI, or get them acquainted with the new technology. *Amazon* and *Netflix* help customers to filter thousands of products and the one most relevant to them. These recommendations engines function like *assistants*[7].

A second phase focuses on setting up an AI system that provides real-time feedback. If a user is about to make a choice that is inconsistent with his or her choice history, an AI system providing accuracy – as *a monitor* – can flag this discrepancy. This is especially helpful during high-volume decision-making, when human employees may be tired or distracted. In a remarkable study concerning legal decisions, it was found that judges grant political asylum more frequently before lunch than after, that they give lighter prison sentences if their football team won the previous day than if it lost, and that they will go easier on a defendant on the latter's birthday[8] – all instances where unconsciously emotions resulted in certain bias that affected the final decisions.

C. Architectural Design to Turn AI in Teammates

Companies, boards and their members – as anybody making decisions that affect many people – should set up an architectural design[9] and particular rules about designing and interacting with AI to ensure some minimal consistency in implementing norms and "best" practices. Secondly, some rules in the AI system might specify the level of predictive accuracy required to show a nudge in a particular more sensible and reasonable decision, or to offer reasons to convince the decision-maker. It might provide the conditions under which an employee or manager is advised to follow the AI's instructions or recommendations or refer it to a superior who could overrule if necessary.

In a subsequent third phase, AI could function as *a coach* by analyzing and improving key decisions and actions[10]. Such coaching requires that expectations about outcomes are documented, and compared at a later stage after receiving feedback. The more the individual is involved in the process, the less this person will feel threatened by the AI algorithm. In fact, the feedback provided by the system could help the individual to better understand the decision patterns and practices. With the necessary feedback put back into the AI system, continuously capturing new data helps the system to become more refined and to provide upgraded insights.

Those insights coming from an AI system could evolve in a fourth phase of *extended mind* which posits that cognitive processing and associated mental acts such as belief and intention are not necessarily limited to our human biological brain. External tools and instruments may start to play a role in cognitive processing as in a coupled system where AI is seen as *a teammate*. Those situations where AI has become a teammate as in a virtual-physical collaborative world is still in its infancy. But this phase could be quite promising, especially because in such a close collaborative working relationship between the individual and the AI system, trust and understanding may increase.

Ultimately, AI may become part of our individual and organizational organism, as an extended tool that significantly may improve our abilities. The ultimate examples are, for instance, "virtual glasses" that allow us to immediately virtually see data on phenomena we observe and becoming our extended mind, allowing us to make speedier and more accurate decisions.

By engaging people in the collaboration with AI system, making those systems more transparent, it will facilitate trust to be gained. In all those stages, humans determine the ground rules; the objectives of this partnership are completely aligned to the individual or organizational objectives. Such partnership between AI and humans is possible when the organization is able to redefine itself as an emerging intelligent enterprise.

D. Responsible Artificial Intelligence Partnering with Humans

AI technology – used in a responsible manner – should be used to augment human skills, not aim to replace them. It should allow to reinvent operating models in full collaboration, or even a partnership. At BMW's plant in South Carolina, robots are installing door-sealing gaskets, a difficult, time-intensive and tiring job for workers. Having AI robots helping the manufacturing process speeds up the line by more than 25 percent time saving, improves quality and gives workers more time to do higher-value work[11]. BMW workers regard these robots as helpful helpers. Some organizations take the opportunity to redefine jobs and rethink the organizational design.

For instance, at *Stitch Fix*, an online clothing subscription service company, about 3,400 human stylists work with the AI recommendation engine to make personalized suggestions for customers. The AI algorithms give stylists the speed they need to be productive, and stylists provide the additional personal judgement needed for accurate recommendations and fewer returns[12]. These stylists hugely contribute to the value created by the human personal touch that any customer esteems when paying a premium price.

Workers will trust and cooperate with AI systems only when they don't feel threatened and see the immediate collaborative value in the potential partnership. Boards and executives should make employees their own partners in building an "intelligent enterprise", by unleashing the human talent that machines can't match and that are essential for growth[13]. It is those human unique talents of *creativity, empathy, communicational skills, adaptability* and *problem-solving* that will become even more valuable in this human–AI collaboration, and result in smarter decision-making. The obvious example of the pharma company *Moderna* that was able to rapidly develop a now widely-used Covid-19 vaccine with the help of AI proves the point[14].

2. Business Competing in the Age of Artificial Intelligence

The benefits of AI go well beyond improved individual efficiency. AI can improve organizational effectiveness and strengthen teams and enterprise cultures; it can generate cultural as well as financial benefits for organizations. Building a culture that supports innovation with AI has an effect on competitiveness: those organizations that use AI to explore new business opportunities – and not just improve existing processes – were 2.7 times more likely to agree that their company captures opportunities from adjacent industries[15].

2.1. Keep Up with the Quants and Learn to Work with Artificial Intelligence

Executives and managers must learn to partner effectively with their "quants" to make better strategic and tactical decisions – which will require a good understanding of the process of making data-driven decisions, and be able to frame and communicate those decisions with the teams in an organization[16]. Maybe installing a culture of inquiry and finding the truth rather than advocacy may garner evident support from these teams. Indeed, it is believed that managers who know their quants, understand their calculative and probabilistic thinking, their analytic processes, and be able to effectively interpret, translate and communicate these findings will likely make smarter decisions. In today's data-driven world, you will need to combine the science of analysis (explicit knowledge) with the art of intuition (tacit knowledge).

Pernod Ricard, the world's second-largest wine and spirit seller, uses AI technology and data diagnostics to optimize salespeople's store visits, augmenting – rather than replacing – their own knowledge. In interviews and the subsequent feedback by experts, this data feedback was fed into the AI system, bolstering the tool's credibility among the experts and improved the effectiveness of the tool itself. Interestingly, the chief digital officer at Pernod Ricard mentioned that not only unexpected insights were provided, but also that "the system is recommending listing only relevant products matching the store profile, for instance, because of the category of consumers living around the store and other factors. That gives salespersons more confidence, more clarity, and higher morale.[17]"

Analytics officers at *CBS*, for instance, describe the broadcast network's efforts to critically assess long-standing organizational assumptions behind the KPIs of allegedly well-performing TV shows. Interestingly, the AI analysis affirmed the utility of some of those KPIs but also added new ones. In other words, AI led to changes in their KPIs, in directly revealing new performance indicators that enabled stronger performance. And realigning behaviors to achieve newly defined objectives often has also a direct positive effect on the organizational culture.

At *Humana*, a healthcare company in the USA, uses AI in their call centres to improve how employees handle interactions with customers. This "emotional AI" listens to conversations of the pharmacists at the call centre and picks up emotional signals in the conversation; it then suggests what the pharmacist could do to provide better experience for the customer calling. Using this emotional AI system actually ended up with more calls with satisfied customers and consequently a higher Net Promoter Score. By training users and engaging advocates, *Humana* carefully avoided culture rejection that this new AI tool could have sparked. Pharmacists learned something about themselves and how to execute better their role in handling customers more effectively[18].

Some companies are deploying AI and robotics in ways that disrupt traditional techniques such as mentoring and on-the-job-learning. In the industry where I am currently active, executive education and training – an industry where companies globally spent up to USD 360 billion on formal training in 2018 – we could question the effectiveness of all those courses. We should not forget that tacit knowledge can only be learned on the job, by doing and mastering a certain task. Explicit knowledge may be easier conveyed in a classroom, but still, practice counts. Some companies use a new form of learning on the job in collaboration with smart machines; an informal process that is called "shadow learning"[19]. Professor Bean's work on shadow learning is focused in the field of robotic surgery where junior surgeons will need to learn with those robots to practice to master both old and new methods while conducting life surgeries. In other words, these AI robots – intelligent machines – are part of the solution in those advanced medical training programs[20]. Organizations often unwittingly choose productivity over considered human involvement, and subsequently on-the-job training – enhancing tacit knowledge – is getting harder. By applying "shadow learning", experts, apprentices and intelligent machines work together and learn together. AI is part of the solution. The future of work?

Unilever's hiring process has been transformed by artificial intelligence. The many job applicants submit a video-recorded interview via computer or smartphone, answering questions designed for a specific position. The results are analyzed by *HireVue*, an AI application that scores words, body language and tone. The most promising candidates are invited to the Unilever offices for a final interview round, conducted by human experts who make the final hiring decision. Thanks to this human–machine collaboration, job applications have doubled compared to a year ago: the average time to hire plunged from four months to four weeks, the time spent by recruiters plummeted by 75 percent, and to date, a more diverse group applied and was hired.

In healthcare, powerful machine learning and simulation software can churn out hypotheses, straight from the data to find correlations (or relations) in medical health records. They do this through "Reverse engineering and forward simulation". Bad drug combination are a major therapeutic problem and have no standard solution. GNS Healthcare, a precision medicine company, assessed anonymized data from more than 200,000 patients, and its machine-learning platform churned through approximately 45 quadrillion hypotheses. After only three months, the final results emerged: the combination of drugs most likely to interact in troublesome ways. A medical team took more than two years to solve the same task. This is the beginning to approach data pattern recognition in novel and very useful ways. In a similar vein, AI is enabling the era of personalized medicine based on genetic testing: powerful machines analyze and manage huge combination of possible treatments for a given patient. These individualized treatments could solve a critical problem in clinical trials: 80 percent typically fail due to some mismatch between patient and drug[21].

2.2. Optimizing AI Aligned with Human Core Competencies

Algorithms are essential tools for planning, but they can easily lead decision-makers astray. Why? First of all, algorithms are extremely literal. These AI machines have no real (emotional or contextual) understanding at all. They'll do exactly what you ask them to do.

A. Algorithms Need Managers Too

An algorithm "understands" only what it is explicitly told. Secondly, algorithms are black boxes. They do not explain why they offer particular recommendations. The "Why" behind their suggestions or solutions is completely absent, and hidden in the black box. As consequence of those very clear limitations, organizations and their managers or operators need to be very explicit about all the goals when formulating algorithms. They need to consider long-term implications of data one examines and make sure that one chooses the right data inputs. In other words, algorithms need managers too[22]. Algorithms that may have found a particular correlation in big data, but these correlations do not necessarily fit a theoretical model that could indicate a causal relationship. For that reason, managers and researchers are necessary to establish whether those connections are the result of cause and effect, or pure random correlations. Those pattern-seeking efforts by AI can be extremely powerful to generate accurate insight and inform better decision-making. They can be quite impressive since identifying these patterns are too subtle to be detected by human observation. However, despite the enormous usefulness of those accurate predictions, they are definitely not a replacement for controlled experiments. The challenge for human employees, managers and executives in organizations is to understand the risks and limitations of those impressive AI tools.

When suggesting collaboration, we assume to take advantage of the strengths of both and the potential synergies in this cooperation between humans and machines. Although it is obvious that AI can augment decision-making, these AI applications often create fundamental and difficult changes in workflows, roles and culture – which leaders will need to carefully shepherd. It is not technology by itself but cultural change that is most often the biggest obstacle for AI integration[23]. And unfortunately, there are many obstacles that easily could derail such a human–AI collaboration, all organizational culture related[24].

Artificial intelligence is changing the kind of work that corporate leadership is looking for, anticipating future needs and increasing employee productivity. What should be the focus of boards and their top executives in terms of adopting to AI and its changing employee landscape: (1) reallocation of capital resources and use machine learning where applicable, and rebalance the human capital to tasks still best performed by humans; (2) invest in workforce reskilling and training by helping employees to partner with "smart" machines as tasks transform and changes in value creation occur; and (3) advance new models of education and lifelong learning to be prepared for the future today, with the understanding that in the remodelling of the value chain activities, the demand for specific skills and thus wages has risen faster in the lower- and high-wage tiers than in the mid-wage tier[25]. Moreover, "new-collar" technical jobs such as cloud computing, cybersecurity and data analysts and data architects are promising fields.

B. What Kind of Future Proof Jobs?

Traditionally, technological change has been driven the human desire to innovate. And those technological innovations have strengthened the uniquely human skills. As argued above, technology such as AI may also "destroy" some jobs. But on average AI seems to improve their jobs, by freeing them from the tyranny of repetitive, mundane tasks and allowing to focus on more rewarding higher value work. I like *The New York Times* technology expert Kevin Roose's summarized recommendations for humans in terms of being "*futureproof*": these jobs need to **be surprising, social and scarce**", quite akin to my thoughts on **combining a cognitive and socio-ethical pathway**.

For years, we have been told that if machines were the future, we needed to become more like machines ourselves. I take a contrarian view: we need to become more human and distinctive from smart machines, because it is those skills and abilities that distinguish us the most from those AI robots. "Rather than treating ourselves as pieces of biological hardware to be debugged and optimized, we need to develop the kinds of unique, human skills that machines couldn't replicate.[26]" And what can humans do so much better than the most advanced AI system: "be surprising, social and scarce". It must be clear by now that AI is better than humans at operating in stable environments with static, well-defined rules and consistent inputs. Humans, on the other hand, are much better than AI at handling surprises, filling in gaps, connecting missing dots, in tasks requiring empathy and compassion, or operating in environments with poorly defined rules or incomplete information.

While AI may be good at meeting some mathematical challenges or meeting some material needs, humans are definitely superior at meeting social and ethical needs. And finally, AI may be better than humans in resolving challenges that involve big data, but humans exceed AI ability at work that involves unusual combination of skills, high-stake situations, or extraordinary special talent. These jobs are labelled "scarce" because they are difficult to precisely define and sometimes "impractical", and hard to automate. Humans are great connectors; they bend, blend and remix genres, and hold vast amounts of random, disparate information that can be mashed together at a moment's notice. It is this ability to combine insights from distinctively different fields that makes human talent unique and scarce. This combinatorial creativity is a uniquely human skill, allowing for unusual combinations of perspectives and insights. And when a job requires *human accountability* or *emotional empathy* – representing intrinsic needs – humans are no match for AI robots. We humans love being witness to human greatness in all fields, and we don't yet accept machine substitutes. Our talent, our relationships, our unique moral courage make us more valuable than the smartest machine. And the major factor of difference is that humans are able to build a life with meaning and purpose, making us "futureproof" against the probable onslaught of AI automation.

C. Focus on Creating on Memorable Human Experiences

It is clear that human managers and employees should not compete on the machines' terms, but focus instead on leaving their own distinctively human mark on the things they're creating. Quite counterintuitively, Yan LeCun, one of the eminent AI researchers and head of Facebook's AI division – and being seen as one of the inventors of multilayered convulational networks that power our recommendation engines, and Godfather of deep learning – said recently at an MIT conference that the people with the best chance to coming out ahead in the economy of the future were not programmers and data scientists, but artists and artisans[27]. I could add that anybody who provides a real human experience – requiring human intervention – can make an impact in business, really creating value to customers. Organizations should figure out strategies for leaving "handprints", or designed compelling experiences. Those that relegate themselves to the diminishing world of goods and services will likely be rendered irrelevant over time. It's all about *creating a memorable experience*. Successful companies have a competitive edge by creating experiences, which can't be easily copied. *Starbucks* or *Nespresso* and so many others are not selling products – coffee in this case – but experience of a unique experience to drink in a suave comfortable homy place and/or drink superb coffee, respectively. I also see the movement for artisan products in the West but definitely also in the East, as in Bali, for instance, that thrives on artisanship, "unique" handmade craftmanship artistic products.

D. Machine-Age Humanities

What are the skillsets that humans should focus on? Technology columnist Kevin Roose labels these skillsets as "Machine-Age Humanities"[28]: (1) attention guarding or mindfulness; (2) room reading or understanding the delicate social maneuvering that requires a high level of emotional intelligence; (3) resting as in turning off our brains and recharging our bodies preventing burnouts, chronic sleep deprivation, stress or exhaustion; (4) digital discernment allowing to distinguish true from false by learning to navigate through hazy, muddled online information ecosystems and media manipulation, which boils down to be able to filter information more effectively; (5) analog ethics in which values will come from our ability to relate to other people – that includes developing empathy and emotional literacy; and finally (6) a form of consequentialism to foresee unintended consequences of planetary-scale AI systems such as Facebook and YouTube, and find blind spots that need to be urgently addressed by people who understand psychology, risk and probability. Making sure that AI is used "responsibly" may turn out to become one of our biggest challenges.

E. Embracing Multiplicity

We should be prepared for the danger of ideas, ideologies and institutions that allow information to feed collective decisions and understanding that may be contrary to an open and less dogmatic perspective of the world. If intelligence is the ability to deploy novel means to attain a goal, then we should allow some competitive forces to drive evolution. At this point, the progress of machine learning, particularly multilayered artificial neural networks, is not resulting yet in achieving general intelligence, but it is mainly restricted to specific problems of mapping well-defined inputs to well-defined outputs. Likely the real danger lies not in the machine itself but in the way humans may use it. Instead of focusing on singularity, Berkeley scientist Ken Goldberg claims, we should embrace **multiplicity** – a hybrid view of how new technologies and humans might collaborate in partnership towards meaningful human solutions. Qualities such as intuition, empathy and creativity remain crucial human qualities. Hence why a more holistic approach by humans could be blended with the precision that machines provide.

Never before have digital devices and machine tools (Internet of Things is currently estimated to reach 20 billion devices) been so responsive to us. This kind of IoT technology may radically alter how works gets done and who does it. However, the impact may be even larger when AI technology will complement and augment human capabilities, not replacing them.

Some thoughts to take away:

- Human intelligence can be aligned and unified to improve the decision-making at boards. AI and transformative digitization of our life cannot be avoided. This chapter assessed how collaboration between humans and AI could make quite some progress in resolving a number of our challenges.
  - Artificial intelligence and digitization provide us the technological marvels that help us to connect with each other and to navigate easier through our daily life.
  - But social media algorithms can also entrap users in ideological echo chambers or even nudge them towards extreme or false beliefs.

- AI can demolish those fundamental social *relationships* by focusing on the divisions instead of the interdependencies of humans as social animals. And surely enough, AI can put millions of workers out of job. Indeed, AI is going to fundamentally change society and transform the global economy.

- How should young individuals prepare themselves for a possible job onslaught by AI? By learning how to be creative, innovative and caring (i.e. emotionally attuned). By being uniquely human, and doing what computers can't do (any time soon): taking other stakeholders' perspectives into account.
  - Caring for those (relations) who matter, be it customers, employees or suppliers in first instance. Without them, there is hardly any business to speak of.
  - Creating (and "sharing") value will ultimately benefit its shareholders.

Chapter Twenty Three

The Geopolitical "Battle" for AI Supremacy

"The future of humankind will be determined what is happening in China in the 21ˢᵗ century".

Economics Nobel laureate **D. Kahneman**

"In the United States, there have long been warnings of a 'cyber-Pearl Harbor' – a massive digital attack that could cripple the country's critical infrastructure without a single shot being fired".

Michèle Flournoy & Michael Sulmeyer, 2018, *Foreign Affairs*

The trend towards "techno-nationalism", where a nation relies on its own resources to become a leader in Artificial Intelligence (AI), machine learning and other crucial strategic tech areas, is fully underway. The groundbreaking deep learning approach to AI has turbo-charged the cognitive capabilities of machines. This "narrow artificial intelligence" – versus the as-yet-unachieved "general artificial intelligence" – can now do a better job than humans in a range of specific domains, from identifying faces and recognizing speech, to issuing loans and weaponized drones. Unsurprisingly, many companies, and the countries from which they originate, are eager to master them. We will need sensitive geopolitical leadership to manage these tensions and defuse potential antagonistic escalations where necessary.

How these countries, especially the USA and China, the two most advanced in AI with the deepest pockets, choose to compete and cooperate will have a dramatic effect on global economics, and geopolitics in general. Firms prepare for a new sort of corporate but also political leadership in those AI-enabled eco-systems where autonomous learning machines are assumed to be aligned with the unlocking of continuous human learning capabilities. It also means that organizations will need to become adaptive and agile to react more "improvisatory" to those numerous changes that take place in the economic but also geopolitical arena.

That begs the question: how to govern Artificial Intelligence in relationship with human intelligence and its profound impact on the lives of millions or billions human lives across borders? How are the corporate and political leaders preparing themselves for the next decade in which AI and Machine Learning will play an increasingly important role? It seems that a geopolitical battle between the USA and China for technology supremacy is under way. Somehow, the current reemergence of geopolitical tensions is translated in a battle for innovation between Western "liberal democracies" (USA, UK–Australia–Canada and the EU) and Eastern "illiberal autocracies" (China–Russia). How to avoid the potential destructive consequences of such an antagonistic mindset?

1. The Geopolitical Battle for AI Supremacy ...

This new Intelligent Economy with numerous scientific and technologic developments (in the field of data analytics, AI, and supercomputing, for instance) requires multifaceted management talent; professionals with a sound knowledge of technology, people and operations. These people are in scarce supply.

1.1. Artificial Intelligence on Turbo Charge in China?

The stakes for global economic pre-eminence in AI are enormous. "Winner-take-all" and "first-mover" dynamics in internet-based industries will enable successful countries to sustain economic growth, meet GDP targets and become more independent of the hegemony of the US economy – assuming that such a decoupling would be possible or desirable. A similar decoupling effect is desired by US hawks and to a lesser degree EU politicians who are confronted by their dependency on the Chinese economy and thus (indirectly) to the China Communist Party, and vice versa.

If data are the new capital for digital connectivity[1] or knowledge economy, then who controls these data and how they are regulated will be crucial. How the countries, especially the USA and China, the two most advanced in AI, choose to compete and cooperate will have dramatic effect on global economics, and geopolitics in general. We argue that in such a increasingly tense geopolitical context, the world will need statesmen with a very reasonable mindset but above all with (feeling of) empathetic responsibility. Such a rational and responsible mindset is assumed to emphasize collaboration over antagonistic grounding, but able to retaliate if commitments do not follow – as any geopolitical realist would require.

A. A Desire by Two Superpowers for Global Standardization or Regional Influence?

Most of the significant network platforms originated in the US (Google, Facebook, Uber) or China (Baidu, WeChat, Didi Cheixing). As result, commercial competition between those network platforms – and the desire for global "standardization" – can affect geopolitical competition between governments. In diplomatic circles, this increased competition in AI has become a top agenda point, especially because these networks and their services seem to become indispensable for our daily lives. "The question of how network platforms establish community standards provides a crystallizing example of the incongruity between the modern digital space and traditional rules and expectations[2]." These rules are currently set by each operator – often administered with the assistance of AI – and govern the context of what is permissible and not.

It is not too difficult to see that USA's "defense policies" are pushing China to become even more "techno-nationalistic", relying on its own resources to become a leader in AI's machine learning and other crucial strategic technology areas. It is hard to deny the fact that China has regularly violated WTO rules since it joined the WTO in 2001 where it pledged US companies to handover their technology to China's companies or authorities in return for access to its market. Many countries have a national interest in employing AI technology to maintain social stability (including judicial reviews, medical care, defence and public security). AI is seen by many thinkers as a revolutionary technology that could significantly impact the balance of power. US policies seem to push the Chinese authorities to become even more self-reliable on high tech. Russian's President Putin quipped that the nation that will control and has supremacy in the field of artificial intelligence will control the world.

B. AI Surveillance Systems and the Master Spies

A lot attention has been on the potential "infiltration" of spyware of Chinese-owned *TikTok* and *Huawei* in the West. But China has concerns of its own. After whistleblower Edward Snowden's release of "secret" documents, Chinese government began a campaign to replace all Western technology in government offices. And recently, Elon Musk insisted Chinese government officials and later on social media that Tesla's cars are very secure, and the numerous cameras on their vehicles were "not activated outside North America", and so could not be used to snap on Chinese customers. Nonetheless, it seems that the Chinese government's insistence on being able to monitor and control the information that flows through the country's digital networks indicates that the Chinese digital security is very precarious. As long as the Chinese Communist Party demands access to data on their citizens, those data can never be robustly protected[3]. Personal data privacy is not a legal aim in China. And it is not an exaggeration that the CCP's focus on surveillance and censorship of its own people is growing.

China's AI industry, in particular, is under the spotlight. This vast country is fully embarked on a journey to be in line with the most advanced countries. By 2025, China aims to lead the world in some AI fields (with AI industry output exceeding USD 60 billion and AI-related output grossing USD 750 billion). By 2030, according to some observers, China may become the world's primary AI innovation centre (worth USD 150 billion and in AI-related industries, USD 1.5 trillion). AI could create USD 600 billion in economic value for China annually – in comparison, the 2021 GDP of Shanghai, China's most populous city of nearly 28 million, was roughly USD 680 billion[4]. This value could be generated by AI-enabled offerings, or cost savings through greater efficiency and productivity.

The stakes for both global economic pre-eminence are high. With the understanding of the "winner-takes-all" and "first-mover" dynamics in internet-based industries, China's endeavour to sustain economic growth and meet GDP targets is to become more independent of the US economy. China also has a national interest to employ AI technology to maintain social stability (including judicial reviews, medical care and public security). In the military arena, some Chinese thinkers view AI as a revolutionary technology that could significantly affect the balance of power. If data are the "new oil" and the connecting network as the "new electricity" for economies[5], then who controls these data and networks and how they are regulated will be crucial.

C. China's Sputnik Moment Waking Up a Dragon

In ancient China, "Go" represented one of the four art forms any Chinese scholar was expected to master, leading to Zen-like intellectual refinement and wisdom. In May 2017, the DeepMind learning machine AlphaGo (backed by Google, arguably the world's top technology company) beat the best Go player, Ke Jie. This was China's "Sputnik" moment[6]. From that experience the mindset changed and the CCP government mobilized for national AI innovation.

The groundbreaking deep learning approach to AI has turbo-charged the cognitive capabilities of machines. These programs are known as "narrow artificial intelligence" (versus the as-yet-unachieved "general artificial intelligence"). They can now do a better job than humans in a range of domains, from identifying faces and recognizing speech, to issuing loans. Unsurprisingly, many companies, and the countries from which they originate, are eager to master them.

AI is a primary driver of China's rapid development towards an *Intelligent Economy*. Set to have a massive impact on billions of lives worldwide, the intelligent economy is having a transformative effect on China. It sits together with other enabling technologies: 5G connection network[7], Cloud, Big Data, Internet of Things, Mixed Reality (MR), Blockchain and Edge Computing. In China, as elsewhere, it will catalyze demand creation, transforming business models and manufacturing processes. It will change our lifestyles ("smart living"), the cities we live in ("smart cities") and how we travel within and through them, how we learn and are kept healthy. It will also have a profound effect on government administration processes and security.

China's efforts in developing AI should be taken seriously. For instance, China developed a software system – called *Wu Dao* 2.0 or "enlightenment" 2.0 – that emulate lowlier types of speech, deriving its power from a neural network with 1.75 trillion variables and other inputs[8]. GPT-3, a similar model built by a team of researchers in San Francisco, considered just 175 billion parameters. We could interpret that Wu Dao represents a leap in this type of machine learning that tries to emulate the workings of a human brain. And currently, China has been deploying more AI-assisted industrial robots than any other country. China can also feature a few prominent AI companies competing with the best: *Hikvision* (producing AI-driven cameras), *Megvii* (image technology) or *SenseTime* (specialized in surveillance technology). A cluster of four startups focused on facial surveillance technology – *SenseTime*, *CloudWalk*, *Megvii* and *Yitu* – has achieved "unicorn" status (i.e. market valuation exceeding USD 1 billion). In a number of AI areas – including facial and visual recognition, 5G technology, digital payments, quantum communications and the commercial drone market – China has surpassed the USA[9]. Despite these leaps forward and successes, it is believed that China almost certainly still lags behind the USA in terms of investment and cutting-edge innovation.

1.2. Follow the (Digital) Silk Road

From a geopolitical perspective, mastery of AI can be seen as part of the New Silk Road that President Xi Jinping has put forward as the next big step for the superpower. The New [Digital] Silk Road[10] is part of the broader Belt and Road Initiative (BRI), a project to link economies via a series of trade networks connecting Asia, Africa and Europe. China is preparing to play a dominant role in financing trading routes through land, sea and digital reality. President Xi Jinping's vision is to develop a world-class technological superpower, an international community of practice built around top Chinese AI talent, with China becoming a primary exporter of AI technologies around the globe. The BRI economic model seeks to transform China's reputation: from a manufacturing-based society that exports cheap goods abroad, to one of cutting-edge technological leadership based on AI and other high-tech innovation. This geopolitical repositioning is aimed at allowing China to cement partnership and export opportunities, advancing its technical and geopolitical leadership objectives.

A. China's Expansion of Traditional Silk Road into a Digital Silk Road

From a geopolitical perspective, it is not too hard to argue that the mastery of Artificial Intelligence can be interpreted as part of the "**digital silk road**" that Xi Jinping has put forward as the move forward by the emerging superpower. China obviously wants to strengthen its geopolitical impact through economic and other means. The **New Silk Road** is an initiative to link economies together whereby China plays a dominant role in financing trading routes through land, sea and digital reality. China's so-called digital silk road can be considered a technological plank of its infrastructure- and investment-driven Belt and Road Initiative, through which it will try to influence its exports network and platform technologies, attempting to shape the infrastructure and norms that govern information in other countries. The installation of Chinese 5G equipment through satellite network connectivity – such as *Huawei* or *Beidou*[11] supported by the Chinese government – around the world will enable to tap in huge data sets. China also distributes its surveillance technologies to Western democracies: the French city of Marseille is working with the Chinese telcom company *ZTE* to establish a public surveillance network[12].

President Xi Jiping's dream is to develop a world-class technological superpower. Developing an international community of practice around top Chinese AI talent, and secondly to become a primary exporter of AI technologies around the globe, fits in the model to further China's One Belt, One Road (OBOR) initiative that in fact seeks to construct a modern-way Silk Road trade networks connecting Asia, Africa and Europe. This economic model somehow hopes to transform China's reputation as a manufacturing-based society that exports cheap goods abroad into one of cutting-edge technological leadership based on AI and other high technology innovation. Such geopolitical positioning would allow China to cement partnership and export opportunities advancing China's technical and geopolitical leadership objectives.

And although China's BRI initiative is promoted and supposed to be China's "soft power" to create a win-win situation, we are less sanguine about the possible outcome on debt-ridden countries who have received "generous" BRI investments. These indebted countries are and will be pushed hard for compromises in case economic returns cannot be returned, and be used by China to get access to harbors to strengthen their military presence, for instance, in Sri Lanka or Pakistan, or make subtle inroads in Greek Piraeus for instance. Superb *Realpolitik* on the international scene, some might say.

B. US–China Competing in Both Fundamental AI Research and AI Applications

A lot of the difficult work in **AI development and discovery** has been driven by a handful of elite researchers, virtually all clustered in the USA, Canada, Israel, UK and France. We are entering the age of **AI implementation** where we see real-world applications. In this age of big data, successful AI algorithms need data, computing power and some good AI algorithm engineers to make a difference. However, once computing power and engineering talent reach a certain threshold, data become the decisive factor in determining the overall power and accuracy of an algorithm. What are China's prospects, going forward? By looking at the four critical success factors for successful AI implementation – *abundant data, hungry entrepreneurs, AI scientists* and *an AI-friendly environment* – we can assume that China has a good chance to emerge as a leading power in the domain, inching ahead of the USA in the near future.

Researcher and venture capitalist entrepreneur Kai-Fu Lee argues that moving from discovery to implementation reduces the traditional disadvantages of one of China's weak points ("outside-the-box" thinking about research questions) and leverages its most significant strength, "scrappy entrepreneurs with sharp instincts for building robust businesses" – something that requires speed and adaptability. China's alternate digital universe now creates and captures vast reservoirs of new, real-world data, and this will prove invaluable in an era of AI implementation. Kai-Fu Lee believes that the US will likely continue to produce state-of-the-art research at the very front of AI. China, on the other hand, will take the lead in doing the practical nuts-and-bolts work for actually implementing AI technology in real functioning applications used across the Chinese economy[13].

Jack Ma's description of Alibaba's goal[14] indicates a clear ambition to play a global role in business (and even beyond): *"to globalize e-commerce so that small businesses and young people all over the world can buy and sell globally"*. Jack Ma's own ambitions may have been clipped in 2020 by Xi Jiping and the China Communist

Party so far, reinforcing the power of the Party over the Chinese economy, both public and private sector.

Nonetheless, Chinese AI entrepreneurs have everything to play for, and with. They are already finding ways to implement data in commercially viable AI-powered applications, drawing on China's huge population of 1,3 billion people, of whom 731 million are active internet users and 685 million mobile users, versus 287 million internet users and 262 million mobile users in the USA in 2019. Additionally, China has roughly 286 million digital natives versus 75 million in the USA[15]. Direct and indirect competition between US and Chinese firms will very likely "ramp-up" into a fierce struggle for AI supremacy.

2. Competitive Intelligence in This Geopolitical AI "Battle"

US firms that widely use AI algorithms for their applications include Google, Amazon, Microsoft, Facebook and WhatsApp, but also Apple, IBM, Netflix, Airbnb and Uber or Lyft. Chinese-backed equivalents include Alibaba and its online shopping website Taobao, the Alipay payment platform (occupying 54 percent of the Chinese market) and Tencent, with its social messaging app WeChat and WeChat Pay (32 percent of the Chinese market), but also QQ Wallet, Baidu, Didi Chuxing and Meituan-Dianping. And the list is obviously not exhaustive.

2.1. Poking the Rising Dragon or Clipping the Mighty Eagle?

In line with its strategy to lead, China's government has supported its "national champions" with substantial funding, encouraged domestic companies to acquire chip technology through overseas deals and made long-term bets on supercomputing facilities. *Baidu* and startups such as *Cambricorn* are designing chips specifically for use by AI algorithms. Early 2021, there is a shortage of chips used in cars and many other devices. The major basic chip manufacturers are located in Taiwan and South Korea, raising the geopolitical stake in those two territories.

A. Access to Data ... Developing AI Talent

Above everything else is the desire to have access to large quantities of data – a crucial driver for any AI system. China has a distinct advantage, given the sheer size of its domestic market. Consider China's progress in allowing for AI uptake, driven by big data from one fifth of all humans on the planet, combined with its gladiatorial entrepreneurs, unique internet ecosystem and a proactive government push, and it's not too hard to imagine a shift of AI supremacy in its favour. In robotics, however, European firms – especially German – may still play a global competitive role. Germany's AI strategy plays to its industrial strengths, drawing on data use in cyber-physical manufacturing and the industrial Internet of Things. The US and EU should build on existing advantages in research and technology – not only because of China's rapid development in this AI field, but because there exists a lack of agility and creativity among federal planners and policymakers[16]. Some public-private sector collaboration may be favourable to create an ever more dynamic ICT industry in which AI can thrive.

Geopolitics will increasingly be determined by power struggles in the AI field, and who wins most from this new technology. Even if China has a numbers advantage over the USA when it comes to data as the new oil, this alone will not be sufficient to gain AI supremacy. The theoretical frameworks for deep learning innovation remain indispensable. And here, the US is still in the lead. Although China may currently have the edge in face recognition algorithms, and smartphone apps for financial services are leapfrogging, Google and other US companies in Silicon Valley are still ahead of the AI game. Moreover, China does not yet have the international data necessary to reduce biases for apps that could be used beyond its national borders.

B. The Geopolitical Perils of AI Networks

The fact that China's government applies a utilitarian view (in contrast to Europe's market-determined deontological approach) means that a "policy-push" will encourage faster adoption of those technologies. Moreover, the Chinese government has a strategy to support its lead: a strong degree of state support and intervention, the transfer of both technology and talent, and investment over a long-term period[17]. Today, there is direct and indirect competition between US firms[18] and Chinese-backed corporations. Among those Chinese firms we find *Alibaba* and its online shopping website *Taobao*, or *Tencent* and its social messaging app WeChat, and *Baidu*, but also *Didi Chuxing* which drove Uber out of China is now battling with *Meituan Dianping* (a tech unicorn backed by *Tencent)* or other AI firms. They all face a fierce struggle for AI supremacy. China's government has supported "national champions" with substantial funding, encouraged domestic companies to acquire chip technology through overseas deals and made long-term bets on supercomputing facilities.

The battle between China and the US is well-installed and looks set to intensify. The White House political involvement to keep *Tencent* and especially *Huawei* at bay to install 5G networks on US soil can be seen as a first shot in front of the bow of China's global aspirations. Huawei has become – alongside Nokia and Erikson – one of the biggest suppliers of high-tech kit used to build mobile-phone 5G networks around the world. Western critique argues that Huawei's commercial self-interest (to comply to Western cybersecurity ICT concerns) is irrelevant, pointing to a Chinese law that compels private firms to assist the intelligence service when asked.

Huawei's sales of surveillance equipment are often financed by loans backed by the Chinese government. A number of countries such as Kenya, Laos, Mongolia, Uganda, Uzbekistan and Zimbabwe can be considered clients – in some case as part of Beijing's global Belt and Road Initiative that funds infrastructure initiatives in nearly 70 countries. Africa is an increasingly important continent for China's AI-driven business. Nations such as Saudi Arabia and UAE are eager customers for Chinese technology as they expand their own surveillance system whereby facial recognition has become routine aspects of daily life[19].

C. AI Innovation Promise Higher Productivity: Really?

Although the productivity growth has been stagnating over the past couple of years, it is expected that the positive impact of AI on productivity will be felt in the coming years. It sometimes takes decades, as in a prolonged period of gestation, before we are able to create complementary innovations, and before we get adjustments in human capital to adapt to structural changes that AI is expected to bring. Professor Brynjolfsson and his team admits that productivity growth is often hidden in intangible assets – like human capital that is in the process of being "upgraded"[20]. An interesting comparison is a defect rate of about 1 percent in production lines among China's leading companies versus a lower defect rate of 0.2 percent in German and Swiss companies. It is this challenge of the middle-income paradox that China[21] currently faces: how to become more productive in comparison with their Western competitors. In order to become a competitive champion, China will need to learn how to improve its quality of value-added in the supply chain, or how to make consumer-facing AI applications such as face recognition even more accurate and predictive.

2.2. A Talent Angle in AI Strategy

The new intelligent economy requires multifaced management talent: professionals with sound knowledge of technology, people and operations. These people are in scarce supply. This said, it is not too difficult to imagine that China may gain an advantage by having established clusters of world-class AI innovation centres by 2030. Developing AI systems depends on quantity *and* quality. China has a significant manpower advantage in "training" and labelling the data that are needed by AI applications, consumer uses or domestic surveillance, for example. Certainly, as late as 2018, China was still dwarfed by the US regarding the number of highly experienced AI professionals in its ranks: 50,000 versus 850,000[22].

A. An Insatiable Hunger for AI Talent

Still, China has been highly creative in the application layer of AI, with rapid user adoption and acceptance, creating a strong feedback loop. Its fundamental AI research is focused on image and speech processing, image recognition, machine vision, speech recognition and natural language processing (NLP). These key AI-enabling technologies – first developed at Canadian and US research centres – are now applied to all market-leading smartphones. Particularly in image recognition, China has already become world-class, dominating in global competitions. Leading companies in NLP include *Flytek, Baidu, Megvil* (Face+++) and *SenseTime*.

The think tank, MacroPolo[23], recently studied the national origins of elite AI researchers[24]. It found that 29 percent of oral presentations at a major conference were made by undergraduates from the US (in terms of their country of origin, and/or the institution to which they were affiliated). But the second highest country was China (9 percent). Looking at where elite AI researchers work today, it found that the US absorbs an even greater share (61 percent), observing a "global brain drain, US brain gain". In short, the majority of elite (and upper tier) research happens at US institutions relying on foreign-born talent for over half their research output. Chinese researchers are an important source of global AI talent, and most end up studying in the US, and working for US companies. Elsewhere, however, there is evidence that ethnic Chinese researchers are also returning from the US, and that China is turning the tables on the brain (and corporate) acquisition flow.

Despite China's lead over USA in overall number of AI-related publications, it still ranks below India and USA in the number of skilled AI coders relative to its populations. And there are a few reasons for this that may persist for a while: first, capital may not be allocated efficiently. For instance, China's government has created a system for rewarding local officials that favours loyalty and debt-fuelled spending and seldom penalizes them for wastefulness.

AI researcher Jeffrey Ding, currently at Stanford, calls many of these state AI investment as "reckless and redundant". Second, China seems to be unable to recruit the world's best AI minds. For instance, more than half of top-tier researchers (including Chinese) in the field were working outside their home countries, for the simple reason that USA and EU research centres at universities are more appealing. Although a third of the world's AI top talent is from China, only a tenth actually work in China. And finally, the Chinese government's master plan ignored the cutting-edge semiconductors that power AI. Virtually all of China's used microprocessors are either American or made with American equipment (Taiwan) which will be subjected to certain restriction amidst the increased geopolitical tensions. It will likely take years for China to catch up in the global cutting-edge semi-conductor business. And yes, for instance, Wu Dao 2.0 was a huge improvement on GPT-3; it did not add anything new of strategic value. As long as China trails behind US–EU–Canada in paradigm-shifting developments of greater strategic value, the battle is on.

B. How to Measure China's AI Power?

How to measure the geopolitical competitive position of a country in terms of artificial intelligence? The following criteria should be considered in making such an assessment:

- the quality of scientific research on AI – especially in the field of sophisticated algorithms;
- the availability of data, with the understanding that data may be very culturally contextual that may not be easily "exportable" to other cultures unless retrained;
- the access to hardware that is needed for calculative power, which may include quantum computers – an area in which China is fast catching up;

- a dynamic entrepreneurial context in which new ideas can thrive, including the necessary eco-systems in which platforms can thrive. Another area in which China is moving fast and catching up with Western innovators; and
- a supporting and stimulating government.

The key features of China's AI strategy are based on the overall development of (1) hardware in the form of chips for training and executing AI algorithms, (2) data as an input for AI algorithms, (3) research and algorithm development and (4) the commercial AI ecosystem that benefits from government guidance funds set up by local governments and state-owned companies.

How to assess the current state of AI capabilities across the four drivers of AI development of both superpowers? The Artificial Intelligence Potential Index (AIPI) approximates a country's overall AI capability, whereby recently, China's AIPI score is 17 percent, which is about half of the US's AIPI score of 33 percent[25]. AI researcher Ding concluded that China trails the US in every driver except for access to data. The overall AIPI-score is reflected in the four quadrants of Figure 1. However, we need to keep in mind that such AIPI score is relative and that individual companies may gain a specific competitive advantage that is

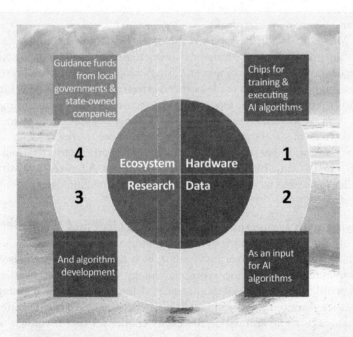

Figure 1: The China's AI strategy is based on the development of four interrelated factors

Source: Verhezen, P. & S. Gande (2020), *Geopolitical War for AI Supremacy*, Amrop Series on AI, based on Ding, J. (2018)

not necessarily quantified at this aggregate AIPI level. Also, a lot can happen in two to three years in the field of AI and in China in particular. Indeed, just a year later, another report suggested the gap was closing. Whilst the US led in four out of six categories – talent, research, development and hardware – China was found to lead in two areas – adoption and data. Overall, the US scored 44 out of 100 available points, China 32, and the European Union, 23 out of 100[26]. Furthermore, even if the US is in the lead in theoretical potential, China is implementing at speed, with fewer legacy systems to unwind.

C. Does Quantity Trump Quality in AI?

In overall terms, it is probably fair to assume that economic benefits are the primary and immediate driving force behind China's development of AI. It can enable the country to dramatically improve its productivity levels and meet GDP targets. Estimates place AI's impact on the Chinese economy at USD 7 trillion by 2030–2035, or a quarter of future GDP. AI's contribution to GDP growth is estimated to be 1–2 percent annually.

Economic benefits are the primary and immediate driving force behind China's development of AI since AI systems could enable China to drastically improve its productivity levels and meet GDP targets. However, digital expertise remains rare. And we should not forget that the artificial intelligence race, after all, remains a very human struggle.

Microsoft Asia in Beijing was the first major foreign computer science research institute in China. Many of China's top technology and AI scientists have passed through its doors. However, China's adoption of AI technologies could also have implications for its mode of social governance whereby AI is intended to play an "irreplaceable" (i.e. supervisory and security) role in maintaining social stability. And AI undeniably will benefit a broad range of public services, including judicial services, medical care and public security. However, the growing concern for privacy and willingness of private companies to participate in various social credit systems in China highlights the potential threats. Admittedly, Washington and Berlin–Paris need to invest more in key emerging technologies.

D. Playing with Dangerous AI-Military Devices and Weapons

Finally, military applications of AI could provide a decisive strategic advantage in international security. Direct investment, be it federal or corporate, is vital to progress in quantum computing, synthetic biology, semi-conductors and even in the field of military-use artificial intelligence[27]. Moreover, with the digitization of our daily socio-economic and political life, cyber-threats have become one of the most serious economic and national security challenges that sovereign nations face today.

Western countries should prepare for stronger answers to foreign cyber-attacks because the do-nothing or do-little-approach is no longer a realistic or appropriate deterrence strategy. Cyber-deterrence policy must reflect the reality that failing to respond in the face of an (international) attack is itself a choice with consequences. Cyberspace has become a domain of international geopolitical contention, information warfare and intense economic competition.

For too long, the United States and its allies have responded to rapidly changing realities too slow. For many of the Western democracies, cybersecurity has been seen as a matter for the IT help desk to address. But considering the massive development in AI-driven weapons and (dis)information tools, new vulnerabilities rapidly crop up in Western societies[28]. One must safeguard against potential AI-enabled cyberattacks and potentially intrusive AI surveillance.

Some thoughts to take away:

- The idea behind the growing **antagonistic battle for AI supremacy** between the two economic superpowers USA versus China is the idea that those who control AI and its underlying data, algorithms and network will **control the future**.

- Political leaders have understood the importance of AI for our daily lives, and AI has become the hot topic in global geopolitics. Indeed, the **geopolitical battle** for AI supremacy **between the USA and China** has been **intensified** over the past five years.

- Does quantity trumps quality in AI: not really. But *China* will lead in *nuts-and-bolt functional AI applications*, whereas the *West* will continue to lead in *fundamental AI research*.

Chapter Twenty Four

A New Geopolitical Order with AI as Defining Lines

"The deepest principle in human nature is the craving to be appreciated".

William James, philosopher and founder of modern psychology

"AI-powered algorithms will allow autocracies to microtarget individuals with information that either reinforces their support for the regime or seeks to counteract specific sources of discontent. Likewise, the production of deepfakes will make it easier to discredit opposition leaders and will make it increasingly difficult for the public to know what is real, sowing doubt, confusion and apathy".

A. Kendall-Taylor, E. Frantz & J. Wright, 2020, *Foreign Affairs*

How will this new competition for AI supremacy between the USA and China unfold on the international scene? Will it rather be a "confrontational" or "cooperative" competition? Will the West start fiercely competing with a Beijing perspective? The Washington consensus is overwhelmingly focused on the power of the free markets to drive growth and is critically dependent on a host of complementary institutions. The autocratic Beijing view, however, takes a very different stance: a socialism with Chinese characteristics.

It is well documented that China's data protectionism favours Chinese AI companies in accessing data from China's large domestic market. Consider China's progress allowing for utilizing artificial intelligence, driven by big data from one fifth of all humans on the planet, combined with China's gladiatorial entrepreneurs, unique internet ecosystem and a proactive government push, and it is not too difficult to imagine that there may be a shift of AI supremacy in favour of China.

However, Germany's AI strategy, for instance, relies on using data in cyber-physical manufacturing processes and the industrial Internet of Things – that plays to German industrial strengths. Indeed, in Robotics, European firms – especially Germany – still play a global competitive role. But other European centra could become important players as well, such as the Belgian *IMEC*, a university spin-off and R&D hub for nano and digital technologies[1]. How to interpret this increasing focus on geopolitical AI-independency?

1. The Mastery of Artificial Intelligence in a Geopolitical Context

Anticipating AI's challenges for the global order requires a better understanding of the different fields in which they would have an impact. Georgetown Professor Wright distinguishes three facets which we summarize as: (1) *Political Regimes*: competing types of political regimes in the global order, as the *Huawei* case clearly has shown us. Liberal democracies could compete with authoritarianism: new AI-related technologies may help reinvigorate the idea that more authoritarian regimes are better placed to enrich their citizens and maintain social order. Particularly, the latter seems to be harder to achieve in polarized democratic regimes. (2) *Social Sectors*: change in the means of production across social sectors. Practical AI applications will transform multiple, fundamental fields: whether in the transport sector (e.g. in autonomous driving cars), in beneficial healthcare applications, social or the more potentially evil military use of AI. And finally (3) *Singularity*: seeking singularity and a sense of self. Fundamental research in AI algorithms claims to inch towards a point of "singularity". This irreversible technological growth may have profound consequences on our self-concept as humans. Indeed, any unequal power fight over AI supremacy could undermine the current world order; the distribution of power between and amongst states and other key actors. If this distribution has previously allowed a relatively stable pattern of relationships and behaviors, then AI could turn that all around in a potentially destructive manner. Artificial intelligence and its force of full-blown digitization could allow those in power to control the life of many by flooding people with (irrelevant) information. That means that today having power means *knowing what to ignore* and sift through the overload of data for essential information[2]. And yes, our liberal democratic system is probably threatened, not by the lack of individual freedom or the idea that there are no free individuals, but rather by powerful technologies in the hands of a few.

1.1. Autocratic System Versus Democratic Processes

AI in general is interpreted by a number of scientists as part of a surveillance system, be it by a Silicon Valley company that can accurately predict the behavior and thus potentially manipulate it, or by any government that is able to closely monitor its citizens. The way Western tech companies have turned human experience into the raw material of the new economy – resulting in *surveillance capitalism*, to quote Professor Shoshana Zuboff[3] – is actually narrowing the gulf between the application of digital technologies in democracies and their application in autocracies such as China. The Western high-tech firms are motivated by profits, whereas China's surveillance systems are more geared towards cementing government control over their citizens and companies[4]. Whatever the motivation, both forms of surveillance prioritize mass collection of data and have developed the power to shape how citizens perceive the world.

As a consequence, any equal power fight over AI supremacy could undermine the current world order, the distribution of power between and amongst states and other key actors. If this distribution has previously allowed a relatively stable pattern of *relationships* and behaviors, then AI could turn that all around in a potentially destructive manner.

For this reason, it may become the newest tool to aim for some kind of global supremacy in the form of increased soft power, through (for example) the concrete impact of AI applications on domestic behavior. Indeed, global institutions and norms create a significant arena for competition.

A. Output Legitimacy Justifying Social Control

The fight for superior AI applications is definitely linked to the question whether an autocratic system – with a primacy of *output legitimacy*[5] – can possibly outperform a democratic system – where *input legitimacy* is assumed. China's adoption of AI technologies could also have implications for social stability in a supervisory and security capacity. Even if the USA is in the lead in the theoretical potential of AI today, such temporary competitive advantage can easily be lost. Indeed, China, is implementing at speed, with fewer constraining legacy systems; it's catching up with the West in the arena of digitization and in particular AI development. This competition between two fundamental different systems may have deep consequences for determining how global governance may look like in the future.

The great firewall of China proves that an authoritarian regime is able to deliver a sophisticated alternative system, and it seems to be tightening this system over the past couple of years where Chinese have hardly freedom of expression on the internet. Western scholars often take democratic rules at face value and dismiss autocratic systems as inferior because this system allegedly lacks (majority input) legitimacy. However, if one emphasizes material(istic) outcome results, political leaders in China have definitely some economic argumentation on their side: they get things done in a relative short time period, especially because any form of (democratic deliberative) contest or consensus voting process is avoided. And this attitude of "output" performance goes very far.

The "citizen credit" scheme in China, for instance, announced in 2014 intends to compute various metrics for every citizen's good conduct. China's planned social credit system is been promoted as a way to reward "trustworthiness" and discourage illegal or immoral behavior – all defined by the CCP of course. Eventually, a genuinely Orwellian system of comprehensive and carefully orchestrated social control will emerge. One could argue that no regime has exploited the "political" potential of AI quite as thoroughly as China. The CCP collects an incredible amount of data on their individual citizens and businesses, be it tax returns, bank accounts, purchasing histories, or criminal and medical records. The regime then uses AI to analyze this information and compile "social credit scores", and then subsequently uses a set of parameters of acceptable behavior to improve citizen control. Any individual or company deemed "untrustworthy" could be excluded from state-sponsored benefits or even banned from air and rail travel[6]. The most complete surveillance system may have been developed in the restive Xinjiang province, a capability that could be rolled out across China.

Artificial intelligence may become the newest tool to aim for some form of global supremacy, be it in the form of increased soft power as result of AI abilities, or through concrete AI applications' impact on domestic usage, and the impact on the military dimensions of global competition. Indeed, global institutions and norms form a significant arena for competition. More broadly, China and Russia have pushed back against a conception of a free borderless global internet.

B. China Competing Against Western ("Imposed") Standards

China uses its market power to influence *technical standards*, "normalize" domestic control and shape norms of behavior through international organizations. However, China's overhyped government plans often under-deliver. And megaprojects have diverted funding from high-quality labs towards more politically connected entities.

It is likely China's frustration of having no say in international standards so far that pushes them to become such assertive competitors in the AI field. Chinese authorities are trying to set up more comprehensive AI ecosystems that could challenge the Western standards. A lot of industrial policy and development is happening at the local Chinese government level: AI centres in Hefei and Hangzhou are obvious examples. Hefei is known to have developed specialized knowledge in speech recognition, with the help of *iFlytek* – a natural language processing tech giant in China – and USTC (the University of Science and Technology of China). This collaborative efforts have focused on developing a cluster of companies with expertise in intelligent speech and natural language processing. In Hangzhou, a comprehensive AI ecosystem has been developed, based on the collaboration between Alibaba – which has incorporated its headquarters in Hangzhou – and the elite Zhejiang University. It is well-known among Chinese AI scientists and industry that third-tier companies make products, second-tier companies make platforms, and first-tier companies make standards. For the Chinese, it is essential that some of their platform techno logies could become international standards – like Microsoft and their Word formatting standard.

According to some Chinese policymakers, China has been excluded from setting any of the rules of the internet, and they do not want that to happen with AI technology[7]. This partially explains the China government-led and top-down-driven approach to push for AI development. China has a lot of products-related AI development, and some huge companies in China have established their own AI cloud platform standards. China's real objective is to set standards that has been exclusively Western till now[8].

C. The Potential Growing Struggle Between the AI-Haves and AI-Have-Nots

For all these reasons, AI may become the newest tool to aim for some kind of global supremacy in the form of increased soft power, through (for example) the concrete impact of AI applications on domestic behavior. Indeed, global institutions and norms create a significant arena for competition.

Another threat posed by AI is the possibility of social disorder and political collapse stemming from widespread unemployment and the gaping inequality between the AI "haves" and "have-nots". Ethical concerns require a robust civil society as we do have in Europe. It is unclear to what extent an open ethical debate can be conducted in China where overall the civil society is more bound by China Communist Party oversight. Authoritarian states have learnt to use digital tools to quell dissent. Although technology and online communication may have helped to facilitate protests, today's savvy authoritarian regimes are using the same technological innovations in AI and social media to push back against dangerous popular mobilizations[9]. As these autocracies have co-opted the same new digital technologies and AI, they have become a formidable threat to democracy, in particular because today's autocracies have grown more durable.

Similarly, populists have used these digital tools to threat democracies from within. These new technologies are particularly dangerous for weaker democracies: AI and digitization can be used to enhance government efficiency and provide the capacity to address challenges such as crime and terrorism, but no matter the initial intentions with governments acquiring such promising technology, they can also use these same tools to muzzle and restrict the activities of their opponents.

The growing battle between the economic superpowers, aggravated by an increased animosity between nationalistic and populistic political leaders, is making economics even more transactional than it already is. One of the major risks is that one party or another chooses only to magnify the capabilities of AI without regarding the safety aspects of AI.

1.2. How to Defuse International Antagonism in Misusing AI's "Darker" Side?

Regulations and some form of global governance may become necessary, and these will need to be implemented without stifling AI research. As always, we only can hope that the rewards will outweigh the downsides of this innovative technology. However, this will require social and political choices that align our interests as a community and society. The aim should not just be to outsmart the other party, but to be wise enough not to allow destructive forces to prevail.

And yes, we should understand the limits and darker side of artificial intelligence, without underestimating the scale, scope and speed of potential AI disruption. Only wise, measured and mindful leaders will be able to define and imagine some form of global good for these innovative but ethically-neutral techniques, realistically implementing them in our specific world context.

The new intelligent economy requires multifaced leadership talent: professionals with sound knowledge of technology, and understanding human resources and operational management skills. Obviously, this kind of executive talent is in scarce supply, especially in China. Digital experts are a new breed, emerging only recently in China. As mentioned earlier, the artificial intelligence race, after all, remains a very human struggle.

Sovereign countries should attempt to agree on some framework for international order based on "sovereign obligation that would prohibit on carrying out or in way support terrorism, defined as the intentional use of armed violence against civilians and non-combatants by nonstate civilians in pursuit of political objectives[10]". In other words, the international political community should come to an agreement in which it is made clear that "dangerous AI-devices" cannot and should not be used to interfere. This notion of "sovereign obligation" differs from the classic notion of (Western) Westphalian sovereignty as it attempts to establish an international (non-Western) order in a highly connected world where individual citizens need to take their respective responsibilities that secure community harmony – a notion that may sound very foreign to Western scholars. China aims to obtain a similar respect that the USSR got in the agreements on the nuclear arsenal and the non-use of these dangerous weapons, the MAD strategy as agreed between USSR (the smaller Russia nowadays) and the USA at the end of the Cold War period.

2. How to Turn Antagonistic International Conflict into Agonistic Relations?

One of the main challenges in this "battle of AI supremacy" is the "Western" assumption of liberal democracy as the main universal legitimatized political framework. Such an assumption undermines our thesis that plural intelligences and frameworks can and should collaborate and be allowed to thrive. However, in geopolitical terms, especially today with rising tensions between these superpowers, it seems that the "hegemony" of liberalism is back on the table[11]. Such (Western) misplaced pretension of "moral" supremacy of this liberal political system undermines the democratic political process itself[12]. Indeed, allowing different paradigms or frameworks to compete fits in the idea of Wittgenstein's family-similarities and games. However, this hegemonistic thinking on both sides makes the other – who may not share the ideas or assumption behind a certain (political) framework – an enemy instead of an adversary. The unbalanced undialectical moralistic thinking of neo-liberal democracies turns the (international) relations into an antagonistic battle that easily destroys any form of dialogue and peace-meal progress. Not exactly a wise approach. How to avoid such zero-sum thinking in international relations? Aggravating this potential zero-sum approach is the potential danger of real war. In other words, the additional question to be asked is to avoid the "Thucydides trap"[13], that indicates that the rise of China and the fear that this may instil in the USA may make war inevitable according to some hawks, unless the trend can be reversed, unless a rebalancing can peacefully take place. A black and white thinking or zero-sum approach is not exactly encouraging.

2.1. Antagonism Versus Agonism

The idea that only a rational liberal democracy – and no other political alternative – has legitimacy to control AI denies the inherent character of power struggle in (international) politics. Some scholars believe that liberal democracy – based on individual personal free choice and the rational belief in an universal consensus based on reasoning only – will likely result in a form of global governance. Under a supra-national authority such as the UN, these liberal democracies believe that such international forum may be the only solution to resolve our global problems. However, denying inherent ambiguities and potential antagonistic conflicts in international relations may make the matter worse. Although a laudable ideal, the supra-national UN is less effective than one may have hoped. Despite my personal scepticism about the UN's effectiveness and its limited power to impose sanctions, it's one of the few supra-national mechanisms we have today to resolve potential or actual international politically inspired disputes in a rather peaceful manner.

A. The Power Play in International Relations Should Diffuse Antagonism into Agonism

It is crucial to acknowledge that (international) politics is about power and resolving military conflict, allowing differences to be expressed, but through appropriate channels. Not imposing a presumed finalized end product through subtly forced consensus. A democratic process – with its differences[14] and a plurality of interpretations what this could mean – may channel the inherent antagonistic relations into more "manageable" and less violent *agonistic* relations[15]. We could possibly label the process more neutrally as "dialectic dialogues" among participating nation-states, or plainly, diplomatic negotiations.

Agonist(ic) relations acknowledge differences in opinion, perceptions and approaches, but fundamentally accept the legitimacy of this potentially conflictual outcries and thus the legitimacy of those conflicting parties. The conflicting parties here assessed – as in the US versus China – should be seen as adversaries instead of enemies. Indeed, in *an antagonistic relationship*, those conflicting parties aim for the complete annihilation of the other; the enemy should be conquered. Such antagonistic conflicts are much more eruptive and dangerous, because each party is convinced about his rightness – a moral and not a political term. Russia with its autocratic leader Putin has apparently fallen in this trap of unbalanced thinking by demonizing the "enemy" (Ukraine and to a certain extent USA). Democracy should transform antagonistic relations into agonistic conflicts that potentially constitutes the possibility of a dialectic synthesis or a political alternative solution than mere supremacy of one over the other. An agonistic conflict is a configuration of power relations which are not necessarily settled by rational cognitive argumentation. In any power struggle, political or otherwise, emotions are involved and they need to be properly channelled to remain constructive.

I admit that I changed my perspective and argumentation over the past decade and that I am not that supportive anymore to mere consensus-seeking solutions such as a Kantian cosmopolitical ideal[16]. A consensus around a cosmopolitical order *sub specie aeternitaties* is almost a *contradictio in terminis*. Cosmopolitics remains an ideal that will be hard to effectively materialize in the current international context. The idea of globalization, for instance, that is positioned to be preferable to an actual nationalistic structure may itself be a captured confirmation of certain powerful elite controlling the major financial sources and channels in a globalized world economy[17]. Such processes are either (unconsciously or consciously) captured by the most powerful players imposing a consensus on the prevailing political or scientific paradigm, or a consensus may be used to force differences to be absorbed or squashed in the name of the greater community good. Consensus-imposed politics often kills progress or innovation, because dissent seems to be forbidden.

B. Avoid Claiming Moral Superiority

Both liberal democratic tendencies (*in casu* the USA, UK or EU) and autocratic-led emerging economies (such as China or Russia) aim not just to proof their political muscles in the world, but even are convinced by their own moral superior correctness, by painting the enemy as "morally wrong". Bringing in a moralistic tone in a political conflict precludes to find a joint discourse or to create new institutions that could handle political agonistic conflicts. In other words, moralizing the international debate about AI benefits and dangers makes finding an international solution extremely hard. Exactly because the opposing party has been de-legitimatized, as morally inferior. When politics is replaced with (misplaced overconfident) morality, the actions in the (international) political arena are played according to moralistic terminology where one is right and the other is deadly wrong.

When we argued in Chapter 22 about the possibility of human collaboration (with AI) and international cooperation in terms of cognitive improvement and socio-moral progress, then we did not mean to say that it is a zero-sum game. Whereas international conflicts expressed in moralistic antagonistic terms, instead of political agonistic vocabulary, become dangerously deadly in its earnest meaning, it has become an ideology that is convinced about its own superiority. That is exactly what terrorism is meant to achieve, playing politics in terms of an extreme ideology conquering the world: "we are right and the rest are infidels, and to be destroyed". Similarly, if the West uses the argument of universal liberal democracy as a way to demonize Russia, China or other alternative political (admittedly more autocratic) systems, we risk to end up in dangerous zero-sum perceived situation. Compromises become almost impossible in such a context. In such situations, fundamental economic and military conflict may be the logic answer to settle the score. Something we should avoid at any cost.

Relations are part of an eco-system, determined by socio-moral values. But these agreed community-accepted values and norms do not need to result in a universal "consensus" perspective – potentially perceived as hegemonistic[18] – where there is hardly place for alternative options, and different opinions and perspectives. An open-minded society – and organizations thriving in such a context – will embrace *la différance* or different viewpoints. It are those differences and ambiguities and tensions that could allow internally dialogues to take place and externally dialectic agonistic conflicts to unfold in a relatively "peaceful" manner. Either way, these internal and external tensions potentially may paradoxally result in a new perspective. At this time of historical evolution, humankind is not ready for a global universalistic discourse with global governance structures that function. We will need to settle for a second best solution in international relations context in which agonistic politics, not antagonism, allows differences to be expressed in a legitimate manner.

2.2. Agonistic Solutions for Conflicts Acknowledging Legitimized Differences

Artificial intelligence should make progress in an agonistic legitimized international context – where national sovereignty can play its role – rather than being played out in antagonistic zero-sum calculations. A *pluriversum* that plays by certain agreed rules may be more desirable to resolve the inherent potential political conflicts. Global governance may be an interesting idea, but we don't have a super-institution – which likely would not be very democratic either – to enforce those rules and norms. At this point, it is destined to fail. An effective multilateral system within a unipolar world is an illusion. Hence why outright hegemonistic tendencies – from whatever side – are not desirable.

A. Establishing Collaborative Co-Existence in Cyberspace: How Realistic Is This?

The action-radius of AI in cyberspace is a new domain of international activity – characterized by a paradox in which both cooperation and conflict co-exist. Some activity in cyberspace and AI is very benign and has little impact on national security, whereas other activities are intimately connected to foreign policy, intelligence and national competitiveness. Here, some international arrangements should be created to encourage benign use and discourage malign use of AI. Achieving such a consensus will require enormous efforts – similar to international agreements to address pandemics such as SARS and Covid-19, or like addressing the enormous challenges around climate change and its negative impact on the survival of our planet.

And despite making efforts to establish such an international order that globally addresses challenges such as pandemics, international (cyber-)terrorism and global climate change, it is clear that the existing arrangements are inadequate in dealing with those contemporary challenges. Abandoning the idea of a more "balanced" global order would make matters worse. It is what some scholars in international relations would label "a world order 2.0"[19] – definitely beyond the scope of this chapter, but crucial nonetheless. The recent pandemic has shown the importance of some form of cooperative coordination, which admittedly was far from perfect, but it could have been worse. We have no choice but to continue to communicate within this international community. Probably, it will involve the major powers, including China and the US but also Japan, France, Germany, UK, Russia and India, and likely initial bilateral talks would be a good start since the UN Security Council and the G-20 may not be the ideal place to get such agreements sealed.

States carrying certain obligations is viewed as pragmatic, not an idealist wish. We have no choice but to coordinate and *co-exist*, like it or not. This idea of co-existence implicitly acknowledges the political legitimacy of the adversary and may lead a discourse in which solutions can be found. Call it a slow and sometimes painful dialectic process – without explicitly wishing for a unified cosmopolitical global order. The reality of such a new cosmopolitical order usually is nothing but a cosmetic materialization of fundamental power relations – grabbed by the existing political and economic elite. One need choices and differences to grow. Unification and a consensus-based new liberal political order is likely not the (only) solution to our global problems.

B. Who Is the Champion of a Peaceful Global Order?

Since China has gained a voice as a champion of globalization, now is the time for the Chinese elite to show that "deeds speak louder than words"[20]. Because the rise of digital flows is increasing competition in knowledge-intense sectors such as AI, protecting intellectual property is growing, generating a new form of competition around patents[21]. It is clear that in this new era of AI, digital capabilities will serve as the "rocket fuel" for a country's economy, be it China, US or any other country. Development in artificial intelligence does not stop at political borders. Digital literacy will become essential for any economy. Hence why we should encourage the development of the "good" of AI – wherever its origin – and minimize the potential harmful effects of the "bad" and the "ugly" of AI. Data governance and privacy beyond borders will prominently be part of such a benign development, whatever the political system. And let us not forget either that in today's competitive global environment, technology is too important to be left to the technologists or technocrats[22]. Relying on a cognitive argument that describes the facts is necessary, but human life is entangled with a unique socio-ethical sphere that evolves.

History has shown us that people and their governments have demonstrated resilience[23]. But the accelerating pace of technological change and its direct impact on so many lives is driving the current international system. And within the foreseen timespan, nation-states will keep holding walls and protect the sovereignty where necessary. We hope that there is a middle way in between outright protectionist antagonism and the danger of a unilateral autocratic superpower demolishing any hope to democratic accountability and responsibility.

We are all responsible to keep AI humane and aligned with human (moral) values, without being trapped in another (geo)political MAD strategy of potential extremely destructive AI weapons, or the desire to destroy the "adversary". The most terrifying threat by AI is autonomous weapons with the ability to kill without the intervention of any (moral thinking) human agent, authorizing such a killing.

Avoiding such potentially disastrous discourse is necessary, according to "senior diplomat" Henry Kissinger. Faith in the future is the indispensable quality of successful leaders showing us an elevated purpose people can believe in[24].

Describing myself as an "Asianized" proud Western democrat, I nonetheless strongly advocate the Western democracies to collaborate together to "develop an updated information model that reflects democratic (*I would personally prefer the notion "dialectic"*) principles and puts individuals, not companies or governments, in control of how data are collected and used[25]." However, I equally prod those democratic nation-states[26] to diplomatically collaborate with other political systems and attempt to reach some common ground to reach some minimal conditions to prevent mutually destructive politico-military disasters to occur. Political and corporate leadership needs to ensure that the promise of technology in the 21st century doesn't become a curse. And that some minimal form of "wisdom" may hopefully prevail.

Some thoughts to take away:

- The need to find new ways to channel this battle for supreme power (in fields like AI or other means to an end) over existing adversaries. Unfortunately, *most geopolitical thinking* has been reduced to **a zero-sum game**. Scholars refer to the 3Cs – confrontation, competition, and cooperation – when talking about the tensions between the two superpowers, the USA and China.

- Because of the **growing interdependencies** of our global economy, and global development challenges and goals (inclusive environmental concerns), a peaceful *co-existence* based on genuine (dialectic) dialogue, appropriate (global) governance practices (including transparency) and designated agreed boundaries is suggested.

- Turn **Antagonistic Relations** into **Agonistic Relations**, allowing peaceful co-existence and potentially some form of "containment".

PART V:
Making Wiser Decisions: Through *Paradoxal* and *Algo-Tuitional* Thinking

The final fifth part attempts to reconcile the notions of smart and wise decision-making with a deeper understanding of the strengths of human versus artificial intelligence. This synthesis may provide some preliminary suggestions on how executives could strengthen their decision-making, especially in turbulent uncertain times amidst increased global tensions and ambiguities – in the era of artificial intelligence.

How to deal with this kind of tensions? A tension looks like an either-or choice, whereas in reality, creative thinking may result in unexpected solutions that resolve those tensions through *paradoxal thinking* and leadership that understands how to deal with them. Paradoxal thinking allows boards and executives to transcend seemingly opposing ideas, and dialectically integrating them into a new innovative product or service could strengthen the competitive advantage of the organization.

These last chapters explain how statistical rational and algorithmic thinking should and could be combined with the more tacit intuitive gut feelings of many experienced leaders. Combining this form of algorithmic leadership that embraces intuitive emotional gut feelings and moral empathy may result in taking advantage of the best of both – akin to the logic behind dialectic paradoxal thinking in finding a synthesis between the cognitive sphere and the socio-ethical realm. I have labelled it "*algo-tuitional*" leadership to indicate that it is not a question of choosing one over the other, but trying to dialectically synthesize both forms of thinking. The research to understand superforecasters – as a counterintuitive force to artificial intelligence – highlights the importance of continuous adaptation, refining and updating of (new) information.

At the end of the day, AI can be helpful to organizations to improve the trustworthiness to both share- and stakeholders. In other words, to become a more mindful leader may help to improve the overall organization's sustainability, both in economic as well as in socio-ecological meaning. If making good and smart decisions that generate future cash flow while doing good is the new adage in business, this fifth part goes deeper into the manner leadership could achieve those objectives.

Artificial intelligence will become an incredible ally in automating repetitive processes and in augmenting the human cognitive ability to "see sooner" certain emerging patterns appearing on the horizon. Supported by AI's predictive powers within a relatively stable context, one could become a better forecaster. However, only humans (and likely some mammals) are fully aware of themselves; they are self-conscious about themselves and about the world around them. Only consciousness – that definitely goes beyond computational calculations[1] – is associated with wisdom. A mindful or fully conscious decision-maker carries (moral) responsibility. Only humans can make wise decisions, which AI is incapable of.

Chapter Twenty Five

How to Optimize
a Paradoxal Mindset?

"Yesterday I was clever, so I wanted to change the world. Today, I am wise, so I am changing myself".

Rumi, 13th-century Muslim poet

"There is little difference between obstacle and opportunity ... the wise are able to turn both to their advantage".

Machiavelli, 1513–1532, *The Prince*

"La science bien comprise ne peut qu'aider les croyants à se concentrer sur l'essentiel, et la religion, bien comprise aussi, donne sa veritable dimension à la science. Chacune a sa fonciton, et désormais dans chaque être humain doivent coexister un religieux et un savant. Oui, pour que la religion et la science ne se combattent plus dans la société, elles doivent cesser de se combattre dans l'être humain. Car, c'est là que se produisent les plus grands dégâts".

Omraam Michael Aïvanhov, spiritual educator, 1986

Life is an accommodation of contradictions and paradoxes. In times of change, uncertainty and scarcity, people experience enormous tensions and competing demands. Our world is increasingly characterized by contradictions, tensions and dilemmas. However, trying to look for trade-offs in making decisions and thus postponing or ignoring them is a form of intellectual laziness, if not dated thinking. Most of those trade-offs are imagined and not real. The boundaries you put around yourself or people – the model you apply – will obviously colour your perspective, but it will also limit it. Often, the model is too narrowly defined.

1. Paradoxal Thinking Beyond Dualistic Tensions
Maybe firms and their boards face an *emotional* innovator's dilemma[2] in which firms hesitate to move away from shareholder primacy thinking because others

seem to stick to the old traditional thinking. Others may stalk to embrace a stakeholder's perspective because it may or may not bring expected higher returns on investments. Most successful companies are so entrenched in mainstream thinking that they do not see the need to fundamentally change and move to another paradigm, what often can be uncomfortable, especially in the initial change process. The late Harvard Business School Professor Clayton Christensen has convincingly argued that entrenched companies can't shift to new, disruptive technologies because they have so much invested in the status quo[3]. Well, companies are equally afraid of paradoxes or ambiguities and shun away from a form of paradoxal thinking. Obviously, they are afraid to lose the current advantage and don't immediately see the real advantage yet to broaden their thinking. The current status quo has made them rich: why change a winning team?

1.1. Overcoming Tensions?

Well, the team may run out of fuel gas soon – by clinching to traditional ways of production. Firms and their boards need to dare to think more broadly – an *outside-in view* that extends beyond the colloquial in-the-box-thinking. But they also are encouraged to think big – an *inside-out view* – in terms of aspirations and goals, even though in the short-term they may feel like unreachable and unrealistic. To make

> *The* **Leading Question**:
>
> *Business and Politics face the increasingly daunting job of managing paradoxes under uncertainty. How to resolve those tensions and dilemmas into integrating them into manageable paradoxes?*

real changes, to make real progress, you need goals and objectives that nudge or genuinely change behavior. Claiming to properly treat your customers, suppliers and employees as you would for your own family remains an idle talk unless you adapt the incentive systems that pay out managers and employees alike for their performance and productivity. That requires a transformational change or adaptation in the structure and processes of an organization and its board functioning[4]. Adopting objectives to hope for "profit with purpose" – an alleged paradoxal goal to many boards – may lead to nothing if one does not adapt the remuneration package and its underlying criteria or goals to measure it.

Firms are used to squeeze the margins out of suppliers, employees and customers, who are all crucial stakeholders for a firm. However, we have learned that deeper relationships with these stakeholders pay off in a rather paradoxal manner: if you look only at the price, you won't get the lowest price. If your focus on the bottom line to maximize profit, you won't achieve that objective. Only by *focusing on the entangled relationships*, on the creating of value for the different crucial stakeholders, you jointly will more likely obtain a more optimum "equilibrium" with optimal prices and a bigger pie for all. By not just focusing on the transactional side with your stakeholders, but on the *relationships* with the share- and stakeholders, you'll paradoxally optimize your own goal, facilitated through the process of trust in the value creation process. Corporations such as *IKEA, Unilever, Pantagonia, Puma* and a number of other well-known brands have made this paradoxal approach on treating business relationships with generating genuine trust among stakeholders as their competitive trademark.

1.2. Overcoming Paradoxes?

The industry 4.0 context has even become more complex by the explosion in tech devices and algorithms that shape our lives and are transforming the business landscape. Fortunately, there is increasing empirical evidence from researchers and business practitioners alike that teach us to overcome contradictions and tensions – something wise sages in any field have been doing for centuries[5]. *Governing and managing and resolving paradoxes* remains a unique human (leadership) characteristic.

Since a paradox contains two contradictory, yet independent elements that operate simultaneously, resolving paradoxes demands a particular mindset. This new kind of *paradox mindset* suggests an alternative perspective, by accepting and learning to live with tensions associated with competing demands. Accepting instead of "fighting" these tensions allows executives and board members to balance and avoid a zero-sum perspective where you choose either of the two sides. This "paradox mindset" realizes that one demand enables the other and "combining" both may cultivate innovation and allow organizations and their leaders to thrive. Such a mindset is a key characteristic of wise decision-making. It's an approach that acknowledges opposing ideas and tensions, taking a more holistic view by embracing the ambiguities of fast-moving contexts. Wise paradoxal leaders do not choose between *"either/or"* but allow *"both/and"* to unfold into a new reality, transcending opposing ideas and creating innovative, competitive avenues.

Most organisms are interlinked and interdependent. Equally, the socio-economic sustainability of an organization is embodied in a paradigm of complex adaptive systems. These systems are interconnected with other systems: energy and resources, environmental and ecological, social and political. A dynamic equilibrium means that leaders must constantly navigate across opposing forces, creating a virtuous cycle that unleashes creativity and potential. This contextual ambidexterity is a quest for uncompromising solutions: a focus on operations *and* innovation, a more global *and* local focus. Such a synthesis requires culturally strong organizations, driven by unifying values, beliefs and principles. Even here we can find more paradoxes: *unity and diversity, globalization and localization, coherence and autonomy* – all to be synthesized in a dialectic intellectual process.

This is all fine in theory, but how does paradox management work in practice? Of course, you could follow your gut when tackling a paradox, but this is a rather unorthodox way of making important strategic decisions. Most business schools teach aspiring corporate leaders to apply analytical methods, using the available data to deal with contradictions and come up with the "best" option as argued in the first chapters. Wise leaders link their financial-oriented thinking to non-financial objectives. This matters very much because as any leader knows, financial and non-financial objectives often conflict, creating an existential struggle that has to be resolved. Usually, in times of crises, executives have to choose between keeping a consistent expected dividend for its capital providers versus keeping a job for all those providing their time and expertise to the company. That looks like a paradox where the executive has to make a choice between one over the other.

How do you reconcile apparently opposing perspectives? We've examined the ways in which people tend to approach a paradox. We can crystalize these into *avoidance, confrontation* and *transcendence*[6]. Clearly, wise decision-making should emphasize the third wherever possible.

A holistic perspective allows wise executives and board members to step back and reflect constructively. The best practitioners apply a "question-and-answer" approach, or *"dialectical synthesis-oriented deliberation"*. They bring moral and ecological values into the equation. In so doing, they move the debate beyond the constraints of purely financial objectives. A holistic perspective also enables leaders and boards to answer rising calls for transparency and flexibility. A trusted, mature and resilient leadership team needs integrity (MQ), competence and contextual understanding (IQ), foresight (RQ) and the capacity to feel empathy and *relate* with others (EQ). Only then will it be able to deliberate, communicate and execute in a win-win solution.

However, finding an appropriate decision in paradoxes remains a difficult task. Often those paradoxes and dilemmas contain "ethical" characteristics or choices to be made. And character in itself is a continuous work in process, principled but also fluid and adaptable to the changing circumstances. How does the American President deal with potential dilemmas like allowing (or not) the mining of lithium – a raw material used in microchips and batteries – in the pristine valleys of Nevada, the habitat of the Shoshone and Paiute Indians? Do you preserve nature and its ecologic bio-habitat for rare animals, or do you create economic opportunities for young people by providing green light for mining companies to create value in the area – with the unavoidable polluting activities as a negative externality? No clear answers for such a conundrum. Smartness may not suffice here. Wise decision-making may help. But no guarantees exist to serve all concerns.

2. Managing Paradoxes

From the 2008 financial crisis to the tsunamis of digitization and machine learning and now Covid-19, and the Russian invasion in Ukraine early 2022, life for leaders has never been more complex. Contradictions and tensions are multiplying by the day. Can we solve them? Research suggests that we can: by governing and managing paradoxes through *wising up*.

2.1. Incapability of AI to Resolve Paradoxes

At the firm level, the board functioning itself can be considered paradoxal – an ability that artificial intelligence cannot take over from humans and therefore cannot be digitally automated. The paradox at boards lies in the dual apparently contradictory function of supervising and coaching top management.

A. Intelligent and Conscious Humans Are Able to Transcend Paradoxes

The board's duties focuses on supervising and probing top leadership that is assumed to execute the strategy while also remaining constructive by supporting and coaching the management team and allowing it to take the lead in setting priorities for the future. This is a complex challenge and requires experience – especially emotional and cognitive abilities, and above all a high level of integrity that creates trust – to simultaneously fulfil these two main duties.

A similar paradox takes place at the national economic level as well. How to reconcile the financial pressure on the bottom line while managing firms with a more human face? Is it possible to simultaneously and harmoniously pursue (infinite) economic growth at national and firm level while keeping the growth within the ecological (finite) planetary boundaries and within socio-ethical standards as stipulated by our (contextual) relational norms and values? Maybe one could "consider" a transition from an economy driven by the goal of endless gross domestic product growth and quarterly profitability to one that "secures material sufficiency and spiritual abundance for all, in balance with the regenerative systems[7]" (of living organisms like the planet earth or adopting organizations).

Wise leaders go beyond being smart and reasonable[8] and navigate towards a form of *mindful consciousness and intelligence*. This enables a broader, even holistic perspective, to better "manage in the gray"[9]. Doing so means addressing complex situations with ethical or ecological consequences and moral duties[10], without necessarily cutting corners.

B. The Rider and the Elephant Jointly Deliver the Job

Both ethical *deontology* and *consequentialism* focus on the **reasonableness (and possibly also on the moral responsibility)** of the decision-maker – **the rational rider** metaphorically riding **the emotional elephant**. There is another third ethical road possible: *virtue ethics*[11]. Here, virtue resides in a well-trained "elephant" by the conscious "rider". Or like the 17th-century philosopher Spinoza eloquently argued in his *Ethica*[12] that emotions can't be mastered by our rational mind. These emotions can only be "controlled" by *nudging them* towards more powerful (positive) emotions. Spinoza basically argues that subduing of (negative) passions should be accomplished by reasons-induced positive emotions and not by pure reasons alone[13]. He even went further by suggesting that the norms that govern our social and personal conduct should be shaped by a deeper knowledge of humanity, one that "made contact with Nature within ourselves" – possibly a form of panpsychism[14]. If this would be true, then fundamental feelings like empathy may reveal something about our own "individual purpose" or "embodied soul".

Training takes daily practice and a great deal of repetition, as in *mindfulness training*. The proverbial conscious rider must take part in the training, but if moral instruction impacts only explicit knowledge – i.e. the rider who can clearly express and communicate – it will have no effect on the metaphorical elephant, and therefore little effect on behavior[15]. Moral practicing imbued in the unconsciousness of "affect" allows us to become virtuous and become more responsible. Only through practicing until our behavior is firmly engrained in our (unconscious) emotions and (conscious) feelings, our decisions will ultimately become more virtuous and responsible. And logically also wiser. *Only enhanced consciousness and broadened awareness can trigger more responsible and virtuous (moral) behavior.*

If morality is about dilemmas, then moral education is training in problem-solving. The rational rider may see the right way, but it remains ineffective until a strong emotion – the elephant – comes along to provide some force. The strength of character allows one to immerse self-consciousness in what one is doing well, as in a flow[16]. Moral education must also impact tacit knowledge – skills of social perception and social emotion so finely tuned that one automatically feels the right thing in each situation, knows the right thing to do, and then wants to do it. Morality, for the ancient sages, was a kind of practical wisdom, as in *wising up*. A wise leader attempts to gain a clear understanding of the net consequences of his/her actions, the core obligations and the inspiring virtues that one incorporates in his/her behavior through trained practices. However, you will also need to accept a struggle you may face in making wise decisions, since these may disrupt the status quo.

C. *Wise Corporate Leaders Being Mindful About the "Elephant" Who Can Be Nudged but Not Controlled*

Business and economics focus on the external material world. However, our internal mindset determines our perspective and the way we see and interpret this external world. Hence why **mindfulness** and **meditation** that positively affect and fine-tune our internal modelling are crucial for any leader. Literally and figuratively, *meditation* positively affects our brain by strengthening and increasing the neural networks of synapses and dendrites in the brain[17]. As in paradoxes, a wise leader is able to balance an internal mindset with the desire to "control" an external world. Moreover, if our perception changes because of increased meditative practices, managers and leaders will see the world differently. Let us try how that may work out in an organization.

Within *Toyota*, researchers found two opposing forces – expansive and integrative forces – that constantly create dilemmas and paradoxes. The expansive forces lead Toyota to initiate change and improvement. To prevent disintegration as result of the expansive forces, Toyota also harnesses integrative forces: the founders' values, open communication and up-and-in people management (commitment to long-term employment)[18]. All practices that stabilize the company help employees internalize their expectations and make sense of the environment in which they operate. Toyota's story makes contradictions and paradoxes a way of life, making the state of perpetual change the norm within Toyota. In a way, Toyota seems to be able to pursue both unpredictability *and* stability, and both analog (relations) *and* digital (efficiency transformation) at the same time.

By practicing and relying on "*both/and*" approach, Toyota cultivates simultaneously ideals and realism, synthesizing those apparent opposing ideas in a new dialectic reality that made Toyota one of the most formidable competitors in the car industry. Toyota being ambidextrous benefits from the best of two worlds and attains a dynamic equilibrium of *yin-yang*, to negate and preserve at the same time. The idea behind this dynamic dialectic and fragile equilibrium assumes that the apparent contradictory demands are often connected to, and dependent on one another. To resolve the contradiction, wise leaders look into where and how the contradiction emerges, and what the relationships between the contradictory demands are[19]. By grasping the bigger picture, or broaden the context of the problem, fully conscious – and thus potentially more conscient – wise leaders embrace a more holistic and often more effective solution.

2.2. Paradoxes Unpacked

How to unpack the tense anatomy of a paradox? We define a paradox as containing contradictory yet interrelated elements. Taken in isolation, these may seem logical. Taken simultaneously, they seem irrational, even absurd[20]. Paradoxes are sticky, they seem to persist over time. They are tricky and can easily lead to perceptions of inconsistency. The tensions they contain can provoke conflict and defensive reactions. No wonder leaders often feel paralyzed by paradoxes.

What exactly makes paradoxes so uncomfortable? One reason is our attitude to paradoxes. When we come up against one, we react defensively to this thorny or wicked problem. We seek to reduce our anxiety by suppressing its inconsistencies, "pushing them under the carpet". We seek pain relief by emphasizing one aspect of duality over the other. We frame the tension or contradiction as an either/or choice. Likely the result of the most "comfortable" option as in system 1 thinking. But doing this can make matters worse, leading to deep "mixed feelings" and the sense of feeling stuck. When we choose one option over the other, it's rather like a seesaw; sitting on one seat only pushes the other seat up, re-emphasizing its demands. Simplistic ways to avoid balanced, complex decision-making, or to hide a lack of courage, always lurks around the corner.

More than a *dilemma*[21], the notion of a *paradox* is rooted in the acceptance that logically and socially-constructed contradictions are *a natural part of reality*. Opposing yet interdependent, these elements pre-suppose each other for their existence and meaning.

Academic literature has surfaced numerous paradoxes in the individual and organizational contexts[22]. In all the research, it has become clear that, whatever the lexicon or definitions, executives will need to handle tensions and translate their conclusions directly into action. And the stakes become particularly high at CEO or board level. CEOs and their organizational boards will need to handle those tensions and therefore become very action oriented. Organizations have moved into a continuous state of dynamic equilibrium, where it is assumed to move across opposing forces, and attempt to create a virtuous cycle that unleashes creativity and human potential. It is through contextual ambidexterity – seeking

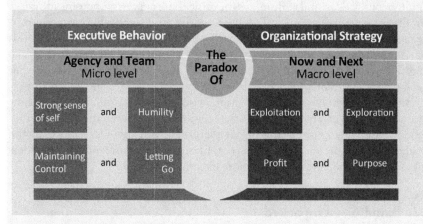

Figure 1: Key paradoxes inherent to executive behavior and organizations

Source: Interpretation by Verhezen & Gande (2020) of Waldman, D. & D. Bowen, (2016), "Learning to be a paradox-savvy leader", *Academy of Management Perspectives*, Vol. 30(3): 316–327

an uncompromising solution with a simultaneous focus on operations and on innovation, being more profitable and more purposeful.

Organizations face the immanent choice of exploitation of the now and the need for continuous explorations of the new. Or alternatively formulated, the paradox of simultaneously enacting both continuity and change. We here conceptually distinguish two paradoxes at the executive leadership level and two at the organizational level – as Figure 1 clearly visualizes.

A. *Individual Behavior*

At an individual agency level, executives show a talent to synthesize seemingly opposing characteristics. Two paradoxes draw our attention:

1. *Strong Sense of Self Combined with Humility*
   Good leaders are likely to display humility by putting themselves in perspective, admitting their uncertainties and incompleteness, drawing on the strengths of their peers and followers. More difficult is the ability to maintain a strong sense of self while maintaining this kind of humility. Put together, these characteristics are extremely effective in generating the envisaged outcomes. It really takes personal confidence and humility to reconsider our past commitments and/or beliefs. Wharton Business School Professor Adam Grant calls it *confident humility*[23]. This confident humility allows us to rethink them and find ways to integrate or balance opposing ideas.

2. *Maintaining Control While Letting Go of Control*

    Another persistent paradox for leaders is that of maintaining control and letting go. Recent research confirms the growing need to give up control and allow for more autonomy on the part of employees. Executives need to learn to combine "natural" self-centredness (as in high personal performance and rewards) with other-centredness (as in serving the team to achieve organizational objectives). Remember that contexts continuously change, and boards need to acknowledge those changes and let go in order to adapt strategy and paradoxally try to keep a certain control over the organization to steer it away from threats towards commercially apt business opportunities.

B. Organizational Strategy

At the organizational strategic level, executives skilfully combine variables, ideas of the "two opposing sides" in a dialectic way, as in transcending those tensions into a coherent and inclusive narrative:

1. *Pursuing Profits and Maintaining a Higher Purpose*

    Times of crisis present executives with a particularly painful paradox: consistently meeting the dividend expectations of capital providers "versus" preserving jobs. Covid-19 has created an even more daunting choice. Should all companies be saved at all costs? And how do we preserve the financial interests of investors while limiting unemployment and supplier bankruptcies? Let's recall that wise decision-making combines the pursuit of profitability *and* the sustained survival of an organization while embracing the concerns of other stakeholders – nowadays often expressed in ESG criteria. A rather challenging and very difficult task, but I'm confident that the right leadership will be up to the task. This was indeed the initial idea that allowed me to collaborate and advise Amrop's board to rethink their own vision on what kind of new leadership is necessary today.

    We can rephrase this paradox as *now and next*, or *short term and long term*. Wise decision-making transcends the long-running debate around corporate social responsibility "versus" mainstream neoliberal economics. The latter perspective considers the purpose of business to be simply making money within the boundaries of legality. The rather traditional view is increasingly shifting to consider the intrinsic moral value of *doing well by doing good*. It is about being profitable and giving meaningful purpose at the same time.

    Leaders who are led by a deep purpose[24] challenge themselves easier to deliver both social benefits and exceptional financial results. It seems that by narrowing the leader's vision to a clear purpose, it facilitates the allocation of innovation budgets. This focus in turn enables firms to think more broadly and holistically inside this narrower area, taking a *systems approach* to arrive at innovations they might never thought to pursue. It is a paradox indeed: "by going narrower, you wind up going much broader and having more impact. In this respect, purpose helps companies to address complex or "wicked" problems that require collaborative solutions[25]". It is clear that purpose almost always confers *relational* benefits, enabling close bonds to form between the organization and external stakeholders, including customers, suppliers, NGOs and local communities. Purpose provides a logic for building an ecosystem of collaborative partnerships – facilitated by defined shared superordinate goals that all partners agree upon and can rally behind those[26].

The beauty of the *now and next* paradox is that it highlights the importance of economic objectives (without which organizations will not sustainably survive) while creating value that respects other objectives: at the strictest minimum, that of doing no harm to other people, communities or the environment. Over a longer term, a good reputation and "sharing" corporate created value will play an increasingly important role in convincing customers and employees alike — beyond focusing only on the shareholders who provide the capital. Somehow this paradox can be rephrased as the *now "versus" next*, or short term versus long term.

This paradox highlights the importance of economic objectives without which organizations will not sustain, but also the importance of creating value that respects other objectives of not harming others or communities.

2. *Exploitation and Exploration*
    Organizations face another core strategic choice: the *exploitation* of the *current* competitive position and the *exploration* of *future* business opportunities. Companies maintain continuity by exploiting their current assets and optimise the cash flow while simultaneously pursuing change through exploring new innovative opportunities. This is also known as the paradox of *continuity and change*. Any investor knows that the value of a company is based on both its competitive position that exploits its current assets to the fullest, as well as the expectation that the company will innovate and explore to generate superior returns on the investment made.

    The electric car manufacturer *Tesla*, for instance, has currently anno 2022, a quite high valuation in comparison with most automotive brands. This is mainly based on the expectation of investors that Tesla will outmanoeuvre its competitors in electric vehicles, giving it a higher potential for profitability, and a chance of meeting their financial objectives. Or in financial jargon, Tesla is expected to generate considerable alpha returns above the industry average, and paradoxally its current financials seem to beat the current expectations, pushing up the stock price even more.

Paradoxes involve contradictory yet interrelated elements that exist simultaneously and persist over time. The essence of paradoxes that two opposites coexist and must be dealt with as a joint interdependent pair. Thus, for executives, to act paradoxically is to adopt a both/and rather than either/or strategy.

Companies like the *Swiss-based* ABB have learned to embrace paradoxes, to embrace the contradictions like being global and local, being a big and small and being radically decentralized and centralized. ABB taught how the engineering multinational is learning to embrace paradoxes: global and local, big and small, decentralized and centralized. This paradoxal view at ABB is nicely expressing in the following statement: "We as a global company need to work out how we adapt to changing standards, and local regulations. If the world gets too fragmented, we won't get the scale to be efficient. But if we find a way to share our global platform, doing local adaptation in a smart way, then we might be able to find a way to win"[27].

Embracing contradiction in the hotel industry enabled the Canadian entrepreneur Isadore Sharp to found the *Four Seasons* hotel group. Its new, paradoxical concept changed the industry forever. Four Seasons stands for the ultimate in luxury. Yet its humble beginnings could not have hinted at this. Isadore Sharp used his "opposable mind" to create a new model[28]; a hotel with the intimacy of your home and the amenities of a large convention hotel. He combined the best of small and big, redefining luxury as a service in the hospitality industry. Integrative thinkers such as these take a broader view while zooming in on what is salient. Instrumental to Isadore Sharp's winning resolution was his choice to attend not just to the stated demands of his guests, but also to their unstated but deeply-held longing to be at home or at their office. Because that wish was in his field of vision, he was able to take into consideration things his competitors couldn't, because they simply didn't know these things existed. The creation of an intimate luxury business and convention hotel reflects the integrative, or paradoxical mind at work, with service at centre of this synthesis. Great leaders actually welcome complexity, ambiguity and paradoxes because they know that the best answers arise from this fertile terrain.

The organizational paradox of *competition* and *cooperation* is one of the most famous. A form of co-opetition[29]? From a standard economic viewpoint, these two elements are like oil and water. *Visa* embraced this paradox from its origins – reconciling the tension. Its member financial institutions were fierce competitors. They – not Visa – issued the cards. So they were constantly chasing each other's customers. But they also had to cooperate with each other. For the system to work, participating merchants had to be able to take any Visa card, issued by any bank, anywhere, abiding by certain standards, participating in a common clearing house operation. To resolve this contradiction, Visa sets the following parameters: its members were free to create, price and market their own products under the Visa name, even as they engaged in intense cooperation. This allowed the system to expand worldwide within 10 years, even in the face of different currencies, languages, legal codes, customs and cultures.

Technological innovation is allowing many companies to collaborate in selected domains while competing in the product and service arenas. In the open-system approach, many different stakeholders are invited to participate in the innovation process. With its open innovation platform, *Procter & Gamble* is an example. And in cybersecurity, companies and government institutions are hiring hackers to help them to close virtual loopholes.

Effective leaders are likely to display humility by putting themselves in perspective, admitting their uncertainties and incompleteness, and fully utilizing strengths in their peers and followers. More difficult is the ability of an executive who can simultaneously have a strong sense of self while maintaining humility. Together, these characteristics are extremely effective to generate the envisaged outcomes. Another tempting paradox for leaders is the one of maintaining control and letting go of control. Recent research seems to suggest the need to give up control and allow for more autonomy on the part of employees[30].

Crucial for executives is not to be trapped in fixating on one pole of the paradox while avoiding the other. Indeed, executives have traditionally been rewarded based on a strong sense of self, showing high degrees of self-confidence and boldness, and basking in the limelight of success. They usually deal with short-term pressures and results – maintaining continuity – because their accountability is tied to short-term results. As in many things in life, most organisms are interlinked and interdependent: similarly, the long-term socio-economic sustainability of an organization is embodied in the paradigm of complex adaptive systems that are pervasively interconnected with energy, resources and interdependent environmental and ecological, social and political systems.

Some thoughts to take away:

- **Ethical thinking** – constituting the crucial *socio-ethical pathway* to fully understand a context more holistically – is here linked to the collaboration within our mind of **unconscious emotions** – the "elephant" – with **enhanced consciousness** that may result in a more sentient and conscientious "rider".
  - Only a higher form of consciousness can lead to taking responsible decisions, and thus to wiser decision-making.
  - Consciousness is sentient and goes beyond calculative computation.
  - Consciousness and wisdom are likely causally associated.

- **Paradoxes** involve **contradictory yet interrelated elements** that exist simultaneously and persist over time. The essence of paradoxes that two opposites coexist and must be dealt with as a joint interdependent pair. Thus, for executives, to act paradoxically is to adopt a both/and rather than either/or strategy.

- Moral practicing imbued in the *unconsciousness of "affect"* allows us to become virtuous and become more responsible. Only through **practicing** until our behavior is firmly *engrained in our (unconscious) emotions*, our *decisions and actions will ultimately become more virtuous and responsible*.

Chapter Twenty Six

"Dialectic" Dialogues in a Business Context

"We do not receive wisdom, we must discover it for ourselves, after a journey through the wilderness which no one can make for us, which no one can spare us, for our wisdom is the point of view from which we come at last to regard the world".

Marcel Proust

"The test of first-rate intelligence is through the ability to hold two opposed ideas in the mind at the same time, and still retain the ability to function".

F. Scott Fitzgerald, "The back-up", *Esquire*, 1936

"The most profound technologies are those that disappear. They weave themselves into the fabric of everyday life until they are indistinguishable from it".

Mark Weiser, computer pioneer, 1991

W ise leaders benefit from an integration of diverse and opposing ideas. It is this kind of paradox mindset that allows CEOs and their board to take a different perspective beyond prioritizing of either/or choices. Managing paradoxes implies that wise leaders direct the organizations beyond a mere zero-sum calculation towards some form of dialectic synthesis that often results in a competitive advantage because of its unique dynamic, often surprising and integrated "system" approach. This kind of *dialectic synthesis* will require culturally strong organizations – driven by values, beliefs, principles and interdependent practices that unite the organization, its leaders and employees alike. More often than not, such integrated solutions – with a both/and approach – advocating integrated solutions – often result in some form of competitive advantage. You can label it *contextual ambidexterity*.

Intelligence adapts to new changed contexts. The moment there is a form of internal representa-tion of part of our world; we likely can talk about a level of general intelligence. Remarkably, humans are born with an innate form of representation – an unconscious form of intelligence – that is characterized by a complexity unraveled yet.

Our intelligence has enabled us to find innovative solutions for numerous challenges: smart executives may be very innovative and able to increase the efficiency and profitability of the firm in the short time. However, this alleged smartness often (unconsciously or consciously) omits the concerns of other stakeholders. The tension is been interpreted as a dilemma – not even a trade-off – where one takes one side over the other. Only the creation of value for shareholders counted; the creation of value for stakeholders is deliberately omitted, or in best scenario seen as a beneficial positive side-effect for some "lucky" stakeholders.

> **Recommendation:**
>
> *Wise Corporate Leaders – chosen by boards and often assisted by executive search companies after a lengthy search process – need to adhere to a more integrative and dynamic perspective beyond zero-sum choices. This kind of paradox mindset allows boards and their leaders to resolve tensions and paradoxes without usual trade-offs. Such dynamic and "contextual ambidexterity" allows to go beyond mere either/or choices and often create a more coherent and integrated new narrative.*

1. Integrative Synthesis-Thinking

Wise decision-making opts to find a balance between those apparently opposing perspectives of shareholders on the one hand, and concerned or anxious employees, (un)happy customers and other affected stakeholders on the other hand. Better able to deal with such tensions, dilemmas, contradictions and paradoxes, instead of letting it festering on. When well-managed, this paradoxical "energy" (resulting from the tension itself) can potentially generate solutions that are *potentially also* more ethical and ecological.

Paradoxal leadership is described as *quiet leadership* by my colleague Professor Steven Poelmans[1] at the Antwerp Management School. Indeed, this paradoxal leadership resonates with a more "sustainable" form of leadership these days. In its discretion, wise or paradoxal executives lead by example. It is inclusive and definitely not limited to a traditional control and command style. These days, *self-organizing teams*[2] seem more sensible to effectively adapt to learning opportunities.

It takes cognitive complexity – or in other words, sophisticated brainpower – to juxtapose the contradictions and tensions in a paradox, to explore potential synergies and question simplistic either/or answers or assumptions.

Former Rotman School of Management's Dean, Professor Robert Martin, joins other strategic thought leaders in proposing *integrative thinking*[3]. This is a way of reframing the relationship between tensions, capturing both the distinct features and interwoven nature of these opposites. By holding opposing ideas in our minds simultaneously, we can find new intersections, creative perspectives and frameworks. Wise corporate leaders, chosen by boards- often assisted by executive search companies after an intensive process – need to adhere to a more integrative and dynamic perspective beyond zero-sum choices. This kind of paradox mindset allows boards and their leaders to resolve tensions and paradoxes without the usual trade-offs. This contextual ambidexterity allows leaders to go beyond mere either/or choices and create a more coherent and integrated new narrative.

Motions of tension in business create ambiguity and may frustrate executives who seek to convey clarity and stability in their decision-making and communication with others. Integrative thinking is not just cognitively tricky. It demands confidence and inner strength to take risks, to act on uncertainty, to create a new or different context and to embrace ambiguity. The alternative, as we've seen, usually leads to anxiety and defensive behavior.

1.1. A Dialectic Approach De-Constructed

We know that confident leaders accept setbacks as learning opportunities. They seek to excel at seemingly conflicting goals, embracing challenges at each turn in the road. The paradox road is a rocky one indeed; as a tension becomes more prominent, conflict can easily rear up. This is particularly true when opposing demands are held by different groups of stakeholders. Juxtaposing these, wise leaders push themselves and others to question existing assumptions and seek out new possibilities.

The dialectical approach in action reaches a "higher" form – a better, more integrated solution. Most able and wise executives will be able to manage these conflictual tensions and paradoxes through juxtaposing competing demands and pushing themselves and others to question existing assumptions and seek out new possibilities. It should not surprise us that all forms of intelligence should be switched on to enable this difficult process of integrating apparently opposing fiduciary duties and required features elements at a board[1], both in its supervisory as well as in its coaching and advisory role.

Finally, communication skills are an essential part of paradoxical leadership; articulating an overarching vision and purpose across competing demands, engaging with people and helping them to deal with wicked problems like these. Effective communication skills and effectively articulating an overarching vision and purpose across competing demands become critical in engaging with others to deal with those opposing ideas and tensions – as yin and yang visualized in Figure 1 that dialectically results in a new synthesis. Leaders stress a *both/and* approach that is effectively communicated in a consistent and confident but humble manner. In other words, cognitive complexity not only offers novel responses to paradoxes but also helps surface new information, fuelling opportunities for communication, and bolstering confidence. These effective paradox leadership skills reinforce each other when they are integrated.

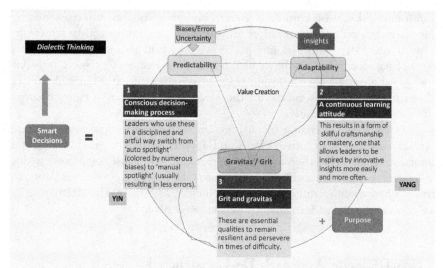

Figure 1: Accomplished and reasonable decisions = smart decision-making through a dialectic lens

Executives, somehow, need to learn to combine the "natural" self-centredness of high self-performance and rewards, with other-centredness that is based on serving the team to achieve the organizational objectives. In that sense, one could argue that *paradoxal leadership behavior*[4] is structurally and individually *ambidextrous*. The two sides of behaviors coexist, like *yin and yang*. In fact, a lot of the decision-making is characterized by seemingly opposing ideas, such as control versus autonomy, treating subordinate uniformly and fairly while allowing individualization, enforcing work requirements while allowing flexibility. Research indicates that the combination of holistic thinking, integrative complexity and organic (versus mechanistic) structures helps leaders to deal with paradoxes and help to think "paradoxally"[5]. Such attitude towards paradoxes and ambiguities often engender more *proficient, adaptive* and *proactive* behavior on behalf of the executive leader, but also on behalf of their followers or subordinates.

Resolving a paradox demands a "***dialectical***" approach. Simply put, this is about viewing issues from multiple perspectives based on discourse and genuine conversations. One should not underestimate the relational power of good conversations and respectful dialogues. A satisfying conversation is one that usually stimulates us to think or reflect in a way we never thought or did something before. It's in (virtual or physical) conversation and dialogue that we progress and come up with new ideas. It is a quest for the most economical, reasonable reconciliation of information and positions. More than pursuing the *middle ground* or a *trade-off*, the paradox-savvy executive is actually transcending the opposing ideas to build something new. S/he seeks an optimization, a simultaneous pursuit of both poles over time. Skilfully addressing a conflict within a paradox often produces a new set of arrangements and practices: a transformation that releases and transcends the core tension. So, in paradox resolution, it's the *tension itself* that has provided the synergy for a novel idea or perspective. Taking a paradox perspective, we deliberately attempt to *dialectically* reframe a tension and give sense to decision-making. In the most basic sense, **"dialectical thinking"**[6] refers to the reconciliation of opposites. We often fall into the habit of thinking of things in very black-and-white terms. We either love or hate something. We are either strong or weak. We are either happy or depressed. We either accept and move on, or reject and rebel. Dialectical thinking encourages us to consider that both of these things – which seem like opposites – can coexist and that they can combine to create a "new" truth. It emphasizes "and" (both/and) instead of "but" (or either/or).

A defensive response, however, seeks to minimize anxiety by suppressing the inconsistencies. These responses emphasize one aspect of the duality over the other. A dialectical approach like the paradox perspective, however, is rooted in the premise that human understanding of reality is often composed of logically and socially constructed contradictions. In the dialectic process, the potential or effective conflict produces a new set of arrangements and practices as in a transformation that releases the tension. In a paradox, the tension has provided synergy for a new novel idea or perspective which gives sense to this decision-making process.

1.2. Distinctive Western and Eastern Perspectives on Paradoxes

Western philosophical traditions have struggled with vexing tensions, though some great thinkers, leaders and artists have integrated them. For example, German philosopher Hegel puts dialectical thinking at the core of understanding of the past and the present. Abraham Lincoln – who has been considered as one of the best US presidents in history – was able to overcome opposing ideas and promoted the adversaries in his cabinet to keep the North and the South united while attempting to abolish slavery in the South. Beethoven and Mozart translated paradoxes into a source of creativity, combining the rigour of the sonata form with fluidity of expression. Picasso used angularity to express vulnerability, and Van Gogh united the everyday and the divine. Moreover, over the past 150 years, Western scientists have started to embrace more holistic theories. This is particularly the case in quantum physics, a domain in which paradoxes have been described and discussed by a host of eminent thinkers, such as Einstein, Bohr, Heisenberg and Schrödinger.

A. "Holistic" Balancing: An "Asian" Perspective

Western tradition has tended to regard the components of a paradox as "twin" (related but distinct entities). In the Chinese context, a paradox is composed of two interdependent opposites, or dualities. The interplay between them is like the way in which silence and sound dance together – they are inseparable, and each makes no sense without the other. Balance is essentially about the wholeness in which all dualities, polarities and complementary forces find their resolution.

The "Eastern" perspective – though admittedly that is in itself an oversimplification – is culturally quite different from the Western view. If Western traditions tend to see contradictions as conundrums, then Eastern equivalents have often embraced them, weaving them into a more coherent, practical philosophy. Consider Chinese *Taoism*. This philosophy of the Way proposes that two sides of any contradiction exist in an active harmony. They are opposed, but connected and mutually controlling. Taoist *yin-yang* philosophy sees the world as holistic, dynamic and dialectical. All universal phenomena are shaped by the integration of these two opposite cosmic energies: *Yin* represents the "female" energy, and *yang*, the "male". Both forces operate in a universal and integrated way, dynamically shaping reality and generating constant change.

The Asians interpret the universe as a dialectic process in which any "sphere" is divided along two planes with a curved division separating them: one side is *yang*, and on the other is *yin*. Each side contains within it the seed or core of the other. According to Taoist Chinese thinking, what is now yang will potentially produce yin, and yin will probably change into yang again. The yin-yang circle is in continuously spinning motion – as attempted to visualize in Figure 1 above. Both yin and yang coexist in harmony or are able to compensate each other – even neutralize or balance each other. Yin and yang describe functions, or stages in the process of a constantly changing context[7]. In this Chinese or rather Asian philosophy, nothing is yin or yang of itself. In this sense, the Chinese universe presents itself as one big correlative network, wherein everything is linked to everything, or wherein each element requires the presence of the other for it to be able to fulfil its full potential.

Quite interesting is the I-Ching (the revered Chinese Book of Change) that symbolizes the notions inspiration, integrity and harmony as perfectly balanced between yin and yang[8]. Not coincidentally that these three notions are directly linked to the *relational* socio-moral pathway of learning and thinking. Wise decision-makers need to walk a fine line, a balancing act of sustaining a high moral integrity, inspiring the internal and external stakeholders forward to a meaningful purpose and attempting to harmonize the numerous stake-brokers' interests.

Other Eastern systems such as Buddhism also embrace contradictions. In Zen Buddhism, the *koan* – a proposition that defies rational logic – is a paradox or question designed as a meditation discipline. "Listen to the sound of one hand clapping" is perhaps the most famous example of a Koan.

We don't generally find a purely rational, truth-seeking perspective in Eastern traditions. With a tendency to embrace contextual ambiguities, the Eastern view has been less concerned with clearing the path for an ultimate truth. In that sense, it is close to Aristotle's quest for balance and *eudamonia* ("human flourishing"). Confucius and Lao Tzu (the founder of Taoism) believed that the truth is often found in the middle. This conveys a dynamic concept, an active harmonious integration of opposites, rather than a reactive compromise. The *middle kingdom* – as its emperors considered China to be for many centuries – calls for maintaining an integrated life by balancing these extremes. In this way, opposing elements are woven into exactly the holistic and paradox thinking that we're emphasizing.

B. A "Western" View on Balancing

Meditation is the Eastern way of training oneself to take things "philosophically". It is the opposite of "judgementalism" or naïve realism[9]. The Eastern approach to paradoxes, however, indicates to embrace, integrate and transcend apparent opposites, in contrast with pre-dominant Western thinking, in which information is processed by breaking up the whole into parts that need to be analyzed in detail.

Judeo-Christian and Muslim beliefs revolve around a single deity that assumes "one absolute truth". Hence the desire in Western philosophy to find that truth – preferably with capital T – or establish rational foundations for it. A prime example in search for (absolute) truth is the German philosopher Immanuel Kant's attempt to separate emotions from pure reason[10]. This allegedly allowed humans to "touch the absolute notion of truth", *das Ding an Sich (Thing-in-itself)*, though this (speculative and regulative) noumenon can never be fully "grasped" as opposed to what Kant defines the phenomena that appear to a human observer[11]. But rationalizing life to its purest form ignores the shape-shifting nature of historical and contextual "truth". We have to understand Kant's thinking in the context of the Enlightenment, a movement that subordinated faith and emotions to reason. However, after Immanuel Kant, many thinkers reintroduced the importance of emotions, from David Hume to Charles Darwin. Evolutionary theory in particular demonstrated the importance of emotions in our thinking and very survival. In the same vein, research in ethical theory and ethical development encompasses different aspects of ethical sensitivity, of **care** and **control**, a *female "relational"* component, and a more *masculine "pure reasoning"* component[12].

More recently, neuroscience has indicated the value of combining cognitive, "moral" and emotional qualities, as in empathy and care. We could even see this as the new Enlightenment, one that is increasingly proving its metal in the business world and is captured in our concept of wise decision-making.

Western languages have a rich vocabulary for reasoning, logic and analysis, much less for introspection. So it has been hard for many executives in the West to accept intuition as legitimate. Sanskrit, in contrast, has about 20 terms for "consciousness" alone. And Mandarin elegantly visualizes the notion.

Perhaps the most famous paradox is *wei-ji*, the Mandarin word for "crisis", formed by combining the characters for "danger" and "change point". This expresses the Chinese view that adversity and change are inextricably linked in a dynamic relationship. So crisis is not an insurmountable problem but a function of transformation, in which paradoxical thinking can lead to opportune action.

Quite a number of Asian (most often overseas Chinese-originated) companies emerged after the Asian financial crisis of 1997–2001. Their founders sought new opportunities and responded quickly. As Jack Ma, founder of Alibaba, puts it: "one must run as fast as a rabbit, but be as patient as a turtle". I have first-hand experienced the dire consequences of this Asian crisis that lead to bankruptcies and social dramas, all because of the one-sided approach to grow business, a quite "*yang*-oriented" perspective where caring (as in *yin*) hardly played an important role in decision-making – with imbalances as result.

In essence, we must be willing to accept our own fallibility and find common ground because, after all, our concerns are roughly the same: to identify and solve challenges that daily affect our lives. In business terms, boards need to create shared value, as a common ground, that minimizes harm of stake-brokers and optimizes the (long-term) sustainability of the organization and its (equity blockholding) owners.

2. Paradoxal Leadership

Given the power of the paradox lens, it's not surprising that paradox management is becoming an ever more important skill. A recent study by my colleague Prof. Ans De Vos of the Antwerp Management School confirms that one of the most important characteristics expected from executives is the ability to adapt to change and lead transformation[13].

Paradoxal leadership can definitely help to adapt to change. Business success lies in the ability to go beyond the existing frame of reference to find the common ground that can hold the interests of all parties. Paradoxical integration provides a framework for discovering areas of convergence beyond conventional reference points. Moreover, paradox-savvy executives are not pursuing a middle of the ground in terms of the paradoxal poles, but instead involve an optimization or simultaneously pursuit of both poles over time. Embracing paradoxes implies an integration of both poles. As recent neuroscientific insights seem to indicate, an ideal pursuit is a combination of cognitive, "moral" and emotional qualities (as seen in socio-moral relations), and not the overblown pure rational sensitivity-deprived approach that aims to control the world and inform in "digits". Maybe this is what we can describe as **consciousness**, a human ability to not just be rational but allowing cognition to be affected by affect, feelings, values and creative imagination as argued earlier. Only an enlightened form of consciousness – possibly evolving in conscience – can facilitate ethical or responsible decisions. It is this mindfulness of our responsibility that generates or is associated with wisdom.

Let's look at the profile – and "equipment" – of the paradoxical leader.

2.1. Paradoxal Leadership Capabilities

In Figure 2, we are looking at two main variables that are crucial for any leader to resolve paradoxes: strategic sensing and integrative ability of corporate leadership. *Strategic sensing* is about being forward looking, with an eye on the best opportunity. Think of it as anticipating change, spotting (weak) signals, subtle trends, connecting dots, rather than reacting to a crisis. *Integrative abilities* enable leaders to make sense of a situation and manage contradictions, as we have explored. We here distinguish four kinds of leaders, with the understanding that the higher the strategic sensing and intuitive experienced way of making decisions, the more holistic and easier paradoxes can be overcome.

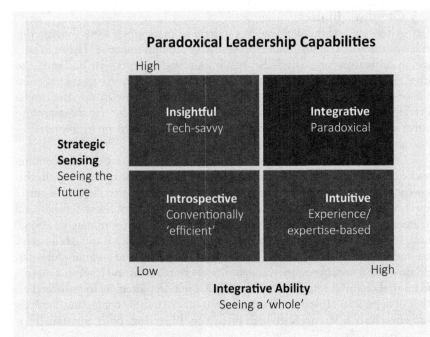

Figure 2: Paradoxal leadership capabilities

Insightful leaders are usually tech-savvy and have a clear understanding of where to direct the company, but are not necessarily attuned to the needs of all different players and stakeholders, and inclusive of these.

Introspective leaders are somehow operating in a psychic prison. They may have no real clue about what's going on in the wider environment, lacking a 360 degree awareness, and are focused on efficiencies. These conventional leaders settle paradoxes by choosing one pole over another.

Intuitive leaders may be low on strategic scanning but have a kind of sixth sense. Instinctive operators, some actually continue to do well, based on their experience and expertise. Their returns are no worse or better than others; however, the variance in terms of performance is huge.

Integrative leaders are capable of very sophisticated interpretations and are able to manage contradictions. As mentioned, integrative paradox leadership is set to become one of the big competencies that we'll be talking about moving forward and when we're thinking about organizational change.

2.2. From Collaborator to Trusting Integrator
We've looked at the human tendency towards a "flight" reaction when facing the teeth of a paradox. The zero-sum or either/or approach is a feature of this stress response, a basic attempt to prioritize, to choose a trade-off.

A. A Paradox Mindset

Alert, self-aware and mindful leaders can help team members work through this tendency, towards a mature, more thoughtful or mindful response. They can help them to cultivate a paradox mindset[14]. We allow both aspects – yin and yang – to thrive. The paradox mindset frees mental resources and drives us towards new solutions, cultivating innovation in the process. Such a paradox mindset can be cultivated. One can learn to balance and make decisions for the short term to survive *and* the long term to thrive, or to ensure physical isolation in corona times while also enabling social connection.

What other characteristics are needed to be effective in transcending paradoxes? First, diversity to bring different cognitive views to the group. In this moment, when problems are no longer routine, teams who provide cookie-cutter answers won't be successful. Diversity allows for varied insights. Second, behavioral integration combines individual behaviors, so a group can coordinate its efforts. Third, high flows of information need to be shared, which leads to high levels of trust and better collaboration. Leaders – when they are aware and mindful – can help their team members work through their flight reaction and towards a mature and more thoughtful response. Such a paradox mindset attempts to transcend an either/or approach. However, learning how to manage these competing demands more effectively is strangely enough often very liberating. Both emotionally as well as cognitively.

Resolving tensions in a paradoxical "yin/yang" situation requires wise leaders to acknowledge, deliberate and integrate the opposing ideas to reach a higher (dialectic) understanding. It can be argued that these leadership capabilities can be translated into an organizational context in which the different forms of intelligence can be integrated to form trust and social capital.

Can we really grow a paradox mindset? Yes, a paradox mindset will (1) reframe the question, (2) accept the tension and develop comfort with the discomfort and (3) distance oneself and search for new possibilities – as visualized in Figure 3.

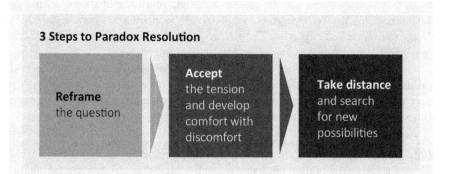

Figure 3: Paradox resolution

By *reframing the initial question*, we may achieve a new dialectic synthesis, at a higher level, where we discover new ways to do both (instead of either/or) that can even reinforce each other. *Acceptance* allows us to reach the understanding that tensions are a natural part of reality and that we all experience these opposing ideas to a certain extent. Once we accept inconsistency, we eventually learn to feel more comfortable in its natural habitat – the paradox. *Distancing our ego* allows us to take decisions for others rather than for ourselves. Cultivating our awareness and mindfulness (via meditative practices for instance) helps. Distancing our ego often facilitates the creative solutions that are a feature of good paradox management. Surprisingly, this often leads to creative solutions. Moreover, and as mentioned, the humility to share our struggle with others provides comfort and helps us see the bigger picture. A paradox mindset may not be able to resolve all problems or tensions. But it will allow us to look at the challenge with fresh eyes, understand the need to adapt and uncover a different way of working.

B. Paradoxal Dialectic Thinking Creates Trust

One of the side effects of dialectic thinking is that it usually engenders trust. The reason is quite simple, because the notion trust also consists of a number of components. Trust in the Chinese language, *xin-ren* clearly shows two distinctive elements[15]: (1) a cognitive component "*xin*" that is usually associated with competence. A confident executive with a high IQ and RQ, typically showing a high level of professional competence, can be expected to take reasonable risks that likely will pay off. This is a typical Western interpretation of trusting the most competent manager to execute a task. However, (2) "*ren*" refers to a second affective component of trust. Asians will only trust someone who is also emotionally tuned in (EQ) or has the reputation of moral integrity (MQ). In other words, without that emotional affective component, most Asians will not feel comfortable with trusting some "competent" professional who is not perceived to be "social" or having the integrity that will protect the family interests and not just his or her own. Trusting someone is a form of intelligence, risking your own vulnerability by relying on someone else without any certainty that the trust will not be misused.

Overall, we here simplify the complexity behind the notion of trust[16] and reduce the determining factors to four major features that we have consistently used throughout this book. Two are related to the *cognitive* path to learn, competence (IQ) and safeguarding or sensing the future (RQ). The two others are closely linked to the socio-moral path to learn, empathy or emotional intelligence (EQ) and moral integrity (MQ) as the basis for *any relation*. However, these four notions themselves can be viewed from a dialectic or paradoxal perspective where at least two seemingly opposing ideas form a this new unity – as seen in Figure 4.

Interesting to note that the Chinese Confucian philosopher Mencius expressed some similar cardinal virtues that fit our model: he speaks of (1) sympathy

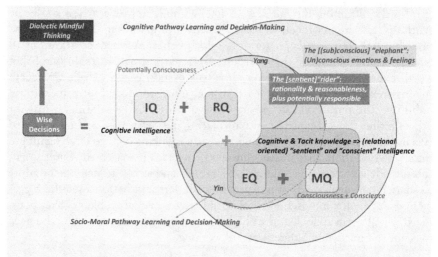

Figure 4: Reasonable and responsible decisions, driven my emotions, through a dialectic integrative lens

and pity as in humanness or *ren*. A feeling of shame needs to specify the feeling of rightness or *yi*. Modesty and deference are expressed in a sense of propriety or *li*. Finally, a sense of right and wrong emerges in the application of wisdom or *zhi*[17].

Deconstructing the notion of trust, I assume to translate Mencius' cardinal virtues that generate trust into our four forms of intelligence. The ability to make smart and wise decisions – rooted in these forms of intelligence and energized and steered by an enhanced level of consciousness – could be described as decisions that are accurate, sincere and truthful[18].

Competence and cognitive learning involve relying on exploiting what you know and continue to explore new knowledge. Safeguarding an investment requires to dare to get in unexplored waters by taking real risk – as having your skin in the game[19] – while also trying to minimize the potential negative effects of such a daring move. Only then organizations and their leaders will be able to regain some trust – see Figure 5 – from society and its stakeholders.

Sharing our struggle with others provides comfort and helps us see the bigger picture. A cultivated paradox mindset may not be able to resolve all problems or tensions. But it will allow us to look at the challenge with fresh eyes, understand the need to adapt and uncover a different way of working. Information is not self-explanatory; it is context-dependent and therefore to be interpreted through a model. In other words, to be useful – or at least to be meaningful – it must be understood through the lenses of culture and history. When information is contextualized, it becomes knowledge. When knowledge compels socio-moral convictions that aim at some common ground, it may become wisdom. The digital world, however, has little patience for wisdom. The digital "values" are shaped by approbation, not introspection or self-awareness. The digital world

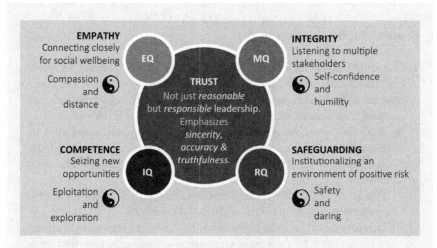

Figure 5: Paradoxal leaders integrating different forms of intelligence = creating trust in organizations

only "understands" mathematical numbers and proffers the connection between contextual history that imposes itself on human conduct by distance or space, time and language. Unfortunately, the digital world often remains situated in a material "objective" interpretation of data – completely unable to give meaning to phenomena that play a role in the socio-ethical sphere. In the analog relational world, however, (ethically accepted) values and emotions play a constitutive role that are absent in a *machina sapiens*.

Resolving tensions in a paradoxal situation – characterized by yin/yang – requires sage leaders to acknowledge, to deliberate and to integrate the opposing ideas in a "higher (synthesis) understanding".

Some thoughts to take away:

- *Integrative thinking* is a way of reframing the relationship between tensions, capturing both the distinct features and interwoven nature of these opposites. By holding opposing ideas in our minds simultaneously, we can find new intersections, creative perspectives and frameworks.
  - ○ Wise corporate leaders, chosen by boards and often assisted by executive search companies after an intensive process, need to adhere to a more integrative and dynamic perspective beyond zero-sum choices.
  - ○ This kind of paradox mindset allows boards and their leaders to resolve tensions as paradoxes without the usual trade-offs.
  - ○ This contextual ambidexterity allows leaders to go beyond mere either/or choices and create a more coherent and integrated new narrative.

- More than pursuing the *middle ground* or a *trade-off*, the paradox-savvy executive is actually transcending the opposing ideas to build something new. S/he seeks an optimization, a simultaneous pursuit of both poles over time.
  - ○ Skilfully addressing a conflict within a paradox often produces a new set of arrangements and practices: a transformation that releases and transcends the core tension. So, in paradox resolution, it's the *tension itself* that has provided the synergy for a novel idea or perspective.
  - ○ Taking a paradox perspective, we deliberately attempt to *dialectically* reframe a tension and give sense to decision-making. In the most basic sense, "*dialectical thinking*" refers to the reconciliation of opposites.

- A paradox mindset will
  - ○ (1) reframe the question,
  - ○ (2) accept the tension and develop comfort with the discomfort, and
  - ○ (3) distance oneself and search for new possibilities.
  - ○ Following this process, a paradox mindset will integrate the notions of (IQ + RQ) (*cognitive pathway*) and (EQ + MQ) (*socio-ethical pathway*) into a coherent framework that will *synethesize* these least two seemingly opposing ideas (what is versus what should be) into a new unity that can be viewed from a dialectic or paradoxal perspective.

Chapter Twenty Seven

Is Intuition or Heuristics Useful in an Ambiguous Volatile World?

"Vision without Execution is hallucination".

Thomas Edison

"You are what you repeatedly do. Excellence, then, is not an act but a habit".

Aristotle

The future favours the prepared mind. Experience isn't enough; calibration and feedback are desirable to make smart decisions. And decisions are often made within teams. Leaders' success depends partially on the ability to make good decisions, but even more so on the ability to help others to make smart and wise decisions, according to Moore and Bazerman[1]. Leaders are most effective when they guide others towards wise decisions[2]. Concretely, it means that we need to create a *decision or choice architecture*. It's a structure that *nudges* others towards smart decisions[3]. Next to a sound *decision architecture*[4], one still expects leaders to show ethical character to be loyal to the organization but above all to stick to ethical principles[5].

Ideally, executives combine, synthesize and integrate two opposite approaches to make smart and wise decisions within an architecture of open-minded and deliberating supporting teams. On one hand, intuitive creative thinking, based on expertise and experience – enhanced by useful "codified" heuristics – allows executives and entrepreneurs to follow their gut feelings and initiate innovative solutions in the absence of data and/or information. On the other hand, an analytical logical mind – strengthened by augmented abilities of predictive power as result of the use of big data analytics – allows to "predict the future". Call it probabilistic thinking based on experimenting. Risk management is akin to this dual approach to assess an uncertain future: a quantifiable future based on probabilities that allows measurement within grades of likelihood, also a non-quantifiable or qualitative approach. These two distinctive capabilities (of system 2 and system 1 thinking) can be compared to a certain extent to the *yin* and *yang* of integrative and paradoxal decision-making. Let's focus in this chapter on the first component: intuitive tacit knowledge and heuristics that can be quite effective in turbulent times or under extreme uncertainty.

1. Tacit Knowledge Using Intuition and Heuristics (the Yin Approach)

For many complex decisions, all the data in the world cannot trump the lifetime's worth of experience that informs one's gut feeling, instinct or what is labelled *intuition* or "*heuristics*". This intuitive thinking is useful when data are completely absent. Heuristics (or "constructed" formalized rules of thumb) are usually quite intuitive.

1.1. When to Trust Your Gut (Intuitive) Feeling?

Intuition – or "blinking"[6] – is usually defined as the capability to act or to decide appropriately without deliberately and consciously balancing alternatives, and without following certain rules of routine, and most probably without full awareness[7]. Intuition commonly stands for rapid reactions that result in effective outcomes. Intuition is the fast way of how we translate our experiences into judgements and decisions: it reflects system 1 thinking.

Intuitive executives (sometimes) perform better than others because of their ability to make effective fast decisions under pressure. Because intuition utilizes tacit knowledge, it's not dependent on conscious deliberate reflection. The intuitive system engages the rich basis of tacit knowledge (stored in our associative memory[8]), and intuitive decision-making can be quite biased. Logically, we need to ask when

Business people and executives need to be aware that most cutting-edge applications are based on probabilistic reasoning. Not only high-tech companies such as Netflix, Amazon, Alibaba, Tencent, Google, Facebook, Uber and Airbnb to just name a few international brands, but also the many traditional firms to implement algorithms use Bayesian thinking that result in personalized services. They are mainly based on the combination of **network cooperation** *and* **data intelligence**. *The latter is a combination of (1) economics that provide the mathematical models of human behavior (2) optimization theory that ensures that models and methods of calculation are efficient provided the time and budget constraints and (3) machine learning methods (part of artificial intelligence) that can be used to obtain and clean the relevant data, and calculate the desired objectives for the business in question.*

Important to acknowledge is the fact that though the probabilistic logic and methods of machine learning (such as backpropriation) represent a revolutionary change to tactical decision-making, machine learning in itself is not the golden goose egg. It is the combined use of data and network effects to a particular business challenge that allows entrepreneurs to take advantage of the improved machine power and big data availability.

we can we really trust our intuitive fast system 1 thinking?

A. Can Intuition Be Accurate?

Intuition's great flaw is not that it can be biased and clumsy; in fact, it can be quite accurate. The flaw for many reasonable people is that you cannot audit it. Because intuition emerges fully formed from the unconscious, there is no way to check its validity or calculations. Hence why it is hard to tell when a decision based on gut feeling is biased or not.

Good intuition is a skillset learned over years through practice, experience and intimate knowledge in a certain field. This system 1 registers the cognitive ease with which our mainly unconscious emotions process information, but it does not generate

However, when data are not really available, **creative intuition**, *artistic insights and vast experience translated in tacit knowledge and* **heuristics** *play then an important role. Experimenting – as in scientific progress – is what creates the future. In an age of uncertainty and change, being able to sense what to do in advance could make business or non-profits smarter, more inventive and more relevant. Sense-making – the intuition to "see" change faster and the capacity to pursue this emerging future energetically – is what markets applauded in Steve Jobs, a man who wasn't an artist but thought like one.*

a warning signal when it becomes unreliable. Hence the precaution that is necessary when following our gut feelings. Intuitive answers come easily and quickly to our mind. Indeed, intuition is very "fast and frugal". Intuitions are not just simplifications of presumed rational models but are also quite biased. Hence why it is advisable that this intuitive system 1 thinking – that is not immediately educable, because it is mainly unconscious – needs to be slowed down by system 2 that could check for possible biases.

The more attentive system 2 seems to articulate judgements and choices, but it sometimes forget the importance of system 1 thinking by rationalizing ideas and feelings that in fact are generated by system 1. Yes, system 2 is not a paragon of rationality either because its (cognitive) "abilities are limited and so is the knowledge to which it has access[9]."

It is well documented that when it comes to really serious business decisions, leaders often rely on their intuition. Similarly, chess grandmasters rely on their intuition – and therefore their experience and expertise – to make the right move within seconds. A chess master sees a pattern behind potential configurations of the game. What is called "intuition" is really one's ability to recognize patterns – a process that often happens unconsciously. Subconscious or unconscious pattern matching generates an action queue of plausible responses, options, to be considered, starting with the most plausible.

Complex decisions, however, bring into play a process in which (tacit) knowledge, experience and emotions are linked and constitute to what we call intuition[10]. Emotion precedes cognition since the *amygdala* – the site in the brain where it is assumed that emotions are memorized – categorizes stimuli and triggers behavior faster than cognitive processes.

Emotions and experience lie at the basis of intuition. Experience emerges into tacit knowledge. Thus, I could argue that EQ => MQ[11], or more precisely: Experience + Emotions => Intuition => Morality[12].

Subconscious intuition is able to "recognize patterns" with a small amount of data which makes it superior to the big data fuelling artificial intelligence or machine deep learning[13]. After the subconscious process of data gathering, taking about 300 milliseconds, consciousness gets involved and selects the most useful data, as it reflects upon them as trying to apply these data in the model.

Intuitive leaders are (better) able to filter out the many ambiguous, contradictory and frequently deceptive pieces of information from those pieces of information that are required for strategic decisions. Intuition is based on large numbers of patterns gained through experience, resulting in different forms of tacit knowledge. Experts have a rich repertoire of patterns, being able to make fine discriminations that may be invisible to novices, having sophisticated mental models of how things work, and having resilience to adapt to complex and dynamic situations. This sense-making requires a deep understanding of the phenomena at stake. What differentiates the skilled decision-maker is the ability to make perceptual discriminations, to recognise patterns, to draw on rich mental models and to judge sensibly[14]. Strengthening intuition means building experiences that result in more accurate and comprehensive tacit knowledge. And obviously, experience does not automatically translate into expertise.

Some neuroscientists claim that intuition indicates how the middle prefrontal cortex gives us access to the wisdom of the body. This integrative cortical function shows that our conscious and cognitive thinking is in fact really dependent on the non-rational processing of our bodies[15] or "affect"[16]. Hence why intuition can potentially generate smart and occasionally wise decisions that are not just logical decisions, but decisions that take a much broader holistic perspective. Some of these decisions encompass both a *cognitive view* as well as a *socio-moral perspective* – my main argument in this book.

Smart leaders are able to single out noise from patterns[17]. And most importantly to note: *quantitative historical data most often do not predict new trends.* Quantitative market research failed to predict the massive enthusiasm for pocket-sized personal computers, text-messaging, wireless email services or even smart phones. In an age of data overload, the intuitive and visionary confidence of a smart leader is necessary to guide the organization. "Analytics can never trump the intuition – wrought by years of experience and accumulation of knowledge, tempered by emotional intelligence. Under the right conditions, companies can help foster a climate in which such people are developed"[18]. But intuitive insights that are often innovative should be checked through experiments where possible.

B. The Siren Song of Intuition – Potentially Prevented by Pre-Mortem Thinking

Even if it would be neuro-scientifically true that intuitive insights constitute "tacit" (subconscious) knowledge, it is equally true that this kind of implicit knowledge can be rather *biased*[19], and potentially be quite "*noisy*" as well. Well-known psychologists Kahneman and Klein note that it is often hard to know when there are enough valid cues to make intuition work[20]. Even where it clearly can, caution remains advisable.

It is obvious that the distinction between fast and slow thinking, popularized by Kahneman, allows us to understand the different brain activities in making reasonable decisions. The more rational[21] and deliberate the decision is, the more justified the process and the outcome likely is. However, the point is that such slow deliberate information process is not always possible, especially when swift decisions need to be made in the absence of any perceived relevant data and information. That's where heuristics and intuition can play a role. And yes, if possible, the intuitive and deliberative processes may diverge, maybe each process should audit the other[22], if applicable and viable.

There is another quite neat solution to help us against the potentially misleading siren song of intuitive thinking: a *Premortem* approach, a notion quipped by eminent psychologist Dr. Gary Klein. The *Premortem thought experiment* tries to curb the bias of overconfidence. It would not be the first or last time that disaster has been induced by powerful emotional and intuitive over-optimism. The *Premortem* procedure is simple: when the organization has almost come to an important decision but has not formally committed itself, one proposes to gather for a brief session with those who are knowledgeable about the decision. The premise of this session could be a brief speech: "imagine that we are a year into the future. We implemented the plan as it now exists. The outcome was a disaster. Please take five to ten minutes to write a brief history of that disaster", a *Premortem* (before death) thought. Like the Devil's Advocate procedure, this thought experiment has the advantage to overcome system 1 thinking, and it also unleashes the imagination of knowledgeable individuals in a much needed direction. In a *Premortem*, the group tries to anticipate a plan's weakness[23], and it also provides a format that supports a productive critique and deliberate dialogue or debate about a plan. A *Premortem* begins with the assumption the plan has failed; it's an exercise to find key vulnerabilities in a plan. May I also add: highly adviceable for most boards to apply when taking important (investment) decisions.

1.2. Applying Heuristics

A *heuristic* is a word from the Greek meaning: "to discover". It is an approach to problem-solving that takes one's personal experience into account – similar to intuitive information processes.

Heuristics are similar to intuitive processes, especially when one is not consciously aware of how one makes a decision. A heuristic is a strategy

– formulated as a rule of thumb – that ignores part of the information, with the goal of making decisions more accurately, quickly and frugally (i.e. with fewer pieces of information) compared to more complex methods. Heuristics can be defined by common building blocks from which an organizing principle is constructed: (1) to search rules that specify in what direction search extends in the search space, (2) stopping rules that specify when search is terminated and (3) decision rules that specify how the final decision is reached[24]. The challenge is to know in which environments a heuristic can be successful applied, and when not.

Heuristics are a subset of strategies that include complex regression or Bayesian models. A heuristic is a mental shortcut that allows people to solve problems and make judgements quickly and efficiently. These rule-of-thumb strategies shorten decision-making time and allow people to function without constantly stopping to think about their next course of action. Heuristics are helpful in many situations, but they can also lead to cognitive biases. Let's explain the term.

A. Satisficing and Thinking Through Systems 1 and 2

Heuristics are simple strategies or mental processes that humans, animals, organizations' and machines use to quickly form judgements, make decisions and find solutions to complex problems. This happens when an individual focuses on the most relevant aspects of a problem or situation to formulate a solution. Nobel laureate Herbert Simon – who did not believe in pure rational thinking but rather in *bounded rationality* – for instance, formulated "*satisficing*" which combines *satisfying* and *sufficing*. Satisficing is a very useful heuristic that significantly improved decision-making. Heuristics can lead to fast, frugal and accurate decisions in many real-world situations that are characterized by uncertainty.

As said before, the psychologists Tversky and Kahneman took a different approach, linking heuristics to cognitive biases[25]. Their typical experimental setup consisted of a rule of logic or probability, embedded in a verbal description of a judgement problem, and demonstrated that people's intuitive judgement deviated from the optimal rational rule.

Even if we would be able to repress our own biases, even if we could become entirely rational – becoming cold and calculating Dr. Spock-like decision-makers in complex real situations, it would be a bad idea. Despite undisputable biases when emotions and intuitions are given free range, excluding this *yin*-perspective is like cutting off one leg. As argued in previous chapter, we need both legs. Biases are the by-product of heuristics. Biases, sometimes but not always, cause mistakes at the individual level of decision-making. However, there exists some methods at the organizational level to reduce such potential strategic errors as result of those biases. It involves what team and how decisions are made within the team to reduce some of those biases[26]. It is true that obsessing over own biases and how to reduce them is a waste of time. Improving the decision-making practices and architectural design to make decisions within organizations is likely much more fruitful and effective[27].

Heuristics play important roles in both problem-solving and decision-making. When we are trying to solve a problem or make a decision, we often turn to these mental shortcuts when we need a quick solution – assuming we don't have the necessary AI tools at hand, or the context itself if too volatile for an AI algorithm. The world is full of information, yet our brains are only capable of processing a certain amount. If you tried to analyze every single aspect of every situation or decision, you would never get anything done. In order to cope with the tremendous amount of information that we encounter and to speed up the decision-making process, the brain relies on these mental strategies to simplify things so we don't have to spend endless amounts of time analyzing every detail.

For instance, the "regression to the mean" is an elegant rule of thumb that applies to athletes, stock analysists and CEOs or Boards alike. Michael Mauboussin, a financial strategist and author, claims that *regression to the mean* is an indispensable tool for testing the role of luck in performance[28]. It seems that *slow regression* is more often seen in activities dominated by skill, while faster regression is likely more associated with pure luck or chance. Again, this law of large numbers describes a situation where having access to more data is better for making predictions, as long as they're operating in a rather stable situation. However, when volatility and ambiguity start to reign, all bets (using AI-tools or for good prediction, or both) are off.

Why do we rely on heuristics? Psychologists have suggested a few different theories: (1) **Effort reduction:** according to this theory, people utilize heuristics as a type of cognitive laziness. Heuristics reduce the mental effort required to make choices and decisions; (2) **Attribute substitution** suggests people to substitute simpler but related questions in place of more complex and difficult questions; and finally (3) **Fast and frugal:** this theory argues that heuristics are actually more accurate than they are biased. In other words, we use heuristics because they are fast and often reasonably useful or correct.

Under uncertainty, simple rules are highly effective in comparison with complex algorithms. And it should not be forgotten that in order to successfully predict the future, one needs a **good theory** that explains the causal relationships, **reliable data** and a **stable** not too volatile world[29]. Artificial intelligence may find invisible patterns that indicate correlations – sometimes very impressive but completely non-sensical or useless – but they cannot provide any theorical framework that proves causality. The reliability of data by AI has been proven over and over with an alarming level of false or misleading information output. Finally, the computational power and big data are of rather limited help when uncertainty reigns. For these reasons, it should not surprise us that an *"intuitive" heuristic* – encapsulating tacit knowledge – can be described as a *fast and frugal "algorithm"*, with the advantage of being *transparent* and *explainable*, in contrast to the black-box AI algorithms.

B. Less-Is-More Heuristics

When my team of financial and industry experts was assigned – by the Ministry of Finance in Indonesia aligned with IMF's standards and rules – to renegotiate and restructure the nationalized bank loans and bond obligations of defaulted companies in Indonesia and Singapore, we regularly applied some financial and industry heuristics. We needed to come up with viable solutions under extreme uncertainty and deliberate opaqueness – this non-transparency was partially caused by the Asian debt crisis and partially by bad corporate governance to say the least. We could not rely on reliable data – even when this data were sometimes verified according to general accepted accounting practices and thus audited[30]. We often applied regressive deductive reasoning combined with some useful rule of thumbs in a particular industry – occasionally enhanced by some gut feeling with respect to the reliability of suggested data sets and the honesty of the agency we were dealing with. Though sometimes proven to be erratic, these heuristics allowed us to gauge for the right direction and resolve immanent deadlocks in the negotiation to come up with feasible solutions. These outcomes were not perfect or optimal but were good enough and doable under great uncertainty and incredible time pressure. It allowed us to take satisficing and appropriate decisions within the boundaries and uncertainties we faced.

There are many kinds of heuristics that can be tailored to solve various problems in everything from psychology to technology design to economics. Heuristic processes are used to find answers and solutions that "fit" or work. This does not mean, however, that heuristics are always correct or right. While they can differ from answers given by logic and probability, judgements and decisions based on a heuristic can be good enough to satisfy a particular need. They can also be quicker to calculate, serving as a quick mental reference for everyday experiences and decisions, or in situations of uncertainty where information is incomplete. Heuristics allow for less-is-more effects, where less information leads to more accuracy. Less-is-more effects have been shown their value through experimenting, analytics and by computer simulations.

A question, for instance, that executives like to be answered is who among the thousands of customers will continue to be active and make purchases in the future? In other words, who are the loyal customers? To do so, one can rely on algorithms based on Pareto/negative binomial distribution (NBD) model that relies on complicated math, or use a simpler but accurate *hiatus heuristic*. In other words, less-is-more can be superior in explaining future behavior. Sometimes, transparent rules can match or even beat black box neural network algorithms at making prediction under uncertainty. For a retailer, for instance, it's crucial to have a good idea how much inventory to store, and to know which previous customers are likely to return again in a given frame. That's exactly what my team and I offered our clients in Southeast Asia and Australia with our CRM system in the late 90s to early 2000s. However, using this data base posed a number of challenges: how complex do we make the algorithmic program in the CRM software to provide useful predictions, or to inform the retailer or hotelier whether or when a customer may get back to you. The so-called hiatus heuristic predicts customers' new purchases even better than current complex machine learning methods. This rule of thumb claims that if a customer at a retail shop (or checked in to a hotel) has made a(nother) purchase (or paid a room) within the last nine months (or about 18 months in business hotels), the customer is likely to purchase in the future, otherwise not. Of course, this hiatus (number of months) varies from industry to industry. We were able to provide very useful information about repetitive customers' purchase for one of our own loyal clients – a three/four star hotel service company or chain with outlets all over Southeast Asia and Australia – that competed with others for the same hotel guests. Knowing beforehand who could be considered "special" and potentially deserving expensive personalized service could make all the difference in this very competitive lodging industry. Our expert CRM software system helped them in the late 90s to predict to identify their most loyal customers with limited data. This *transparent* algorithm[31] is very explainable and can be routinely tested and fine-tuned – definitely an antidote to the current opaque black-box algorithms.

This hiatus heuristic knows that by classifying customers as active, only if they have made a purchase within the last nine months (the hiatus), it was able to predict customer purchases more accurately than the Pareto/NBD model, despite using less information. This hiatus heuristic does not calculate any variance because it does not estimate any parameter. Admittedly, the heuristic may be more biased than the Pareto/NPD model (algorithm)[32]. But a cognitive system needs to draw a balance between being biased and flexible (variance), rather than simply trying to eliminate all possible bias. Heuristics can be fast, frugal and accurate by exploiting the structure of information in environments, by being robust, and by striking a good balance between bias and variance.

A heuristic leader uses a mental shortcut that helps to make decisions and judgements quickly without having to spend a lot of time researching and analyzing information.

2. Ambidextrous Decision-Making in a Cloud of Ambiguity

Human creativity is rooted in our capacity for conceptual modelling, imagining and integration[33]. Cognitive operations can be interpreted as a choice of some basic strategies which can be interpreted as bending, breaking or blending of reality. At the end of the day, adapting to a changed context – and thus Darwinian *fitness* of beliefs and models in a certain situation – claims victory over truthful ideas[34].

2.1. Expert Intuition That Recognizes Patterns

When it comes to the future, what matters is to invigorate the search, not to determine the outcome. Wise leaders embrace the advantages of **probabilistic** Bayesian thinking[35] (also currently the basis for useful AI devices) that enables accurate prediction. However, when date are unavailable, or when the context is too volatile, the frugal and powerful use of **intuition** (that relies on unconscious and conscious neural processes) or the fast heuristics (or rules of thumbs) can be useful.

But first things first: let us try to understand how we form ideas in the first place and then attempt to formulate some integrative way of improved thinking that likely includes a reverse mimicking of algorithmic machine learning. How to embrace the best of both worlds, optimizing human creativity supported by machine learning (AI)?

Unconscious biases prohibit clear, reasonable and responsible decisions. Indeed, it is well documented that executives and we all make decisions that are heavily distorted by biases – often unconsciously. Competent and smart decision-makers should be wary of such biases.

Gary Klein's research on fireground commanders – the leaders of firefighting teams – made him believe in the power of intuition. He sees intuition as recognition of patterns, such as master champions in chess. Klein's recognition-prime decision model[36] acknowledges the importance of the automatic function of associative memory of system 1. The next phase is a deliberate process of system 2 in which the plan is mentally simulated to check the plan. It was Herbert Simon who came up with the idea of pattern recognition, stating that the situation has provided a cue that has given the expert access to information stored in memory, and the information provides the answer. "Intuition is nothing more and nothing less than recognition[37]". An experienced firefighter intuitively knows the danger, without explicitly knowing how he knows. Developing such experience and expertise takes time and a lot of practice.

It is fair to conclude that one can rely on intuition as a real skill, as long as the environment is sufficiently regular to be predicable, and when these regularities are learned through prolonged practice. When both these condition are fulfilled, intuitions are probably very skilled and reliable. Experienced firefighters have learned to recognize highly valid cues that the expert's system 1 has learned to use, even though it may not have named them[38], or be conscious of them. In short, these are the limitations and contextual constraints – data, practice, recognition, regularity, etc. – that determine "intuitive expertise", or not[39].

2.2. Intuition as Tacit Knowledge Steering Decisions

In this context, I argue that intuitive and heuristic thinking by leadership is often the result of affective tacit knowledge, whereas algorithmic or rational probability thinking is directly derived from a cognitive calculative or explicit knowledge.

A. The Rider and the Elephant Revised

Any observation is influenced by our own thinking and models applied. That thinking can be either tacit or explicit. Research has proven that explicit knowledge is clearly distinguished from tacit knowledge. The former adds the facts you know and can consciously report, independent of context. Using the metaphor of the conscious reasonable "rider" and the unconscious emotional "elephant", the rider gathers information and is able to file it away, ready for use in later reasoning[40]. Implicit tacit knowledge is procedural – knowing how rather than knowing that. It is acquired without help from others, and it is related to goals that a person values.

Tacit knowledge resides in the "elephant". It is the skills that the metaphorical "elephant" acquires, gradually, from life experience, and is completely depending on the context. Some may go that far that wisdom is based on tacit knowledge, subconsciously balancing different perspectives[41]. It can be argued that wise people are able to balance their own needs, and the need of others, even the needs of people or things beyond the immediate interaction. Ignorant people, on the other hand, see everything in black and white and are strongly influenced by their own (immediate) self-interest (of self-gratification) and emotions. Wise people are able to see things from others' point of view, appreciating the shadows of grey, and then choose or advise a course of action that works out best for everyone in the long run. Indeed, wise people are able to balance different responses to different situations[42]. Hence why wise people could "claim" to grant [them] serenity to accept things they cannot change, courage to change things they can, and wisdom to know the difference.

How to optimize your decision? Do you have all the data needed to make an accurate prediction of a particular desired outcome? What options do executives have? Deep knowledge and experience is usually required through the executive's curiosity, openness and propensity to seize opportunities. This combination of conscious explicit knowledge and sub- or unconscious tacit knowledge or experience, fueled by emotional intelligence, allows intuition to play a crucial role in smart decision-making. However, Peter Drucker clearly indicated the limitations of intuitive power in decision-making: "I believe in intuition if you discipline it", an idea that later has been explicitly echoed by Nobel laureate Kahneman and his co-author Tversky. In other words, executives should reflect on their intuitive decisions before they execute them.

B. Optimizing Decisions in Turbulent Times

You probably make hundreds or even thousands of decisions every day. What should you have for breakfast? What should you wear today? Should you drive or take the bus? Should you go out for drinks later with your co-workers? Should you use a bar graph or a pie chart in your presentation? The list of decisions you make each day is endless and varied. Fortunately, heuristics allow you to make such decisions with relative ease without a great deal of agonizing.

While heuristics can speed up our problem and the decision-making process, they can introduce errors. Just because something has worked in the past does not mean that it will work again, and relying on an existing heuristic can make it difficult to see alternative solutions or come up with new ideas.

Heuristics can also contribute to things such as stereotypes and *prejudice*. Because people use mental shortcuts to classify and categorize people, they often overlook more relevant information and create stereotyped categorizations that are not in tune with reality. Boards often expose an organization to inconsistent risk and therefore decrease its overall expected value or long-term performance. Boards should therefore reward good decisions, and not good results – known as an outcome bias.

Despite the usefulness of intuition and heuristics, we agree that it is always a good habit to adhere to a "trust but verify" attitude. It means that intuition may be quite useful and frequently results in good and smart decisions. But intuition is not perfect, and it can easily err in predicable ways. Hence the suggestion to verify with data if available, or take into account the rational approach in business to choose the option with the *highest expected value* at every opportunity minus the potential negative impact on ecological and social environment. According to Berkeley Professor Moore and Harvard Professor Bazerman, the essence of reasonable decision-making is to minimize any form of biased heuristic and simple to choose the option with the highest value at every opportunity. One should focus on promoting decisions that maximize the organizational *expected value*[43]. The expected value simply multiplies an option's value by its probability. Bazerman argues to pursue a policy of risk neutrality[44]. Although it is easy to find examples of intuition leading to good decisions, it's as easy to find counterexamples of intuitive decisions over science that led to suboptimal or even catastrophic results. The *expected value* – equalling probability multiplied by actual pay off – helps us to make better decisions in business[45]. Indeed, in business, it is not how likely an event is to happen that matters, but how much you make or loose when it happens that should be your main consideration. How frequent the profit may occur is irrelevant, as any investor with a skin in the game would testify[46]. It is the magnitude of the outcome of your loss or profit that counts[47], that is often more the result of (bad) luck than by following the right approach.

A more optimal thinking may be a question of paradoxally combining system 1 and system 2 thinking. Because our intuition and deliberative process may diverge, each process may be a "verification" factor to the other. Intuition, which represents tacit invisible knowledge, could be a good check on the deliberate process, especially if calculative thinking may omit an important consideration because it was difficult to quantify. The deliberative process can confront our intuition and heuristics about what we might be overweighting. Comparing different methods and decision-making processes steer towards greater deliberation and probably better decisions[48]. However, when there is no data available, heuristics and intuitive tacit knowledge can prove to be very useful.

Some thoughts to take away:

- **Intuition is useful, fast** and **frugal**. Indeed, managers and executives have learnt to make decisions when data were hardly available or when the decision was so unfamiliar that one did not have much to fall back on.

- **Intuitive insights** and **heuristics**, somehow the result of **experience and practices**, help managers to navigate through the enormous uncertainty and turbulence, especially in the absence of reliable data.

- Those simple **rules of thumb** are extremely useful and **transparent** and can be as accurate as current black-box AI algorithms.

Chapter Twenty Eight

Algorithmic Intelligence Predicting Under Stable Uncertainty

"People cannot be faulted for failing to predict the unpredictability, but they can be blamed for a lack of predictive humility".

Kahneman, Sibony & Sustein, 2021

"We are not to tell nature what she is going to be. That's what we found. Every time we take a guess at how she's got to be and measure, she's clever. She always has a better imagination than we had and she finds a cleverer way to do it what we haven't thought of ".

Richard Feynman, 1979, Robb Memorial Lecture-Auckland

"The premise of the (Hegelian) dialectics is that the path of truth is a moment of truth itself: truth is ultimately nothing other than the systematic articulation of a succession of errors".

Slavoi Žižek, 2022

Defenders of algorithmic management point out, quite correctly, that many managers show many flaws in making rash (and sometimes presumably intuitive) decisions. That shouldn't surprise us, given that quite a number of results in probability are rather counterintuitive and hard to grasp by "intuitive thinkers".

The situation gets even more messy when these managers occasionally violate boundaries, or worse, play favourites. They can be quite egomaniacal and cruel, even narcistic. In theory, automation could replace the worst human bosses and make the good ones better by equipping them with better AI tools and information to make smarter decisions. Let's explore this a little more.

For instance, it may be hard to predict individual behavior that can be described as pure random behavior from the outside. However, the aggregate of many individual behaviors is a large group which often display statistical regularities absent at the level of the individual. Randomness turns into statistical trajectories that can be measured and even be "predicted" – as in a physical law[1]. Instead of jettisoning detailed consideration of individual (potential) behavior, one should focus on statistical statements describing the average behavior of large groups of individuals. It makes measured calculations mathematically tractable. And on an aggregate macro-level, that is what matters in business. This is exactly what an algorithmic mindset attempts to achieve: *how to improve risk-taking by having more accurate measurements or probabilistic "predictions" of an uncertain future.* The quintessential quality of the future is that it differs profoundly from the past. But *as long as the "future" is not too different – on aggregate – and not too volatile, big data and algorithmic probability thinking allows us to extrapolate and thus to "predict" the future.* That is where artificial intelligence will become a very useful tool to assist us to improve our decisions.

1. Explicit Knowledge (*the Yang Approach*) Turned into an "Algorithmic" View

Using aggregate (as in "big") data allows executives to fine-tune their decisions – seeking to explain (future) behavior and potential future business outcomes. Numbers, be it big or small, however, cannot speak for themselves. They need to be interpreted to be really understood. A *statistical* **model** is required. Let us not forget either that big data are most useful in situations that are stable, where data are reliable and where theory can guide the search[2]. This is obviously the case in astronomy, in health records, in certain fields of finance. Big data is much less promising in volatile situations, where changes unexpectedly take place. This is the case of stock traders over a longer period or geopolitical predictions – where prediction is extremely difficult (see our next chapter). For that reason, economic theory and human behavior are notoriously difficult to accurately predict, because of the huge number of variables – including the possibility of "free choice" – affecting the dependent variable. As impactful is the indeterminate "randomness" affecting our daily life.

1.1. Smart Machines Augmenting the Decision Power of Wise Leaders

If intelligence is the ability to accomplish complex goals, then (weak) Artificial Intelligence can help businesses to find new applications to either augment the decision-making power of executives and managers, or to automate repetitive familiar tasks.

How to prepare for a future where smart computers (AI) will take over a lot of tasks and where AI will enable businesses to "predict the future" through pattern recognition in reasonably stable environments? How (smart) executives need to make decisions when machines are smarter than them? Likely it requires the executive to apply a different approach in decision-making.

A. Algorithmic Leadership

The futurist Mike Walsh has labelled it as *Algorithmic Leadership*, a term that he derives from the field of computer science. Because business needs to focus both on keeping your current customer happy, but also to think about what your future customers might want will ensure that you start to solve problems today that your competitors won't be thinking about until tomorrow. This ability to adapt, learn and achieve proficiency within narrow domains explains why machines are becoming "smarter" than us in specific domains[3].

Artificial intelligence can be considered a form of "augmented intelligence" helping individuals and organizations to provide better customer experiences. No doubt, algorithmic leaders embrace uncertainty as they view the information probabilistically that enables them to describe one of the many possible outcomes, some more or less likely than others.

Developing such a **probabilistic mindset** allows these new leaders to be better prepared for the uncertainties and complexities of the algorithmic age. Even when events are determined by an infinitely complex set of factors, probabilistic thinking can help them **identify the most likely outcomes** and the best decisions to make. Probability is not a mere computation of odds on the dice. It is the acceptance of the lack of certainty in our knowledge and the development of methods for dealing with our ignorance. However, it is also true that "Probability is not about the odds, but about the belief in the existence of an alternative outcome, cause, or motive[4]". Somehow, we can formulate that a certain conscious experience $Q(x)$ could take place as the probability of this experience occurring $P(x)$ to multiplied with a quantum possibility of an alternative possible outcome $R(x)$[5]. The higher this $R(x)$, the more $R(x)$ deviates from the normality, the stranger this unlikely event may take place, possibly a black swan: $Q(x) = P(x) + R(x)$.

Nothing should be accepted with certainty; conclusions of various degrees of probability could always be formed. In that sense is probability the core of sound "Humean" scepticism. It was David Hume who clearly criticized the problem in induction: all swans occur to be white, till one sees a black one (in Australia). Computing is not the same as clear critical thinking[6].

Considering that alternative outcomes could have taken place, that the world could have been quite different, it is the core of probabilistic thinking. Nassim Thaleb even claims that mild success can be explainable by skills and hard work, while wild success is attributable to variance or luck[7]. But someone aware of the risk of being fooled by randomness has a higher chance to be a real performer. How then is such probabilistic or algorithm mind related to AI? And will experience always result in useful expertise?

B. Probability Thinking Only "Sees" Associations, but Cannot Change or Imagine Things

A narrow defined goal, plus the ability to learn, allows today's algorithmic platforms to gain rapid mastery of tasks such as pattern recognition, navigation, optimization or personalization. While machines will get dramatically better at extracting insights from data, spotting new patterns and even making decisions on our behalf, only humans will have the unique ability to *imagine* innovative ways to use machine intelligence to create experiences, transform organizations and reinvent the world.

After recently re-reading some passages of Homer's Iliad, it stuck to me that Homer did not judge his heroes by the result, but judged them by their actual behavior or character (of integrity and honour) or their lack thereof. It is as if Homer understood that fortune or randomness can be quite cruel, but that does not diminish the value of the (moral virtuous or deontological) agent trying to intervene and make the "right" choice, regardless of the actual outcomes. Only humans can think and act in terms of moral agency and counterfactuals; they also can intervene and change the course of action; something the smartest computer cannot do.

Smart computers can only "see" in making associations but cannot intervene in the matter or change that reality. Or even imagine another reality that could be based on counterfactual argumentation – as the brilliant mathematician Judea Pearl argued when suggesting a methodology to understand causality[8]. Something no computer is able to "understand" by itself; these smart computers are limited to correlations and associations without any possibility to intervene in the course of action or think in causal models. This ladder of causality clearly shows the limitations of artificial intelligence algorithms today – as visualized in Figure 1 below.

The best way to imagine a future shaped by AI is not to focus on machines and their current capabilities, but to think about the potential interactions

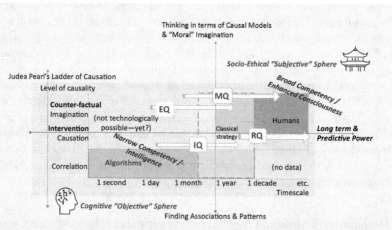

Figure 1: AI can help executives to become smarter, but not wiser

Source: Personal Interpretation of Boston Consulting Group (2020) and Pearl, J. & D. Mackenzie (2018), *The Book of Why. The new science of cause and effect*, London, Penguin

between algorithms, human behavior and identity. We are just entering a new age of algorithmic experiences that will be fuelled by big data and exponential advances in machine intelligence. AI has the potential to transform the way we interact with the world. However, the corporate or political leader can imagine what that future might look like and figure out how we get there. These leaders need to think about the *relationships* between *intentions* (often unarticulated needs or desires of user/customer), *interactions* (the method or manner by which you use a platform, product or service) and *identity* (the cognitive or emotional impact of the experience and the degree to which it has become integrated into a participant's sense of self), allowing them to come up with new insights[9]. The new way of thinking or imagination provides the argumentation to change or to act upon this insight. We cannot expect that from even the smartest computer. Probabilities are useful to detect certain patterns, but they won't provide us really insights in the way we handle our business relations. The major reason in my opinion is that integrity and relations belong to a different (epistemological) sphere or reality that is normative. We humans seem to be only species that can deliberately change the expected normal course of an activity, or evade patterns. We have a free choice within the socio-ethical realm of choosing one action over another.

1.2. A Probability Mindset

Any forecast without a time frame is absurd. Although we advised to broaden the space- and time-vector to transform smart into wise decision-making, we caution to be attentive to the immanent limitations of making those suggestions untestable (as in a too broad space- or too long time frame).

Forecasts must have clearly defined terms and timelines. Forecasters who practice get better at distinguishing subtler shades of grey. In addition, those smart forecasters "adopted" their numerous forecasts by continuously adding (new) data or information. Those pragmatic "experts", who think more like foxes than hedgehogs, combine calibration and resolution. They always talk about possibilities and probabilities, not about certainties.

Amazon, for instance, obtained a patent for "anticipatory shipping"[10] – as having the intention to deliver goods before consciously expressed by the (potential) customer, being convinced that this will augment a personalized algorithmic experience for many customers. This patent for "anticipatory shipping", clearly indicating the intention of Jef Bezos, Amazon's owner. Instead of customers making their own decisions, Amazon decides for them, sending before they know they want the product or item. It could be once more a step towards cutting out agency altogether.

Part of the journey to becoming an algorithmic leader is being brave enough to pursue opportunities that deliver results in multiples, not just achieving some higher margins. Again, Amazon's founding concept of the "flywheel of growth" is structured around learning models built on data loops that reinforce a cycle of profitable business opportunities.

The capability to think carefully about **data availability**, **data acquisition**, **data labelling** and **data governance** will become crucial. Moreover, think computationally is becoming one of those necessary capabilities for any algorithmic leader. This new kind of leadership will need to identify the organization's current assumptions and then break them down into pieces before exploring how the organization might create new solutions from scratch. In other words, besides breaking down a problem into parts or steps (as in the traditional business reengineering processes), leaders need to recognize certain trends and attempt to translate those into principles or insights. By reverse-engineering the future, leaders may be able to capture some of that endless cycle of challenges and opportunities. The fluidity of time – not chronological time, but how we experience technological change – must stay at the forefront of thought processes whenever algorithmic leaders plan for the future.

2. Seeking a Manageable Future Through Algorithmic Thinking

As the apparent opposing forces of *yin* and *yang* are actually interconnected and seem contradictory, when (perceived as) balanced, they are complementary allowing us to see new opportunities. Similarly, the future of our civilization and culture is undoubtedly intertwined with the future of science and technology. In any organization, people are either veering more towards creativity or logic. When not in balance, this (paradoxal) duality can prevent organizations to properly look forward. The prevailing logic at *BlackBerry*, for instance, prevented it to make some audacious and creative moves. BlackBerry fainted not because of the lack of technology, but because it was not able to bring both forces together to forecast trends and plan for a changing context. Instead BlackBerry was fixated on risk (trying to reduce uncertainty) and maintaining their enormous customer base, not imagining that a computer company would enter the mobile phone business, and turn the industry upside down by making a phone part of a mobile computer with access to apps on the internet.

2.1. Exploring and Capturing the Future

Should we try to escape randomness (or luck) and attempt to create our own made future? In other words, how can leaders create and capture a future that is meaningful? Or more broadly, how to balance creativity and probability thinking?

A. About "Flaring" and "Focusing"

NYU Professor Amy Webb has translated this duality of opposing trends or characteristics into an interesting process to "*capture the future*": her forecasting Six-Step Funnel methodology illuminates how an organization can harness both strengths in equal measure by alternating broadening or diverging ("flaring") and narrowing or converging ("focusing") its thinking. Flaring ask questions such as "what if?", "what might be the implications of these actions?", while focusing is about "which option is best?", "what is the next action?", and "how to move forward?" She claims that any organization that intends to prepare for the uncertain future must practice both flaring and focusing.

Part of our human evolution includes the *vision* – the *ability to "see"* – that made the development of complex, intelligent life forms possible. Indeed, the technological advances in deep learning and neural networks, AI and cloud robotics could usher into a new period of technological advancement where algorithmic competence and leadership will be necessary to survive. Robots could learn from the experience of other robots that may result in rapid growth of robot competence, particularly as the number of robots grow.

The most highly compensated and coveted people in the future won't necessarily be the most skilled programmers or smartest MBA graduates. They will be the people who can live at the intersection of technology and business, who can devise and drive the domain-specific languages that will allow them to shape and reshape their business model. In short, creative thinking and action-oriented intrapreneurs who master algorithmic logic will be sought after in the future ...

B. Learn to Love Uncertainty

These algorithmic thinkers will somehow embrace uncertainty and "find" opportunities to materialize. Viewing the information probabilistically enables them to describe one of the many possible outcomes, some more or less likely than others. In the end, being an effective algorithmic leader means finding mechanisms and mindsets to cope with uncertainty, both by yourself and with your teams. More, to occasionally "escape" these probabilities, or create a (more meaningful) reality that was unexpected. So, isolate the factors that really matter, have a sense of the odds, check your assumptions, make a decision, and then re-evaluate when new information comes to light. And most importantly, learn to love uncertainty.

Developing a probabilistic mindset allows those practitioners to be better prepared for the uncertainties and complexities of the algorithmic age, even *to "see" the future better* and more intimately than others. Even when events are determined by an infinitely complex set of factors, probabilistic thinking can help them identify the most likely outcomes or understand randomness more profoundly – allowing to make better decisions.

Interestingly, the performance of teams in solving problems and developing new ideas may have less to do with who is part of them and more to do with their shared values (i.e. a degree of emotional safety). Indeed, in particular, the cohesiveness of a group, or how much people talked to each other, is by far the strongest predictor of performance across almost every attribute being measured.

One of the main lessons that Kahneman taught us is not that people who attempt to predict the future make many errors. That's obvious. But more important is that errors of prediction are inevitable because the (by me labelled socio-ethical) reality in which business decisions evolve what will happen there is unpredictable. Very different from a more stable descriptive reality of physics or chemistry. Subsequently, high subjective confidence by an expert – be it a specialist in a certain field, or a CEO or a board – is not to be trusted as an indicator of accuracy. Humble agents with low(er) confidence could be more precise and informative than their (over)confident colleagues. To be fair, experts may have valuable insights about the near future. However, one should be aware of the line that separates a possible predictable near future from the unpredictable distant future that is yet to be drawn.

In the realm of socio-ethical learning, our future is inherently unpredictable. However, when studying science and the natural environment, the future is less uncertain and be understood in terms of probability. Those business or economic situations that are reasonable stable allow possible accurate predictions. However, they are rather rare and only valid for a certain period in which the phenomena are stable: for instance, inflation almost disappeared from the economic scene until recently. It is in this realm of cognitive sciences and physics–biology–chemistry that artificial intelligence could become very helpful in augmenting our understanding of finding (in)visible patterns speedier.

Business, however, sits on the verge of both realms, where certain objective facts are entangled with the socio-ethical realm. These objective facts can be accurately predicted, whereas the subjective choices are fickly but can be measured on an aggregate level. However, the socio-ethical sphere requires political and moral choices to nudge us in a certain direction, in a world we have chosen to live in ... We can't and shouldn't undo the entanglement of both spheres, but we should remain aware of its distinctive features.

2.2. AI-Platforms Promises to Predict Behavior

One way to help executives to become more "algorithmic" is the use of experimentation through data. Entertainment, retail and even transportation may soon be disrupted by new AI-driven digital platforms.

A. *Leave Command and Control Behind and Accept the Power of Creative Teams*

Uber and *Lyft* in the USA, *Gojek* and *Grab* in Southeast Asia and *Didi* in China are not disrupting but colliding with the traditional taxi corporations. *Airbnb* and *Booking.com* are colliding with the incumbent hotel businesses. In other words, today's businesses are transformed again, this time by digital technologies where data and their algorithms play a crucial "predicting" role. Digital platforms[11] and algorithms connect companies and potential customers in an unseen manner across geography, scale and scope. Executive leaders will need to adapt and transform themselves as well. Professor Mukherjee urges executives to embrace AI and digital technology to lead this transformation, away from "a command-and-control" approach to a more inclusive and coaching role for their subordinates. These new generation leaders must continuously navigate between the in-between-spaces that experts avoid; they must learn rapidly and embrace and encourage productive collaboration across borders, which requires a high level of trustworthiness to materialize such much needed (global) collaboration.

This new kind of leadership will foster creativity and learning in others to stay ahead as a team or organization. And this means that modern creativity will trump uniformity. Only diversity and multiple inputs will allow a place where creative innovation can take place. And finally, this new kind of leadership reflects more the attitude of a guardian than that of a chief commander. Embracing new technology requires enormous flexibility and emotional savviness to get all team members on board whereby technology will need to be assessed for being feasible, organizationally valuable and socially usable.

B. The Algorithmic Leader as a Facilitator

Technology may have changed businesses, but culture is the organizational true operating system. Hence why principles can't be vague mission statements. They have to be concrete enough to be useful, but fluid enough to adapt to a wide variety of circumstances. The algorithmic leader sets the proposition that the organization is trying to solve as the aspiration and will use it as a resource for aspiration with the people who can extract the data and action it. The job of a leader is not to enforce their views and ensure compliance, but rather to provide the nutrients and the space to allow things to grow. Therefore, the algorithmic leader is more of a gardener, rather than a prison guard.

Traditional leaders inadvertently use metrics that preserve, rather than challenge resulting in maintaining a status quo, with questions as "are we meeting the targets? How are we tracking against our key performance indicators? Is the team exceeding expectations? Is the employee engagement survey up or down this month?" Rather than just trying to improve a score, time or some other indicator, an algorithmic leader takes a meta-perspective and questions the ultimate premise of the job itself. The question you should be asking is not "are we getting results?" But "do we have the right approach"? Digital transformation requires you to not only automate your processes but also reimagine what you do and to reimagine/ offer an entire new customer experience. For instance, the *Rolls-Royce* Trent engine is fitted to a wide variety of aircraft from the Airbus A330 to the Boeing 787 Dreamliner. Nowadays, Rolls-Royce – and its competitor *General Electric* – developed a new subscription model that let the airlines buy power by the hour. For a flat hourly rate per engine, Rolls-Royce would handle everything from installation to maintenance. In order to make the transition, Rolls-Royce had to stop just making engines and start collecting data about engines as well. It started filling its engines with sensors that provided real-time data analytics about their performance. This leads to a new understanding that allowed them to predict future failure, discover what types of maintenance were effective, and uncover new ways to optimize fuel consumption. And becoming more sustainable in the process. Designing work, rather than "doing work", is thinking about the digital version of what organizations do. Machine intelligence may assist us with data gathering, analysis and simulation, but it is ultimately up to algorithmic leaders to explore and design smarter ways of using those outputs.

Some thoughts to take away:

- Smart executives know how to **improve risk-taking** by having more accurate measurements or **probabilistic "predictions"** of an uncertain future – as long as the "future" is not too different – an aggregate – and not too volatile, big data and algorithmic probability thinking allow us to extrapolate.

- An **Algorithmic Mindset** incorporates a more statistical and (exponential) systemic thinking – a clear fiat of combined general human intelligence (IQ) and risk intelligence (RQ):
  - Algorithmic probability thinking may proof to contain the necessary ingredients to make smarter decisions – deliberate decisions that will benefit the organization and its relationships with stakeholders.
  - These smart leaders usually have a probability mindset that somehow can be expressed in explicit knowledge, next to experience that evolved into an intuitive tacit knowledge.

- Seeing the future faster enabling them to create and capture the future allows these smart leaders to remain competitive.

Chapter Twenty Nine

About Foxes and Superforecasters (in the Socio-Ethical Sphere)

"The first principle is that you must not fool yourself, and you are the easiest person to fool".

Richard Feynman, 1985, Nobel laureate physicist

"Most of the greatest evils that man has inflicted upon man have come through people feeling certain about something which, in fact, was false".

Bertrand Russell, 1950

"People with a surplus of confidence and a shortage of character never fail to disappoint. [...] Leadership skill is inversely related to the size of fragility of the ego. Humility, generosity, and honour are underrated virtues. The most principled person is the best poised to serve".

Adam Grant, Organizational Psychologist at Wharton (2020)

A prediction is really nothing but a hypothesis. What matters most is not the predictions themselves but how we respond to them, or whether we respond at all. Forecasts that provoke fresh thinking are useful. Nobody should surrender to predictions but use them to broaden and map one's conceptual and imaginative horizons. Nobody is able to fully accurately predict the future in a consistent manner, and when there is any chance of (normative) values and ideology involved, the forecasts do not become more reliable. Niels Bohr, a Nobel laureate in Physics, allegedly said that predicting is hard, especially about the future.

1. How Optimistic Are You in Using Human Intelligence to Predict the Future?

Penn University and Wharton Professor Tetlock's well-known punchline has stirred some feathers: *"the average expert was roughly as accurate as a dart-throwing chimpanzee"*. However, Tetlock considers himself as an optimistic sceptic who believes that it is possible to "see" into the future, at least in some situations and to some extent and that any intelligent open-minded and hard-working person can cultivate the requisite skills. The question remains: Is the future predictable or not? Is a reality clocklike or cloudlike? Unpredictability and predictability coexist in an intricately interlocking eco-system that encompasses our human bodies, our societies and the cosmos. Predictability depends on what we're trying to predict, how far into the future and under what circumstances. Separating the predictability from unpredictable is rather difficult.

Professors Tetlock and Gardner laid out an interesting experiment in the form of a tournament, initiated by IARPA, the US Intelligence Advanced Research Projects Activity. A big part of what American intelligence does is *forecast global political and economic trends*. Good forecasting does not depend on what one does, not who (as expert) you are. It is the product of particular ways of thinking, of gathering information and of updating beliefs and assumptions[1]. How you think about self-improvement (through feedback) will determine the success of forecasting.

With billions of dollars of invested interest in useful intelligence that is to inform decisions about terrorism, security, energy, environmental and societal policies, the IARPA project aims for clear and objective accurate insights. The first year, Tetlock's team proved 60 percent more accurate than the control group, and superior to university teams at MIT and the University of Michigan. In the subsequent second year, the team did 78 percent better than the reference group, outperforming professional intelligence analysts of IARPA who has access to classified information. What did turn Tetlock's team into "good judgers" and superforecasters? The team almost never gave an absolute yes or no to any question. Instead, they assessed in probabilities, i.e. how likely was it that an event would occur or not?

Probabilities – not presumed precise forecasts – changed the way that they thought about the future, allowing them to accept uncertainty and to reject the dramatic absolutism so beloved of popular audiences, and abhorred by anyone who understands to make sophisticated decisions about the future. Thinking like scientists – hypothetical thinking – made them more thoughtful and more accurate. The result was these teams were considered **superforecasters**, and being much better than others, including experts. What made them superpredictors?

1.1. The Illusion of Full Control

The illusion that we believe to understand the past fosters overconfidence in our ability to predict the future. That luck has determined the outcome of history is utterly shocking[2]. Not underestimating randomness, these superpredictors were first and foremost open-minded, humble, educated, prepared to change their minds, aware into what might happen in the next year or so, and attentive to any source that would provide them insights. Consistency was not their main priority, because they learned from mistakes and through trial and error and were willing to drastically change when deemed appropriate. All forecasts were seen as mere probabilities, not absolute facts to happen. And by working in teams and be open to dialogue and discussion, they improved this attitude of trial and error. The team got well versed in asking the "better" questions and were ready to adapt the forecasts with new information. They were continuously calibrating their model and forecasts through trial and error, by open-minded discussions and anxiously seeking new information. Interestingly, the time horizon for accurate forecasts is dauntingly small. Usually, these superforecasters were often very accurate within about 150 days but started to be hesitant to make any forecast beyond 400 days.

That fact should raise questions. Any organization that invests time and effort into intricate five-year plans or 30-year estimates should not believe that they represent any kind of absolute truth, hardly mere potential scenarios. By the way, not many did forecast that Trump would win the 2016 elections, or that the UK would vote for Brexit.

A. About Two Systems of Thinking and Judgements in Two Realms

A foresight about predicting the future is dependent on our cognitive ability to be smart and intelligent, be open-minded and hard-working and to continuously update new relevant information in our forecasts. But we also need to get acquainted with the inherent uncertainty of the future; we should get comfortable with existential uncertainty of the future. The future is unknowable – especially in the socio-ethical realm. The best we can hope for is to think in terms of probabilities – which themselves may be incorrect. Even statisticians and mathematicians sometimes find probabilities counterintuitive and often at odds with gut instinct. Hence why one should treat predictions as mere hypotheses and ask whether these advertised forecasts are part of propaganda, bad science, careerism or entertainment. Hardly the foundation on which you want to build your future.

Nonetheless, data and reliable information can help to improve decisions. And if one has access to a well-validated statistical algorithm, it likely beats subjective judgements. Machines may get better and better at mimicking human decision-making and even "digitally copy" (the notion of) meaning to a certain extent (without understanding it), and thereby becoming better in predicting human behavior. However, there still exists a gap between mimicking and reflecting about meaning. The latter is a unique human judgement. Indeed, those judgements are prone to biases, cognitive limitations and/or subjectivity.

Scientists have supposed that growing knowledge about the physical world would lead to greater predictability because the reality was assumed to function like a mechanical clock with universal laws of physics. And some mathematicians like Pierre-Simon Laplace took this to extremes by assuming that having all data on the movements of the greatest bodies of the universe would make "the future just like the past would be present before its eyes[3]", call it Laplacean predictability if you like. But that's only part of the story. Business faces two spheres of reality: a "cognitive (objective) reality" and a "socio-ethical (subjective) realm" with each its peculiarities and characteristics.

Obviously, making *cognitive judgements* about the future may be partially predicable in case the context remains reasonably stable – as is the case in most positive scientific contexts. However, it should be clear by now that predictability has its limits. Even more so in the field of socio-moral reality, when we need to make a *moral judgement*. As mentioned a few times, the gap between what is objectively true and what is perceived as a subjective prescriptive and desirable reality is quite distinct.

Just imagine thinking about a decision to be made on an ethical dilemma. In an open-minded deliberative dialogue, that process of decision-making can go all directions. As said, these cognitive and socio-moral judgements are two different though entangled realities that do not necessarily mix very well. But we will need to learn to blend computer-based forecasting and subjective judgements – in boardrooms or in courtrooms, for instance – in the future. This predictability and unpredictability coexist uneasily in an intricately interdependent eco-system in which we and organizations thrive. How predicable something is depends on a high extent *what* we are trying to predict, *how far* into the future and *under what specific circumstances*. We can't predict the weather in a few months, but we manage to do so for the immediate future of days, for instance.

B. *Attempting to Predict and Falsify*

As Karl Popper, an Austrian-British philosopher of science, once said, we can only progress by trial and error, through piecemeal moving forward. Theories are so far true until *falsified* and a better one takes over. Good foresight is possible, and good superforecasters excel not because who they are but because what they do. Foresight is real but very piecemeal; good forecasts are the result of a particular statistical way of thinking, of gathering information, and continuous updating of beliefs and data.

Good predictors consult other perspectives[4]. It all boils down to a trial and error method – in line with Karl Popper's fallibility theory[5]. Because we suffer from the illusion of control[6] or the illusion of (precise) prediction, we often forget how we hardly grasp randomness in experiments – which time after time seems to succeed to fool us[7].

Superforecasters also use introspection to capture a tiny fraction of the complex unconscious and conscious processes that take place in our brain. The more intuitive system 1 thinking comes first and runs in the background, allowing system 2 to choose certain parts about which we become conscious of. The analytical system 2 scrutinizes answers provided by system 1; the conscious analytical system starts with an examination of what system 1 decided or offered us as answer. Snap judgements are often essential to survive, based on little evidence. That is exactly what system 1 does, functioning as the propulsive force behind all human efforts to comprehend reality. The interplay between system 1 and system 2 can be quite subtle and creative. Scientists have learned to wonder and to continuously doubt and to test hypotheses. That doubt can be reduced by better evidence from better studies or data. But it can never fully be eliminated because we are never 100 percent sure.

C. *The Rigour and Adaptability of Foxes as Superforecasters*

Let us remind readers that board members, executives or politicians may declare in high confidence that x will happen; it does not mean anything. It only indicates that this individual constructed a coherent story but that story is not necessarily true[8]. Proper deliberation and more conscious thinking (system 2) can improve our (cognitive) judgements. These superforecasters bring some rigour of measurement to forecasting: they must be clearly defined terms and timelines, using numbers, and preferably a lot of forecasts that can be used as feedback to continuously improve the forecast – called calibration in statistics. Paraphrasing Isaiah Berlin, good forecasters are like foxes who know many things, whereas the hedgehog knows one big thing or One Big Idea. An eclectic fox easily beats a hedgehog because it continuously update information and forecasts – as Darwinian evolution theory has taught us to adapt to a changing context.

Famous experts often grab and hold audiences with an animated big idea, like a hedgehog. These coherent and often convincing stories are simple and clear. But not necessarily reflecting a reality. And "the more famous an expert was, the less accurate he was[9]". Foxes, however, aggregate different perspectives, which allows them to progress to the mean. Just like "the wisdom of the crowd" allows diversified opinions or views to aggregate to the mean, which is often more accurate than any expert's advice.

D. Who Does Likely Predict Better: Dr. Spock or Captain Kirk?

In fact, a sophisticated thinking combines Dr. Spock's superb cognitive rationality and Captain Kirk's emotional and ethical intelligence – to speak in Star Trek's TV metaphors. In short, combining system 2 and system 1 thinking provides the best "predictions". Humans seem to relate more to "real humans with emotions" than to cognitive super-rational robots without emotions. However, it should be said that emotions are often overrated. Nonetheless, it is also true that affect and feelings constitute reasonable thinking. It is innate in the human being to feel a little uneasy about "unnatural" mere rational mechanistic robots.

The potential mis-judgement of an individual subjective finding about certain "facts" can be overcome by aggregating different opinions or judgements that will have more accurate and thus more refined predictable outcomes. Unfortunately, aggregation in bringing together different perspectives does not come to humans very naturally. We are squeezed between an objective reality and a subjective experience. Combining both requires a special effort. But foxes are likelier than hedgehogs to give it a try; they consult other perspectives and ideas. Our minds are full of models – simplifications of reality to understand without which we could not function. We often function reasonably well because some models are decent approximations of a physical or other reality. Statistician George Box would have quipped that all models are wrong, but some are more useful than others.

E. The Illusion of Accurate Predictions and the Art of "Seeing" the Future

Superforecasters update much more frequently, on average, than regular forecasters, resulting in a "better-informed forecast" that is more accurate[10]. Intriguingly, they don't consider themselves experts, and they suffer less from a big maniacal ego, and consequently less possible dilution. Good updating is all about finding the middle passage – the mean – and avoid under- and overreaction to new information. It's almost like a continuous *Bayesian belief-updating* whereby the *posterior odds = likelihood ratio multiply with prior odds*. Bayes's luminous idea – that these superforecasters apply – is the core insight of gradually getting closer to the truth by constantly updating in proportion to the weight of the evidence – akin to Popper's scientific progress through a falsification process.

Ultimately, it is *not the crunching power* (of humans augmented with the use of smart machines) that counts. It's *how one uses the information*, by breaking the raw data in different pieces that are more manageable – *separating the knowable from the unknowable*. Any belief needs to be tested, likely resulting in a better more refined forecast.

We also need to be wary of overconfidence in some situations[11]. Although confidence and accuracy are positively correlated, too often people equate confidence with competence. A smart executive will not expect everybody to agree on one suggestion or option. On the contrary, the executive will treat a possible immediate consensus as a warning flag that group-think has taken hold. An array of different opinions or judgements likely indicates that people are actually thinking for themselves by offering unique views. Simply averaging those numerous views would be a good start, as "the wisdom of the crowd" enables a synthesis of the different judgements. However, there are "wise crowds" whose mean judgement is close of the correct answer, but there are crowds that follow tyrants, that fuel market bubbles, or that are under the sway of a shared illusion[12].

To give advice on geopolitical events or predictions is extremely difficult. How accurate are the forecasts of intelligence analysts? That's hard to say. Did they consider alternative hypotheses? Did they look for contrary evidence? Hence why there is no meaningful way to hold intelligence analysts accountable for accuracy, unless accuracy metrics are used and demanded. For instance, in economics, one makes forecasts that can be measured and verified. For instance, will the Euro fall below USD 1.02 in the next 12 months? Most economists fail to accurately predict that exchange rate. That can be measured and traced back.

It seems that most humans poorly grasp the notion of randomness[13], and by extension, luck or fortune. We suffer from the *illusion of prediction* – forecasting with enough confidence that we know what we are doing – and from illusion of control[14] – believing that we have great control over events, mixing up correlation and causation. People who start being successful – hitting a string of pure luck, not due to really strategic insight – feel very confident about their own ability after a while. For instance, someone who correctly calls a coin toss is not demonstrating a special coin-tossing ability or special gambling expertise, whether he succeeds 10 or 100 times. It is called luck or randomness. Of course, it takes a lot of luck to correctly predict 75 percent of all coin tosses. However, if you have a sufficient big group of coin-toss callers, then the assumed "unlikelihood" of reaching such a high correct prediction rate becomes easily much more "likely". Ask any statistician: they call it a regression to the mean. That regression to the mean is quite indispensable for testing luck in a presumed performance.

Fast regression is likely more associated with real luck or chance or randomness, whereas slow regression may indicate a real skillset[15]. Wall Street analysts know very well that is hard to beat the market for a long time; nobody can defy the rules of statistical "gravity" for very long. Even superperformers or superathletes will have lesser years. Each year, about 30 percent of these superperformers – on average – fall from the ranks of the top 2 percent the subsequent year. However, this means that 70 percent can consistently perform above average: that remains very impressive, and most likely due to real skill. It means that superperformers are not infallible – they all will have bad years over an enough long time period – but their above-average performance indicates real skills. The same applies to good strategists.

1.2. Probability Thinking for the Information Age 4.0 Versus Stone-Age Thinking

Ultimately, it is not the level of statistical knowledge or expertise that counts in becoming more accurate in making decisions; it is how one uses the available information and the continuous flood of new data to make those smarter decisions.

A. The "Subjective" Inside View Aligned with the "Objective" Outside View

Like with everything, in cognitive puzzling challenges, one needs to break down the question in a number of subquestions that can be assessed and analyzed. Secondly, the so-called subjective opinion – an *inside view* – may need to be tested or verified or falsified by external data – or an *outside "objective" view*. That outside view is often abstract or is a model that does not lend itself well to story-telling. Narrating a story is a typical expression of an internal (subjective) perspective.

It's interesting that Kahneman considers probabilistic thinkers as "taking an outside view toward even profoundly identity-defining events, seeing them as quasi-random draws from distributions of once-possible worlds[16]". Interestingly, the more forecasters embrace probabilistic thinking, the more accurate they were. And yes, Tetlock and Gardner provocatively state that finding meaning in events is positively related with well-being but negatively with foresight. It means that boards and executives need to understand to focus on probabilities and concrete mathematical or financial metrics to make smarter decisions and secure a fair return on investment for shareholders. At the same time there is a huge need to express meaning and purpose to inspire and aspire the stakeholders in the organization.

A superforecaster remains open-minded and will always reflect in a dialectic manner through putting forward a thesis, seeking contrary facts to come up with an antithesis – or adapting to a changed situation – that may then ultimately result in a new synthesis. In other words, a scientific mind – and superforecasters – sees beliefs as mere hypotheses that need to be tested, not guarded as treasures against questioning. It is this affinity with data and probability thinking that partially explains their superb results.

B. About Foxes and Hedgehogs, Once Again …

Experts are people who spend their time and earn their living studying a particular topic. Despite this intellectual knowledge, they produce poorer predictions than dart-throwing monkeys. Even in the region they were assumed to know best, to be an expert in, these expert-hedgehogs were not significantly better than non-specialists. Those with the most expertise and assumed explicit knowledge are often less reliable, mainly because these presumed experts become unrealistically overconfident. Randomness seems to be a stubborn ingredient in our socio-political and economic lives.

Professor Tetlock even provokes his academic colleagues where hyperspecialization is demanded. However, there is no reason to suppose, he says, that contributors to top academic journals – be it distinguished professors in political science or economics – are any better than informed journalists or any attentive reader of Le Monde, the Financial Times or The New York Times, in "reading" emerging situations. The education level is an imperfect measure of intelligence, and probably un-correlated to wisdom.

The more famous the expert, the more flamboyant their forecasts can be. And they hardly admit they had been wrong, or bring in numerous excuses to "justify" their forecasts, such as timing or unforeseen events. Humility is not often a characteristic of experts. Of course, the exceptions on the rule are well-known Nobel Prize winners in Economics like Rob Shiller, Dan Kahneman or Bob Thaler who are unassuming in their Socratic approach: they likely know they don't know that much … after studying the ability to predict …

Hedgehogs are often dazzled by their own presumed brilliance and hate to admit they were wrong. Foxes, by contrast, are complex thinkers. They recognize that reality emerges from the interactions of many different agents and forces, including randomness that can result in unpredictable outcomes. These hedgehogs are led astray not by what they believe, but rather by how they think.

The advantage in the expert's ability to filter out irrelevant information also means that the expert is less likely to consider all elements of a problem systematically, potentially causing them to miss important nuances or variances that do not fit their mental maps. And like anyone else, expertise based on intuitive gist (system 1) rather than careful analysis (system 2) is also more swayed by emotions and expectations that confirm their "expert-correctness". Consequently, cognitive biases such as framing and anchoring are as rampant in the mind of experts as anyone else. Of course, the expert can override their intuitions and return to a more detailed systematic analysis, potentially reducing some of those biases. The opposite is also true: when this fallible gist-based processing is combined with over-confidence and "earned dogmatism", it probably creates an "intelligence trap"[17] – and the consequences can be devastating. This intelligence trap is the potential curse of all expertise, when these "hedgehogs" refuse to seek or accept another's opinion. In worse cases, intelligence can become a tool for propaganda rather than truth-seeking[18].

C. Eternal Questioning Almost Always Trumps Presumed Objectivity of Data

Most of the time, a majority of the forecasts of these superforecasters are simply the product of careful and nuanced informed judgement. Admittedly, their superior numeracy – and probability thinking – helps these forecasters. Not because the algorithm is superior to others, or that they would have access to some divine future. But they continuously question the so-called objectivity of the data, one is never really sure. It is this fundamental doubt and eternal questioning that makes them more accurate forecasters than others. And because one is never sure, only thinking in terms of probabilities – disguising a fundamental uncertainty – allows to move towards a more clear picture of what is going on, or what could happen.

Most people would equate science with certainty. It's the exact opposite: *all scientific knowledge is tentative.* Read any serious tractate on philosophy of science – be it Kuhn, Popper, Lakatos, Feyerabend or anymore contemporary one – and they tell you all the same: science slowly progresses through stages and paradigms follow in each other's footsteps. Nothing is absolutely sure[19]. Not even in the science of physics, let alone in management or economics. The only setting is "maybe", exactly what most people intuitively try to avoid, looking for serious grounding and firm objective truth. Unfortunately for them, life is more a matter of probability.

It is foxes who scored the best in Tetlock's study – though *not* with "stellar" scores. The reason for this predictive underperformance: geopolitics belongs to the socio-ethical and political sphere in which any precise prediction is notoriously difficult – because in this normative sphere individuals often make "free choices" or historical events "evolve (un)expectedly". But it are the hedgehogs (with not so steller performance) who get invited to participate in television debates to inform the less-informed masses, forgetting that the wisdom of the crowd always overclasses them.

2. Creating Meaning in a Socio-Ethical Realm

One of the most distinctive capabilities of any human is asking the question "why"? We are innately looking for meaning, for reasons to understand why something is happening. We should never forget that scientific knowledge is always tentative, never 100 percent sure. However, science sticks to *"how"* questions that focuses on causation and probabilities: they hardly tackle *"why"* questions about purpose. To the extent that we allow our thoughts to move in the direction of fate, we undermine our ability to think probabilistically. Personally, I take a Humean view to think in empirical and algorithmic terms, but apply the Pascalean adage that fate and faith may help to answer the ultimate question of meaning. In a way, *"why"* directs us to metaphysics, faith and socio-moral thinking, whereas *"how"* sticks with physics and a tangible physical reality that we cognitively can grasp and know ... Our socio-ethical thinking alludes to "provide a meaning" that seems to be an existential human need. A socio-ethical reality is per definition non-deterministic, granting people to make (moral) choices and wise judgements. This seems to be a quite different realm than the more objective scientific reality of "what is".

2.1. Foresight Versus Meaning: Two Different Spheres of "Reality"

Admittedly, the probabilistic thinker is less concerned with the "why" behind phenomena and focuses on the "how" that can be cognitively explained in terms of probable existence or metrics. Probabilistic thinkers – like superforecasters – take the outside objective view towards even profoundly identity-defining events, and even see them as quasi-random draws from distributions of once-possible worlds[20]. The superforecaster is less inclined towards "it-was-meant-to-happen thinking", but rather embraces probabilistic thinking, making the forecasts more accurate and less ephemeral.

A. The More Meaning Given, the Less Foresight Is Possible

As mentioned before, *finding meaning in events is positively correlated with well-being but negatively correlated with foresight*. Intriguingly, it seems that "misery is the price for accuracy"[21]. In other words, to become more *accurate in forecasting*, one needs to *unpack the general hypothesis* or *question into components*, and distinguish as much as possible *the known and unknown*, and try to scrutinize assumptions as much as possible. Subsequently, one adopts the outside view and compares different perspectives on that view – downplaying its uniqueness – and treats it as a special case of a wider class of phenomena. Then, one adopts the inside subjective view that plays up the uniqueness of the problem. Explore similarities and differences between one's own view and those of others – and pay attention to prediction markets and potentially extract info from the wisdom of the crowds. Synthesize those different views into one single vision as acute as possible, and then express one's judgement – using a finely grained scale of probability.

Any updated forecast is likely slightly more accurate and therefore a better-informed forecast or decision. In trading, for instance, this is a very challenging task. Many studies have found that those who trade frequently get worse returns than those who lean towards old-fashioned buy-and-hold longer-term strategies[22]. And good forecasting is about being aware of under- and overreaction to new information, "the Scylla and Charybdis of forecasting". Indeed, good updating is all about finding the middle passage. It also means *avoiding noise and biases* that undermine the accuracy of the forecast[23]. One of the best ways to improve your prediction is to update often, and bit by bit – using Bayes' theorem. Bayes' core insight was of gradually getting closer to the truth by constantly updating in proportion to the weight of the evidence[24].

B. Seeking Certainty or Rather "Verstehen"

Hedgehogs give us the feeling of (false) certainty – and they come in all forms and formats in life. There is no magical formula; randomness plays its role in the objective world[25]. One needs an open growth mindset, and it is equally true that fortune favours the prepared open mind.

There are a couple of characteristics and features that significantly improves the odds of becoming good predictors: being cautious, humble and non-deterministic; be actively open-minded, knowledgeable and a desire for cognition, reflective (introspective and self-critical) and numerate (i.e. being comfortable with numbers) at the same time; being pragmatic and analytical-probabilistic, but also have a good intuition, being determined, showing grit and having a growth mindset[26].

2.2. "Foxes" Asking the Questions That Count, Competing with "Hedgehogs"

Superforecasters appears to be roughly 75 percent perspiration and endurance, and 25 percent inspiration. And in addition, leaders seldom make judgements about the future entirely in isolation. As social species, even in organizations, leaders – especially at boardrooms – decide together.

A. How Foxes Resolved the Cuba Crisis in 1962

Working in teams is crucial to improve judgements. And of course, groupthink always linger around the corner, as the "Bay of Pigs fiasco" invasion in Cuba under President Kennedy clearly has proven. Fortunately for the world, the subsequent nuclear Cuba missile crisis short thereafter was approached in a much better manner where dissent was actively sought by President JF Kennedy, in which the team creatively engineered a positive result with the USSR under enormous pressure. Indeed, internally in the Oval Office, the cabinet used this time a *"devil's advocate"* – in the figure of Robert Kennedy, the trusted brother of John F. Kennedy – to stimulate deliberate and open discussion. These two geopolitical crises in 1961–1962 show that groups can be smart or mad, or both. What makes the differences is not who belongs to the group, but how the group makes a decision. Practicing constructive confrontation can make a huge difference. Diversity is most often a positive thing in decision-making. Consensus-seeking – that easily falls into the trap of group-think – is not always a good thing in making smart decisions.

Many leaders underestimate the value of aggregating other's opinions and perceptions, and they equally overestimate their own ability to provide accurate guidance or be able to distinguish real expert advice from sales talk. However, when a group veers towards group-thinking – consequently lacking any diversity within the group – the individuals within that group may share "correlated" errors. The knowledge of the individual then becomes redundant with another's. Indeed, as diversity shrinks in group-thinking, so do the benefits of the wisdom of the crowd. At the end of the day, the logic of averaging estimates across many experts or individuals depends on having uncorrelated errors. Interpersonal influence in boardrooms, for instance, that squashes independence of opinion – a fiduciary duty in corporate governance – will result in suboptimal decisions. Independence requires that each individual assess the question, separately from the other participants in the group. Only independent individual opinions aggregated will provide some wisdom of a crowd.

B. *Stimulate Open Debate and Dissent to Improve Decisions*

One can even solicit independent opinions or estimates from a group and formalize it into a deliberate process of synergistic interaction, where independence is recorded prior to the deliberate dialogue. Leaders are recommended to accept the advantages of gathering insights from multiple experts, value the benefits of diversity and aim to gather its valuable independent assessments where practically it is possible. A strong chairman can easily influence the discussion within a boardroom, and falsely believe that the subsequent group interaction will provide a real independent opinion.

For instance, Reed Hastings, CEO of *Netflix*, adjusted the decision process at Netflix to elicit the best evidence and stimulate sincere healthy debate, even dissent when necessary. This culture of open debate and dissent has handsomely paid dividends to the owners of Netflix. When the idea of developing children's content emerged, the CEO initially opposed it, arguing that no one would sign up for a subscription to Netflix to watch children's cartoon. Nonetheless, the topic was openly discussed and debated in 2016 with the top 400 Netflix employees and managers who favoured the new idea. The group was persuasive – the wisdom of the crowd – and Netflix adapted the idea, resulting in a sounding success among parents. Netflix was winning new customers and winning awards for its children's films. And thus, for any new idea, one better tests it out. Just like pragmatic foxes would.

C. *Caring Liberates You from Hubris*

On average, teams were 23 percent more accurate in their predictions than individuals[27]. However, successful CEOs get sometimes too confident and ignore dissent. That *kind of hybris* is of all times and can affect the most accomplished individuals. It is sometimes called *the CEO disease*. How a group thinks collectively – in a boardroom, for instance – is an emergent property of the group itself, a result of communication patterns and social chemistry among the group members, not just the smartness or thought processes inside each member. A group of big egos who do not care for each other and the organization is most likely less effective than a group of opinionated individuals who engage with other and really care for the organization – especially in pursuing a truth.

Hence why the fostering of a culture of caring, according to Wharton Professor Adam Grant, can make a big difference[28]. Leaders must be decisive, but at the same time, they need to be able to rely on reliable information of their subordinates whom they care for. It is for this reason that caring CEOs are more trusted and likely also perceived to be more trustworthy[29]. Sharing information in an open mindset where dissent is welcomed – and thus people feel comfortable being pushed out of their intellectual comfort zone – and where psychological safety is guaranteed, is in itself a good predictor for proper smart decision-making. Paradoxically, this open-mindedness allows to develop leaders who can deal with uncertainty, where using conscious system 2 reflection to catch potential mistakes arising from rapid unconscious system 1 operations strengthens smart and possible wise decision-making.

D. Are We Dealing with (Normal) Black Craws or (Unexpected Rare) Black Swans?

And yes, occasionally, history makes jumps, as in black swans – a metaphor for an event so far outside our individual experiences that we can't even imagine it until it happens. A black swan is usually very impactful[30]. That said, both Kahneman and Taleb's critiques can be seen as strong challenges to the notion of being able to make a good forecast. I share that critique on the limits of predictability. Basically, the profound critique indicates that any prediction in the socio-economic and geopolitical world far away is non-sensical. Anything predicted beyond three to five years should be taken with extraordinary caution, because of the non-linearity and potential butterfly dynamics of such prediction far away. Our world is vastly more volatile than we like to, which makes predictions extremely difficult. And maybe Nassim Taleb is right in believing that the world we live in is but one that emerged, quasi-randomly, from a vast population of once-possible worlds[31].

Human foresight can be quite puny, and although AI algorithms may help to slightly improve our predictions, especially if we assume a reasonable stable world where preferences remain quite constant. However, in a fast-changing world, assumptions need to be constantly re-evaluated. But of course, it is also true that fuzzy thinking can never be proven cognitively wrong. And prediction is trying to reduce fuzziness. Likely, we may try to follow a middle path – usually a wise choice. We aim to make progress, but we also know that perfection is unattainable. Foresight – running through a scientist's mind and algorithm – and good judgements remain a work in progress. Collaboration between these two realms is needed. Cognitive abilities that allow us to make reasonable smart decisions and forecasts should be "aligned" with our socio-ethical skills to become more responsible, making fine judgements about the direction we want to go forward, about the societal reality we want to create. This can be seen as the combination of political ethical choices (focused on interdependencies and relationships) underpinned by cognitive analysis and technological (digital) innovation. Indeed, transforming smart decision-makers into wise leaders has been the aim of this book.

E. Explore Through Experimentation Beyond Exploiting Recognized Patterns

To improve predictions, experimentation through trial and error and continuous updates are crucial to be precise and credible – just like machine learning algorithms with a feedback system function. And in case of a stable environment that is not too volatile with a lot of data available, algorithms will do a superb job, speedier and likely more accurate than humans.

Technology companies such as *Netflix* and *Amazon* have discovered how easy it is for them to experiment with changes in their recommendation platforms that allows them to test how to nudge (potential) customers even more efficiently. Experimentation allows organizations to fine-tune product offerings to maximize their appeal and thus effectiveness. Companies such as *Google* alone continuously test their offerings or changes in the recommendation engine. It is advisable for most companies to experiment and test more, and to identify the best option. The power of experiments cannot be overstated.

Some thoughts to take away:

- Why and how some people have the ability to make **better predictions** than others: accurate predictability depends on *what we're trying to predict, how far into the future* and *under what circumstances*.

- Machines may get better and better at mimicking human decision-making and even "digitally copy" meaning to a certain extent (without understanding it), and thereby becoming better in predicting human behavior. However, there still exists *a gap between **mimicking** and reflecting about **meaning**.* The latter is a unique human judgement. And yes, those judgements are prone to biases, cognitive limitations and or subjectivity.

- Any prediction far away in the ***socio-economic*** *and geopolitical world* is non-sensical. Anything predicted beyond three to five years should be taken with extraordinary caution, because of the non-linearity and potential butterfly dynamics of such prediction far away. Our world is vastly more **volatile** than we like to, which **makes predictions extremely difficult – especially in the normative socio-ethical sphere.**

Chapter Thirty

Entanglement of Smart and Wise Decision-Making

"Silence is the language of god, all else is poor translation".

Jalauddin Rumi

"What can be said at all can be said clearly; and whereof one cannot speak thereof one must be silent".

Ludwig Wittgenstein, *Tractatus Logico-Philosophicus*

"Don't hold back … the imagination is the limit".

Elon Musk, 2012, Carnegie-Mellon Commencement Speech

"The support that believers in, and advocates of, self-interested behavior have sought in Adam Smith is, in fact, hard to find on a wider and less biased reading of Smith. The professor of moral philosophy and the pioneer economist did not, in fact, lead a life of spectacular schizophrenia. Indeed, it is precisely the narrowing of the broad Smithian view of human beings, in modern economics, that can be seen as one of the major deficiencies of modern economic theory. This impoverishment is closely related to the distancing of economics from ethics".

Amartya Sen, Nobel Prize laureate in Economics 1998

Smart decision-making is crucial to create competitive advantage in business, and that counts for a big portion of what business value creation and business efficiency is all about. However, the argument put forward is that managerial wisdom will be increasingly needed to address the global challenges in our competitive business world, especially if those challenges are characterized by tensions, conflicts and dilemmas. Moreover, a huge number of companies have invested in artificial intelligence (AI), but fewer than 40 percent had seen business gains from it in the previous three years.

We highlighted the enormous business opportunities from AI apps but also the obvious limitation – especially in the second often ignored socio-ethical sphere. Reality is usually not straightforward, and "seeing" the future is hard, in some instances even impossible. However, in a more "objective" physical sphere aggregate measurements give us a good idea of what can be expected. Artificial intelligence will prove very useful in helping business and customers predict a future that is relatively "stable". This chapter looks at the dialectic power of some features that help to prepare for a meaningful future, by bringing together a variety of intelligences and the entanglement of values and facts.

In a first paragraph we'll attempt to decipher the different intelligences. The cognitive abilities necessary to achieve some digital competency will also require some relational competency that requires some form of consciousness. This consciousness allows managers to become more mindful, a necessary ingredient for wise decision-making – that focuses on the broader socio-ethical and ecological impact of businesses. Smart decisions emphasize the operational efficiency and strategic effectiveness. The second paragraph subtly deconstructs the "objective sphere" that can be distinguished from a more "subjective" often normative reality for which consciousness is necessary to comprehend this distinction.

In previous chapters, we argued that resolving paradoxes may require executives to combine the forces of different intelligences. Even our brains apply innate *a priori* structures combined with personal *a posteriori* hypotheses testing and confirmation that result in concrete (subjective) experiences. As neuroscience has shown us, our physical bodily brain and embodied mind are completely entangled.

Similarly, we explored the potential of combining both *intuitions* (often fuelled by gut feeling and emotions) and *algorithmic* reasoning (using big data or probability thinking) that could help to strengthen smart, good decision-making. The interdependency of intuitive and algorithmic reasoning, which I have labelled "*algotuitional*" thinking, does not necessarily provide any fundamental insight in the often ignored entanglement of facts and values. In other words, avoiding a sharp dualistic perspective of either or requires a more subtle view.

Let's tap into all the potential of our intellectual abilities, be it explicit or tacit knowledge, but also focus more on self-reflection – as in self-consciousness – about our own mindset and thinking. Boards and executives could vastly benefit from such improved ability, embracing different cognitive competencies and an enhanced (self-) awareness to envision or see these subtle differences – most often completely ignored in decision-making at boards and corporations.

1. *Intelligence* Potentially Capturing the Fuzziness and Complexity of Our Reality

Wise leaders who are able to think "algotuitionally" – i.e. combining a probability algorithmic mindset and intuitive knowledge or intelligence – are very much aware of the limitations of our ability to understand and to predict. A *bounded rationality* indicates the rational limitations of decision-making. These leaders will use data analytics and artificial intelligence where possible, and still "mentalize" new insights that are experiential, probably entrepreneurial and often unexpected. And thus hard to predict. It is the fundamental unpredictability of the future that allows executives to alter status quo and to launch new products, technology or business models. Reality more often than not does not always follow a linear path.

1.1. Competencies to Make Smart and Wise Decisions

Making business decisions is often a "fuzzy" process acknowledging that reality is not black and white, or binary right or wrong. In fact most board members are aware that our own thinking can be quite fuzzy, continuously adjusting for a changing context[1]. Many options should be considered. Indeed, as in fuzzy logic – the technique used to help an algorithm operate in situations where there is no certain truth – not every factor can be categorized as either/ or. We often are situated in a grey area where "facts" are not right or wrong, where we need to navigate through these grey areas of business life. Accepting a form of fuzzy logic allows managers to achieve necessary compromises. It also implies that executives need to accept that our answers may not lie at either extreme poles, 0 or 1, but more likely in between[2]. Having such "fuzzy" arguments may help to get us to understand the assumptions and experiences of both the shareholders and relevant concerned stakeholders, for instance.

A. Raising the Executives' Digital Competence (IQ + RQ) ...

Understanding human biases, and being willing to flex our own convictions and assumptions in light of that self-knowledge is crucial for making decisions that acknowledges the firm as a *nexus of relationships*, and not just as a *nexus of contractual agreements*. This undoubled perspective of the organization encompasses both a fiduciary obligation to the organization and its *shareholders*, but also expectations and a responsibility to its *stakeholders*. In that sense, cognitive abilities, IQ (intellectual "coefficient" or ability) and RQ ("risk coefficient"), allow managers to prepare the competencies needed to prepare for the future. The IQ is the basic skillset to comprehend abstract and other phenomena in the physical sphere. The whole discussion around the predictability of phenomena is associated with the RQ of managers and executives. My argument claims that this predictability is possible for an objective natural reality as one observes in the physical world and to a certain extent in the economic reality. However, once we talk about business in creating and capturing of value, we enter a different sphere, one where values and giving meaning determine to a certain extent the outcome of the actions undertaken. "Sensing" the future in a paradoxal entangled world[3] is different from predicting a more deterministic "objective" reality as shown hereunder in Figure 1.

Obviously, management and leadership will try to reduce potential errors and biases, and limit uncertainty as much as possible. Some tools enable us to make smarter judgements to reduce biases and errors (with increased predictability and more perfection): impose stricter standards, increase controls, document all sources, identify assumptions, estimate uncertainty value for these assumptions, increase the number of reviews, justify conclusions with greater rigor, rely on checklists and procedures, and increase the precision of schedules.

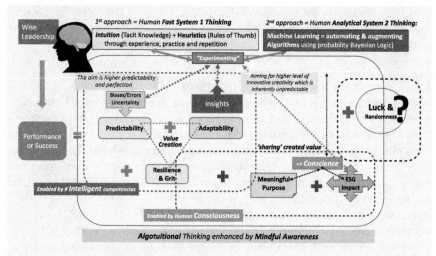

Figure 1: Intelligence underpinning smart decisions transformed through enlightened consciousness into wise decision-making

Explicit knowledge can be codified and to an extent digitized. That allows AI to augment our decision power to resolve certain challenges. But AI is rather helpless in the domain of socio-ethical domain where normative decisions are made about our relations with the world. As visualized in Chapter 28, only human executives can (tacitly) think in terms of causality and see the future in terms of imagined scenarios. Smart computers can only gauge to prepare us for a smarter future by "calculating" correlations or associations that can be very helpful for business of course. Business is embedded in a socio-ethical and political sphere where relations count.

B. ... And Enhancing Relational Competencies (EQ + MQ)

The ability of executives to increase the "insights" through intuitive thinking and heuristics on the one hand, and through the extensive use of data experimentation and self-learning algorithms on the other hand, is adamant to improve performance. Smart leaders attempting to make wise decisions cannot ignore the socio-ethical and environmental impact of their decisions. When (non) executive leadership values the relational competencies – expressed in EQ (emotional "coefficient" or emotional intelligence) and MQ (moral "coefficient" or moral intelligence) that itself depends on conscience associated with consciousness – to provide meaning to those that affect the organization, to those who have a real stake in the organization, one needs leadership that is aware of those stakes, that is mindful about the organization's actions and its consequences. Making wise decisions is only possible through enhanced mindfulness or consciousness[4]. Without the valuation of meaning, leadership would not be able to make responsible decisions.

Decision-making uses broadly both conscious and unconscious processes, preferences, inference, classification and judgement. The fact that non-rational theories – like intuitive thinking and heuristics – postulate agents with emotions, limited data and little time – rather than omniscient "rational" beings – need not to imply that these executives fare badly in the real uncertain world. Continuous adaptation by those (non) executives to an evolving and often volatile reality will make the organization fit to explore new opportunities.

Social psychologist Adam Grant's research shows that the pro-social example of someone who naturally gives can improve the behavior of others in the team. Such an attitude of generosity is helping everyone in the team, including the giver. That explains why "givers" or their teams tend to come out on top of the performers. Fostering a culture of sharing within a team and an organization is crucial to outperform competitors. This attitude of giving is akin to strategically "*sharing*" *created value* with employees, customers and suppliers-partners. Such sharing is relational-oriented – and part of practical wisdom.

In boardrooms – just as in a courtroom – it is not enough for a decision-maker to be virtuous. The individual must also be able to collaborate with others because important decisions in organizations should not be made alone. True, collaboration and processes are the principles on which sound decisions are based – comparable to the principles found in good corporate governance practices[5]. As a "due process of law" in a courtroom that acts as safeguards against arbitrariness and human error, board members and executives should follow particular procedural requirements. Unfortunately, corporate decision-making has not really evolved: "In essence, CEOs still make decisions in much the same way Louis IX did under his oak tree"[6]. Making wise decisions must arise from collaborative processes underpinned by individual virtuous thinking and behavior. Self-consciousness and an enhanced level of self-reflection and mindful awareness will definitely contribute to making wiser decisions.

1.2. Why *Phronèsis* & *Sophia* Constitutes Wise Decision-Making

Making wise decisions is materializing *phronèsis*. Aristoteles saw practical intelligence – or *phronèsis* – as *knowledge in action*, based on logos or the ratio. With the knowledge we have acquired through neuroscience, we now are aware that emotions and feelings – the proverbial "elephant" – somehow partially constitute our reasonable logos. Without those emotions, reasoning and making smart decisions would be hard. The rational "rider" sits on and steers the "elephant" to a certain direction, be it reasonable or ideally responsible decision-making.

To be able to transform our human intelligence and capture this new appealing *Zeitgeist* to become more sustainable, other forms of intelligence may need to be tapped into – using Aristotle's old but useful distinction – such as *epistème* (or science, as in the knowledge of universals), *technè* (or specific expertise as in the knowledge of particulars) and *philo-sophia* (or love for *wisdom* as in the "universal" knowledge).

A. A Smart Manager Can Learn to Become Wiser

I have argued that we should not limit ourselves to one particular field of knowledge, but trying to expand our radius allowing us to see a broader picture that possibly may also generate new ideas to resolve challenges.[7] It is this idea to combine (1) **reasonableness** (possibly found in historical past data and expressed in *epistemè* and *technè*) and (2) **responsibility** that is really future-oriented where risk orientation with prudence but especially a socio-ethical understanding is needed to imagine a world that makes sense – as found in the domain of *phronèsis* and *philo-sophia*. Business has been traditionally focused on science and expertise and thus smart decision-making. Much less on *phronèsis* and *philosophia* that did not fit the mainstream economic model of the *homo oeconomicus rationalis*.

Today, our business leaders are assumed to be purely rational, and stay away from allegedly distorting emotions. Algorithms seem to enable to illuminate this view of pure probability thinking and rational perspective, deprived from any presumably subjective individual emotions. However, neuroscience explained us a more complicated and complex story where consciousness and reflective rationality is somehow fueled by unconscious or subconscious "sensing" of the world (as it were emotional not-yet-structured data). Recent studies in cognitive sciences do not make this hierarchical distinction between emotions and rationality anymore. Emotions are even seen as the driving fuel of many moral conscious convictions.

Similarly, AI and human (executive) intelligence can fertilise each other, nourish each other. And maybe we need to prepare to the next evolution in the progress of an evolving *homo sapiens*, not just a transgression into a new paradigm, but a new way to view the future. At the interface of AI and bioengineering on the one hand, and human intelligence on the other hand. This evolution into "augmented intelligence" – and hopefully also a more attentive mindset that generates more consciousness – will affect business.

The philosopher and pragmatist John Dewey argued that a process of deliberation is reasonable by virtue of its leading to the resolution of a problematic situation[8]. Reasonableness is enacted and achieved, rather than being given and found. Conscious deliberation is an imaginative process of inquiry that arises when changes in our situation call into question our ordinary habits of thought, feeling, appraisal and action. Such deliberative moral imagining often implies intuitive values that are inherited from prior experience.

An unreasonable choice occurs when some single value is allowed to dominate our motivational economy, without any consideration of other competing values. A reasonable choice, by contrast, is one that finds a way to harmonize to a certain degree the competing values we entertain. Paradoxal leaders make more reasonable than unreasonable choices. The deliberative dialectic processes are at once emotional, rational and imaginative. It is not a question of reason versus desire, but rather a question of the reasonable ordering and harmonizing of desires. Moral deliberation is a process of composing life situations, and, as such, it is form of artful remaking of experience.

Similarly, *ecological and socio-ethical objectives* (expressed in the occasionally misused and badly defined notion of ESG) and moral thinking is about finding and creating sensible meaning – not (necessarily) about "the Right and the Good"[9]. Executives have obviously the liberty to apply those ESG goals, or not. However, in close collaboration with their board, they will undertake a process of deliberation to assess the situation and find out how to apply those non-financial objectives that will make an organization more sustainable and therefore likely more competitive over the longer term. Quite a number of companies, such as *Novo Nordisk, Johnson & Johnson, Natura* and *Unilever* to name a few obvious ones – who all built some reputational capital over the years based on a broader stakeholders' perspective – have succeeded to bring those non-financials in their performance criteria. But it remains a work in process, a never-ending challenge. Quite a number of institutional investors may even argue against ESG as dilution of the single-focused objective of maximizing return on invested capital. That begs the question which perspective makes most sense today.

B. *Integrating Diverse Opinions into a Coherent Framework*

We are convinced that combining and balancing certain opposing ideas – as in shareholder profit maximization versus taking into account the goals and objectives of different concerned stakeholders – may require thinking in terms of resolving paradoxes and deliberate ethical reasoning. Wise leaders can be perceived as ethically sensitive pragmatists who not only create and capture, but also "share" that corporate value.

The moral implications of any (business) decision require us to enhance self-reflection and consciousness. Whatever your IQ[10], you can learn to think more wisely with a high(er) level of self-awareness and consciousness. The smartest kid on the block – with incredibly high IQ and/or RQ – can be very unwise or socio-ethically inept. AI can help humans to augment their smart decision power, but never to become a wiser person. Wisdom plays out on a different level than cognitive intelligence. Responsible leadership provides clues to overcome ethical biases or blind spots[11]. Either way, taking into account the questions around *"What are the net consequences of executive decisions"*, *"What are my core obligations when making an executive decision"* and *"What can I live with as a (virtuous) human being when taking an executive decision"* will likely lead to more morally sound and thus wiser decisions.

2. (Enlightened) Consciousness Understanding the Entanglement of Facts and Values

When talking about responsibility, we refer to creating "meaning" in the corporate value proposition. How to understand the inherent entanglement between "objective" facts and "subjective" experiences and values? How can a smart executive transform into a wise decision-maker? The key, I will argue, is an enhanced level of mindfulness and enlightened consciousness.

2.1. Counterfactual Thinking and Ethical Deliberation

In our terminology, **ethical deliberation** refers to (1) *reasonable accountability* that aims to comply to corporate governance practices (i.e. smart decisions) and (2) *engaged responsibility*. Making wise decisions[12] creates but also "shares" value. It transcends the seemingly opposing perspective of shareholders to optimize annual profitability and employees to sustain job security or customers to have access to competitively high-quality products. Responsible leadership minimizes harmful effects of firms on the surrounding environment in the community.

Wise Leaders can mould, shape and transform current realities; they express the ability to distinguish between what we can control and what we cannot. They are aware of the continuous struggle but also able to inspire others to go beyond what may seem possible, in other words, enabling to change reality itself.

Wise leaders may provide us a glimpse of a newer (theoretical causal) model or toolkit that allows a more sustainable business world. Responsibility implies to embrace the latest competitive technological innovation, especially if it links with an updated perspective of humans in an *interconnected* and increasingly *digital* world[13].

How do wise leaders deal with uncertainty? We have argued that these executives have practiced their ability to become **algotuitional thinkers**: (1) allow experience and expertise to guide your "gut feelings" (system 1) and fall back on possible heuristics; (2) once you feel or "foresee" the future, embrace reflection (system 2) to check and verify the real trends that will determine the future plus use algorithmic digitization where possible; (3) as social animals, with the distinctive feature to linguistically communicate and bond, we need to build relationships, be in teams within organizations or between organizations, to create some kind of common good as possible purpose and (4) once we have acknowledged such a purpose – answering the why we are doing what we are undertaking – we also need to share responsibility.

Algotuitional decision-making combines intuitive tacit knowledge with algorithmic predictive power and allows someone to fine-tune smart decisions. However, when we talk about meaning and values, we enter a different sphere where (self-) consciousness and mindfulness take over.

Obsessive managerialism, with its measurable, predicted targets, stifles creative minds. This traditional managerial style unnecessarily narrows perspectives and often obscures context and genuine meaning. Wise leaders, on the other hand, enable teams and organizations to balance broad targets or objectives with adventurous and explorative team members to work on creative innovative solutions. What does constitute "new" counterfactual knowledge?[14] It is part of an often ambiguous adventurous journey full with traps. Only through piecemeal engineering and in *trial and error* one can make progress: intuitive minds are allowed to wander while sometimes supported by data analytics.

We need to disentangle the different kinds of intelligence, and distinguish them from consciousness. It may help us to understand why apparently clever people with the right academic credentials may lack good judgement. Wisdom has in essence nothing to do with IQ. Although my conceptual visualizations were simplifications, I argue that smart decision-making is associated with the expression of (cognitive) intelligence. In that sense, AI will help us to make smarter decisions provided there is enough data available within a relatively stable situation. However, wise decision-making relies on enlightened consciousness and conscience that is more associated in evolving relations – supported (or not) by unfolding new moral norms in a particular society.

2.2. Philosophical Pragmatism Deconstructing the Entanglement of Facts/Values

Let me recapitulate: David Hume's famous doctrine states that one cannot infer an "ought" from an "is". However, Hume's natural fallacy was more about the metaphysical dichotomy between "matters of fact" and "relations of ideas". An "ought" judgement cannot be derived from an "is" judgement that describes a "matter of fact". What Hume really claims, however, is that there is no "matter of fact" about *right* or *virtue*, two ethical values-laden notions. Hume's interest in the non-cognitive character of ethical concepts was part of his wider interest in the nature of ethical judgements. That led to the idea that ethics is not about "matters of fact". That there is a distinction between facts and values may be true, but the distinction is not metaphysical, and therefore facts/values dualistic dichotomy is suggested to be disinflated a little. First of all, even theories and the selection of a theory over another pre-supposes values. Secondly, ethical reasoning about "should be" can be objectively evaluated with notions that we apply in any scientific context. Maybe it is time to stop equating objectivity with description only – as philosopher Hilary Putnam convincingly argues.

A. The Rational Homo Oeconomicus Revised and Reinterpreted?

The assumptions of mainstream economics are based on being rational and reasonable – in line what we have attempted to apply for smart decision-making. I have argued that smart decision-making is necessary but not sufficient to make a business thrive and sustainable. The notion of *(ethical) meaning* and *non-financial objectives* were brought into the thinking of business, in the belief that socio-ethical sphere is complementary to our cognitive intellectual abilities to make smart decisions, but nonetheless necessary for business to become more meaningful.

In fact, Professor Amartya Sen provides us with a more appropriate reinterpretation of Adam Smith's writing in which he reintroduces ethical concerns into economic discourse. Many have misrepresented the technical analysis of the economist Adam Smith by those who would construe him as the prophet of "economic man" that still haunts us: "It is not from the benevolence of the butcher, the brewer or the baker that we expect our dinner, but from their regard to their own interest. We address ourselves, not to their humanity but to their self-love, and never talk to them of our own necessities but of their advantages"[15]. However, in *The Theory of Moral Sentiments*, Adam Smith argues that the emotion of sympathy is a better guide to moral action than is reason. The notion of sympathy relates and identifies how basic rules of prudence and justice could unfold to survive and thrive in a "fair" society. Both rationality and sympathy are necessary ingredients for economic exchanges.

Sen's critique in his *On Ethics and Economics* sought to challenge standard economists' view of what economic rationality requires, what the motivations of economic actors can be realistically assumed to be and what criteria of economic performance are legitimately used[16]. The vision of a *homo sapiens* as a logical human being, situated between animals and God (or the gods), has been the predominant view in our society and culminated in the age of Enlightenment. Economics is assumed to deal with ascertainable "objective" facts whereas ethics is concerned with valuation and (moral) obligations. "The complex procedure of equating self-interest with rationality and then identifying actual behavior to be thoroughly counterproductive if the ultimate intention is to provide a reasonable case for the assumption of self-interest maximization in the specification of actual behavior in economic theory"[17].

This mainstream standpoint says that valuation can't possibly be a (statement of) "fact" and are presupposed to be "subjective". The fact/value dichotomy – "is" versus "ought" – and the analytic/synthetic dichotomy – "matters of facts" versus "relations of ideas" – was foundational for logical positivism and classical empiricism[18] that became the paradigm for modern scientific thinking. We ended up in a Cartesian dualistic reality that I have underwritten to a certain extent by distinguishing cognitive learning from socio-ethical learning. However, some nuances need now to be brought in to amend this dualism.

B. Warranted Assertability Suffices to Talk "Objectively" About Ethical Values

Perception is not innocent; it is always an exercise of our concepts. Our brains uses models to understand the world around us. That also applies to businesses and their executives, both in the cognitive and socio-ethical spheres that are rather entangled and affecting our perception of facts and values. As neuroscience has now confirmed, John Dewey's astute pragmatic reasoning was very sensible. He asked "What makes something valuable as opposed to merely being valued?" The entanglement of both facts and values become clear when valuations should be seen as inseparable from all our activities, including our "scientific" ones. For philosophical pragmatists, the distinction fact/value is real but not absolute because of the entanglement between those different kind of thinking and learning. "What holds good for inquiry in general holds for value inquiry in particular" – Harvard philosopher Hilary Putnam says, quoting John Dewey[19].

Indeed, it can be argued that the "ascertaining" of "facts" and "values" are interdependent activities. Although cognitive learning and socio-ethical learning belong to two different realms, we need to shade this dualistic separation a little since both spheres are intertwined. The description of economically relevant behavior, in fact, assumes the use of a variety of thick ethical concepts – used by agents for their ethical reasoning. The prescriptive ethical theories are equally entangled with the possibility to be properly evaluated in an "objective" reasonable manner.

It should not surprise that our ethical judgements – in the socio-ethical sphere – can claim objective validity, while still recognizing that these values are shaped by a particular culture and a by a particular problematic situation. A cultural context of values and objective validity do not have to be incompatible. For both science and socio-ethical values, there does not exist an Archimedean point of view, an "absolute conception" outside all contexts and problematic situations[20]. Our perspectives on the world and its situation – the way we investigate and discuss – is always fallible. If the idea of a frozen "final truth" does not make sense in science and physics, this is even more so in the socio-ethical realm. But in contrast to most post-modernist philosophers, pragmatists like Richard Rorty do not conclude that therefore we cannot speak of truth or *warranted assertability* in ethics[21]. One can even argue that ethics may have some objectivity. Yes, we may not find some form of recognition transcendent truth here, but we can treat value judgements[22] in the socio-ethical sphere as capable of truth and falsity. Similar as any scientific objective fact, and thus we can treat those values as capable of *warranted assertability* and *warranted deniability*, as we do apply in positive science. This shows that a clear and absolute dichotomy between facts and values is untenable. Ethics does not really conflict with physics[23]. Ethical notions like "just," "good" and a "sense of justice" (by looking into the consequences for instance) are indeed part of a discourse that is not reducible to physical discourse.

Within such an understanding of fallibility, facts and values are really entangled, which subverts the dichotomy a little. "If agreeableness is precisely the agreeableness or congruence of some objective condition", according to American pragmatic philosopher John Dewey, this notion can be applied to a moral agent as to a describable impulse or habit[24]. Admittedly, the "objectivity" that ethical claims require is not interpreted in Platonic Ideas. As argued, ethical talk does not necessarily need a metaphysical foundation to support it[25]. In the way we deal with problematical situations and in the relationships with other agents and stakeholders we discover which ones are more applicable or better than others and which ones are worse. Following the philosophical pragmatists John Dewey and Hilary Putnam, we don't need an epistemological or even ontological foundation of facts or values (or their dichotomy) to be able to use them and effectively understand in a particular situation.

Although the notion of consciousness refers to personal "subjective" experiences – in contrast to the "objective" natural laws of physics, for example – the dichotomy between facts and values is less strict than proclaimed. Indeed, these personal experiences can contain some "element of objectivity". In a sense, one could establish some warranted assertability about the truthfulness of such experience or moral value, and thus I could even label it as a form of objectivity. In other words, (ethical) values may be *non*-scientific without being *un*scientific[26]. Ethical values can have a warranted assertability because the values could be plausible, coherent and simpler than others to understand. These conditions determine what is considered as "objective", but can be applied as well to subjective experiences. In other words, that dualistic dichotomy is less strict than David Hume and many others – and also myself when referring to the naturalistic fallacy – have argued for.

I started this book by saying that philosophically speaking I can be considered a "pragmatic realist". Philosophical pragmatic realism adheres to *fallibilism* – i.e. one does not regard the product of inquiry or a conclusion or warranted assertability as immune from criticism – but it should not result in a form of skepticism. Pragmatism believes that doubt requires both justification of theoretical inquiries about facts as much as beliefs about values. The distinction between facts/values may be seen as too dualistic, and in reality those two spheres are more entangled than often acknowledged.

Let me try once more: criticism usually is interpreted as an intelligent reflection about a certain phenomenon. When claiming cognitive value, it means that scientists have enough reason to believe that there is warranted assertability to claim objective truth. The argument here – in line with Hilary Putnam – is that knowledge of facts pre-supposes knowledge values, confirming the inherent entanglement of both spheres. Judgements of coherence and simplicity are pre-supposed by physical science. Yet these notions are values themselves. Again, clearly an entanglement of both facts and values. And any rational inquiry, be in the sphere of objective cognition or "subjective" socio-ethical reality, is always under the scrutiny of the methodology of fallibilism. In other words, both the arguments for more reasonableness and responsibility in business decisions – though belonging to two different epistemological spheres – carry the possibility of objectivity. The distinction between facts that are objective and values that are perceived as subjective is less dualistic and clear as often assumed. As this book argues, different spheres and distinctive components are all part of a coherent entangled reality.

Indeed, both facts and values are needed to make good, smart or wise decisions. Both intelligence and consciousness are part of our decision-making process, especially if executives aim to embrace wisdom to tap into more fulfillment and meaning in business. Even the notion of meaning carries some objectivity that allows organisations to be distinguishable in order to potentially become competitive[27].

C. How Awakened Consciousness Strengthens and Broadens Our Understanding

It is clear that business and management does not provide us the tools to really understand the entanglement of values and facts. Only consciousness – that somehow constitutes the EQ and MQ in the socio-ethical sphere – is able to guide us through this philosophical and spiritual journey that allows us to create meaning and purpose.

(1) Reaching out for meaning beyond the objective "*Geworfenheit*"

Managers and executives have learned to determine and analyze the crux of a problem[28]. Strategy then indicates to turn the problem statement into a value proposition supported by tailored value chain activities that aim to act in an effective and efficient way to optimize minimal input into maximal output. This unique value proposition is constituted as such that it cannot be easily copied ensuring the firm a (temporary) competitive advantage. Management focuses on the external factual exchanges optimizing the net input/output that is expected to maximize profitability. The glue that keeps organizations together is more internally oriented and the topic of organizational studies.

Intelligently managing an organization and those who have a real stake in it also will require some form of enhanced consciousness to find that balance of profit cum effectiveness and dignified caring for customers and employees.

This book emphasized the distinction between two different though entangled spheres, the factual sphere of "external" exchanges that need to be managed – the subject of most business schools – and the normative sphere of socio-ethical values, often supported by some spiritual notions of meaning. AI operates in the first factual sphere that can be "objectively" measured and controlled. The different forms of human intelligence are reasonably well equipped to deal with this factual sphere. Admittedly, in some well-defined narrow aspects of this reality, AI is a superior performer compared to human intelligence. However, in the second sphere of values other variables count: norms and values that somehow find their origin in EQ and MQ, but more importantly, are underpinned by human consciousness that allows us to understand and give meaning to our experiences. It's this same ability to understand our world in which we are thrown in – to use Heidegger's philosophical metaphor of *Geworfenheit*[29] – that can create another reality.

(2) Solving the *"hard problem of consciousness"*?

That leaves us with the notion of consciousness, more specifically the "hard problem of consciousness". Management studies and economics do not even touch this notion, and psychologists, neuroscientists and philosophers have not provided a convincing answer either so far. Now what? I am aware that this book is not the place to explore in detail how to reach such form of enlightened awareness. Allow me though to indicate some very rough contours of a possible path that executive and managers could follow: meditative contemplation and yoga practices have proven to enhance awareness, and even to awaken our brain[30]. The Buddhist interpretation of consciousness can indirectly help us in partially addressing this "hard problem of consciousness". But there are numerous other ways to bring wisdom of our awaked brain into our daily lives, through integrating awakened mindful attention, awakened connection[31] or relationship, and through awakened heart. In a way, such enlightened consciousness crushes the binary ways of knowing – that in some instances can be considered to toxicate our judgments. Modern people and their algorithms think in terms of binaries and divisions. We should not be bound by binary algorithmic thinking only, but beyond, and probably more in terms of **relational, reciprocal**[32] and **interconnected** beings[33].

Yes, I was fortunate to attend such Buddhist practices for a couple of years in Solo in Indonesia near the Buddhist Borobodur temple in the early nineties, allowing me first hand to understand and to feel the impact these exercises had on my own mind and attitude in general. This Buddhistic introspective power – though brought up by a Catholic Jesuit education – never left me during all my years living in Asia and later Australia, before heading back part time to my place of origin in Belgium. This combination of "subjective" spiritual exploring that allowed me to enhance my own consciousness of being thrown into specific contexts, with the forces of down-to-earth management practice over those years as an entrepreneur and as a consultant helped me to balance my own view of an entangled and occasionally confusing reality in which we live.

(3) Standing on the shoulders of (ancient and modern) sages

The stories of personal spiritual journeys of sages can be quite useful to be inspired by to determine some wisdom we all aspire. The ancient Ionian Greek philosopher Pythagoras (570–496 BC) – who had an enormous influence on Plato and Aristotle and thus the Western culture – was convinced that meditative tradition attended to our "harmony of the spheres", combining music, mathematics and astronomy. Pythagoras was a strong believer that the highest life is one devoted to passionate sympathetic contemplation, which produced a kind of ecstasy derived from a direct conscious insight into the nature of reality. These ideas are quite akin to what the Gautama Buddha (circa 563–483 BC) taught us: consciousness could be used for meditative investigating the nature of suffering and its causes. Gautama became an "awakened one" – a buddha – due to his mind being utterly freed from all afflictions and obscurations, realizing a state of "nirvana", a sheer nothingness of sublime peace. In short, Buddhism – but in a way most mystical oriented venues in the religions such as the *Kabbalistic string of Jewish mysticism, Christian mysticism, Sufism in Islam* – showed us to realize genuine well-being through purifying our mind of its afflictions, cultivating virtue and gaining insight in the nature of reality.

Often these sages went through meditation and "mystical" experiences to reach an enlightened form of consciousness[34] – and we find them in almost all different religions. Such mindfulness could enlighten us to become more "effective" in the socio-ethical sphere. The more we become aware of ourselves and the world, the more we will recognize the fundamental interdependency and *relational* innateness of our humanness. How is that all relevant for boards and executives?

(4) How executives benefit from *meditative mindfulness* and from understanding the *objective-subjective entanglement?*

This book asserted the inherent strong entanglement of different spheres of reality, more particularly the cognitive "objective" factual sphere that is accessible to our intelligence, and a more subjective sphere of values that is accessible by enhanced consciousness. I stipulate that this enhanced consciousness can be quite helpful and even necessary in becoming wiser decision-makers. The incredible usefulness of mindful introspection and meditative practices reconfirm the hypothesis in the initial 2016–2017 Amrop survey, stipulating the constructive useful force of meditation and contemplation in business.

Outward management goals are important, but are not a substitute for "finding" meaning and purpose, so crucial to enable organizations and their boards-and-executives to enlighten their stakeholders, especially their employees and customers.

Increased mindfulness usually include a heightened sense of compassion[35] and is able to understand a state in which one is acutely aware of and focused on the reality of the present moment. Being-in-the-present does not contradict the "sensing of a future" since they are spiritually speaking almost indistinguishable. Mindfulness[36] is a kind of non-elaborative, non-judgemental, present-centred acute awareness in which each thought, feeling or sensation that arises is acknowledged and accepted. We have assumed that such mindfulness is a *conditio sine qua non* to enable some wise decision-making. Taking responsible decisions implies an agent who is mindful and astutely conscious about the impact of these decisions. In some way, those authentic board members with a clear North Star[37] in sight and mind – paraphrasing former Metronic CEO and now Harvard faculty Bill George – are seasoned and smart (non) executives. They pursue material prosperity for the organization and its talented leadership while also being attentive and sensitive for the impact of these decisions. Corporations and their leadership are obviously accountable and responsible for their decisions and actions.

(5) Wise decision-making implies balancing objective facts and subjective experience, integrating *intelligence* and *consciousness*

Being reasonable or smart takes place in the "objective" material world in which those executives optimize input/output. Responsibility, however, refers to the wisdom to balance this presumed "objective material" aspects of business with the more "subjective personal awareness" and even spiritual (self-) consciousness of the socio-ethical sphere. Both the executive's *intelligence* and *consciousness* (or *soul*) play their respective guiding roles in these two entangled realities, constituting an infinite arena of possibilities and probable opportunities. When the two realities transcend the usual dualistic awareness about object versus subject to an *inverted consciousness* – where this dualism disappears into the feeling of a *common deep purpose* – then this "synthesis" allows us to experience a sense of (immanent promising) future.

Especially when facing adversity, such an experience of serenity through enhanced acute awareness and highly focused attention will allow to build resistance and enlightened grit. This focus is (almost) a meditative inversion process of consciousness that Mahayana Tibetan Buddhism has embraced for centuries. This radical empirical approach by the Buddhist tradition[38] is akin to William James's description of spiritual perspective in which the notion that all physical and mental phenomena arise out of some primal material "stuff" is rejected. The pragmatist philosopher William James – often considered the founder of psychology – would argue that the primal substance of the universe is pure experience[39] – or consciousness. He proposed introspection – an inward-oriented direct observation of mental phenomena – as the primary means of investigating the mind. Indeed, he was deeply skeptical of the mechanistic materialism that already dominated science during his time and is now predominant in all branches of science.

(6) Consciousness, cognizance and conscience – crucial for making wise decisions

Historically, modern science progresses based on objective (empirical) observation and testing. However, consciousness or the soul cannot be directly observed objectively or publicly with those "current materialistic tools", but can only be observed in terms of our own subjective experience. According to the Mahayana school of Buddhism, consciousness[40] is characterised by a form of bliss or luminosity and by a "superior" multidimensional "cognizance". Our argument is against scientism – the belief that the natural world consists only of physical phenomena explainable according to the laws of physics and biology only – not against science. The hard problem of consciousness is still unresolved within such a Western "objective scientific" context[41] – because it seems to escape in invisibility, not comprehensive to the objective physical realm. Nonetheless, consciousness is very "subjectively" real and constitutive for the reality of the normative sphere of values that steers our organizations. Maybe we should take Nobel Prize-winning physicist Richard Feynman more seriously when he told an audience that "we should try to prove ourselves wrong as quickly as possible, because only in that way can we find progress"[42]. Even when we won't be able to fully materialize our spiritual potential, enhancing our consciousness and listening to our inner voice, part of a vital energy, has proven to have a positive impact on our mental and physical health[43]. Be it that we feel less stressful and more in tune with our team members, as well as a much smaller chance to get into depression or burnout.

If we are able to maintain some enlightened mindfulness – as in a continuous and unwavering flow of opportunities – we may be able to really "broaden" our mind. Such an attitude will help to see the fundamental connectivity and interdependency of our reality, of how an organization itself is related and connected to invisible forces within a very objective "factual" world. Finding "silence" in ourselves, escaping the imposed artificial rat race, meditating to re-create ourselves and our relationships from day to day may help to address our fundamental challenges, to start with in our self in relationship with our own interactions, be it in business, politics and beyond. Obviously, I am not ignoring the daily managerial concerns of any executive or board member in this fierce competitive economy, but I am trying to argue that changing our individual mindset and enhancing our own awareness is a necessity to turn ourselves, smart executives, into wise leaders – **outmaneuvering** any artificial assumed intelligent device in the process. Tapping into our inner strengths, doing mind-training, broadening our mindset and becoming more aware of how we think – aligned with the traditional organizational strategic and operational steps taught at our business schools – will deepen the understanding of our *smart intelligent executives*, and potentially transform them into *wise highly conscious decision-makers*.

Some thoughts to take away:

- Without a theoretical model, it is hard to steer organizations towards more sustainability. Being responsible – something AI completely lacks –. will determine the fate of the organization in the not too distant future.

- Although I underwrote the **dichotomy** of cognition (facts) and ethical thinking (values) – as quipped by philosopher David Hume – I believe that this dualism *need to be shaded a little*. A slightly more dialectic approach of both realms may be preferable to indicate the strong **entanglement** of both spheres:
  - Combining in*tuitive* thinking (System 1) and *algo*rithmic thinking (more System 2 related) in a smart way can result in a form of "algo-tuitional" thinking. This new term "algotuitional leadership" indicates how the *homo sapiens* currently already makes reasonable decisions, but with this specific understanding that "a more holistic mindset" is strengthening our consciousness and conscience, allowing us to steer towards more responsible behavior.
  - Similarly, as explained in part 2, our thinking presumes an objective structured innate natural *a priori* structures and personal nurtured *a posteriori* experiences.
  - The distinction between objective material reality versus subjective personal experience may be less dichotomous than previously thought. This chapter argues that **facts and values are entangled** and not completely separable. Both facts and values carry some form of objectivity. And even objective knowledge assumes the use of values, reconfirming the fierce entanglement of both the cognitive and socio-ethical spheres.
  - Infusing some Buddhist meditative practices will allow managers and executives to enhance their **personal awareness** and **astute enlightened mindfulness** – allowing to transform from a *smart intelligent person* into a *wise highly conscious person*.

- Intelligent leaders are likely smart decision-makers, but not necessarily responsible leaders. **Wise decision-makers** who are conscious about their moral obligations and about consequences of the activities of their organization and themselves, likely aim to be virtuous and will likely also be emotionally and morally intelligent. Binary artificial intelligence could be described "intelligent" (as in reaching and fulfilling certain clearly defined objectives) but not "*fully consciousness*" or *mindful*, and therefore not really wise. Artificial intelligence remains amoral without conscious. Only enlightened conscious beings are able to take moral steps and act accordingly. Achieving awakened awareness and enlightened consciousness is directly linked to the fundamental principles of relations, reciprocity and interconnectedness.

Conscious and Mindful Leadership
Making Wise(r) Decisions in a Smart World

"The kind of hope that I often think about ... I understand above all as a state of mind, not as a state of the world. Either we have hope within us or we don't; it is a dimension of the soul, and it's not essentially dependent on some particular observation of the world or estimate of the situation ... Hope is not the conviction that something will turn out well, but the certainty that something makes sense, regardless of how it turns out".

Václav Havel (1990: 181)

"The notion of obligations comes before that of rights, which is subordinate and relative to the former".

Simone Weil, *The Need for Roots: Prelude to a Declaration of Duties Towards Mankind,* 1949

"Man is by nature a social animal; an individual who is unsocial naturally and not accidentally is either beneath our notice or more than human. Society is something that precedes the individual. Anyone who either cannot lead the common life or is so self-sufficient as not to need to, and therefore does not partake of society is either a beast or a god".

Aristotle, *Politics,* c. 330 BC

The world becomes smarter by the day. Nonetheless, our entangled challenges seem to grow by the minute. Can a real homo *sapien* stand up, *wise up* and change course?

The real world is likely far too complex to fully comprehend. In our attempt to understand, we structure through models that simplify[1]. "*Making Wise Decisions in a Smart World*" is not different. I argued that *our future will be digital*, with its enormous benefits of making us smarter. But I also highlighted the limitations of smart machines and its darker side of taking out (individual responsible) agency and installing continuous surveillance. This increased digital connectivity carries a possible destructive force of making people so co-dependent with inescapable ties that could become "toxic"[2]. However, the human inherent *thumos* – the desire for recognition and respect – will likely make *our future also more relational.*

Again, balancing these potentially opposing forces will be the ongoing challenge for us all. It is no coincidence that consciousness is inherently dialogic; that self-awareness emerges in connecting and interacting with others. Consciousness is fundamentally relational, potentially allowing us to create and find profound meaning and purpose.

1. Being Smart Does Not Legitimatize Your Business, Wise Decision-Making Probably Does

The crux of my argument is that *smart decision-making is necessary but insufficient to stay relevant in business and society*. And sure, artificial intelligence (AI) brings benefits to customers and organizations: smart computers will make business executives smarter and render their business more competitive. Unfortunately, smart computers won't be able to make us any wiser. On the contrary, paradoxically, these smart computers will make our life more convenient but potentially also less meaningful and our dependency on those few powerful oligopolistic tech companies may lead to "big brother guiding us", not just watching us – probably taking away individual agency.

1.1. How to Really Interpret Wise Decision-Making in Organizations?

Making sense of the future is less straightforward as often suggested, especially in turbulent times where the past may not be the best guide for decisions about a volatile, complex and ambiguous future, simply because the context has changed[3]. Combining smartness with practical wisdom may help.

Making wise decisions likely engages different spiritual traditions to bring about a renaissance of contemplative heritages as a potent counterforce of material modernism that mainly focuses on the outward exploitation, control and exploration of our environment. Indeed, time has come now[4] to balance our outward-looking management perspective with a more inward emphasis of making enlightened wise(r) decisions in an ever-"smarter" world.

Wise leadership is often seen as interchangeable with "ethical intelligence". However, ethical intelligence is only one facet. A **wise** executive who is most probably also **smart** will likely possess certain competencies (IQ), accustomed to be risk sensitive (RQ), tuned in to its important stakeholders through a high level of emotional intelligence (EQ), as well as being a beacon for many through a developed moral intelligence (MQ). Indeed, sage leaders combine:

1. *Making sense of the new context (IQ)* by directing the company with sufficient *competence* to new business opportunities. Basically, these competent managers draw on experience (without being locked in to the past success) to **exploit** the current assets and *explore* new opportunities with their teams, exercising multi-dimensional thinking, avoiding false dilemmas and by synthesizing seemingly opposing arguments or alleged facts after thorough analysis.

2. Becoming *good (super) forecasters (RQ)* to sense the future and **explore** new trends. Taking reasonable decisions likely contain particular risks. It is therefore important to improve forecasting methodology and knowing how to predict an uncertain future – albeit with the assistance of AI.

3. *Creating a "safe" and healthy environment* in which managers care for organizational teams *(EQ)*. Partially unconscious, EQ engenders **trustworthiness** and creates bonds between stakeholders. Showing care or EQ for your team often results in a safe environment that facilitates the conditions for taking reasonable risks; brace yourself for pushbacks and failures, and allow a longer term horizon; use trust as a key indicator and care for your employees and customers; back up trust with compliance and installing proper corporate governance practices; exercise zero-tolerance to bad governance. And finally …

4. *Guiding the organization with integrity (MQ or moral intelligence)*, which implies that the board and executive have the courage of conviction by being clear on the **principles** (the moral compass); by blending courage, instinct/intuition and sophistication (multi-dimensional learning); and by thinking in terms of value, not in terms of securing tenure. Being able to assess and resolve ethical dilemmas in organizations is of course an enormous asset.

1.2. Mindful Leadership "Seeing" Purpose That Transcends Mere Legality and Efficiency

Mindful executives and managers understand the importance of both the objectives of efficiency and effectiveness established through smart decision-making. But they are aware of the necessity to create a narrative around a meaningful purpose that comes alive through valuable interactions with stakeholders. Such mindfulness allows executives to tap into **the Owl of Minerva's wisdom**[5].

By infusing meaning and purpose, wise decision-making may prolong the relevance of a business, but is not the elixir that makes business immortal. My aim is rather more modest: how to deal with technologies like AI that may enhance reasonable or smart decision-making, but potentially jeopardizes our own (human) responsibilities. The desire of many young people to belong to a community [or to create a more ideal alter-self] partially explains the push of a "metaverse" world in which they feel like a member with a real stake, not a mere commercial "user". This virtual metaverse world indicates that we're moving towards a digitized gamified living context where relationships nonetheless count.

By integrating or balancing the sphere of ethics, ecology and governance into a commercially viable utility view, boards or executives at organizations may intuitively "see" the future or detect trends much sooner and faster than anyone else. However, whatever the organization's or entrepreneur's ability to sense the future trend, "it remains hard to make predictions, especially about the future".

Thriving in the future will require business to "share" some of that created value with a number of crucial stakeholders, be it the obvious customers, but also engaged and loyal employees, as well as trusted long-term suppliers. When local communities grant the metaphorical "licence to operate" to corporations, the *legitimacy* of business is strengthened beyond mere legal or utilitarian efficiency grounds.

2. AI Is a Useful Tool Making Us Smarter but Not Wiser

Complex AI algorithms function best in well-defined and stable situations where large amounts of data are available. Narrowly focused AI algorithms enhance our accurateness in decision-making, making us smarter in the process. Repetitive tasks with a lot of data available will likely be automated and laborers will probably be replaced by smart robots. However, our versatile human intelligence has evolved to continuously adapt to uncertainty, independent of big or small data.

Today, AI is deeply felt in the way we use our smartphones, watch movies online, or purchase books online. AI applications having the biggest impact are found in medicine, health care, fintech and some agricultural and manufacturing sectors. The benefits of AI are substantial and potentially enormous.

2.1. Limitations of Smart AI/Machine Learning (ML)

To accurately predict the future, one needs a good theory that explains causality, reliable big data, and a relatively stable world. That is the reason that AI is very good at predicting the future outcome in stable situations, such as face recognition for unlocking your phone or any secured entry point, to finding the fastest route to your destination, to sorting and analyzing large data in accounting. Understanding the Knightian distinction between uncertainty and risk is crucial. By measuring risk, we assume to know the possible outcomes, their probability and impact or consequences. However, in unstable situations or high uncertainty, we cannot envisage all possible outcomes or their consequences in advance. Many situations today are characterized by a mixture of risk and uncertainty, which means that both ML and human intelligence have an important role to play. The more precisely defined and more stable a situation is, the more likely it is that AI will outperform humans.

However, predicting human behavior is extremely difficult since our lives are characterized by so many different variables, while a free choice could do things differently or prescribe certain alternative behavior or solution. It is human choice that makes human behavior hardly predicable, though making the summation of many aggregated individual preferences may give us a statistically relevant idea of the "average" behavior.

The developments in digital technology[6] and AI's ML are vast and promising. The argument to embrace AI/ML is compelling. However, the limitation and the darker side of AI/ML should not be omitted on the agenda of board meetings. Although we do not think that "broad general AI" is immanent any time soon, we do believe that the danger of misuse and even monopolization of AI/ML is real and evident. Politicians and corporate leaders can be easily swayed to misuse the power of AI technology for their own benefit. Just look at the increasing surveillance systems in autocratic regimes where citizens will be nudged, coerced or forced to comply with the leaders' rules, or oligarchic technology companies, which will take advantage of their predictive AI power to manipulate the needs of potential customers, persuading them to enter the digital world (in which they will be unconsciously monitored, continuously under digital or actual real surveillance and assessed ...). And one can wonder what question the metaverse, for instance, is exactly trying to resolve ...

Why do so many people and organizations believe in *techno-chauvinism*, which claims that technologically advanced solutions are always superior to human ones? To what extent is this techno-chauvinism legitimatizing these new technologies? Consensus tells us that useful tech improves our daily lives, moving into every corner of our real *analog* lives. But the debate around privacy and human dignity remains unresolved in quite a number of jurisdictions. What about the rights and security in work in our gig economy? Or what about our privacy rights in unaccountable facial recognition on the street, or the use of wearable tracking devices that workers need to carry with them to improve productivity? The legitimacy of these technologies should be questioned not only by citizens and politicians, but also by the boards of organizations who develop those AI applications and devices, or who consider to apply them in their own organization. We may need more balance between insightful innovation, ethical reflection and proper legal oversight. The technology's dark side can be felt in the violations of privacy in the name of necessary (Orwellian) surveillance, or in potential cyber-wars which could undermine our security and potentially even threaten our Western values.

Indeed, AI can help in resolving cognitive challenges. Imagining a different more sustainable and probably more meaningful future, however, will require values and insights that are related to "should be" questions that cannot be necessarily derived from existing data. In this normative sphere, (self-) awareness through introspection and meditative practices pursues an advanced consciousness function as a bridge between the dualistic two realms of objective factual "truth" and subjective personal values–oriented experiences. Balancing diverse competencies of intelligence and an enhanced level of consciousness constitutes practical wisdom. Such mindfulness may provide us a fertile context in which a new future is imagined, prescribed and created potentially addressing some of the most pressing current challenges.

Innovation in the field of AI holds enormous promises, but, if unregulated, citizens will cede more power to already-powerful oligopolistic companies. History has taught us over and over that too much power in the hands of one or a few should be avoided. It would be wiser to prevent such situations to occur in the first place by installing or voting for politicians who have the courage to provide some more fairness in terms of regulation and law enforcement.

AI needs to be ethical and respond to the normative tenets of our society, and a higher level of accountability from those who initiate and innovate the applications, i.e. boards of tech companies. The same kind of scrutiny and global norms should be wrapped around AI, with the same dedication that we bring to consensus-seeking discussions around nuclear energy or nuclear "power". Only a more responsible leadership will enable this dialogue to happen …

The starting point remains to define the crux of a certain problem, and then resolve it. That is exactly what intelligent or smart decision-making aims to achieve. Boards need to assess the quality and impact of AI and whether AI is more than a new technology to be given to the IT department for implementation, or whether AI is affecting human relations in the organization – potentially even perceived as an ideology. AI systems are complex and often very contextual requiring C-level continuous strategic oversight. A clear meaningful purpose or soul could inspire. It is this *strategic foresight* of a board that makes the organization unique and so special.

2.2. Cognitive Abilities Versus a Moral Normative Conscience: A Neuroscientific Perspective

Making wise decisions occurs in a fundamental different reality than mere digitizing a known relatively stable world. This book argued why human learning definitely outsmarts smart computers. Don't we all occasionally confuse correlations with causation? Well, that's true. But only the human brain is able to think in terms of counterfactuals and is able to imagine a new world. Factual "cognitive" thinking differs from "socio-ethical learning", although both realities are closely entangled. Similarly, the human brain combines innate "objective" *a priori* structures allowing babies to learn a language and meaning, combined with the personal and thus "subjective" *a posteriori* experiences that is built up over the years.

Neuroscience teaches us that our "unconsciousness" in our brain envisions a landscape of probabilities whereas our conscious mind samples from it. The global information broadcasting within our cortex arises from an incredibly dense neuronal network whose *raison d'être* is the massive sharing of pertinent information through the brain. It seems that our unconsciousness is like an automatic algorithmic computer that helps us to create conscious meaning. Some aspects of problem-solving are better dealt with at the fringes of unconsciousness, rather than with an analytical full-blown conscious effort. It seems that our brain uses a clever division of labor: an army of unconscious statisticians and a single conscious decision-maker. From an information processing view, this unconscious is interpreted as subliminal subconscious or "consciousness-in-waiting". This information is already encoded by an active assembly of firing neurons and this could become conscious at any time, if it were attended at. Conscious access corresponds to a transition towards a higher state of synchronized brain activity. Putting that analogy at work for our subject: smart (unconscious but "intelligent") computers process enormous amount of data. By becoming fully self-conscious or aware in understanding and potentially deliberating what is "good" or "right" in (business) life, we take a step further than mere objective cognition.

We humans are able to take socio-ethical decisions in which we take our responsibility for the (utilitarian) *consequences* of our actions, for the (deontological) *obligations* we have vis-à-vis others, and being able to be *virtuous* in difficult circumstances because it is the right thing to do. You can call that "wisdom" in which "ought-to-do" reasons play a role next to "what-is-going-on". Only conscious agents can make ethical decisions. Smart computers, lacking any form of self-consciousness, are unable to help us to become wiser decision-makers.

3. Better Bet on Human Consciousness and Creativity than on Smart Machines

Judgement by boards and their leadership is often the result of multiple (cognitive) paradoxes and (normative) dilemmas. In today's high tech, data-driven societies, many smart judgements rely on statistical knowledge. But in the *ethico-political reality* and *social spheres*, assessments are usually "grounded" in the combination of intuitive abductive capacities, tacit skills, and affective and moral imagination. The cognitive "objective" pathway uses reasonable deductive (logic) and inductive (empirical) argumentation to come to valid conclusions. For instance, algorithm-supported induction could even help executives to strategize about partnerships[7], potentially giving rise to innovation. Yes, deductive and inductive logic may generate intelligent smart judgments but does not automatically lead to wise judgments.

3.1. Intelligence and Enlightened Consciousness Constitute Pragmatic Wisdom

Practical wisdom pertains to matters that cannot be defined by a single truth, but rather by a complex reality with different perspectives. Indeed, practical wisdom combines smartness and responsibility. Smartness pursues analytical rigour that supplements rather than supplants the exercise of intuition and abduction – as in emotional and moral intelligence. To make a wise decision and to judge well is to reject the extremes of sterile logic and reactive impulses, and to embrace the multifaceted intelligences by being a fluent reader of the hearts and minds of fellow members on boards for instance, or in any team for that matter. We are not essentially rational animals, but rather *social* or *relational animals*, capable of rationality **and** reasonableness, of being *intelligent* **and** *conscious*.

Our life as humans will be increasingly organized by intelligent machines. However, strengthening our uniquely human skills and attitudes will allow us to stay ahead and to determine ourselves what choice for the future we want to make. Only humans can see and create the future. We are the future. We humans should hold our own destiny: we should be "futureproof"[8]. We and our organizations should be adaptable to (necessary) changes, embrace digitization and AI that allows to make some more predicable decisions, while strengthening our resilience or grit for crises. However, uncertainties and ambiguities will inevitably occur. Our cognitive skillset should be accompanied by a socio-ethical attitude that sees phenomena in a more holistic context, that can hopefully limit negative externalities and see opportunities to be optimized that are shared by both the organization as well as the community. These interdependencies[9] will be a guiding beacon for making wiser decisions.

Trust in business is at an all-time low. Although government has its role to play to serve as a corrective and as an arbiter to impose the boundaries, the global business community must put its house in order by reinterpreting its fiduciary duties and broaden its perspective, both in time and space. I did not concur to blindly accept a stakeholder's perspective to replace the shareholder's view, but I argued that without taking these relevant and engaged partners with a real stake in the organization seriously there would be no business or cash flow to talk about. What can be commonly agreed? Survival is a primary driving force of "life". But it also reminds us of our (moral) responsibility to pass on opportunities to the next generation. The key to a workable definition of sustainability[10] is the realization that business and communities are already part of a natural and now increasingly digital ecosystem.

Although a strong believer in AI, but also vehemently warning us against super-intelligent AI, Elon Musk tweeted: "excessive automation at *Tesla* was a mistake. Humans are underrated". That leads to the interesting idea that we should not train people to do machine things, but we should be training people in uniquely human capabilities. *Toyota's* philosophy of *monozukuri* or craftmanship has somehow bucked the automation trend as well. They have even started to de-automate some tasks of the production lines, bringing in humans to do jobs that were once performed by robots. Even in the age of advanced robotics, their human skills can make all the difference. The one thing that humans are good at is creating new ideas, being creative and be extremely ambidextrous and adaptable.

Most likely, *creativity* is a necessary and unique ingredient of humans to resolve some of our challenges in the future. Creativity is here defined as the interdependent relationship of *visioning, relating* different notions and different stakeholders, *inventing* or *innovating* new products and services, while also emphasizing some *sensemaking* of the reasons why one is in business. However, one of the biggest reason for success in entrepreneurship is not brilliance. Nor is it just its creative genius. It's the simple ability to keep going when the going gets tough, and adapt to a changing context. It is all a question to be best fit and adapted to a changing context[11].

3.2. Awakened Consciousness in Corporate Life's Decision-Making

Humans can fundamentally imagine different scenarios, whereas smart computers can superbly calculate different scenarios, but not imagine counterintuitive or completely different out-of-the-box models or new solutions. Smart executives[12] are able to change the way things unfold in the organization and the industry, they see beyond the mere associations. We humans inherently think almost always in causal models. Building businesses in the future will increasingly be built on relations and corporate alliances. Those crucial business-oriented network power will allow leverage and be key to ensure that anti-fragility can take root again, slightly tilting the swinging (geopolitical and economic) movements from mere (global) efficiency thinking to (localized) resilience[13]. Digitization (and AI in particular) will improve cognition in many ways, but socio-ethical values will grow again in importance, determining in what kind of economy, political and ecosystem we want to live in. Efficiency will always play an important role in business, but it can be enriched by a dialectic dialogue underpinned by prescriptive socio-ethical reasoning.

Wise decision-making is not limited to ethical superheroes. Nor are we at the mercy of a clockwork brain over which we would have no control. Instead, wise decision-making is the result of a continuous practice of mentalizing. Mindful awareness is a must for any executive who wants to make more reasonable and responsible decisions. Our ability to predict and contemplate the future, our creative foresight may be the defining attribute of human intelligence. Becoming conscious or aware of its implications is a uniquely human ability. Wise decision-making is, in essence, allowing to take multiple perspectives in account, enabling leadership to manage in the grey, overcoming paradoxes and dilemmas.

Our more philosophical contemplative heritages function as a potent counterbalance of this material modernism that almost solely focuses on an outward "presumed objective" control and exploitation of our environment. Time has come to emphasize an enlightening consciousness and a "clear light awareness" aiming to make wise(r) decisions in an ever "smarter" world – allowing the organizations and its many stakeholders to flourish more equally as well as more sensibly.

This book advocated (1) imagining "*deep time humility*" that attempts to escape the tyranny of the gratifying now; choosing meaning in *eudamonia* above instant *hedonia*[14], (2) caring for some intergenerational justice, which requires a much longer *stewardship mentality*[15] than what is currently taught at business schools and (3) planning for *a legacy* in the future that goes beyond mere (socio-ethical or even political) *legitimacy* and *legality*, beyond our own life time span. It is the power of prospection what makes us wise. Our journey reveals that wise leadership is holistic. When we exercise wise leadership, we avoid ill-being[16] and are activating the potential of a highly evolved organic mechanism – our brain. Its power on learning, abstraction, innovation and imagination is unmatched, and something we are only just beginning to understand. What we do know is that all leaders can and should learn to exercise its incredible potential to become more mindful and spiritually self-conscious.

At the end of our (professional) life, the only thing that endures is who we became, the real difference we made for other people and the organization. Being wise is discovering our inner consciousness – as in a sudden glimpse of insight that gives us deep meaning – that makes a deliberate (ethical if not "spiritual") choice of responsibility. It is about the engaged judgements we make that have a positive beneficial and meaningful impact on the organization and on society at large. We all can make a choice in the way we perceive to broaden or even change our view, to achieve "awaked" awareness[17], almost to feel **consciousness**[18] that **relates** to "the other". Committing to an *ethic of responsibility* has never been more important than it is today. *Making wise choices* probably transcends a rather mechanistic future that seems to have pushed us to the brink of dangerous unsustainability, ill-being, instability and chaos. Indeed, it is our thoughts and respective actions that could conceive and create an emerging and more meaningful if still contested future. **A future** that will be **digital** and definitely *smarter*. But also a future that will be **relational** – including and beyond social contracts or legal obligations. A future, hopefully, supported by *wise* judgments while recognizing our limited understanding of a vast world …

REFERENCES

BIBLIOGRAPHY

INDEX